Applications of Artificial Intelligence for Smart Technology

P. Swarnalatha
Vellore Institute of Technology, Vellore, India

S. Prabu
Vellore Institute of Technology, Vellore, India

A volume in the Advances in
Computational Intelligence and
Robotics (ACIR) Book Series

Published in the United States of America by
    IGI Global
    Engineering Science Reference (an imprint of IGI Global)
    701 E. Chocolate Avenue
    Hershey PA, USA 17033
    Tel: 717-533-8845
    Fax: 717-533-8661
    E-mail: cust@igi-global.com
    Web site: http://www.igi-global.com

Library of Congress Cataloging-in-Publication Data

Names: Swarnalatha, P., DATE- editor. | Prabu, S., 1981-
    editor.
Title: Applications of artificial intelligence for smart technology / P.
    Swarnalatha and S. Prabu, editors.
Description: Hershey, PA : Engineering Science Reference, 2020. | Includes
    bibliographical references and index. | Summary: "This book addresses
    the difficulties and challenges that various fields have faced in
    implementing artificial intelligence for smart technology"-- Provided by
    publisher.
Identifiers: LCCN 2019051918 (print) | LCCN 2019051919 (ebook) | ISBN
    9781799833352 (h/c) | ISBN 9781799833369 (eISBN) | ISBN 9781799833376
    (s/c)
Subjects: LCSH: Artificial intelligence--Social aspects. | Intelligent
    control systems. | Technology. | Identification.
Classification: LCC Q335 .A6715 2020 (print) | LCC Q335 (ebook) | DDC
    006.3--dc23
LC record available at https://lccn.loc.gov/2019051918
LC ebook record available at https://lccn.loc.gov/2019051919

This book is published in the IGI Global book series Advances in Computational Intelligence and
Robotics (ACIR) (ISSN: 2327-0411; eISSN: 2327-042X)

British Cataloguing in Publication Data
A Cataloguing in Publication record for this book is available from the British Library.

For electronic access to this publication, please contact: eresources@igi-global.com.

Advances in Computational Intelligence and Robotics (ACIR) Book Series

ISSN:2327-0411
EISSN:2327-042X

Editor-in-Chief: Ivan Giannoccaro, University of Salento, Italy

MISSION

While intelligence is traditionally a term applied to humans and human cognition, technology has progressed in such a way to allow for the development of intelligent systems able to simulate many human traits. With this new era of simulated and artificial intelligence, much research is needed in order to continue to advance the field and also to evaluate the ethical and societal concerns of the existence of artificial life and machine learning.

The **Advances in Computational Intelligence and Robotics (ACIR) Book Series** encourages scholarly discourse on all topics pertaining to evolutionary computing, artificial life, computational intelligence, machine learning, and robotics. ACIR presents the latest research being conducted on diverse topics in intelligence technologies with the goal of advancing knowledge and applications in this rapidly evolving field.

COVERAGE

- Intelligent control
- Computational Intelligence
- Computational Logic
- Artificial Intelligence
- Heuristics
- Neural Networks
- Pattern Recognition
- Cognitive Informatics
- Automated Reasoning
- Machine Learning

IGI Global is currently accepting manuscripts for publication within this series. To submit a proposal for a volume in this series, please contact our Acquisition Editors at Acquisitions@igi-global.com or visit: http://www.igi-global.com/publish/.

The Advances in Computational Intelligence and Robotics (ACIR) Book Series (ISSN 2327-0411) is published by IGI Global, 701 E. Chocolate Avenue, Hershey, PA 17033-1240, USA, www.igi-global.com. This series is composed of titles available for purchase individually; each title is edited to be contextually exclusive from any other title within the series. For pricing and ordering information please visit http://www.igi-global.com/book-series/advances-computational-intelligence-robotics/73674. Postmaster: Send all address changes to above address. Copyright © 2021 IGI Global. All rights, including translation in other languages reserved by the publisher. No part of this series may be reproduced or used in any form or by any means – graphics, electronic, or mechanical, including photocopying, recording, taping, or information and retrieval systems – without written permission from the publisher, except for non commercial, educational use, including classroom teaching purposes. The views expressed in this series are those of the authors, but not necessarily of IGI Global.

Titles in this Series

For a list of additional titles in this series, please visit:
http://www.igi-global.com/book-series/advances-computational-intelligence-robotics/73674

Handbook of Research on Natural Language Processing and Smart Service Systems
Rodolfo Abraham Pazos-Rangel (Tecnológico Nacional de México, Mexico & Instituto Tecnológico de Ciudad Madero, Mexico) Rogelio Florencia-Juarez (Universidad Autónoma de Ciudad Juárez, Mexico) Mario Andrés Paredes-Valverde (Tecnológico Nacional de México, Mexico & Instituto Tecnológico de Orizaba, Mexico) and Gilberto Rivera (Universidad Autónoma de Ciudad Juárez, Mexico)
Engineering Science Reference • © 2021 • 554pp • H/C (ISBN: 9781799847304) • US $295.00

Applications of Artificial Neural Networks for Nonlinear Data
Hiral Ashil Patel (Ganpat University, India) and A.V. Senthil Kumar (Hindusthan College of Arts and Science, India)
Engineering Science Reference • © 2021 • 315pp • H/C (ISBN: 9781799840428) • US $245.00

Analyzing Future Applications of AI, Sensors, and Robotics in Society
Thomas Heinrich Musiolik (Berlin University of the Arts, Germany) and Adrian David Cheok (iUniversity, Tokyo, Japan)
Engineering Science Reference • © 2021 • 335pp • H/C (ISBN: 9781799834991) • US $225.00

AI-Based Services for Smart Cities and Urban Infrastructure
Kangjuan Lyu (SILC Business School, Shanghai University, China) Min Hu (SILC Business School, Shanghai University, China) Juan Du (SILC Business School, Shanghai University, China) and Vijayan Sugumaran (Oakland University, USA)
Engineering Science Reference • © 2021 • 353pp • H/C (ISBN: 9781799850243) • US $195.00

For an entire list of titles in this series, please visit:
http://www.igi-global.com/book-series/advances-computational-intelligence-robotics/73674

701 East Chocolate Avenue, Hershey, PA 17033, USA
Tel: 717-533-8845 x100 • Fax: 717-533-8661
E-Mail: cust@igi-global.com • www.igi-global.com

Table of Contents

Detailed Table of Contents

Chapter 1
Artificial Intelligence-Based Robot-Children Interaction for Autism Syndrome ..1
> *T. D. K. Upeksha Chathurani, Sri Lanka Technological Campus, Sri Lanka*
> *Akila Wijethunge, University of Sri Jayewardenepura, Sri Lanka*

Autism spectrum disorder (ASD) is considered a lifelong disability which causes deficits in both social and cognitive functions and affects to the quality of an individual life. The limited human resources, time, and considerable cost have affected the diagnosis and treatment methods of ASD over the world. The state of the art implies how modern technologies and robotics can offer promising tools to reinforce the researches and therapies of ASD. Robots have been shown to have a promise approach as therapeutic tools that can be implemented to diagnose ASD, improve social interaction in the scope of stimulating emotional engagement and physical activity engagement while creating an interactive environment with less anxiety. Nowadays, AI has become a significant and frequent factor in robotic solutions, introducing flexibility and learning capabilities for the applications. Impact of introducing AI for robotics solutions to autism syndrome has been discussed throughout this chapter.

Chapter 2
Wearable Technology as a Source of Data-Generation Tool for Artificial Intelligence...17
> *Gyasi Emmanuel Kwabena, Vellore Institute of Technology, Vellore, India*
> *Mageshbabu Ramamurthy, Sri Sakthi Amma Institute of Biomedical Research, India*
> *Akila Wijethunga, University of Sri Jayewardenepura, Sri Lanka*
> *Purushotham Swarnalatha, Vellore Institute of Technology, Vellore, India*

The world is fascinated to see how technology evolves each passing day. All too soon, there's an emerging technology that is trending around us, and it is no other technology than smart wearable technology. Less attention is paid to the data that our bodies are radiating and communicating to us, but with the timely arrival of wearable sensors, we now have numerous devices that can be tracking and collecting the data that our bodies are radiating. Apart from numerous benefits that we derive from the functions provided by wearable technology such as monitoring of our fitness levels, etc., one other critical importance of wearable technology is helping the advancement of artificial intelligence (AI) and machine learning (ML). Machine learning thrives on the availability of massive data and wearable technology which forms part of the internet of things (IoT) generates megabytes of data every single day. The data generated by these wearable devices are used as a dataset for the training and learning of machine learning models. Through the analysis of the outcome of these machine learning models, scientific conclusions are made.

Jaya S., Sri Sarada College for Women, India
Latha M., Sri Sarada College for Women, India

This chapter focuses on detailed overview of medical images as well as microscopic images to diagnosis the disease based on pattern recognition model in digital image processing. Pattern recognition is leading role in machine learning model which is used to detect the object such as text or character recognition, fingerprint recognition, face recognition, and biometric recognition. This chapter used pap smear images of cervical cancer to diagnosis a tissues by applying various image processing techniques followed by four tasks which are image acquisition, preprocessing, feature extraction, and object recognition. Cervical cancer is one of the very dangerous kind of cancer which may occur on the cervix part of the women. Diagnosis of tissue cells is based on the pixel variations of the images that may predict the cell is normal or abnormal state. This chapter presents machine learning algorithm of principle component analysis (PCA), Singular value decomposition (SVD), and linear discriminant analysis (LDA) under dimensionality reduction to recognize the pattern of the pap smear microscopic images.

Megala G., School of Computer Science and Engineering, Vellore
Institute of Technology, Vellore, India
S. Prabu, Vellore Institute of Technology, Vellore, India
Liyanapathirana B. C., Department of Science and Technology, Uwa
Wellassa University of Sri Lanka, Sri Lanka

The major network security problems faced by many internet users is the DDoS (distributed denial of service) attack. This attack makes the service inaccessible by exhausting the network and resources with high repudiation and economic loss. It denies the network services to the potential users. To detect this DDoS attack accurately in the network, random forest classifier which is a machine learning based classifier is used. The experimental results are compared with naïve Bayes classifier and KNN classifier showing that random forest produces high accuracy results in classification. Application of machine learning, detecting DDoS attacks is modeled based on the supervised learning algorithm to produce best outcome with high accuracy of training algorithm on network dataset.

Sreedevi E., Koneru Lakshamiah Education Foundation, India
PremaLatha V., Koneru Lakshamiah Education Foundation, India
Prasanth Y., Koneru Lakshamiah Education Foundation, India
Sivakumar S., Koneru Lakshmaiah Education Foundation, India

Data which contains noise is termed as uncertain data, and the presence of noise makes a deviation in the correct, intended, or original values. Size and complexity of the software products are the two main reasons for uncertain data set that identifying defective modules in uncertain datasets has become a challenging issue. In this chapter, the authors implemented a multi-learner ensemble model for uncertain datasets for defect detection. In this model, different weak classifiers are optimized to improve the classification rate on uncertain data. They have implemented their proposed model on NASA(PROMISE) metric data program repository. Accuracy is used as performance evaluation metric for our multi-learner ensemble defect detection model and ensemble model outcome achieved higher accuracy rate of 97% and when compared to another classification model.

Lavanya K. Sendhilvel, Vellore Institute of Technology, Vellore, India
Anushka Sutreja, Vellore Institute of Technology, Vellore, India
Aritro Paul, Vellore Institute of Technology, Vellore, India
Japneet Kaur Saluja, Vellore Institute of Technology, Vellore, India

Malware attacks are broadly disguised as useful applications. Many android apps, downloaded to perform crucial tasks or play games (take one's pick), seem to do completely different tasks, which are potentially harmful and invasive in nature. This could include sending text messages to random users, exporting the phone's contacts, etc. There exist some algorithms in place that can detect these malwares, but so far, it has been observed that many of these algorithms suffer from false negatives, which grossly reduced the effectiveness of said algorithms. The aim of this chapter is to introduce a flexible method to detect if a certain application is malware or not. The working can be loosely defined as the source of a set of applications is detected and the list of permissions is studied. The set of relevant and highly close applications is selected, and from the most relevant category, the permissions are checked for overlap to see if it can be stated as a possible anomalous application.

Chapter 7

Ramani Selvanambi, Vellore Institute of Technology, Vellore, India
Samarth Bhutani, Vellore Institute of Technology, Vellore, India
Komal Veauli, Vellore Institute of Technology, Vellore, India

In yesteryears, the healthcare data related to each patient was limited. It was stored and controlled by the hospital authorities and was seldom regulated. With the increase in awareness and technology, the amount of medical data per person has increased exponentially. All this data is essential for the correct diagnosis of the patient. The patients also want access to their data to seek medical advice from different doctors. This raises several challenges like security, privacy, data regulation, etc. As health-related data are privacy-sensitive, the increase in data stored increases the risk of data exposure. Data availability and privacy are essential in healthcare. The availability of correct information is critical for the treatment of the patient. Information not easily accessed by the patients also complicates seeking medical advice from different hospitals. However, if data is easily accessible to everyone, it makes privacy and security difficult. Blockchains to store and secure data will not only ensure data privacy but will also provide a common method of data regulation.

Chapter 8

Tamilarasi R., Vellore Institute of Technology, Vellore, India
Prabu Sevugan, Vellore Institute of Technology, Vellore, India

Dimensionality reduction for hyperspectral imagery plays a major role in different scientific and technical applications. It enables the identification of multiple urban-related features on the surface of the earth, such as building, highway (road), and other natural and man-made structures. Since manual road detection and satellite imagery extraction is time-consuming and costly, data time and cost-effective solution with limited user interaction will emerge with road and building extraction techniques. Therefore, the need to focus on a deep survey for improving ML techniques for dimensionality reduction (DR) and automated building and road extraction using hyperspectral imagery. The main purpose of this chapter is to identify the state-of-the-art and trends of hyperspectral imaging theories, methodologies, techniques, and applications for dimensional reduction. A different type of ML technique is included such as SVM, ANN, etc. These algorithms can handle high dimensionality and classification data.

Chapter 9

   *Saira Banu Jamalmohammed, Vellore Institute of Technology, Vellore,
       India*
   Lavanya K., Vellore Institute of Technology, Vellore, India
   Sumaiya Thaseen I., Vellore Institute of Technology, Vellore, India
   Biju V., Jubail University College, Saudi Arabia

Sparse matrix-vector multiplication (SpMV) is a challenging computational kernel in linear algebra applications, like data mining, image processing, and machine learning. The performance of this kernel is greatly dependent on the size of the input matrix and the underlying hardware features. Various sparse matrix storage formats referred to commonly as sparse formats have been proposed in the literature to reduce the size of the matrix. In modern multi-core and many-core architectures, the performance of the kernel is mainly dependent on memory wall and power wall problem. Normally review on sparse formats is done with specific architecture or with specific application. This chapter presents a comparative study on various sparse formats in cross platform architecture like CPU, graphics processor unit (GPU), and single instruction multiple data stream (SIMD) registers. Space complexity analysis of various formats with its representation is discussed. Finally, the merits and demerits of each format have been summarized into a table.

Chapter 10

   Sivakumar S., Koneru Lakshmaiah Education Foundation, India
   Sreedevi E., Koneru Lakshamiah Education Foundation, India
   PremaLatha V., Koneru Lakshamiah Education Foundation, India
   Haritha D., Koneru Lakshamiah Education Foundation, India

To detect defect is an important concept in machine leaning techniques and ambiguous dataset which develops into a challenging issue, as the software product expands in terms of size and its complexity. This chapter reveals an applied novel multi-learner model which is ensembled to predict software metrics using classification algorithms and propose algorithm applied in parallel method for detection on ambiguous data using density sampling and develop an implementation running on both GPUs and multi-core CPUs. The defect on the NASA PROMISE defect dataset is adequately predicted and classified using these models and implementing GPU computing. The performance compared to the traditional learning models improved algorithm and parallel implementation on GPUs shows less processing time in ensemble model compared to decision tree algorithm and effectively optimizes the true positive rate.

Chapter 11

    Vibhu Dagar, Vellore Institute of Technology, Vellore, India
    Amber Verma, Vellore Institute of Technology, Vellore, India
    Govardhan K., Vellore Institute of Technology, Vellore, India

Sentiment analysis is contextual mining of text which identifies and extracts subjective information in source material and helps a business to understand the social sentiment of their brand, product, or service while monitoring online conversations. However, analysis of social media streams is usually restricted to just basic sentiment analysis and count-based metrics. This is akin to just scratching the surface and missing out on those high value insights that are waiting to be discovered. Twitter is an online person-to-person communication administration where overall clients distribute their suppositions on an assortment of themes, talk about current issues, grumble, and express positive or on the other hand negative notions for items they use in life. Hence, Twitter is a rich source of information for supposition mining and estimation investigation.

Chapter 12

    Francina Sophiya D., Vellore Institute of Technology, Vellore, India
    Swarnalatha P., Vellore Institute of Technology, Vellore, India
    Prabu Sevugan, Vellore Institute of Technology, Vellore, India
    T. D. K Upeksha Chathurani, Sri Lanka Technological Campus, Sri Lanka
    R. Magesh Babu, Sri Sakthi Amma Institute of Biomedical Research, India

Smart environments based on wireless sensor networks represent the next evolutionary development step in engineering, such as industrial automation, video surveillance, traffic monitoring, and robot control. Sensory data come from multiple networks of interconnected sensors with complex distributed locations. The recent development of communication and sensor technology results in the growth of a new attractive and challenging area: wireless sensor networks (WSNs). A wireless sensor network which consists of a large number of sensor nodes is deployed in environmental fields to serve various applications. Facilitated with the ability of wireless communication and intelligent computation, these nodes become smart sensors that do not only perceive ambient physical parameters but also are able to process information, cooperate with each other, and self-organize into the network. These new features assist the sensor nodes as well as the network to operate more efficiently in terms of both data acquisition and energy consumption.

Chapter 13

Smart education derived from information communication technologies (ICT) has attracted various academicians towards it. The growth of multiple sensor devices and wireless networks has brought drastic changes in IoT in the education sector. Applications of IoT in the education sector can improve academicians' and learners' considerable skills. Therefore, this chapter analyses various applications, advantages, and challenges of IoT in the education sector. The multiple applications of IoT in the education sector are identified in terms of smart classroom management, student tracking and monitoring, campus energy management, and intelligent learning. IoT in education's significant advantages are an innovative teaching and learning process, cost reduction, and smart infrastructure development. Various challenges in developing IoT-based applications identify as designing a secure learning environment, efficient resource tracking, efficient access to information, and intellectual plan development.

Chapter 14

In this work, an image retrieval system based on three main factors is constructed. The proposed system at first chooses relevant pictures from an enormous information base utilizing colour moment data. Accordingly, canny edge recognition and local binary pattern and strategies are utilized to remove the texture plus edge separately, as of the uncertainty and resultant pictures of the underlying phase of the system. Afterward, the chi-square distance between the red-green and the blue colour channels of the query and the main image are calculated. Then these two (the LBP pattern and the edge feature extracted from the canny edge detection and by chi-square method) data about these two highlights compared to the uncertainty and chosen pictures are determined and consolidated, are then arranged and the nearest 'n' images are presented. Two datasets, Wang and the Corel databases, are used in this work. The results shown herein are obtained using the Wang dataset. The Wang dataset contains 1,000 images and Corel contains 10,000 images.

Lahari Anne, School of Computer Science and Engineering, Vellore Institute of Technology, Vellore, India

S. Anandakumar, School of Computer Science and Engineering, Vellore Institute of Technology, Vellore, India

Anand Mahendran, School of Computer Science and Engineering, Vellore Institute of Technology, Vellore, India

Muhammad Rukunuddin Ghalib, School of Computer Science and Engineering, Vellore Institute of Technology, Vellore, India

Uttam Ghosh, Vanderbilt University, USA

Cloud computing is a technology that has enabled individual users and organizations alike to implement such functionality. Currently, a large percentage of the data being generated is stored on clouds, and the number of organizations opting for cloud-based technologies is continuously on the rise. With such growing numbers accessing and utilizing cloud resources, data security has become a significant cause of concern. Traditional methods of cloud computing are becoming obsolete and ineffective with each technological breakthrough, and data is thus highly subjected to getting corrupted or hacked. This chapter provides a survey on various trust management techniques used in cloud technology to protect the data with multiple security features.

Debajit Datta, Vellore Institute of Technology, Vellore, India

Saira Banu Jamalmohammed, Vellore Institute of Technology, Vellore, India

Image classification is a widely discussed topic in this era. It covers a vivid range of application domains like from garbage classification applications to advanced fields of medical sciences. There have been several research works that have been done in the past and are also currently under research for coming up with better-optimized image classification techniques. However, the process of image classification turns out to be time-consuming. This work deals with the widely accepted FashionMNIST (modified national institute of standards and technology database) dataset, having a set of sixty thousand images for training a model and another popular dataset of MNIST for handwritten numbers. The work compares several convolutional neural network (CNN) models and aims in parallelizing them using a distributed framework that is provided by the python library, RAY. The parallelization has been achieved over the multiple cores of CPU and many cores of GPU. The work also shows that the overall accuracy of the system is not affected by the parallelization.

Chapter 17

    Sagar Gupta, Vellore Institute of Technology, Vellore, India
    Garima Mathur, Vellore Institute of Technology, Vellore, India
    Venkatesan R, M.I.E.T. Engineering College
    S. Purushotham, Vellore Institute of Technology, Vellore, India

This chapter aims to solve the problem of heavy traffic caused due to a long queue near the toll plaza. The authors design the website with the motive that it will save the maximum time of the public, reducing the problem of heavy traffic. Moreover, the website maintains the entire database containing the details of the staff, pass, receipts, vehicle details, etc., which will reduce any problem in the future. Since they are also aware of the fact that in many villages in India, there are not even proper toll booths to pay taxes, and people are doing it manually, which can result in data loss and even is time-consuming. So, keeping this mind, they aim to design the website that is simple to use such that every people working in toll booth can get habituated to it easily. They also aim to make this website fully secure such that data can be protected and citizens are comfortable providing their details to create their pass and generate receipts. The main feature is that users can also generate receipt for themselves from anywhere through website to avoid waste of time at toll.

Chapter 18

    Ranjani Arsu Mudaliar, Vellore Institute of Technology, Vellore, India
    Sonal Sanjay Rajurkar, Vellore Institute of Technology, Vellore, India
    Mythili Thirugnanam, Vellore Institute of Technology, Vellore, India

Due to negligence by drivers, there might be large number of road accidents. In order to overcome this current issue, various methodologies were used to combine the artificial intelligence theory and road traffic control system. In addition to that, researches were performed regarding driving behaviours which include intelligent driving and artificial driving. These two behaviours were based on cognitive science and as well as simulation. Cognitive science is scientific study of the mind and its processes. In the current research papers, autonomous driving system was implemented but had some drawbacks while overtaking. Therefore, this work aims to modify and implement an intelligent driving system to help the drivers and lower the accident rates.

Foreword

When I was invited to write a foreword for this book *Applications of Artificial Intelligence for Smart Technology,* I felt glad to note the varied tools, challenges, methods are applied in Artificial Intelligence for Smart Technology

This book is a significant collection of 18 chapters covering Artificial Intelligence, Cloud Computing, Data Mining, High Performance Computing and Block Chain, as well as their applications emerged in the recent decades. This book provides an excellent platform to review various areas of Artificial Intelligence and affords for the needs of both beginners to the field and seasoned researchers and practitioners. The tremendous growth of AI (Artificial Intelligence), ML (Machine Learning), Block chain documented in this book, such as Artificial Intelligence Based Robot-Children Interaction for Autism Syndrome, Wearable Technology as a Source of Data Generation Tool for Artificial Intelligence, An Analysis of Pattern Recognition and Machine Learning Approaches on Medical Images, Detecting DDoS Attack – A machine learning based approach, A Novel Ensembel Learning for defect detection method with uncertain data, A Trustworthy Convolutional Neural Networks based Malware Variant Detector in Python: Malware Variant Detector, Security and Privacy for Electronic healthcare Records using AI in Blockchain: AI in Blockchain, Hyperspectral Image classification through Machine learning and deep learning techniques, Review on Sparse Matrix Storage Formats with Space Complexity Analysis, Parallel Defect Detection Model on Uncertain Data for GPUs Computing by a Novel Ensemble Learning, Sentiment Analysis And Sarcasm Detection (Using Emoticons), Smart Sensing Network for Smart Technologies, IoT in the Education Sector in Applications and Challenges: Education, Internet of Things, Challenges, Applications, A Proficient Hybrid Framework for Image Retrieval, A Study and Analysis of Trust Management System in Cloud Technologies, Image classication using CNN with multi-core and many-core architecture, Enhancement of Toll Plaza System with Smart Features and Intelligent driving using Cognitive Science: Intelligent Driving which are focused in various applications.

To the best of my knowledge, this is the first attempt of its kind, providing a coverage of the key subjects in the fields Artificial Intelligence, Cloud Computing,

Data Mining, High Performance Computing, Block Chain and applications. This book is an invaluable, topical, and timely source of knowledge in the field, which serves nicely as a major text book for several courses at both undergraduate, post graduate levels and scholars. It is also a key reference for scientists, professionals, and academicians, who are interested in new challenges, theories and practice of the specific areas mentioned above.

I am happy to commend the editors and authors on their accomplishment, and to inform the readers that they are looking at a major piece in the development of computational intelligence on organizational decision making. I am familiar with your research interests and expertise in the related research areas pf Artificial Intellligence for Smart Technology which would make an excellent addition to this publication. This book is a main step in this field's maturation and will serve to challenge the academic, research and scientific community in various significant ways.

S. Arunkumar Sangaiah
Vellore Institute of Technology, Vellore, India

Preface

Artificial Intelligence plays a significant role in building smart cities. Artificial Intelligence could be deployed in smart cities to discover correlations between circumstances. This book aims to discuss and address various Artificial Intelligence techniques and challenges faced in applying AI (Artificial Intelligence) and handling security issues to store data applied in various applications resulting in Applications of Artificial intelligence for Smart Technology. The editors have received chapters that address different aspects of applying Artificial Intelligence upon Robot System, Health System, Block chain, Cloud Environment and related topics. Additionally, the book also explored the impact of such methodologies on the applications in which the advanced technology is being implemented.

This comprehensive and timely publication aims to be an essential reference source. This book helps the researchers who are working on Artificial Intelligence with the available literature in the field of Artificial Intelligence techniques for Smart Technology and providing for further research opportunities in this dynamic field. It is hoped that this text will provide the resources necessary to the developers and managers to adopt and implement these techniques, platforms and approaches in developing efficient solutions.

NEED FOR A BOOK ON THE PROPOSED TOPICS

Artificial Intelligence is an evolving term that will provide the foundation for smart cities. Even though every city is unique, smart cities do share common characteristics. Primarily, to be considered a smart city a metropolitan area needs to blend the right combination of people, processes, technology, and policies. Every discussion of smart cities should begin with people. After all, the primary objective of a smart city initiative should be to make urban life better for people who live in metropolitan areas. To do that, systems need to operate effectively and resources need to be used as efficiently as possible.

This book looks to discuss and address the difficulties and challenges that various fields have faced in implementing the technologies and applications.

Applications of Artificial Intelligence for Smart Technology is a critical scholarly resource that examines the challenges and difficulties of applying Artificial Intelligence for various purposes. Featuring coverage on a broad range of topics, such as Smart Vision-based Robotic Manipulation, Artificial Intelligence and Machine Learning Smart Sensor networking Ubiquitous and High-Performance Computing, Data Management, Exploration, and Mining, etc., this book is geared towards scientists, professionals, researchers, and academicians seeking current research on the use of Artificial Intelligence for Smart Technology. Additionally, the book will explore the impact of such technologies on the applications in which this advanced technology is being implemented.

ORGANIZATION OF THE BOOK

The book is organized into 18 chapters. A brief description of each chapter is given as follows:

1. Artificial Intelligence Based Robot-Children Interaction for Autism Syndrome

This chapter focuses on the Artificial Intelligence Based Robot-Children Interaction for Autism Syndrome. Autism Spectrum Disorder (ASD) is considered as a lifelong disability which causes deficits in both social and cognitive functions and affects to the quality of an individual life. The limited human resources, time and considerable cost has affected the diagnosis and treatment methods of ASD over the world. The state of the art implies how modern technologies and robotics can offer promising tools to reinforce the research and therapy of ASD. Robots have been shown to have a promise approach as therapeutic tools that can be implemented to diagnose ASD, improve social interaction in the scope of stimulating emotional engagement and physical activity engagement while creating an interactive environment with less anxiety. Nowadays, AI has become a significant and frequent factor in robotic solutions, introducing flexibility and learning capabilities for the applications. Impact of introducing AI for robotics solutions to autism syndrome has been discussed throughout this chapter.

2. Wearable Technology as a Source of Data Generation Tool for Artificial Intelligence

It is fascinating to see how technology evolves at each passing day. All too soon, there's an emerging technology that is trending around us now, and it is no other technology than Smart Wearable Technology. We ignore a lot of data that our bodies are radiating but with the advent of wearable sensors, we now have numerous devices that can be tracking and collecting the data that our bodies are radiating. Apart from numerous benefits that we derive from the functions provided by wearable technology such as, monitoring of our fitness levels, etc. one other critical importance of wearable technology is helping the advancement of Artificial Intelligence (AI) and Machine Learning (ML). Machine Learning thrives on the availability of massive data and wearable technology which forms part of the Internet of Things (IoT) generates megabytes of data every single day. The data generated by these wearable devices are used as a dataset for the Training and learning of Machine Learning models. Through the analysis of the outcome of these Machine Learning models, scientific conclusions are made.

3.   An Analysis of Pattern Recognition and Machine Learning Approaches on Medical Images

This chapter focuses on detailed overview of medical images as well as microscopic images to diagnosis the disease based on Pattern Recognition model in Digital Image Processing. Pattern recognition is leading role in machine learning model which is used to detect the object such as text or character recognition, fingerprint recognition, face recognition and biometric recognition. Used pap smear images of cervical cancer to diagnosis a tissues by applying various image processing techniques followed by four tasks which are image acquisition, preprocessing, feature extraction and object recognition. Cervical cancer is one of the very dangerous kind of cancer which may occur on the cervix part of the women. Diagnosis of tissue cells is based on the pixel variations of the images that may predict the cell is normal or abnormal state. This chapter presents machine learning algorithm of Principle Component Analysis(PCA), Singular Value Decomposition(SVD) and Linear Discriminant Analysis(LDA) under dimensionality reduction to recognize the pattern of the pap smear microscopic images.

4.   Detecting DDoS Attack: A Machine Learning-Based Approach

The major network security problems faced by many internet users is the DDoS (Distributed Denial of Service) attack. This attack makes the service inaccessible by exhausting the network and resources with high repudiation and economic loss. It denies the network services to the potential users. To detect this DDoS attack accurately in the network, random forest classifier which is a machine learning based classifier is used. The experimental results are compared with Naïve Bayes classifier and KNN classifier showing that random forest produces high accuracy results in classification. Application of machine learning, detecting DDoS attacks is modeled based on the supervised learning algorithm to produce best outcome with high accuracy of training algorithm on real life dataset.

5.   A Novel Ensemble Learning for Defect Detection Method With Uncertain Data

Data which contains noise is termed as uncertain data and the presence of noise makes a deviation in the correct, intended, or original values. Size and complexity of the software products are the two main reasons for uncertain data set that identifying defective modules in uncertain datasets has become a challenging issue. In this paper we implemented a multi-learner ensemble model for uncertain datasets for defect detection. In this model, different weak classifiers are optimized to improve the classification rate on uncertain data. We have implemented our proposed model on NASA(PROMISE) metric data program repository. Accuracy is used as performance evaluation metric for our multi-learner ensemble defect detection model and ensemble model outcome achieved higher accuracy rate of 97% and when compared to another classification model.

6.   A Trustworthy Convolutional Neural Networks-Based Malware Variant Detector in Python

One of the most common avenues of malware attacks are broadly disguised as useful applications. Many android apps, downloaded to perform crucial tasks or play games (take one's pick), seem to do completely different tasks, which are potentially harmful and invasive in nature. This could include sending text messages to random users, exporting the phone's contacts etc. There exist some algorithms in place that can detect these malwares but so far, it has been observed that many of these algorithms suffer from False Negatives, which grossly reduced the effectiveness of said algorithms. The aim of this paper is to introduce a flexible method to detect if a certain application is malware or not. The working can be loosely defined as: The source of a set of applications is detected and the list of permissions is studied. The set of relevant and highly close applications is selected and from the most relevant category, the permissions are checked for overlap to see if it can be stated as a possible anomalous application.

7.   Security and Privacy for Electronic Healthcare Records Using AI in Blockchain: AI in Blockchain

In yesteryears, the healthcare data related to each patient was limited. It was stored and controlled by the hospital authorities and was seldom regulated. With the increase in awareness and technology, the amount of medical data per person has increased exponentially. All this data is essential for the correct diagnosis of the patient. The patients also want access to their data to seek medical advice from different doctors. This raises several challenges like security, privacy, data regulation, etc. As health- related data are privacy-sensitive, the increase in data stored increases the risk of data exposure. Data availability, privacy is essential in healthcare. The availability of correct information is critical for the treatment of the patient. Information not easily accessed by the patients also complicates seeking medical advice from different hospitals. However, if data is easily accessible to everyone, it makes privacy and security difficult. Blockchains to store and secure data will not only ensure data privacy but will also provide a common method of data regulation.

8. Hyperspectral Image Classification Through Machine Learning and Deep Learning Techniques

Dimensionality reduction for hyperspectral imagery plays a major role in different scientific and technical applications. It enables the identification of multiple urban-related features on the surface of the earth, such as building, highway (road), and other natural and man-made structures. Since manual road detection and satellite imagery extraction is time-consuming and costly, data time and cost-effective solution with limited user interaction will emerge with road and building extraction techniques. Therefore, the need to focus on a deep survey for improving ML techniques for dimensionality reduction (DR) and automated building and road extraction using hyperspectral imagery. The main purpose of this chapter is to identify the state-of-the-art and trends of hyperspectral imaging theories, methodologies, techniques, and applications for dimensional reduction. A different type of ML technique is included such as SVM, ANN, etc. These algorithms can handle high dimensionality and classification data.

9. Review on Sparse Matrix Storage Formats With Space Complexity Analysis

Sparse matrix – Vector multiplication (SpMV) is a challenging computational kernel in linear algebra applications, like data mining, image processing and machine learning. The performance of this kernel is greatly dependent on the size of the input matrix and the underlying hardware features. Various sparse matrix storage formats referred commonly as sparse formats has been proposed in the literature to reduce the size of the matrix. In modern multi-core and many-core architectures the performance of the kernel is mainly dependent on memory wall and power wall problem. Normally review on sparse formats is done with specific architecture or with specific application. This paper presents a comparative study on various sparse formats in cross platform architecture like CPU, Graphics processor Unit (GPU) and Single Instruction Multiple Data Stream (SIMD) registers. Space complexity analysis of various formats with its representation is discussed. Finally, the merits and demerits of each format have been summarized into a table.

10. Parallel Defect Detection Model on Uncertain Data for GPUs Computing by a Novel Ensemble Learning

To detect defect is an important concept in machine leaning techniques and ambiguous dataset which develop into a challenging issue, as the software product expands in terms of size and its complexity. This paper, reveal about a applied novel multi-learner model which is ensembled to predict software metrics using classification algorithms and propose algorithm applied in parallel method for detection on ambiguous data using density sampling and develop an implementation running on both GPUs and multi-core CPUs. The defect on the NASA PROMISE defect dataset is adequately predicted and classified using these models and implementing GPU Computing. The performance and compared to the traditional learning models improved algorithm and parallel implementation on GPUs, it shows that less processing time in ensemble model compared to decision tree algorithm and effectively optimizes the true positive rate.

11. Sentiment Analysis and Sarcasm Detection (Using Emoticons)

Sentiment analysis is contextual mining of text which identifies and extracts subjective information in source material, and helping a business to understand the social sentiment of their brand, product or service while monitoring online conversations. However, analysis of social media streams is usually restricted to just basic sentiment analysis and count based metrics. This is akin to just scratching the surface and missing out on those high value insights that are waiting to be discovered. Twitter is an online person to person communication administration where overall clients distribute their suppositions on an assortment of themes, talk about current issues, grumble, and express positive or on the other hand negative notion for items they use in day by day life. Hence, Twitter is a rich source of information for supposition mining and estimation investigation.

12. Smart Sensing Network for Smart Technologies

Smart environments based on Wireless Sensor Networks represent the next evolutionary development step in engineering, such as industrial automation, video surveillance, traffic monitoring, and robot control. Sensory data come from multiple networks of interconnected sensors with complex distributed locations. The recent development of communication and sensor technology results in the growth of a new attractive and challenging area - wireless sensor networks (WSNs). A wireless sensor network which consists of a large number of sensor nodes is deployed in environmental fields to serve various applications. Facilitated with the ability of wireless communication and intelligent computation, these nodes become smart sensors that do not only perceive ambient physical parameters but also be able to process information, cooperate with each other and self-organize into the network. These new features assist the sensor nodes as well as the network to operate more efficiently in terms of both data acquisition and energy consumption.

13. IoT in the Education Sector in Applications and Challenges: Education, Internet of Things, Challenges, Applications

Smart education derived from information communication technologies (ICT) has attracted various academicians towards it. The growth of multiple sensor devices and wireless networks has brought drastic changes in IoT in the education sector. IoT is an advanced technology that connects various sensors, processing devices, and actuators to fulfill the desired purpose. Applications of IoT in the education sector can improve academicians and learner's considerable skills. Therefore, this chapter analyses various applications, advantages, and challenges of IoT in the education sector. The multiple applications of IoT in the education sector are identified in terms of smart classroom management, student tracking and monitoring, campus energy management, and intelligent learning. IoT in education's significant advantages is an innovative teaching and learning process, cost reduction, and smart infrastructure development.

14. A Proficient Hybrid Framework for Image Retrieval

In this work, an image retrieval system based on three main factors is constructed. The proposed system at first chooses relevant pictures from an enormous information base utilizing shading second data. Accordingly, canny edge recognition and Local Binary Pattern and Canny edge recognition strategies are utilized to remove the surface plus boundary includes separately, as of the question and resultant pictures of the underlying phase of the system. Afterward, the Chi-Square distance between the red-green and the blue color channels of the query and the main image is calculated. Then these two (the LBP pattern and the edge feature extracted from the canny edge detection and by Chi- square method) data about these two highlights compared to the question and chose pictures are determined and consolidated, are then arranged and the nearest 'n' images are presented. Two datasets Wang and the Corel database are used in this work. The results shown here in the results section belong to the Wang dataset. The Wang dataset contains 1000 images and Corel contains 10000 images.

15. A Study and Analysis of Trust Management System in Cloud Technologies

Cloud computing is a technology that has enabled individual users and organizations alike to implement such functionality. Currently, a large percentage of the data being generated is stored on clouds, and the number of organizations opting for Cloud-based technologies is continuously on the rise. With such growing numbers accessing and utilizing cloud resources, data security has become a significant cause of concern. Traditional methods of cloud computing are becoming obsolete and ineffective with each technological breakthrough, and data is thus highly subjected to getting corrupted or hacked. This chapter provides a survey on various trust management techniques used in Cloud Technology to protect the data with multiple security features.

16. Image Classification Using CNN With Multi-Core and Many-Core Architecture

Image classification is a widely discussed topic in this era. It covers a vivid range of application domains like from garbage classification applications to advanced fields of medical sciences. There have been several research works that have been done in the past and are also currently under research, for coming up with better-optimized image classification techniques. However, the process of image classification turns out to be time-consuming. This work deals with the widely accepted FashionMNIST (Modified National Institute of Standards and Technology database) dataset, having a set of sixty thousand images for training a model and another popular dataset of MNIST for handwritten numbers. The work compares several Convolutional Neural Network (CNN) models and aims in parallelizing them using a distributed framework that is provided by the python library, RAY. The parallelization has been achieved over the multiple cores of CPU and many cores of GPU. The work also shows that the overall accuracy of the system is not affected by the parallelization.

17. Enhancement of Toll Plaza System With Smart Features

Our chapter mainly aims to solve the problem of heavy traffic caused due to a long queue near the toll plaza. We are designing the website with the motive that it will save the maximum time of the public, reduces the problem of heavy traffic.

Moreover, our website maintains the entire database containing the details of the staff, pass, receipts, vehicle details, etc. which will reduce any problem in the future. Since, we are also aware of the fact that in many villages in India, there are not even proper toll booths to pay taxes and people are doing it manually which can result in data loss and even is time-consuming. So, keeping this mind we aim to design the website which is simple to use such that every people working in toll booth can get habituated to it easily. We also aim to make this website fully secure such that data can be protected and citizens are comfortable providing their details to create their pass and generate receipts. The main feature is that user can also generate receipt for themselves from anywhere through website to avoid wastage of time at toll.

18.   Intelligent driving Using Cognitive Science

Due to negligence by driver there might be large number of road accidents. In order to overcome this current issue various methodologies were used to combine the Artificial intelligence theory and road traffic control system. In addition to that researches were performed regarding driving behaviours which includes intelligent driving and artificial driving. These two behaviours were based on cognitive science and as well as simulation. Cognitive science is scientific study of the mind and it's processes. With the help of information processing which is also termed as change of information which was modelled to Artificial and Intelligent driving behaviour. In the current research papers autonomous driving system was implemented but had some drawbacks while overtaking. Therefore, this work aims to modify and implement an intelligent driving system to help the drivers and lower the accident rates.

ACKNOWLEDGMENT

It is obvious that the development of a book of this scope needs the support of many people. We must thank Mr. Lindsay Wertmam, Managing Director, Ms. Maria Rohde, Assistant Development Editor and the editorial team, IGI Global for their encouragement and support enabled the book publication project to materialize and contributed to its success. We especially thank the management of VIT University for their tremendous assistance. The most important contribution to the development of a book such as this comes from peers reviews. We cannot express our gratitude in words to the many reviewers who spent numerous hours reading the manuscript and providing us with helpful comments and ideas.

We would like to express our sincere gratitude to all the contributors, who have submitted their high-quality chapters, and to the experts for their supports in providing insightful review comments and suggestions on time.

Gopinath Ganapathy
Bharathidasan University, India

V. Susheela Devi
Department of Computer Science and Automation, Indian Institute of Science, Bangalore, India

Anantharajah Kaneswaran
Department of Computer Engineering, Faculty of Engineering, University of Jaffna, Sri Lanka

Chapter 1
Artificial Intelligence–Based Robot–Children Interaction for Autism Syndrome

T. D. K. Upeksha Chathurani
Sri Lanka Technological Campus, Sri Lanka

Akila Wijethunge
ⓘD https://orcid.org/0000-0002-7672-6583
University of Sri Jayewardenepura, Sri Lanka

ABSTRACT

Autism spectrum disorder (ASD) is considered a lifelong disability which causes deficits in both social and cognitive functions and affects to the quality of an individual life. The limited human resources, time, and considerable cost have affected the diagnosis and treatment methods of ASD over the world. The state of the art implies how modern technologies and robotics can offer promising tools to reinforce the researches and therapies of ASD. Robots have been shown to have a promise approach as therapeutic tools that can be implemented to diagnose ASD, improve social interaction in the scope of stimulating emotional engagement and physical activity engagement while creating an interactive environment with less anxiety. Nowadays, AI has become a significant and frequent factor in robotic solutions, introducing flexibility and learning capabilities for the applications. Impact of introducing AI for robotics solutions to autism syndrome has been discussed throughout this chapter.

DOI: 10.4018/978-1-7998-3335-2.ch001

BACKGROUND

Statistics shows that 1 out of 160 children has an ASD through worldwide. This is only an average value, estimated on reported cases across the studies. The reported figures might be higher as prevalence of ASD in developing countries is so far unknown (World Health Organization, 2019).

Advances in recent year's progress in robotics technology, tremendous opportunities are open for innovation in emotional therapy treatments. These therapeutically robots, mostly develop as a pet-type animal by providing a companionship to augment patient's psychological comfort and induce social interaction and motivate patients for a positive behavior change.

Nowadays, interactive robots' development for clinical use for the individuals with Autism Spectrum Disorder (ASD) is a promising approach. Autism is a prevalent developmental disorder which causes deficits in correct information processing, difficulties in speech language learning, problems in interpreting social behaviors and situations and impairments in gross motor functioning (A. R. T. et Al,2014; P. Lanillos et al.,2020; She, T. et al.,2018).

Some of characteristic attributes that are often associated with ASD can be discussed as;

1. **Impairment of Social-Emotional Engagement In Communication:** Difficult to share common interests and emotions, lack of response or interest in social interaction, difficulties in keeping eye contact, speech delay, and absence of interest in participate in social interaction and adjusting behavior accordingly, deficit of using and understanding gestures, facial expressions and body language.
2. **Abnormal Behavior Patterns:** Exhibits stereotyped movements or behavior such as repetitive motor movements or speech, Fixated and restricted interest such as endearment to certain objects or activities, attention to sameness, tantrums, aggression hyperactivity to sensory inputs such as lack of concern to pain, offensive response to specific sounds or textures (Centers for disease control and prevention, 2020; P. Lanillos et al.,2020;She, T. et al.,2018.).

Not necessarily everybody with ASD has all these deficits and occurrence frequency of these symptoms can be increased in unfamiliar environments.

Autism begins at birth or shortly thereafter, but the symptoms are visible with their growth and continues throughout adulthood and no exact reason or cure has been found yet. By early intervention, the difficulties to have a normal life routine can be reduced and improving the quality of life can be done (She, T. et al.,2018;J. Shi, 2019).

Robots have been identified as potential assessment and therapeutic tools for accompanying ASD patients as they react and understand the physical world (object related) rather than the social world and are more responsive to social interaction when integrated with technology rather than human intervention (M.V, 2012).

RELATED WORKS

Robot Assistive Treatments

Based on the spectrum level, the respective symptoms may differ and treatment methods need to be adapted accordingly. Most of the researches for ASD focus on early detection and intervention to mitigate the adverse consequences of ASD that affect to the quality of the life (N. Ackovska, 2017;SM.Eack, 2013).

Diagnosis of ASD

Diagnosis is the first step of an effective disease management process. Early diagnosis of ASD has been shown that long-term benefits of clinical therapy for children with ASD (B.Scassellati, 2005). Diagnosing ASD risk during infancy stage will offer opportunity for early intervention and begins the therapies at earliest. Though Autism begins at birth or shortly thereafter, the differences in their behavioral patterns will be visible with their growth. Different type of approaches are available to diagnose ASD with or without human direct intervention. Role of robots or computational systems to diagnose ASD can be explained in two aspects. First one is observing the children's behavior patterns and do the predictions and the second is, analyzing neurobiological changes: For the studies related to neuroimaging, magnetic resonance imaging (MRI) and Positron Emission Tomography (PET) techniques can be used to analyze neurodevelopmental characteristics related to ASD.

Under the first approach, examine the eye gaze behavior is one of common way of diagnosing ASD. Several eye tracking methods for children with ASD has been discussed (Falck-Ytter et al.,2013). Identify ASD children using video data is another way of diagnosing. Combining both of these a novel method was proposed to recognize ASD children automatically, using raw video data for tracking trajectory of eye movement and classifying using SVM (support vector machine) was proposed (J. Li, Y. Zhong et al., 2018)

Under the second approach, analyze neuroimaging data to identify neurobiological changes occur in brain of autistic children. Several researches have been conducted to diagnose ASD using this approach. Classifying brain network-based features using image processing algorithms approach is discussed (S Mostafa, 2019), 3D convolutional neural networks was trained to visualize distinct brain structures of autistic children (Fengkai Ke et al., 2020).

In Italy, researches use three reference sensors to detect abnormalities of infants relating to autism focusing on eye-gaze tracking device with audio system and Ankle or wrist band with set of motion sensing device and toy ball with embedded force and tactile sensors to check and measure their respond accordingly for diagnosis purpose (D.J.Ricks & M.B.Colton, 2010).

Self-Initiated Interactions

The children with autism are reluctant to initiate the social communication. They find difficulties in expressing or requesting their needs. Systems designed to deliver therapies to improve this behavior are focusing on activities which they can be more proactive during communicating with others. The common way of addressing this deficit is to motivate them to engage with such activities where they being rewarded on making request or express their need. Robotics can be incorporated to create such environment while encouraging them for self-initiated interaction.

Engage in a Conversation

Focusing therapies to improve the turn talking behaviors is another type of aspect in treatments for ASD. These children reluctant to turn taking during a conversation and often found rambling without allowing any interference from an external party. Social robotics approach can help to make children interest in communication.

Imitating

Another type of technique used in ASD therapies is imitation therapeutic activities. Most of the children with ASD are not efficient in recognize –their peers, parents or therapist as "Social other". Imitating activities may help them to improve hand-eye coordination, observe and understand the existence of others presence around them. And these activities will make them to realize that communication actions are related and coupled with others. A study was done and to motivate ASD children in recognizing and imitating facial expressions using a robot called Tito which its mouth modeled using LEDs and present a smile or a frown (Duquette, A, 2007).

Emotional Recognition

A child with autism spectrum find difficulties in distinguish the differences of facial expressions. The same emotion could be recognize as two expressions with a slight difference. Since, Robots can repeatable its actions with same intense, robotic intervention for the ASD therapies will be an advantage.

Joint Attention

Another deficit of the children with ASD is lack of focus or joint attention during communication with another person. Joint attention difficulties can range from establishing eye contact with a visual of another person to focusing on a lesson in a classroom (D.J.Ricks & M.B.Colton, 2010). Many researches and clinical studies have been done by focusing on improving joint attention of an ASD child. Sara Ali et al., have discussed the results of applying new mathematical model based on adaptive multiple therapy. Multiple robot system was used to introduce the children with ASD to a concept of multi-person communication (S.Ali et al, 2019). To motivate the eye-gaze towards an object, Keepon robot has been used and once the child make the eye contact Keepon would positively react and show its excitement to encourage the child (D.J.Ricks & M.B.Colton, 2010). Another study was done to perform eye contact exercise in three different levels using Robot-NAO. In easy level robot says "Look at me" and repeat it until child look at the robot, and then says "Good" with adding the name of the child at the end and playing a cheerful music when child make the favorable interaction. In medium level, robot's stimulus is changed into calling by his/her name without using the phrase "Look at me" and successful interaction followed by music. In Final level; robot do not play the music to cheer his/her action (Palestra G et al., 2017).

Vocal Prosody

One among many issues in autistic children vocal prosody and intonation is recognize as another different deficit. They are not capable to recognize and understand the information beyond a sentence's literal meaning (B. Scassellati, 2005). In this scenario, adding prosody to SARs in order to augment speech recognize deficits of autistic children can be implemented. SAR designed with pitch contours signal capabilities can guide autistic children in vocal prosody while interacting them in well-planned activities (Marchi E et al., 2014).

BEHAVIOR AND COMMUNICATION APPROACHES FOR ASD

It is important to have professional assistance and care for most of the individuals with ASD, throughout their lives. To continue the research approach in evidence-based psychotherapy, both clinical expertise and expertise knowledge in applying the study's results are both needed.

The most effective treatment or intervention in autistic therapies depends on the individual's age, strength, challenges and differences. One of the most efficient ways of reducing the symptoms of an ASD child and improving them as an individual is early behavioral intervention programs. Behavioral intervention strategies pivot on social communication skill development and reduction of restricted interests and repetitive and challenging behaviors. Generally, in treatments, individuals with ASD are encouraged for positive behavior and discouraged for negative behaviors. The studies done for analyzing the effectiveness of such interventions has shown a significant improvement in their social skills and deplete of stereotyped behaviors (P. Esteban et al.2017).

Applied Behavior Analysis (ABA) is the most evidence-based treatment method used in researches and studies so far. Simply, ABA is a scientific approach in understanding the behavioral change in different environments, situations and how learning process takes place accordingly. Studies have been done using behavioral therapies shown that ABA has been recognized as the most effective therapy method by both the National Research Council and American Academy (J. Shi, 2019).

Social Assistive Robotics (SAR)

Robots assist the human in rehabilitation processes known as Assistive Robots. For diagnosing and treatment purposes they are modeled in different types such as humanoid, animal type and non-biomimetic (figure 01) around the world (A. R. T. et

Figure 1. Categorization of SARs depending on physical appearance

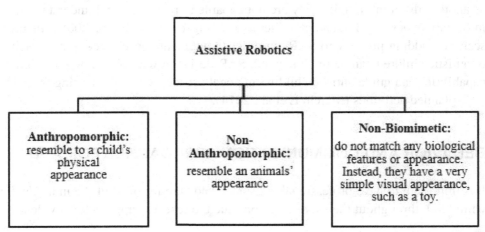

Al,2014). Assistive robots develop as helpful tools for improving social interaction is known as Social Assistive Robots (SAR) (L. S. N. L. Joseph & Pramod S, 2017).

Recent researches have shown that robot interaction can catalyze stimulating social skills in autistic children and encourage them to initiate communication, keep eye contact, imitate the actions and improve the social behavior (M. M. Achraf Othman,2017). SARs are used to establish an effective interaction with users to have a measurable improvement in rehabilitation and recovery processes. They can perform interactions diversely and act as a clinical role under minimal contribution of a professional intervention yet such devices or systems need to be properly validated.

SARs focus on assisting user in social behavior rather than physical interaction which leads to reduce the most possible risk-physical harm that can be encounter in human-Robot interaction (D. Feil-Seifer and M. J. Matarić,2011). Therapeutic intervention for the children with ASD need to be adapted in order to encourage them to initiate and respond with suitable social, emotional and cognitive cues (D. Feil-Seifer and M. J. Matarić, 2009).

Several robots have been used as a therapeutic tool for ASD such as The humanoid robot NAO (Figure 1) (Z. J. & H. M. M. Feng H, Gutierrez A,2013; r H. F. A,2012), Keepon (Figure 2); developed as effective communication tool to use in treatments for autistic children (H. Kozima etal.,2005), Popchilla; designed to improve attention skills in autistic kids (J. K. & D. jiang Bei Li,2017), Robots developed with touchscreens to improve Human Robot Interaction (HRI) such as CARO and iRobi (P. S. Yun SS, Kim H, Choi J, 2016) and a story telling robot (D. Anderborght B et al.,2012) to motive the interaction.

Figure 2. Interaction with NAO (IEEE SIGHT, 2018)

KASPAR(Figure 3) is one of the most used humanoid robot in therapy studies developed for improving social behavior by interaction with adults (Duquette, Aet al.,2007). Another type of humanoid robot designed to help in interacting with humans is Qtrobot (Figure 4) which can simply program for set of instructions and

Figure 3. A companion robot: Keepon performing eye-contact (H. Kozima et al., 2005)

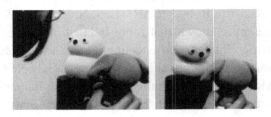

Figure 4. KASPAR: Therapy Robot (Duquette, A et al., 2007)

Figure 5. Qtrobot (Waltz E, 2018)

skills (Waltz E, 2018). Some robots were developed with a cartoonish appearance to attract children with autism and mostly motivate them in imitating facial expressions and joint attention (Ntaountaki P et al.,2020).

AN ARTIFICIAL INTELLIGENCE (AI)APPROACH AS AN INTERVENTION FOR CHILDREN WITH AUTISM

AI Based Approach for SARs

Artificial Intelligence (AI) and robotics are a strong combination for automating tasks that makes the robot capable of sensing, navigating, real-time course correction and calculating their reactions accordingly.

Recent researches indicate that children with ASD are more responsive to robotic/ AI applications because these devices can operate in the same manner without getting frustrated and facilitate less complicated behavior than human beings.

AI can be used to model robots or computational systems with the capacity of learning, understanding and creating appropriate reactions based on sensor inputs and allow prediction-based behavior to the SAR (Anagnostopoulou P, 2020). The children can be familiarized with routine-oriented interactions of the robot to improve their interactions by reducing anxiety to the unfamiliar situations. AI can be used to produce reciprocal peer interactions with use of graphical user interface (GUI) by sharing the control over the robot with any other responsible party such as teachers, therapist or parent. Peer interaction can motivate ASD children to interact with team activities such as playing board games, playing a catch or classroom scenarios (C. Nikolopoulos et al., 2011).

Children with ASD are facing difficulties in recognizing and differentiating emotional states of people around them. A SAR with emotion recognition technique integrated with deep learning that works in real time to predict the behavior of ASD children have been discussed (L. S. N. L. Joseph, & Pramod S.,2017)

The children with ASD find challenge in performing logical and analytical thinking. A human interaction robot head was developed using Convolution Neural Networks architecture for teaching logical and analytical skills to autistic children. It is implemented to engage in activities to identify digits, alphabets, colors and perform simple arithmetic calculations (Aniketh M et al., n.d.).

During social communication, complex behavioral and physiological processes will occur. Guedjou H. et al., have developed a multitasking human -robot posture imitating learning framework based on a neural network (H. Guedjou1et al.,n.d.)

Socially Assistive Robots (SAR) develops to support social and cognitive growth of children with ASD. While interacting with the robot it is important to examine the behavior of the Children with ASD, to have a metric about effectiveness of the therapy. M.Leo et al. (2015), were conducted a research to measure Human Robot Interaction for ASD children. The behavior and level of interaction with the robot were observed under two scenarios: bubble blowing game which is a standard ASD diagnosis method which normally able to provoke children's social behavior and the second was robot engages the user in a game of Simon-Says, where the robot encourage the child to imitate its gesture (M. M. David Feil-Seifer,n.d.). Marco Leo et al., have conducted a research on improving facial expressions of children with ASD. While the robot performs facial expressions, the child is asked to imitate it .An evaluation has been done to determine the effectiveness of the treatment as measure of the emotion imitation capability and processing time between robot request and the child response (M. Leo et al. 2015).

AI Based Approach for Neuroimaging

Neuroimaging is a recent promising approach that has the potential of observing and analyzing what can be the issues in brain development causing autism spectrum disorder and diagnose autism at earliest as possible (J. Lainhart,2015). Neuroimaging approach mitigate the drawback of the conventional method of diagnosing ASD which can do the diagnosing by observing abnormal behavior changes of a child only when they were old enough to disclose the symptoms of ASD.

Most prominent neuroimaging techniques that use to analyze the structure and functioning of human brain are magnetic resonance imaging (MRI) or positron emission tomography (PET). And these techniques can use to analyze the brain abnormalities occur in autistic spectrum disorder. [(J. Lainhart, 2015). It is observed an increase rate of brain growth and enlarged brain volume within first two years from a child birth has a high risk to develop autism disorder (M. Leo et al., 2015; Scudellari M,2017). There are considerable number of researches has been conducted related to neuroimaging approach for early detection of ASD in different scopes. Mostafa S et al., conducted a study to diagnose autism using Eigen values defined for brain network-based features and several machine learning algorithms (S. Mostafa et al., 2019), Jiao Y et al., were researched to develop ASD predictive model using regional cortical thickness of the brain (Jiao Y et al.,2009) a clinical research was done to enhance the features classification accuracy in brain of ASD person using several type of neural networks (F. Ke, S. Choi, et al.,2020).

For a precise diagnosis of ASD is necessary for its management and planning of rehabilitation activities. A review was conducted on Deep Learning for Neuroimaging-based Diagnosis and Rehabilitation of Autism Spectrum Disorder. Further, the studies conducted to diagnose of ASD using Deep Learning (DL) networks and rehabilitation tools modeled by using DL were discussed (M. Khodatars et al,2020)

DISCUSSION

Human-robot interaction (HRI) for social assistive robotics applications is a new and interdisciplinary research area by combining diverse of research fields such as medicine, neuroscience, social science, cognitive science, robotics and smart technologies. A variety of combined assistive robotics with AI platforms in different aspects, progressively being studied and has been generating a considerable impact through years. The major advantages of social assistive robots are they allow to have an interaction with 3D objects that are close to the real scenario and facilitate engaging and encouraging the learning process through imitation and interaction.

As discussed earlier, the conventional method of diagnosing ASD is observing the human behavior patterns. This can be a challenging task for a human observer because the behavior patterns of a child can be affected by several non-autism related factors such as age, living environment and cognitive functioning. At certain ages, it is difficult to differentiate these characteristics to verify a child with ASD. To address these challenges, robotic intervention and training can be augmented to observe human behavior patterns. For the training and automating purpose, a thorough study to the subject has to be done and lots of data need to be collected and maintained, related to human behavior patterns.

One of the main drawback in the all studies discussed here is the strength of the evidence is limited. Though these case studies had shown qualitative statistics for their approaches, but not sufficient in quantitatively. Most of the studies were done using limited number of robots, less number of individuals sample and observation was done over few days, few weeks or few months. And the sample selecting methods are lack of statistical power. In summary, a large scale of experiments and clinical studies are need to be conducted with a proper statistical methods and an appropriate methodology. Further, studies can be done to analyze which exact functions and characteristics of these SARs contributing for the positive outcomes and responses.

Socially Assistive robots integrated with AI platforms for ASD treatments is an emerging field with solution creation to address a variety of challenges that have to be dealt with in therapeutic treatments for autism such as decreasing anxiety during teaching phase that occurs due to spontaneous and unpredictable behavior of human nature, capability of performing repetitive tasks with same intense level, giving much attention and time comparatively to a human therapist, invent as a cost effective solution, flexibility of controlling, monitoring and maintain the treatment level accordingly. Regardless of social skill and interaction development, occupational therapy is useful for some children to improve their life as an individual.

Another important concern is facilitating multi-disciplinary approach in ASD treatments to strength the effectiveness of the therapies. Developing SAR systems with other smart technologies integrated, always need expertise knowledge in different specialization areas such as computer science, mechatronics engineering, social psychology, and clinical research. Every research group is not made of all these interdisciplinary expertise and absence of one of these expertise knowledge may lead for incomplete results. For an example, without psychiatrists and psychologists, long term clinical practices and continuity of research may not possible. This will miss the opportunity to measure the benefits of design decisions and chances in making any modifications to the design.

The hardware of SARs need to be strong enough to tolerate bumps, drops and knocks up to some extent. Developing robotic solutions for ASD treatments with simple, flexible, sufficiently sturdy and nonthreatening is a greater challenge.

Design is the most important stage of developing process of robotics solutions for ASD therapies. It includes altogether mechanical design, control algorithms, mode of control, electronics circuit designs and power distribution. The design can be integrated with smart technologies such as Internet of Things (IoT), machine learning, deep learning and neural network for a better performance. The mode of control can be fully autonomous or either remotely controlled. It is very challenging to operate them autonomously as they are expected to perform and adapt their actions and responses automatically considering the situation while interacting with children with ASD. For an example, SARs developed for imitating activities, the robot need to recognize child's body motion accurately, mapping the body parts movements through space and know when to begin its actions exactly.

Integrating robotics with artificial intelligence will create more opportunities in medical application field. SARs development with Artificial intelligence would create more possible solutions for ASD therapies. AI methods have been used to early diagnosis of ASD. Support vector machine, supervised machine learning algorithms are the most used approaches for this purpose. Applying AI techniques in neuroimaging studies related to ASD is consider as a promising approach for early diagnosing of ASD. The most critical challenge for diagnosing autism spectrum disorder at early stage of a life is inadequate neurobiological evidences. Machine Learning approaches need big data and the most of the studies import collected data from data repositories. Therefore, it is very much required of having proper validated training data set for research purpose. Using neural networks, accuracy level of predictions in diagnosis of ASD or either in human-robot interaction can be improved with the sample size of training.

Broadly divert autistic symptoms with different levels of severity highlight the requirement of adaptability of therapeutic robots according to the situation. It is not much useful to program them to operate within a fixed frame and when they are programmed once for an autistic child, it may not appropriate even for another child with same deficit. Therefore, to have a better interaction, Artificial intelligence integrated SARs can be recognized as a promising approach which can train robot to think, make decisions and act accordingly.

REFERENCES

Ackovska, Kirandziska, Tanevska, Bozinovska, & Božinovski. (2017). Robot - assisted therapy for autistic children. *SoutheastCon 2017*, 1-2. doi:10.1109/SECON.2017.7925401

Ali, S., Mehmood, F., Dancey, D., Ayaz, Y., Khan, M. J., Naseer, N., Amadeu, R. D. C., Sadia, H., & Nawaz, R. (2019). An Adaptive Multi-Robot Therapy for Improving Joint Attention and Imitation of ASD Children. *IEEE Access: Practical Innovations, Open Solutions*, 7, 81808–81825. doi:10.1109/ACCESS.2019.2923678

Anagnostopoulou, P., Alexandropoulou, V., Lorentzou, G., Lykothanasi, A., Ntaountaki, P., & Drigas, A. (2020). Artificial Intelligence in Autism Assessment. *International Journal of Emerging Technologies in Learning*, 15(06), 95. doi:10.3991/ijet.v15i06.11231

Anderborght, Simut, Saldien, Pop, Rusu, Pintea, & Lefeber. (2012). Using the social robot probo as a social story telling agent for children with ASD. Interact. Stud., 13.

Centers for Disease Control and Prevention. (2020). *Treatment | Autism Spectrum Disorder (ASD) | NCBDDD | CDC*. https://www.cdc.gov/ncbddd/autism/treatment.html

Duquette, A., Michaud, F., & Mercier, H. (2007). Exploring the use of a mobile robot as an imitation agent with children with low functioning autism. *Autonomous Robots, 24*(2), 147-157.

Eack, S. M., Greenwald, D. P., Hogarty, S. S., Bahorik, A. L., Litschge, M. Y., Mazefsky, C. A., & Minshew, N. J. (2013). Cognitive enhancement therapy for adults with autism spectrum disorder: Results of an 18-month feasibility study. *Journal of Autism and Developmental Disorders, 43*(12), 2866–2877. doi:10.100710803-013-1834-7 PMID:23619953

Esteban. (2017). *How to Build a Supervised Autonomous System for Robot-Enhanced Therapy for Children with Autism Spectrum Disorder*. Academic Press.

Falck-Ytter, T., Bölte, S., & Gredebäck, G. (2013). Eye tracking in early autism research. *Journal of Neurodevelopmental Disorders*, 5(1), 28. doi:10.1186/1866-1955-5-28 PMID:24069955

Feil-Seifer. (n.d.). *Robot assisted therapy for children with Autism Spectrum Disorders*. Academic Press.

Feil-Seifer & Matarić. (2009). *Toward Socially Assistive Robotics for Augmenting Interventions for Children with Autism Spectrum Disorders*. Academic Press.

Feil-Seifer, D., & Matarić, M. J. (2011). Socially Assistive Robotics. *IEEE Robotics & Automation Magazine, 18*(1), 24–31. doi:10.1109/MRA.2010.940150

Guedjou, Boucenna, Xavier, Cohen, & Chetouani. (n.d.). *The Influence of Individual Social Traits on Robot Learning in a Human-Robot Interaction*. Academic Press.

IEEE Sight. (2018). Humanoid Robots for Therapeutic Treatment of Autism Spectrum Disorder (ASD). *Children*.

Jiao, Y., Chen, R., Ke, X., Chu, K., Lu, Z., & Herskovits, E.H. (2009). Predictive models of autism spectrum disorder based on brain regional cortical thickness. *Neuroimage, 50*(2), 589-599. doi:10.1016/j.neuroimage

Ke, F., Choi, S., Kang, Y. H., Cheon, K., & Lee, S. W. (2020). Exploring the Structural and Strategic Bases of Autism Spectrum Disorders With Deep Learning. *IEEE Access: Practical Innovations, Open Solutions, 8*, 153341–153352. doi:10.1109/ACCESS.2020.3016734

Ke, F., Choi, S., Kang, Y. H., Cheon, K., & Lee, S. W. (2020). Exploring the Structural and Strategic Bases of Autism Spectrum Disorders With Deep Learning. *IEEE Access: Practical Innovations, Open Solutions, 8*, 153341–153352. doi:10.1109/ACCESS.2020.3016734

Khodatars. (2020). *Deep Learning for Neuroimaging-based Diagnosis and Rehabilitation of Autism Spectrum Disorder*. Academic Press.

Kozima, H., Nakagawa, C., & Yasuda, Y. (2005). Interactive robots for communication-care: a case-study in autism therapy. *ROMAN 2005. IEEE International Workshop on Robot and Human Interactive Communication*, 341-346, 10.1109/ROMAN.2005.1513802

Lainhart, J. (2015). Brain imaging research in autism spectrum disorders. *Current Opinion in Psychiatry, 28*(2), 76–82. doi:10.1097/YCO.0000000000000130 PMID:25602243

Lanillos, Oliva, & Philippsen, Yamashita, Nagai, & Cheng. (2020). A review on neural network models of schizophrenia and autism spectrum disorder. *Neural Networks*, ●●●, 122.

Leo. (2015). *Automatic Emotion Recognition in Robot-Children Interaction for ASD Treatment*. Academic Press.

Li, J., Zhong, Y., & Ouyang, G. (2018). Identification of ASD Children based on Video Data. *2018 24th International Conference on Pattern Recognition (ICPR),* 367-372. 10.1109/ICPR.2018.8545113

Marchi, E., Ringeval, F., & Schuller, B. (2014). *Voice-enabled assistive robots for handling autism spectrum conditions: An examination of the role of prosody.* Academic Press.

Michel, P. (2004). *The Use of Technology in the Study*. Diagnosis and Treatment of Autism.

Mostafa, S., Tang, L., & Wu, F. (2019). Diagnosis of Autism Spectrum Disorder Based on Eigenvalues of Brain Networks. *IEEE Access: Practical Innovations, Open Solutions, 7,* 128474–128486. doi:10.1109/ACCESS.2019.2940198

Nikolopoulos. (2011). *Robotic Agents used to Help Teach Social Skills to Children with Autism: The Third Generation*. Academic Press.

Ntaountaki, P., Lorentzou, G., Lykothanasi, A., Anagnostopoulou, P., Alexandropoulou, V., & Drigas, A. (2019). Robotics in Autism Intervention. *International Journal of Recent Contributions from Engineering Science & IT, 7*(4), 4–17. doi:10.3991/ijes.v7i4.11448

Palestra, G., Carolis, B.D., & Esposito, F. (2017). Artificial Intelligence for Robot-Assisted Treatment of Autism. *WAIAH@AI*IA*.

Ricks, D. J., & Colton, M. B. (2010). Trends and considerations in robot-assisted autism therapy. *2010 IEEE International Conference on Robotics and Automation,* 4354-4359. 10.1109/ROBOT.2010.5509327

Scassellati, B. (2005). How Social Robots Will Help Us to Diagnose, Treat, and Understand Autism. *Procs. 12th Int. Symp. on Robotics Research*.

Scudellari, M. (2017). AI Predicts Autism From Infant Brain Scans. *IEEE Spectrum.*

She, T., Kang, X., Nishide, S., & Ren, F. (2018). Improving LEO Robot Conversational Ability via Deep Learning Algorithms for Children with Autism. *2018 5th IEEE International Conference on Cloud Computing and Intelligence Systems (CCIS),* 416-420.

Shi. (2019). The Application of AI as Reinforcement in the Intervention for Children With Autism Spectrum Disorders (ASD). *Journal of Educational and Developmental Psychology*, *9*.

Diehl & Schmitt. (2012). The clinical use of robots for individuals with Autism Spectrum Disorders: A critical review. *Research in Autism Spectrum Disorders*, *6*. PMID:22125579

Waltz, E. (2018). Therapy Robot Teaches Social Skills to Children With Autism. *IEEE Spectrum*.

World Health Organization. (2019). *Autism spectrum disorders*. WHO.

Yun, Kim, & Choi. (2016). A robot-assisted behavioral intervention system for children with autism spectrum disorders. *Rob. Auton. Syst.*

Chapter 2

Wearable Technology as a Source of Data–Generation Tool for Artificial Intelligence

Gyasi Emmanuel Kwabena
https://orcid.org/0000-0001-6801-9013
Vellore Institute of Technology, Vellore, India

Mageshbabu Ramamurthy
Sri Sakthi Amma Institute of Biomedical Research, India

Akila Wijethunga
https://orcid.org/0000-0002-7672-6583
University of Sri Jayewardenepura, Sri Lanka

Purushotham Swarnalatha
Vellore Institute of Technology, Vellore, India

ABSTRACT

The world is fascinated to see how technology evolves each passing day. All too soon, there's an emerging technology that is trending around us, and it is no other technology than smart wearable technology. Less attention is paid to the data that our bodies are radiating and communicating to us, but with the timely arrival of wearable sensors, we now have numerous devices that can be tracking and collecting the data that our bodies are radiating. Apart from numerous benefits that we derive from the functions provided by wearable technology such as monitoring of our

DOI: 10.4018/978-1-7998-3335-2.ch002

fitness levels, etc., one other critical importance of wearable technology is helping the advancement of artificial intelligence (AI) and machine learning (ML). Machine learning thrives on the availability of massive data and wearable technology which forms part of the internet of things (IoT) generates megabytes of data every single day. The data generated by these wearable devices are used as a dataset for the training and learning of machine learning models. Through the analysis of the outcome of these machine learning models, scientific conclusions are made.

INTRODUCTION

It is fascinating to see how technology evolves at each passing day. Technological innovations have led to the reduction of monitoring devices and power sources, unveiling an entire innovative world of opportunities and advancements. Some people call the internet, the summation of human knowledge as they perceive it to be everything that we know at our fingertips. Those with this school of thought are not far from the right since one is seen as haven the entire world in his palm when he is connected to the internet. Smartphones give us the ability to connect to human knowledge anywhere that we find ourselves. What intrigues the masses of technology fanatics is the question of what comes next after the smartphone? And again, the question of whether technology is going to be a new form of human connection to knowledge? All too soon, there's an emerging technology that is trending around us now, and it is no other technology than **Smart Wearable Technology**. Although wearable products are not new, the touch of smartness, the application of Artificial Intelligence, and the implementation of sensor technology to some of these wearable accessories are novel.

What Is Wearable Technology?

Generally, we don't pay the needed attention to the data that our body is radiating even though it constantly radiate data. Not until we fall seriously sick, we usually disregard this message that our bodies are telling us. For instance, waking up early in the morning with a sore throat and backache may be a sign that your body is telling us, that we have not been paying attention or looking after it very well. It's at that point that it will dawn on us to seek for more rest, drink our water, take more vitamins, and indulge in exercise. Sometimes, not until we visit our Doctor and he breaks the bad news of our lab results showing high cholesterol level, and we turned to pay attention to the food that we eat, or the exercise that we get. It's at that point that it occurs to us, the need to eat a well-balanced diet, have rigorous exercise, etc. Certainly, we disregard the massive data that our bodies are radiating but thankfully, the timely arrival of wearable devices promises to change the status quo. Numerous devices can be tracking and collecting the data that our bodies are radiating and allow us to analyze it in real-time and make changes in our lives at the most basic human level. Most scientists, engineers, and researchers have tried defining what wearable technology is about. While some define it as a category of electronic devices implanted in the user's body or tattooed on the skin, embedded in clothes that can be worn as accessories, others too define it as simply the electronic technology or devices incorporated into items that can be comfortably worn on the body. One notable definition among them, which this book will adopt is the definition by Duking P. et al, 2018.

Definition: *Wearable Technology which is also referred to as fashion electronics, wearables, fashion technology, or tech togs are smart electronic devices usually, with micro-controllers or sensors that are worn close to and/or on the surface of the skin, where they can detect, analyze, and transmit information concerning e.g. body signals such as vital signs, and/or ambient and which allow in some cases immediate biofeedback to the wearer, Duking P. (2018).*

BACKGROUND OF WEARABLE TECHNOLOGY

In 1571, Queen Elizabeth received the first wearable device which was a wristwatch, as a new year's gift. Then came the ABACUS Ring in 1644. In 1950, the Button Spy camera was invented which was used mostly by the United State of America's CIA. Then in 1961, the Gambling shoe which is the first computer was introduced. The year 1979 was when wearable computing, which was in the form of helmet, backpack, etc. was introduced. In the 1980s, a pre-modern wearable technology which is a wearable calculator watch was also introduced. A hearing aid is also another earlier modern technology to be invented. Wearables ranging from electronic headbands used as a costume in theaters, Rings as a computational device by traders and a wearable camera strapped to a bird to take aerial photos to mention but a few have since been used by man. In 2000, the first Bluetooth headset was introduced, then followed by the commercialization of Fitbit Tracker in September 2009. A Kickstarter campaign was launched by Oculus in 2012 to start the sale of the first consumer virtual reality headset. Samsung Galaxy Gear which is the first smartwatch was released in September 2013, then followed by the Apple Watch in April 2015.

According to Harito (2020), the Virtual Reality (VR) headset manufactured by HTC Company in 2016 allow users to move freely within a virtual space.

MAIN FOCUS OF THE ARTICLE

Types of Wearable Technologies

Although there are different types of wearable technologies, depending on the manufacturer of a particular type of wearable device, the functions sometimes overlap, as one type of wearable device may have several functions that are found in the other types of wearables. Below are the types of wearable devices;

- Fitness Tracker.
- SmartWatch.
- Head-Mounted Display.
- Sports Watch.
- Smart Jewelry.
- Smart Clothing.
- Implantable, etc.

Smart Watch: This is a digital watch or device that performs many other functions such as receiving of messages, emails, apart from telling time. The smartwatch provides the user with notifications on their calls, social media updates, and many more. It has a touch screen just like the phone, which allows the user to swipe or type text using the screen.

Fitness Tracker: This is a wearable device that helps keep track of the number of steps the wearer walks each day and also monitors the heart rate continuously. Fitness tracker calculates and reports accurate data on calories burn and that of exercises performed by the wearer.

Head Mounted Display (HMD): This is a wearable device or display-device that is worn on the head or as part of a helmet that has a small display optic in front of one or each eye. If the display optic is in front of one eye, it is referred to as the Monocular-Head-Mounted Display. On the other hand, if the display optic is in front of each eye, it is referred to as the Binocular Head-Mounted Display. HMD is used in areas such as medicine, gaming, engineering, and aviation. HMD can be categorized into two groups namely, Virtual Reality Devices and Augmented Reality Devices. Luke Dormehl (2017).

Virtual Reality (VR): This is an artificial environment that lets the user believe and accepts it as a real world. For education purposes, students wear virtual reality devices to study and communicate in a three-dimensional environment. They use it in medical training by allowing both the Doctor (practitioner) and the student to practice surgeries and procedures.

Augmented Reality (AR): This overlays new information on the existing environment. In medicine, it helps improve the surgeon's sensory perception, reduce and avoid the potential risk. For navigation purposes, augmented reality devices with GPS technology helps to reach a destination easier.

Sports Watches: This is a rugged and water-resistant watch or wearable device that provides services such as heart rate monitor, stopwatch, tachymeter (rotating bezel for calculating speed), alarm, tide indicator (for divers), compass, and thermometer.

Smart Jewelry: This is a smartwatch or wearable device that is designed as pieces of jewelry and it is mostly intended for women. This jewelry gives notifications such as calls, text messages, emails, etc. to the users when they are out of reach to their phones.

Smart Clothing: This is also known as high-tech clothing, electronic textiles, e-textiles, smart wear, smart garments, smart textiles, monitors the wearer's or user's condition. Bodysuits and Smart shirts provide biometric data such as temperature, heart rhythm, and physical movements, pulse rate, muscle stretch, and the data is transmitted through Bluetooth to an app (software) in real-time.

Implantable: These are wearable electronics or technologies that are surgically implanted under the skin of the user. The main purpose of the implantable smart device is to help improve the user's health condition. Patients with heart diseases are made to undergo surgery to insert an insertable cardiac monitor to monitor and record the heart rate. Doctors can track the patient if he is fainting, by downloading the information and analyzing it to figure out the exact problem. Implantable smart devices also allow doctors to monitor Parkinson's disease. Parkinson affects the nerve cells that produce the dopamine which leads to body stiffness and slowing. The Implantable smart device called "WAND" is planted into the patient's body to monitor the brain's electrical activity, learn to identify the abnormal signals, and also to modulate electrical signals to prevent the symptoms from occurring once more. Implantable are used for tracking insulin levels, tracking contraception. To use Implantable as contraception, a microchip that contains a tiny reservoir of the hormone levonorgestrel is used for contraception.

Categories of Wearable Technology Products

Wearable Technologies can be categorized into:

§ Health Wearables
§ Security Wearables

§ Sports Wearables
§ Fashion Wearables
§ Entertainment Wearables
§ Pleasure Wearables

Health Wearables

Flagship life-changing wearable technology applications are undisputedly found in medical devices. In recent years, attention has been given to the manufacturing of medical wearable devices purposely for healthcare uses. More often than not, the health condition of the user who wears the wearable device is monitored. Provided, the device is worn or is nearby of the user, it can certainly record the data that the user is radiating. Some of the data that wearable devices can collect from a user's health care; Calories burned, Blood Pressure, Heart Rate, Release of certain biochemicals, Steps walked Time Spent Exercising, Physical Strain, Seizures, and many more. Monitoring of local air quality, measurement of pollutants, and identification of hotspots for residents with respiratory problems are performed by the use of wearable technology or devices made by AIR in Louisville, Kentucky. According to Harito (2020), an intelligent patch called iTBra which can detect signs of breast cancer at the early stage and at the same time transmit the information to a laboratory for analysis has also been developed by Cyrcadia Health. The impaired and the elderly are significantly benefiting from the wearable medical alert monitors since it extends greater mobility and independence. Smart tattoos that contain flexible electronic sensors are being developed to monitor muscle function, sleep disorders, heart and brain activity, etc. Although these are short-term, nothing is left to chance including inks. A wearable device such as smartwatches is made for Parkinson patients to track and transmit data relating to the symptoms. The transmitted data is used to tailor treatment plans solely for the user. Examples of Health Wearables are Apple

Figure 1. Sample health wearable devices

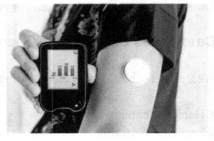

Watch Series 2, Samsung Galaxy Gear Sports, etc. Figure 1. Shows some examples of health wearable devices.

Security Wearables

Recently, attention to the development of wearable devices or technology has been shifted from consumer accessories to several expert and hands-on applications. Keys and passwords are now substituted with microchip implants. The chip which is embedded in a fingertip uses near-field communication (NFC) or radio-frequency identification (RFID) which are akin to the chips used to track missing pets. The military of the United State of America is seemingly making an allowance for the use of radio-frequency identification chips to keep track of its troops globally. Wearable accessories such as KERV Ring is the world's first MasterCard contactless payment ring that has been invented. KERV Ring is fitted with sensors that can be used for authentication and signing into the wearer's Bank Account, Airport gate entries (Boarding pass), London's Tube, and any other public transport network that accepts contactless payments at the point of entry, etc. Child monitoring devices equipped with GPS are available and are used to track and monitor the movement of children. Nimb is also a Smart Ring with a panic button that allows the user to send an emergency alert to preset contacts from the user's mobile app with just a touch of the user's thumb without drawing unwanted attention. Figure 2. Shows some examples of security wearable devices.

Figure 2. Sample security wearables

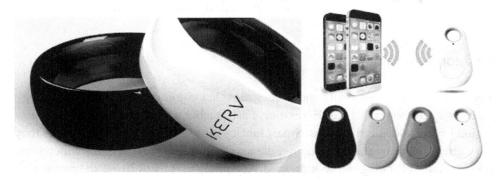

KER V Contactless Payment Ring   Child GPS Tracking System

Sports Wearables

These are wearable devices that are worn by sportsmen and women or are attached to their vest or boots to obtain or collect biometric data such as; global positioning data (e.g. distances covered or the speed reached by an athlete on the field), heart rate, blood oxygen levels, body temperature, sleep data, accelerometry data (e.g. to assess the energy expenditure of an athlete in training). These biometric data can assist athletes and coaching staff to monitor health and injury risks, assess the athlete's physical exertion, and tailor training programs to meet individual needs. These devices also aid the athletes, for instance, Simon Wheatcroft is blind but he has run ultramarathons around the world by himself with the help of wearable technology. Figure 3. Show some examples of Sports wearable devices.

Figure 3. Sample sports wearables

Fashion Wearables

These are designed garments and accessories that combine functional technology with style and aesthetics e.g. E-Textiles. Fashionable wearables are also known as digital textile and smart textiles. Smart fabrics sense the wearer's moves ones they have direct relations and by so doing, the user's concerns such as communications, privacy, and well-being can be addressed. According to Harito (2020), the production of smart fabrics or garments is not reserved for one set of materials or colors since these can change in reaction to the embedded sensors in the gear. Fashion wearables such as Polar Seal are capable of regulating the temperature thereby controlling the heat of the dress worn by the user. This means that users can feel warm in winter and all year round as they will experience instant heat at the touch of a button. Bluetooth Gloves is another fashion wearable.

Entertainment Wearables

The use of Virtual Reality (VR) headsets and Augmented Reality (AR) glasses were mostly used in entertainment. Initially, VR and AR were mostly used in the gaming industry but there has been a paradigm shift, as they are now used more often in medicine and education. ZEROi Smart Cap is a wearable device that allows the user or the wearer of the Cap to listen to music and make phone calls without Bluetooth or the user's phone in hand. ORII is a voice assessment Ring that turns the user's finger into a smartphone all through just a touch of the ear. This is because, how we are using our devices is changing from a world where we use scenes and touch, to one where we talk. ORII uses bone conduction, and bone conduction has been used in many medical-grade devices. It is made in such a way that, it sends vibrations through your finger and directly into your ear, so only the user can hear. And that allows the user to hear and talk through just the finger. Due to bone conduction and the dual noise-canceling microphone, the user can hear and talk even in loud places. ORII is more than just a neat gadget for talking and making calls because behind it, is a powerful voice Artificial Intelligence. It also has a feature called Translation which is supported by Artificial Intelligence. All that the user has to do is just motion upwards and say ORII, how do I say; (e.g. *"Where are the burritos in Spanish?"*). The ORII Ring will then respond with *"Donde Estan Los burritos"*.

Pleasure Wearables

These are wearable technologies that respond to stimuli of the user. For instance, i.Con is a Smart Condom Ring fitness-tracker for the male reproductive organ (penis) which records, stores, and displays the man's sex performance statistics at the end of each sexual intercourse with a woman in addition to detecting signs of sexually transmitted infections (STIs). The smart condom ring can track the duration of intercourse, girth measurements, calories burnt, and the average number of thrusts. Another example of pleasure wearables is the Dress IT UP Wearables which is interactive clothes that change color or light up depending on the wearer's mood. The cloth has an LED studded collar that lights up in different colors based on a change in the electrical characteristics of the skin prompted by pleasure, excitement, stress, or other feelings or based on galvanic skin response. Figure 4. Shows some examples of Pleasure wearable devices.

Figure 4. Sample pleasure wearable devices

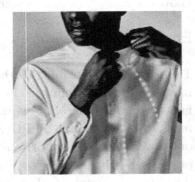

i.Con Smart Condom Ring   Smart Wearable Shirt.

Classification of Wearable Technologies

Two standards are used to classify wearable technology or devices. The first standard is based on product forms, including hand-worn (like a bracelet, watch, and gloves), body dressed (like a coat, trousers, and underwear), foot-worn (like shoes and socks), head-mounted (like glass and helmet). Whilst the other standard is based on product functions, including somatosensory control (like somatosensory controller), healthy living (like a smart bracelet, and sports wristband), information consulting (like a smartwatch, and smart glass), G. Chen (2014).

Characteristics of Wearable Devices

The following are five major characteristics of Wearable devices, L. BASS (2020):

- It should be able to use when in motion.
- It should be able to use even when your hands are free or not.
- It should allow the wearer to maintain his or her control.
- It should be available at all times; meaning, it should be constant and reliable.
- It should be present within the bodily envelope of the wearer, meaning, not only does it has to be attached to the body but also becomes an integral part of the person's apparel.

Table 1. List of some types of wearable technologies, properties, and their applications

	Description	Existing Products	Research Prototype
Accessories			
Wrist-worn			
Smart Watches	Wristwatch devices with a touchscreen display	Apple iWatch Samsung Gear Moto 360 Pebble Time	Smartwatch Life Saver Finger-writing with smart-watch
Wrist bands	Wrist-worn devices with fitness tracking capabilities or other functionalities. Generally without a touchscreen display	UP by Jawbone Fitbit Flex MOOV NOW Nymi Band	Wrist-worn Bioimpedance sensor Wrist-worn Smoking Gesture Detector Ultrasonic-speaker Embedded Wrist Piece and Neck Piece
Head-Mounted Devices			
Smart Eyewear	Spectacles or contact lenses with sensing, wireless communication, or other capabilities.	Microsoft HoloLense FUNKI Ambient Glasses Recon Jet	Google Glass Google Contact Lens Object Modeling Eye-wear iShadow Mobile Gaze Tracker Indoor Landmark Identification Supporting Wearables Chroma
Headset and Ear-buds	Bluetooth enabled headsets or ear plugs Sensor-embedded hats and neck-worn devices are also found in research products.	Sony Xperia Ear Apple Airpods Bragi Dash Pro	-
Other Accessories			
Smart Jewelry	Jewelry designed with features such as health-monitoring and handles control	Smarty Ring Kerv Bellabeat Leaf	Typing Ring Gesture Detection Ring
Straps	Chest straps, belts, arm bands, or knee straps equipped with sensors for health tracking or other functionalities.	MYO Armband Zephyr Bioharness	Pneumatic Armband BodyBeat
E-Textiles			
Smart Garment	Main clothing items that also serve as wearables such as shirts, pants and undergarments.	Athos Hug Shirt Solar Shirt Spinovo	Myovibe Dopplesleep
Foot / Hand-Worn	Shoes, Socks, insoles, or gloves embedded with sensors.	Lechal Sensoria Fujitsu Gesture - control Gloves	LookUp Gait Analysis Foot Worns Foot Worn Inertial Sensors
E-Patch			
Sensor Patches	Sensor patches that can be adhered to the skin for either fitness tracking or haptic applications	HealthPatch MD Thyne UPRIGHT	DuoSkin Tattoo-Based Iontophoretic-Biosensing System Smart Tooth Patch
T-Tattoo / E-Skin	Tattoos with flexible and stretchable electronic circuit to realize sensing and wireless data transmission.	Motorola e-tattoo Wearable interactive Stamp Platform	-

Basic Components of Wearable Technologies

Although there are various kinds of smart wearable devices, the main components of smart wearables are Control (Microcontrollers), Input/Output (Board), Conductive Textiles, Sensors, Actuators, Power, Networking (Wi-Fi or Internet, GPS, Bluetooth, BLE, NFC). Figure 5. Shows the functionality level of Sensors used in Smart Wearables.

Figure 5. The functionality level of sensors used in smart wearables

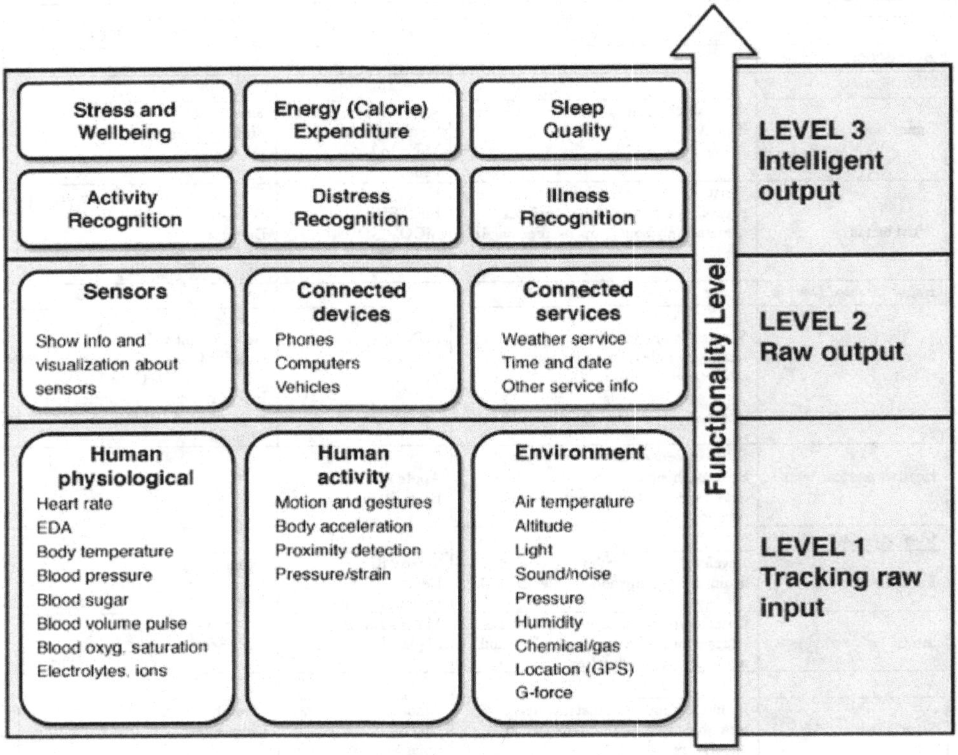

Working Conditions of Wearable Technologies

The wearable device operates as an interconnected system. Apart from the wearable device itself, an associated application running on the user's smartphone and the cloud server services which are the database for the storage and processing of data. In most cases, some third-party vendors render services such as internet connectivity, GPS, Google Maps, etc. Figure 6. Shows an Example of Wearable System Architecture.

Data Collection, Transmission, Processing, Analysis, and Storage of Wearable Device

Data Collection and Transmission

The wearable device which is nearby or in contact with the user gathers data from the user by the use of the sensors that are embedded in the device. For example, an

Figure 6. Example of wearable system architecture

Wearable Device	Smart Phone with Custom Application	Cloud Server Service	Stakeholders
Data Sensing	User Interface	Data Storage	Data Consumption
Some controls and feedback	Network Connectivity	Data Analysis	
	Basic Data Processing		

embedded temperature sensor will respond to the changing heat of the body of the user. A pre-installed software application which comes together with the operating system of the device then collect the changing response of the sensors (data) and then transmit it through the use of either Wi-Fi, GPS, Bluetooth, BLE, or NFC connectivity between the wearable device and the user's mobile phone.

The Smart Phone with Custom Application

The received data from the wearable device is processed through the algorithm of the software application on the mobile phone. The results of the processed data are either send back to the wearable device for it to be analyzed or it's displayed on the phone for analysis or both. In some cases, the results are transmitted to the database (Cloud server) of the wearable device's manufacturer (vendor). The connectivity between each node of the architecture is two-way communication.

Operating System Software for Wearable Devices

An Operating System which is mostly referred to as OS, is the system's software that runs computer hardware, software resource, and render corporate services for computer programs. It controls program execution, improves human-computer interaction, provides services for the users, creates a conducive working environment for the user, and support for other applications. Currently, there are several kinds of operating systems available for wearable devices even though most of them are not user friendly. The existence of several varieties of operating systems makes it difficult for developers to choose which OS is ideal for a particular device. Moreover, the application for the Operating system is not one-fit-all. An operating system meant for the wearable device must take into account the features of the wearable devices to achieve the following objectives.

Scalability: OS must be scalable and accommodate new system functions to be developed, tested, and contained within.

Convenience: The construct of the OS must be expedient to allow users to use wearable devices.

Multitasking: The operating system should be able to run multiple applications concurrently.

Effectiveness: The OS must be efficiently operationalized and maximize the use of resources such as Software, Hardware, and data of wearable devices.

Openness: The OS has to integrate well with other devices and services offered by various manufacturers to allow interoperability of applications and also retain portability, D. Y. Chen, (2000) and Fickas S. (1997).

Network Connectivity

Network protocols for wearable devices are very essential due to the interoperability of wearable devices and other appliances or machines like Computers, Mobile-Phones, and even different brands of wearable devices from different manufacturers. A network-protocol defines the network-communication mode of wearable devices, and decide exchange data-format as well as challenges associated with synchronization. Wi-Fi, Bluetooth (IEEE 802.15.1), NFC (IEEE 802.11), ZigBee (IEEE 802.15.4) are the four most well-known short-range wireless-communication protocol standards, J. S. Lee (2007). At the moment, network-communication-protocols for wearable devices are comparatively modest and centers largely on wireless-functions. Nevertheless, wearable devices will ultimately carry out several functions like those employed in mobile phones, such as GPRS, WAP, GRS, data transmission, or large files, etc. Given this, several dedicated network-communication-protocol supports are needed. Network-communication-protocols administered on mobile phones or tablet computers are to be transferred to wearable devices. Developers can alternatively, design special network-communication-protocols for wearable devices, which are safe, more energy-efficient, and with high-throughput.

Cloud Server Services

These are remote database servers of the vender (wearable device's manufacturer). It hosts the application software of the wearable device and keeps it updated at all times. It also stores the processed data received from the user's mobile phone. Vendors provide services to third parties such as insurance agencies, healthcare providers, etc.

Database Management System: Since wearable devices have different functionalities, the data recorded are interchangeable and might comprise important personal information, external environment changing data, and physical health data, etc. Apart from the local database, Cloud database management systems become necessary. Hence, specific DBMS that can cope and run various data should be designed. It should be lightweight and have a fast response speed. Alternatively, prevailing DBMS on a mobile phone can be transferred to wearable devices.

Stakeholders

These are third party agencies, companies, or organizations that solicit data from the manufacturers of these smart wearable devices.

Importance of Wearable Technology

Apart from numerous benefits that we derive from the functions provided by wearable technology such as, monitoring of our fitness levels, viewing text messages, making and receiving calls without touching our phones, tracking our location with GPS, receiving messages and notifications, etc. one other critical importance of wearable technology is helping the advancement of Artificial Intelligence (AI) and Machine Learning (ML). Machine Learning thrives on the availability of massive data and wearable technology which forms part of the Internet-of-Things (IoT) generates megabytes of data every single day. The data generated by these wearable devices are used as a dataset for the Training and learning of Machine Learning models. Through the analysis of the outcome of these Machine Learning models, scientific conclusions are made. What all these technologies are doing is in three basic premises that involve some form of searching in this life these days is to make us warier of our bodies; To be more mindful and pay more attention to our environment that affect our lives; And to be more existing in this world.

Challenges of Wearable Technology

Although the development of wearable devices is traced back in the 1950s, it is still not mature as their importance has not been fully harnessed enough. Once it is still on the learning stage, wearable technology is destined to suffer numerous setbacks such as OS and software incompatibility, functional singleness, security and confidentiality of the information, the convenience of human-computer interaction, and energy consumption problems due to continuous running, etc.

Table 2. List of some wearable devices

Type	Properties	Capabilities	Applications
Smartwatch	• Low operating power • User friendly interface with both touch and voice commands	• Displays specific information • Payments • Fitness / Activity tracking • Communication • Navigation	• Businesses, Administration • Marketing, Insurance • Professional Sports, Training • Education • Infotainment
Smart Eyewear	• Controlled by touching the screen, hand movement, voice command, and hand shake • Low operating power send sound directly to the ear	• Visualization • Language Interpretation • Communication • Task coordination	• Surgery • Aerospace and defense • Logistics • Education • Infotainment
Fitness Tracker	• High accuracy • Waterproof • Lightweight • Wireless communication	• Physiological wellness • Navigation • Fitness / Activity tracking • Heart Rate Monitor	• Fitness • Healthcare • Professional Sports • Outdoor / Indoor sports
Smart Clothing	• No visual interaction with user via displaying or screen • Data are obtained by body sensors and actuators	• Heart Rate, Daily Activity, Temperature, and Body position tracking • Heating or cooling the body • Automatic payment	• Professional sports fitness • Medicine • Military • Logistics
Wearable Camera	• Making first-person capture attachable on clothes or body • Smaller dimensions • Night vision	• Captures real-time first-person photos and video • Live Streaming • Fitness / Activity tracking	• Defense • Fitness • Industry • Education
Wearable Medical Device	• Pain management • Physiological tracking • Glucose monitoring • Sleep monitoring • Brain activity monitoring	• Cardiovascular diseases • Physiological disorders • Chronic diseases; diabetes • Surgery • Neuroscience • Dermatology • Rehabilitation	• Fitness • Cardiovascular medicine • Psychiatry • Surgery • Oncology • Dermatology • Respirology

CONCLUSION

When one is confronted with the choice of choosing between life and privacy, a sizeable number of people will go for the former. Although the usage of wearable technology is bedeviled by the issue of a potential breach of privacy and confidentiality of the user due to the cloud storage of the recorded data, the benefits accrued by using the wearable device supersedes that of potential confidentiality breaches. A woman in labor pays little or no attention to her privacy at that critical moment in labor. Whether the physician is a male or female gynecologist, she cares less since

all that she is looking for, is safe delivery. Using a smart wearable device should be situated in this context since it is a lifesaving technology that must be given the needed full attention. In the same vein, individually, our bodies are radiating data continuously and loudly. The data are so loud but before the advent of wearable technology, doctors were the only persons that had the speaker to listen to the voice of the data that our bodies are radiating. With these wearable devices, we can simply connect it to our smartphones, and instantly, we get the image of our heart's health shorn of ever going to see the doctor. There's no doubt that the benefit of using wearable technology is enormous hence all must embrace it while we look for possible solutions to the lingering problems. Industry players can adopt the latest encryption technology methods to safeguard and secure the data of their customers whilst researchers continue to dive deeper into the manufacturing and working conditions of these wearable devices.

REFERENCES

Bass. (1997). *Conveners report of CHI ' 97 Workshop on Wearable Computers.* Personal Communication to attendees. http:// www.bham.ac.uk/ManMechEng/ieg/w1.html

Chen. (2014). *Smart Wearable Change the World: The Next Business Tides.* Benjing: Publishing House of Electronics Industry.

Chen, D. Y. (2000). The Evolution and Trend of Wearable Computer (2). [Natural Science Edition]. *Journal of Chongqing University, 23*(4), 142–148.

Dormehl. (2017 November). *8 Major Milestones in the Brief History of Virtual Reality.* www.digitaltrends.com

Düking, P., Achtzehn, S., Holmberg, H. C., & Sperlich, B. (2018). Integrated Framework of Load Monitoring by a Combination of Smartphone Applications, Wearables, and Point-of-Care Testing Provides Feedback that Allows Individual Responsive Adjustments to Activities of Daily Living. *Sensors (Basel), 18*(5), 1632. doi:10.339018051632 PMID:29783763

Fickas, S., Kortuem, G., & Segall, Z. (1997). Software organization for dynamic and adaptable wearable systems. Wearable Computers. *Digest of Papers, First International Symposium on. IEEE, 1997,* 56-63

Harito, C., Utari, L., Putra, B. R., Yuliarto, B., Purwanto, S., Zaidi, S. S. J., Bavykin, D. V., Marken, F., & Walsh, F. C. (2020). Review—The Development of Wearable Polymer-Based Sensors: Perspectives. *Journal of the Electrochemical Society*, *167*(3), 037566. doi:10.1149/1945-7111/ab697c

Lee, J. S., Su, Y. W., & Shen, C. C. (2007). A comparative study of wireless protocols: Bluetooth, UWB, ZigBee, and Wi-Fi. Industrial Electronics Society, *IECON 2007. 33rd Annual Conference of the IEEE*, 46-51.

Chapter 3
An Analysis of Pattern Recognition and Machine Learning Approaches on Medical Images

Jaya S.
Sri Sarada College for Women, India

Latha M.
Sri Sarada College for Women, India

ABSTRACT

This chapter focuses on detailed overview of medical images as well as microscopic images to diagnosis the disease based on pattern recognition model in digital image processing. Pattern recognition is leading role in machine learning model which is used to detect the object such as text or character recognition, fingerprint recognition, face recognition, and biometric recognition. This chapter used pap smear images of cervical cancer to diagnosis a tissues by applying various image processing techniques followed by four tasks which are image acquisition, preprocessing, feature extraction, and object recognition. Cervical cancer is one of the very dangerous kind of cancer which may occur on the cervix part of the women. Diagnosis of tissue cells is based on the pixel variations of the images that may predict the cell is normal or abnormal state. This chapter presents machine learning algorithm of principle component analysis (PCA), Singular value decomposition (SVD), and linear discriminant analysis (LDA) under dimensionality reduction to recognize the pattern of the pap smear microscopic images.

DOI: 10.4018/978-1-7998-3335-2.ch003

INTRODUCTION

Machine Learning and Artificial Intelligence

Machine learning is comes under the Artificial intelligence(AI). The main objective of machine learning is to infer the structure of data and applying the data into training models which can be implied and accessed by people. Machine learning algorithms are implemented into a computer and it is used to train and test the data for obtaining a accuracy level in classification phase. At present there are various machine learning algorithms are available that can be used by multiple fields such as healthcare, remote sensing, pattern recognition, data science and data analytics for business development, information technology, agriculture, home appliances and many more. Machine learning algorithms are utilized to building some models from sample data that provides automatic decision making solution and solves problems based on the input data given by the user. Learn computers by uploading different kind of data samples based on the requirements of the user helping with machine learning models or algorithms. Supervised, unsupervised and reinforcement learning algorithms are comes under the types of machine learning algorithms.

Artificial Intelligence is increasingly helping in medical field to diagnosis a disease stage of the patient. AI can refer the previous records of the patient based on the information hidden behind the image which defines the problems and solutions of patient health. Medical image data set is one of the valuable source collection of data about the patient and more over it is very complex. The development of AI technologies helping in the field of clinical sector in form of CT Scan, MRI images, microscopic image analysis and pathologist to take decision on the images. Automated disease detection is possible in medical sector only after arrival of artificial intelligence. Image processing in one of the image analysis tool for enhancing and improving quality of the image by applying various filters, edge detection algorithms, thresholding, morphological operations, segmentation, feature extraction algorithms. Image processing techniques are mostly used in medical images such as, brain tumor, breast cancer, mammography images, pathology images, fundus images, pap smear images of cervical cancer, lung cancer and many images. The fundamental steps in image processing is enhancement of the image, applying filters and threshold techniques, segmentation of the object, feature extraction from the segmented image and finally classification task by using machine learning approaches.

Machine learning is a part of artificial intelligence. Machine learning is learning huge data and it is automatically make a decision based on the past experience. For this many machine learning algorithms are applicable to take a decision as a human being. Prediction, description are build to predict the future event earlier for example rain fall prediction, business strategies, medical disease diagnosis, agricultural field and many more. In present days, machine learning and artificial intelligence are combined together making a huge development technologies worldwide to solves the problems which human can not do. Basically human beings can able to recognize objects based on past learning experiences. For example, when the human looks at a car, bike, tree, house, toys, devices they can easily recognize the object belongs to because of the repetition of learning and experience only it is possible for quick response when seeing the object. In early days, many researchers used tools mathematical models and statistical methods in that Bayesian decision tree is one of best classifier in statistics. But still there are some drawbacks appeared in imperfect accuracy and difficult in implementation phase. Also another famous method are called template matching and syntactic methods faced some limitations during classification. In Neural network also has some drawbacks such that undefined parameters applied in the model. If the computer want to find a object is car or bike means, the training phase has to be implemented to define a class and features. By doing so, the computer can easily get the matrix form of a image. The computer understands only the numerical value of matrix instead of 2D image. Reinforcement learning is one of the techniques to make a design by the algorithm again and again depends on the trained model. Deep learning defines about the brain neural networks called as artificial neural network. Driver less car, automatic working devices are the best example for deep learning. Deep learning contains large size of data as well as linked with neural network architecture using many layers.

Pattern recognition has many types like fingerprint, face, eye, biometric recognition, whether the mail is spam or not, vein pattern, Iris, palm print. This chapter presents the models and work flow of pattern recognition on Pap smear images. Pap images is microscopic cell images of detection of cervical cancer. The cell contains nucleus and cytoplasm together making the form of cell structure. Most of the women affected by the cervical cancer due to not following screening procedure tests are called PAP test and HPV(Human Papilloma Virus) test. These test sample results will be send to the pathologist lab for analyzing the cancer cells. The input various sample images loaded into the computer for future references to recognize the cell is normal or abnormal. Machine learning algorithm will provide the solution of the state of the cancer whether the presence and absence of the abnormal cell. Image pattern recognition is based on the pixel variations and edge regions filled in the image. Medical image pattern can be recognized with the help of unsupervised machine learning algorithms such as PCA, SVD and LDA under dimensionality reduction techniques. Deep learning is playing vital role in artificial intelligence in order to training lakh dataset with neural network models for the purpose of automatic recognition such as CNN (Convolutional Neural Network) and ANN(Artificial Neural Network).

LITERATURE REVIEW

According to Khan, A., & Farooq, H. (2012) has been presented multimodal biometric system using Principle component analysis and Linear discriminant analysis combined with K-nearest neighbor algorithm. The conclusion of the paper is high accuracy can be obtained by merging PCA and LDA algorithm[1]. This article analyzed by Dass, R. (2018) shown a review on pattern recognition models of statistical model, structural model, template matching model, neural network model, fuzzy based model, hybrid model with machine learning algorithm.

Elie, S. (2013) has been explained overview of pattern recognition as well as process of classification method by following preprocessing, feature extraction and classification. Used Fourier transform, Random transform, Gabor wavelet transform and fuzzy invariant vector for feature extraction. In classification phase discussed Fuzzy ART(Adaptive Resonance Theory), Neural Network, Support Vector Machine, Markov Random Model, Multi-class SVM.Thus the author did not shown any publication details.

Jain, A.K., Duin, P.W., & Mao, J. (2000) has been proposed a review on Statistical pattern recognition on face and handwriting recognition by using dimensionality reduction, statistical model, feature extraction, feature selection and examined various machine learning algorithms.

Ashour, S.A., Samanta, S., Chakraborty, S., & Salem, M. (2015) focused on PCA algorithm on medical images applying image compression, image fusion, image segmentation, feature selection, image registration, image DE-noising and feature extraction.

Suja, K.V., & Rajkumar, K.K. (2019) has been briefly explained about PCA and LDA feature reduction algorithm and also compared with Rough set, Fuzzy set, Hybrid genetic algorithm, Fuzzy and Rough set feature selection based on the SVM, Filter based feature matching techniques.

The author Sadek, A.R. (2012) has been provided singular value decomposition (SVD) on various image processing applications with image properties, image forensic, image compression, image roughness measure, frobenius based energy truncation, fobenius based error truncation.

The main aim of this paper is delivered by Michahical, S. (2016), shown the image compression techniques using SVD by reducing the eigen values to reconstruct the image in better quality and also obtained PSNR value to evaluate the performance. The author denoted that SVD is good compression techniques which were applied on a image.

Sandhu, K., & Singh, M. (2018) has been analyzed compression techniques by using SVD. During the first step, input image has been converted into JPEG format and also those image stored as a array of integers. SVD compression method executed ion RGB color image,

Seth, R., & Shantaiya, S. (2013) has been conferred that survey reports on PCA and LDA with lossy and lossless compression method. The author did not displayed any result images to find the accuracy,

Sahu, K.K., & Satao. K.J. (2013) has been implemented PCA and LDA statistical tool used for the purpose of image compression to reduce the size of the image high dimensional space into low dimensional space,

Tharwat, A., Gaber, T., Ibrahim, A., & Hassanian, A.E. (2017) has been proposed definition, mathematical calculations, implementation of LDA. The main theme of the paper was based on the basic and working calculations of LDA whether it is class dependent or class independent variable.

Mokeev, A.V., & Mokeev, V.V. (2015) has been given detailed tutorial on LDA low mathematics, explained combined algorithm of PCA-LDA that are implemented using facial data set as well as referred LDA-dependent class and LDA-indelendent class methods. Face image recognition was considered in pattern recognition using PCA-LDA where dataset has been downloaded from ORL and FERET database.

PROPOSED METHODOLOGY

Pattern Recognition

Pattern recognition refers about the process of analyzing and classifying input data into different classes based on the properties/attributes of the images. Pattern recognition may has applications in speech and text recognition, character and letter recognition. The result of pattern recognition algorithms will be very perfect and ore accurate as well as can get the quick result. There are various machine learning algorithms are growing up for training and testing the sample data. For example, consider 100 cat images and 100 dog images which are located in a computer database. The first step of machine learning algorithm is to read and import the data file with exact location. After that will move to training and testing phase where 80 cat and dog images are taking for training the data as well remaining images are moved to testing phase. So that the computer learning the objects and also build a models from the images by comparing each and every images based on the features like eyes, nose, ears, shape, color, size and structure of the cat or dog. In testing phase, have to test the sample image from the computer file to analyzing the result of the image whether the given object is cat or dog. Testing phase is used to measure the accuracy level of the system whether the results are correct or not. Machine learning algorithms are working in between the every process by detecting the classes and attributes.

Mean while various statistical methods are working behind the AI and ML. The general architecture of pattern recognition with medical image analysis in digital image processing is given below,

Figure 1. Architecture of Pattern Recognition

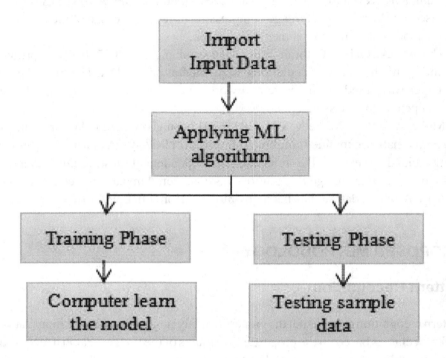

The figure 1 displays the work flow of pattern recognition using machine learning algorithms while in training and testing process.

Applications of Pattern Recognition

Diagnosis a Medical Image

In many fields pattern recognition is used to make a decision as final where especially in medical sector for diagnosis a disease. MRI, CT scan, microscopic images are used for analyzing the pixel variations in feature extraction to detect the disease. Example brain tumor, lung cancer, mammogram images, abnormal cell tissue, pathology images and so on.

Computer Vision

Pattern recognition is used to extract features from the input image by applying image processing techniques such as, morphological operations based on statistical shape measurements or structure of the object in a image.

Speech and Text Recognition

The greatest success of pattern recognition is speech recognition which is used by various algorithms to automatic speech recognition (ASR) and computer speech recognition or speech to text (STT). For example watching film in YouTube with subtitles with the option called caption on or off. Text to speech application is available in android gadgets like mobile, laptop, tab.

Finger Print Identification

Pattern recognition is widely used for identify a fingerprint mark by the forensic department. Feature matching algorithms are implemented to match the pattern with recorded database. Edge detection algorithm is mostly used for fingerprint detection in segmentation phase. Optical Character Recognition is also one of the apt example.

Medical Diagnosis

EEG signal analysis, MRI, CT scan, X-Ray images and pathology images are utilized by pattern recognition techniques. Segmentation is done before feature extraction based on the pixel range. The result will be predicted after analyzing the pattern by using machine learning algorithms.

Face Recognition

For safety precautions face recognition is used by the various fields especially in IT industry, also for security purpose the electronic devices is build with face, fingerprint and palm print recognition system. It has been developed to protect the data from unauthorized access. Also face recognition system is broadly used in forensic department to find the victim where input face image may compared with previous records.

Pattern Recognition in Digital Image Processing

Digital image processing is a process of some operations on the image to make it better visualize using statistical methods and mathematical calculations. Determination of image building with pixels and intensity values in between the range of 0 to 255. Machine learning algorithm works based on the pixel variations by doing training and testing the data. Training data is learning the system with different possible ways which conclude that the system will design the pattern automatically. The main duty of pattern recognition is collecting the similar data from the trained data such as it matches the related information called as label. In image processing feature extraction is the essential task for recognize the pattern.

Figure 2. Work flow of pattern recognition in image processing

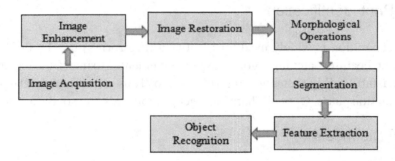

Figure 2 explains the general process in image processing in term of classification and pattern recognition.

Image Acquisition

Image acquisition can be done by electronic device or any suitable camera. It performs capture the event in front of the camera. The use of camera will be differ for every

Figure 3. Process of Image Acquisition

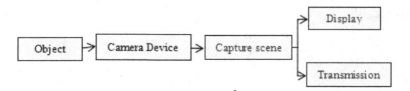

applications to capture the image like, x-ray images. Image acquisition is the primary step in image processing to make all operations. The camera needs some energy to capture the image where the energy is called as electromagnetic waves. Image is produced with the combination of illumination source, reflection of the light and background illumination. The Charge Coupled Device(CCD) and Complementary Mental Oxide Semiconductor(CMOS) are the image sensor technology used for register the scene.

Figure 4. Image Restoration model

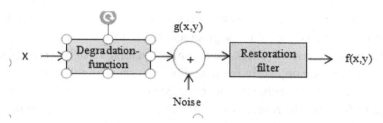

The figure 3 shows the basic form of image acquisition. The object captures from the camera using sensor cable for restore and transmission purpose.

Image Enhancement

Image enhancement is adjusting the pixel values so that the output image will be more quality. The original image may have some noise, to remove those noise image processing has many technologies to resolve the problem by sharpen and brighten the image. Image enhancement algorithms are histogram equalization, filtering methods, linear contrast adjustment, Contrast limited adaptive histogram equalization(CLAHE), mean and median filters and so on. In medical images,

Figure 5. Segmentation of pap smear images

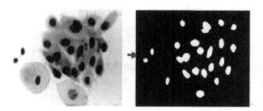

enhancement is the essential task for improve the quality of the image to reach the best classification result to diagnosis the disease.

Image Restoration

Degradation of the image may occur in many case like, motion blur, misfocus of the camera. Degradation model is used to restore the original image where image processing has several methods for degraded image/distorted image.

Image Segmentation

Image segmentation is dividing the part of the necessary object in a image. By doing segmentation, can make use of the segmented image for further analysis. A single image contains set of several pixels, these similar attributes will be grouped together that makes the separate object. In medical diagnosis, cancer and tumor detection is found to be a great part of segmentation in image processing while can detect earlier.

The figure 5 shows the result of original and segmented pap image of multiple cells. Each cell may have different structure, shape and size. Overlapped cells also appeared in the image.

There are various segmentation algorithms available in digital image processing. The accuracy of pattern recognition will get increased based on the segmentation result. Types of image segmentation algorithms are cluster based segmentation, edge based segmentation, region based segmentation, histogram based segmentation, watershed segmentation and statistical methods called morphological operations.

Feature Extraction

Now a days it is quite common to be work with hundred and thousands of dataset together in many fields. If the dataset is larger, it may called as overfitting data. To avoid this kind of problem, can apply regularization or dimensionality reduction techniques. This is called as feature extraction. Using dimensionality reduction could certainly help to reduce the overfitting the data in machine learning model. Feature selection is considered only the essential features. Feature extraction is playing vital role to identify a Pattern recognition in digital image processing. The main advantages of feature extraction given below,

- Can improve accuracy.
- Risk can be reduced in overfitting data.
- Training data will be fast.
- Good Data Visualization.

- Machine learning build model in easy manner.

Classification

Classification is a process of dividing a dataset into two or more classes which can be done on both structured or unstructured data. Based on the given data, the machine learning algorithm determines the data type whether the input image is normal or abnormal in case of cervical cancer. Machine learning algorithm can be divided into two types that is supervised and unsupervised learning algorithm. In supervised learning, class label is used to categories the dataset whereas in unsupervised learning algorithm does not have any class labels. But the possibility of high accuracy obtained in supervised learning algorithm. It will predict the disease based on the training data. So that more information have to load into the system to learn the model, then only the prediction result will be high. The number of neural networks may also work behind the layers such that input layer, hidden layer and out layer. MATLAB has the facility to execute all machine learning algorithm with any kind of dataset. In many algorithm hyper-planes are used for graphical representation to visualize the results in order to separate the classes between line. ANN(Artificial Neural Network), SVM(Support Vector Machine), Naive Bayes Classifier are the example algorithm for classification or pattern recognition model. Machine learning model has the advantage of multi-class classifier that means it may have more than two classes for example, if cervical cancer has many stages. Based on the disease tissue stage, the doctor can find the state of the patients health. So that the stages are, normal columnar, normal intermediate, normal superficial, light dysplastic and severe dysplastic. These are the five classes of cervical cancer which can be used in machine learning algorithms.

Figure 6. Architecture of classification algorithm

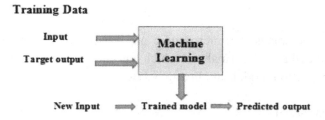

The figure 6 represents the work process in classification phase. The input data loaded for train the model using machine learning algorithm. The sample input data is to be tested to check the correctness of the result prediction.

Diagnosis of Cervical Cancer in Pattern Recognition: Pap Smear Images

In world wide cervical cancer is very dangerous disease which affect the women frequently. Though many technologies are developed, but still the early detection of cervical cancer is not clear and accurate manner by the doctor as well as the pathologist. Cervical cancer has two types that are normal and abnormal cell. This cancer affect the women body in cervix area because of the growth of abnormal cells. This chapter presents the pattern recognition model with cervical cancer images and type of machine learning algorithms. Each and every cell has a unique structure. The combination of pap cell has nucleus and cytoplasm where the abnormal cell can be identified based on structure and shape of the nucleus. Take a look on below sample pap smear microscopic images. The pathologist used to analyse this kind of sample images for further classification to detect the tissue.

Figure 7. Pap smear images of normal and abnormal cells

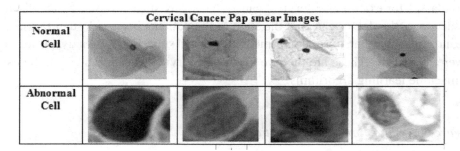

The figure 7 displays the microscopic pap images of detecting the cervical cancer- normal cell and abnormal cell which has nucleus and cytoplasm together.

Pattern recognition models are listing below,

1. Statistical model
2. Structural model
3. Template matching model
4. Neural network model

5.   Fuzzy based model
6.   Hybrid model

Machine learning model builds the pattern recognition. There are different types of ML algorithm implemented by the several fields. They are shown below,

Classification Methods

Classification method is used to predict the categorical labels. This model can be divided into to types, parametric and non-parametric labels. In parametric label has Linear discriminant analysis, Quadratic discriminant analysis, Maximum entropy classifier, logistic regression, multinomial logistic regression. In non-parametric label has Decisiontrees, K-nearest-neighbor algorithms(KNN), Naive Bayes classifier, Neural networks (muti-layer perceptron, ANN), Perceptrons, Support vector machines, Gene expression programming.

Clustering Methods

Machine learning algorithm works on the basis of clustering model which refers the group of data will be collected based on the nearest pixel values in the image. For example the input image contains black and white color. While applying clustering algorithm black color will be grouped together and white color alone grouped together. This is how the data cluster works on the input data. Machine learning based clustering algorithms are Hierarchical clustering, K-means clustering, Correlation clustering, Kernel principal component analysis (Kernel PCA).

Regression Methods

Regression analysis refers about the type of machine learning methods which allows to predict a continuous outcome variable (y) depends on the value of single or multiple predictor variables (x). It deals with the relationship between the outcome and predictor variable. Regression techniques are Gaussian regression, Linear regression and extensions, Neural networks and Deep learning methods, Independent component analysis (ICA), Principal components analysis (PCA). It is simply called as 'predicting real-valued labels'.

Sequence Labeling Methods

It is used to predicting sequence of categorical labels. It is being very powerful methods but still not reached success due to some drawbacks. List of sequence labeling machine learning algorithms are Conditional random fields (CRF), Hidden Markov models (HMM), Maximum Entropy Markov models (MEMM), Recurrent neural networks (RNN), Hidden Markov models (HMM) and Dynamic time warping (DTW). The drawback of HMM and CRF are Markov chain-based model that have few trouble to handle due to longer sequential dependency. For example dependency of the input sequence is more than 3 or larger so that it is ignored.

Tools Used for Pattern Recognition in Machine Learning

Now a days various tools are available for executing the real time data using ML algorithm. Pattern recognition is slightly related to machine learning and artificial intelligence. These tools are mainly used in data science, data mining, data analytics, cloud technology and also image processing. This pattern recognition is commonly used for biometric data like finger print, palm print, face detection etc,.

The below mentioned tools are used for pattern recognition using ML algorithm.

- Amazon Lex
- Google Cloud AutoML
- R-Studio
- IBM Watson Studio
- Microsoft Azure Machine Learning Studio
- MATLAB R2020a Version
- Anaconda Python(All notebooks) & Weka

Figure 8. work flow of proposed methodology

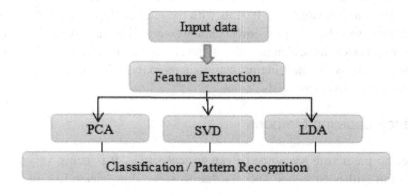

Objective of Proposed Work

The main theme of this chapter is focusing on pattern recognition on pap smear images using machine learning algorithms. Feature extraction is leading role to design a pattern based on pixel variations. PCA, SVD, LDA, LSA are dimensionality reduction algorithm that are applied in pattern recognition.

The figure 8 presents the working flow of the paper using PCA, SVD and LDA for Pattern Recognition of pap smear images.

Principle Component Analysis(PCA)

Principle component analysis is most widely used as statistical tool for analyse the data set. The primary work of the PCA is to reduce the dimensionality or size of the data which consists large number of interrelated data. PCA is a combination of statistical features which are standard deviation, eigenvector and eigenvalues. While applying PCA on a image, it is possible to concentrated on data compression techniques. Data compression means reducing the size of the data for storing purpose. PCA will be used in case of large data set to reduce the size so that it may easy at training the data in classification phase. This algorithm has wide a facility to improve the several image processing techniques such as feature extraction, image fusion, image compression, image registration and image segmentation. PCA used to build a model based on the dataset for identify a pattern and also eigen vector is a vital statistical feature to recognize spatial characteristics of a pixel variations in a image. The main goals of PCA are given below,

1. Extract the most essential features from the data set.
2. Compressing the size of the data is the vital role of PCA.
3. Simplify the features of the data set where easy to handle.
4. Examine basic structure of the observations and the variables.
5. Data compression done without any loss of information.
6. PCA in machine learning used for pattern recognition.
7. Removes correlated features and improves visualization.
8. Avoiding Overfitting data
9. Feature selection in PCA that increase accuracy level.

Principle component analysis is build by statistics and matrix algebra which are the principle goal of PCA by calculating the statistical measurements. Variance and co variance are essential process in PCA work flow which measures the mean value from the data. Principal component analysis (PCA) is a trending technique in form of patterns recognize dataset by containing variations. Feature selection is one of the techniques which can be used to select only important properties from the dataset. PCA contains two work phase, they are training phase and recognize phase. It is a way of cleaning data set to explore and analyse in easy manner. The algorithm of Principal Component Analysis consists by few mathematical. They are,

1. Variance and Co-variance
2. Eigen Vectors and Eigen values.

Co-Variance

It measures the joint variability of two random variable as well as variable refers about the mean value of the dataset.

Vector

It is a combination of magnitude and direction while plotted in XY plane. In linear transformation vector may have changes the direction. The computation of Eigen vectors and Eigenvalues are called as correlation or co-variance which represents in matrix form. Eigen vector determines the direction of new feature space as well as eigen values denotes the magnitude.

Steps for Data set dimentionality reduction using Principle component analysis,

Figure 9. PCA in case of dimentionality reduction of dataset

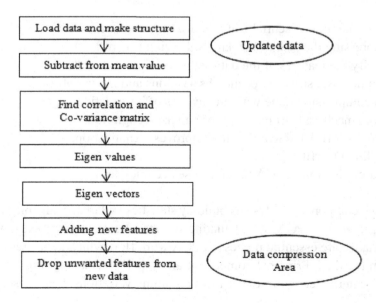

The figure 9 is the PCA algorithms steps that can be applied on a statistical numeric dataset with some mathematical calculations.

Singular Value Decomposition(SVD)

SVD is a matrix decomposition or matrix factorization which including in the applications of image/data compression, denoising and data reduction in machine learning. SVD is used to calculated through iterative numerical methods. Dimensionality reduction is a reducing a input variable for the purpose of predicting event from the input data. By reducing the number of columns from the data where input variable is called as features. It is a most popular approach comes from linear algebra. SVD techniques might be used in case of sparse data. In earlier days SVD is otherwise called as factor analysis.

It transform decomposition matrix into three other matrix.

- A denotes m × n matrix
- U denotes m × n orthogonal matrix
- S denotes n × n diagonal matrix
- V denotes n × n orthogonal matrix
- U called left singular vector
- Where as V called right singular vector

The SVD supplies a statistical way to regulate a low-dimensional approximation to high-dimensional data in terms of dominant patterns. Let see the SVD decomposition of $n \times d$ matrix.

Figure 10 displays the syntax for SVD algorithm in matrix form in order to reduce high dimensional space into low dimensional space.

Mathematical steps of SVD algorithm,

Step 1: Load input image matrix A

Figure 10. SVD decomposition of n × d matrix

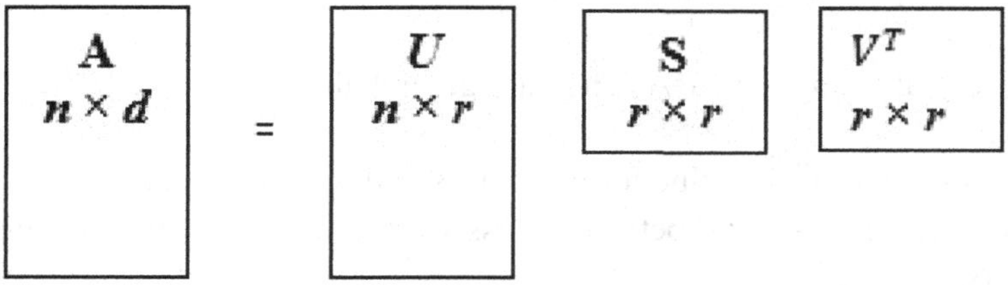

Step 2: Calculate A transpose of A

Step 3: Find eigen values and eigen vectors to make the columns of U by using A and A transpose.

Step 4: Find eigen values and eigen vectors to form the columns of V by using A transpose and A

Step 5: Split each eigen vectors by its magnitude to make the columns of U and V.

Step 6: Now take square root of the eigen values to find the singular values and place it in the diagonal matrix S in descending order.

Linear Discriminant Analysis (LDA)

Linear discriminant analysis is comes under the dimensionality reduction techniques. LDA is mainly used for pattern recognition by doing preprocessing steps. The primary goal of LDA focusing on the higher dimensional space into lower dimensional space in order to avoid the size which may cause to attain the high speed in pattern recognition. LDA is supervised classification techniques that are used by various applications using machine learning models of categorical output variable. LDA can able to implemented both single class classification and multi-class classification. Thus LDA considers that every input variable has the same variance, which used to regularize the data before applying LDA model. It assumes mean value to be Keep 0 and the value of standard deviation to be 1. LDA has the facility for multi-classification. For example this chapter considers the cervical cancer dataset for pattern recognition such that pap smear image dataset may have two class like normal cell and abnormal cell. Dataset of cervical cancer has 2 classes that are normal and abnormal cells where as it has 12 features like, area, perimeter, diameter, radius, homogeneity, Energy, Entropy, Mean, Standard deviation, RMS, Contrast, Correlation.

The following functions are LDA algorithm implementation using MATLAB,

Step 1: Determine the size of the input data

Step 2: Discover and count unique class label(target and class label).

Step 3: Initialize covariance and coefficients()

Step 4: Loop for intermediate calculations. Initialize size of each class and location. Calculating mean vector(group), accumulate all covariance information.

Step 5: Assign probabilities and calculate linear discriminant coefficients.

The essential 5 stage in LDA. They are given below,

1.	Means → find mean value for each class and also over all data.
2.	Scatter matrices → find between-class scatter matrix and within-class scatter matrix.

3. Finding linear discriminant → calculate eigen vectors and eigenvalues using distance and directions.
4. Subspace → sort eigenvector by reducing eigenvalues
5. Project data → display LDA result using plot.

The figure 11 shown to be a classes and features of cervical cancer dataset that has been taken in this entire chapter.

Figure 11. Cervical cancer dataset 2 classes and 14 features can be used in LDA

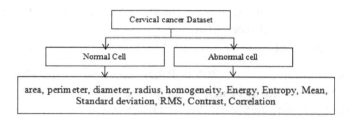

CONCLUSION

Pattern recognition is widely used in several applications to develop the more facility in the fields. Especially in medical field, image recognition is one of the main role to detect the tissues in such a case of cancerous disease. This chapter focus on the importance and application of pattern recognition with machine learning algorithms of PCA, SVD and LDA. Those machine learning algorithms are mainly used for the purpose of dimensionality reduction on dataset to reduce the redundancy of data to attain the best accuracy in classification. The data set has been used in this chapter is cervical cancer of microscopic pap smear images. There are two classes of normal and abnormal cell and 14 features of statistical methods are defined that are compared with machine learning algorithms. Thus pattern recognition of pap smear images is based on the shape and size of the cells which contains nucleus and cytoplasm.

REFERENCES

Ashour, S. A., Samanta, S., Chakraborty, S., & Salem, M. (2015). Principal Component Analysis in Medical Image Processing: A Study. *International Journal of Image Mining, 40*, 65–86.

Dass, R. (2018). Pattern Recognition Techniques: A Review. *International Journal of Computer Science and Telecommunications*, *24*, 25–29.

Elie, S. (2013). *An overview of Pattern Recognition*. Academic Press.

Jain, A. K., Duin, P. W., & Mao, J. (2000). Statistical Pattern Recognition: A Review. *IEEE Transactions on Pattern Analysis and Machine Intelligence*, *3632*(1), 4–34. doi:10.1109/34.824819

Khan, A., & Farooq, H. (2012). Principal Component Analysis-Linear Discriminant Analysis Feature Extractor for Pattern Recognition. *International Journal of Computer Science Issues*, *42*, 267–270.

Michahical, S. (2016). Image Compression using Singular Value Decomposition. *International Journal of Advanced Research in Computer and Communication Engineering*, *7*, 208–211.

Mokeev, A. V., & Mokeev, V. V. (2015). Pattern Recognition by Means of Linear Discriminant Analysis and the Principal Components Analysis. *Pattern Recognition and Image Analysis*, *3*(4), 685–691. doi:10.1134/S1054661815040185

Sadek, A. R. (2012). SVD Based Image Processing Applications: State of The Art, Contributions and Research Challenges. *International Journal of Advanced Computer Science and Applications*, *101*, 26–34.

Sahu, K. K., & Satao, K. J. (2013). Image Compression Methods using Dimension Reduction and Classification through PCA and LDA: A Review. *International Journal of Science and Research*, *4*, 2277–2280.

Sandhu, K., & Singh, M. (2018). Image compression using singular value decomposition (SVD). *International Journal of Latest Research in Science and Technology*, *15*, 5–8.

Seth, R., & Shantaiya, S. *(2013)*. A Survey on Image Compression Methods with PCA & LDA. *International Journal of Science and Research*, 274-277.

Suja, K.V., & Rajkumar, K.K. (2019). Classification of Abnormalities in Medical Images Based on Feature Transformation- A Review. *International Journal of Scientific & Engineering Research,* 1304-1308.

Tharwat, A., Gaber, T., Ibrahim, A., & Hassanian, A. E. (2017). Linear discriminant analysis: A detailed tutorial. *AI Communications*, *127*, 1–22.

Chapter 4
Detecting DDoS Attack:
A Machine-Learning-Based Approach

Megala G.
*School of Computer Science and Engineering, Vellore Institute of Technology,
Vellore, India*

S. Prabu
Vellore Institute of Technology, Vellore, India

Liyanapathirana B. C.
*Department of Science and Technology, Uwa Wellassa University of Sri Lanka,
Sri Lanka*

ABSTRACT

The major network security problems faced by many internet users is the DDoS (distributed denial of service) attack. This attack makes the service inaccessible by exhausting the network and resources with high repudiation and economic loss. It denies the network services to the potential users. To detect this DDoS attack accurately in the network, random forest classifier which is a machine learning based classifier is used. The experimental results are compared with naïve Bayes classifier and KNN classifier showing that random forest produces high accuracy results in classification. Application of machine learning, detecting DDoS attacks is modeled based on the supervised learning algorithm to produce best outcome with high accuracy of training algorithm on network dataset.

DOI: 10.4018/978-1-7998-3335-2.ch004

INTRODUCTION

Network provides communication between two parties using various communication protocol (TCP/IP) suite to link devices and transmission medium. Legitimate and authorized users are allowed to use the network. Illegal users or the attackers try to exploit the network by pretending themselves as authentic and access the others data. To admittance others data, attacker use many strategies which are classified as Active and Passive attacks. The attacker endeavors control access on data or the hardware it resides is known as active attack. Whereas the intruder monitors the communications and listens the aspects of the network devices is known as passive attack. A few attacks DDoS (Distributed Denial of Service) attack which comes under Denial of Service (DoS) attack, masquerade attack and session replay attacks falls under this passive attack category. Machine learning model is preferred to identify and classify these complex attacks.

The network technology was also improved to achieve better performance in communication. But it also opens a great loop hole for the attackers to conduct DDoS more effectively. DDoS is a security problem which degrades the services of the legitimate users. This attack targets the resources which may be a victim's single machine (personal computer) or server or a collection of servers. Since the network is capable of sending large number of packets in small time, the DDoS attackers can easily send a flood of packets to the target through the network, which causes severe damage to the target. The DDoS attack makes the target machine to slow down it's process and make it to hang. If the target machine is a server, then the server will over flow with requests. So the server can't responds to the legitimate requests. It also restarts if the attack conduct for a long period of time. During restart the server is not able to filter the requests. The server's firewall and anti-virus software takes some time to start after server start. At that period of time, the attacker sends malicious files to the target machine to exploit. After exploitation the attacker stops the attack if he wants the data only from the server. Otherwise, the attacker continuously attack the target machine to denial the services provided by the server to the legitimate users. There are many types of DDoS attacks available. But the most famous attacks are, ICMP flood and TCP flood(SYN). Both are capable of denial of service of any type of server. There are many different protection mechanism such as machine learning approach used to prevent the attack as shown in figure1.

Different Types of DDoS Attacks

Denial of service attack is the attack where the victims' service availability is affected and also may provide fake service. Distributed Denial of service (DDoS) attack overwhelms the target network service and disturbs the normal traffic of

Figure 1. DDoS attack detection

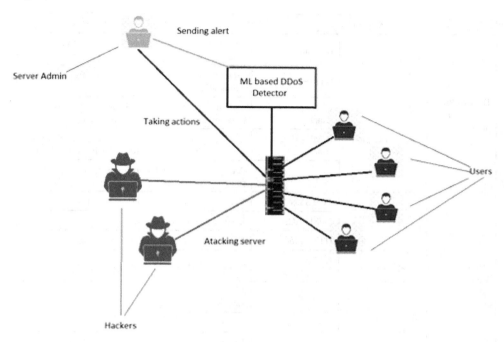

server by flooding of internet traffic. This DDoS attack exhausts the users' network bandwidth, network resources and the infrastructure.

Volumetric Attacks

For denying the legitimate services, the resources and bandwidth of a network are starved out in these kinds of attacks (Goparaju et. al., 2020) with the flooding of UDP traffic. In order to multiply the traffic bandwidth of traffic through the services such as NTP, DNS, and Mem cached, reflection is utilized to hide the identity of a source through the amplification and spoofing source IP address. Sending of a request with spoofs to UDP services is the primary key feature of any amplification attack and the large amount of data is elicited as a response. Through amplification and reflection attacks and ICMP floods are covered in the major part of attacks under this category. Categories of DDoS attacks with its effects are shown in Table 1.

Today, most of the remediation activity of DDoS bots included a manual process. At the firewall or proxy, the required steps are considered by identifying the bots based on certain domains or IP addresses. The traditional approaches to security that becomes less effective since the malicious bots sophistication level and other attacks are increased. The network bandwidth and web applications are targeted if

Table 1. Different categories of DDoS attacks

DDOS Attacks			Effects
Bandwidth Depletion attack	Magnification Attack	DNS attack	Divert internet traffic away from server to fake ones.
		NTP attack	Protocols synchronizing the clock performs degradation to NTP server
	Protocol Exploit attack	UDP - flood attack	The attacker overwhelms the targets host random port numbers by inundating UDP datagram packets.
		ICMP - flood attack	The Attacker endeavors to overwhelm the objective device by flooding numerous ICMP echo-requests
		Fraggle attack	A huge volume of UDP traffic is used to broadcast routers network
Resource Depletion attack	Protocol Exploit attack	TCP SYN	Keeps server with dead open connection
		PUSH ACK	Disrupt the network activity
		HTTP Flood	Floods http request to exhaust network & resources
	Slow HTTP	HTTP fragmentation	Send http traffic to server in small fragments slowly
	Malformed packet attack	Slowloris	Uses partial http request to open connection and slow down target
		Ping of Death	Sends malicious ping to host
		Tear drop	Unable to perform TCP/IP fragmentation reassembly

in case of detecting the DDoS attacks (Goparaju et. Al., 2020). The limitations are included in the traditional approaches like flow-based network parameter, frequency-based detection, poll-based monitoring, and deep packet inspection which depend on the attacks' signature.

Motivation for the work is to detect the anomalous behavior, identifying events in logs by using supervised machine learning algorithms. There are many security products available with the incorporation of supervised machine learning algorithms. There are many interventions in ML based analysis and detection. In this paper, Random forest technique is contrived in automation for identification and classification of DDoS attacks in the network flow.

RELATED WORKS

Netflow protocol is used by (Hou et al.,2018) for gathering information about the network packets, which is very simple to implement and available in most Cisco devices. The classification was done by using Random Forest classification algorithm.

This algorithm produces high accurate results with less amount of training data. Netflow protocol provided high accurate results on data classification and prediction of DDoS attacks. The Cisco network uses protocol to prevent from attacks. Since it uses a large amount of features, the performance of this model was low.

The system implemented by (Doshi et al.,2018) uses the data from the on-path devices like gateways, routers or middlebox. A DDoS attack is simulated using famous DDoS tools. Simulated attack is done, data was captured and used for training. The captured packets are analyzed and subjected to machine learning algorithms such as K-Nearest Neighbour and Neural Network Classifiers. This system also prevents the creation of Botnet inside a local network. Since IoT systems don't have a default security system, this system can provide security to the IoT devices.

DDoS attacks exploits the cloud platform. The attacker launches malwares by software's or virtual bots in the cloud environment which causes security threat. They also try to access the virtual machines of the target cloud and degrades the cloud service provider's reputation. (He et al., 2017) uses Secure Shell Brute-force as its feature to identify the threat and detect them. The network flow of the virtual machines in the cloud are monitored and the data is given to a machine learning algorithm to find any malicious activities. Since it is implemented in a cloud, a variety of protocols like TCP, ICMP, UDP, etc, (Thomas et al., 2020) might be used and all of them are analyzed. This algorithm also checks for any brute force attack implemented in the cloud which is used to gain access to other user's account. Table. 2 shows the techniques used for detecting DDoS attack with its observations.

MACHINE LEARNING APPROACHES FOR CLASSIFICATION

In streaming network transactions, early detection of DDOS attack is still a substantial research objective in existent level of internet usage. Different supervised machine learning models are applied to detect distributed denial-of-service (DDoS) attacks. Prediction of human behavior and simulating it can be model by artificial intelligence with the assistance of machine learning techniques. Many research is being performed in this topic. With the help of ML techniques it is also easier to predict the network behavior too by training the model and testing it with the trained one for classification of unauthorized access and attacks. Intrusion detection in the network can be identified with these ML techniques. There many datasets of network activities and intrusion datasets are publicly available which is helpful for researchers to make use of it of their research work.

Table.2 Summary of ML based DDoS attack detection

Reference	Dataset	Technique	Observation
(Obeidat, Ibrahim, et al., 2019)	KDD Kappa with 41 attributes	Random forest	Achieved 90.57% accuracy.
(Bindra, Naveen et al., 2019)	Real life dataset	Random forest	96% accuracy obtained. K-fold crass validation increased accuracy
(Aamir et al., 2019)	DS00_Full dataset	KNN algorithm	Results 93.5% accuracy. Data preprocessing is tedious.
(Kushwah et al., 2020)	NSL-KDD and ISCX dataset	Voting extreme learning machine	92.11% accuracy is obtained.
(Wang et al., 2020)	NSL-KDD	Dynamic Multi-Layer Perceptron (MLP)	Need to perceive lightweight solutions on detection error
(Çakmakç et al., 2020)	CICIDS2017 dataset	Enhanced Kernel Online Anomaly Detection	Up-to-date dictionary is used to measure Mahalanobis distance providing detection accuracy with optimal threshold.
(Sahoo et al., 2020)	NSL-KKD dataset	Kernel principal component analysis (KPCA) with genetic algorithm (GA)	KPCA is used for dimensionality reduction, GA for optimizing parameters and improved kernel function, Radial Basis Function (N-RBF) with an accuracy of 98.9% for noise reduction.
(Goparaju et al., 2020)	CICIDS 2017 dataset	ANN classifier	88.36% testing accuracy is achieved by extracting and labelling net flow data.
(Tuan et al., 2020)	CAIDA 2007 dataset	K-Nearest-Neighbor (KNN) and XGBoost	Classification accuracy and alleviation efficiency is evaluated by deploying testbed.
(Tuan et al., 2019)	UNBS-NB 15 and KDD99 datasets	SVM classifier, Artificial Neural Network, Naïve Bayes classifier, Decision tree	Bot net is identified using USML (unsupervised learning) from the normal network traffic.
(Polat et al., 2020)	CAIDA 2007 dataset	KNN Classifier	98.3% accuracy rate is achieved

Naive Bayes Classifier

Naïve Bayes classifier is an assumption algorithm which assumes that the feature present in a class is not related to other feature. Independence of each features are measured by this algorithm. This NB classifier is a machine learning algorithm used for classification purpose. This classifier calculates the posterior probability as

$$P(y|x) = P(x|y) * P(y) / P(x) \tag{1}$$

here

P(y|x) is the posterior probability of class y for the given predictor X
P(x|y) is the likelihood. It is the probability of predictor class
P(y) – prior probability class
P(x) – prior probability of predictor

Here the dataset is converted into frequency table. Likelihood is created by computing the probability of attributes. Using Eqn.1 posterior probability for each class is calculated. The class which has the maximum posterior probability is the prediction outcome.

K Nearest Neighbor (KNN)

To solve the deterioration and classification problem, KNN is the simplest and easiest algorithm used in machine learning. Here distance function is computed which calculates the similarity measures on data and classify data points. Based on the majority votes to its neighbors, classification is performed.

Distance is calculated as shown in Eqn.2

$$d(x,y) = \sqrt{\sum_{i=1}^{n}(x_i - y_i)^2} \tag{2}$$

Random Forest

Random forest is an ensemble decision tree based learning algorithm. In order to predict more accurate and stable, random forest algorithm constructs numerous decision tree and merges them together. Individual trees are strengthened so as to reduce the forest error rate.

The frequency of incorrect identification of the random chosen element is measured using Gini Index. The low value of Giniindex is preferred for identification or classification purpose.

$$GiniIndex = 1 - \sum_j p_j^2 \tag{3}$$

Eqn.3 can be used to identify the elements that are incorrectly identified. The gathered data and the chosen features are given as input to the ML algorithm which

Figure 2 Random Forest tree

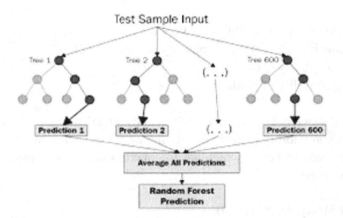

applies the chosen features on the processed data. Since the algorithm is already trained with the different kinds of data sets, it can classify the data.

Decision Tree (DT), a tree structure which consists of nodes is used to define the class elected for the best. Feature selection based on decision tree requires fewer effort and are expandable.

IMPLEMENTATION

The proposed model gathers the raw data of network flow which holds the parameters such as, IP addresses of source and destination, time stamp, length of the packet etc.,. Preprocessing is performed on the dataset to remove noise and extract the features. Feature extraction is being performed on the parameters. Data adaptation is involved which converts these parameters into numerical values. These values are then trained and tested by three different classifiers. Decision tree algorithm makes a decision on the results of the classifier. A web application is designed with Angular as a frontend.

Algorithm

Step 1: Input the dataset with the mentioned parameters.
Step 2: Extract the features such as value of Del, label and size of packet.
Del = difference between two arriving packets timestamps t1 and t2
Step 3: Use transform function to convert data into numerical.
Step 4: Split the encoded information's two different sets as training and testing set.
Step 5: Train the model with the calculated distance and probability value individually.

Step 6: In testing phase, find the accuracy of classification.

Since this system uses supervised machine learning algorithm and since the features are already mentioned, it all makes the prediction process easy. The outcomes can also be predicted using the statistical predictive model.

Figure 3. Packet Information

```
[Protocol:] TCP [Source IP:] 187.11.159.209 [Destination IP:]192.168.78.132 [Length:] 60 [Time :]1576337949.013975000 [Label :]Yes
[Protocol:] TCP [Source IP:] 17.227.230.10 [Destination IP:]192.168.78.132 [Length:] 60 [Time :]1576337949.026457000 [Label :]Yes
[Protocol:] TCP [Source IP:] 187.156.125.11 [Destination IP:]192.168.78.132 [Length:] 60 [Time :]1576337949.039509000 [Label :]Yes
[Protocol:] TCP [Source IP:] 146.34.254.120 [Destination IP:]192.168.78.132 [Length:] 60 [Time :]1576337949.050748000 [Label :]Yes
[Protocol:] TCP [Source IP:] 202.47.171.141 [Destination IP:]192.168.78.132 [Length:] 60 [Time :]1576337949.061258000 [Label :]Yes
[Protocol:] TCP [Source IP:] 58.107.186.206 [Destination IP:]192.168.78.132 [Length:] 60 [Time :]1576337949.074846000 [Label :]Yes
[Protocol:] TCP [Source IP:] 226.50.187.12 [Destination IP:]192.168.78.132 [Length:] 60 [Time :]1576337949.089728000 [Label :]Yes
[Protocol:] TCP [Source IP:] 149.151.6.84 [Destination IP:]192.168.78.132 [Length:] 60 [Time :]1576337949.102827000 [Label :]Yes
[Protocol:] TCP [Source IP:] 115.192.27.111 [Destination IP:]192.168.78.132 [Length:] 60 [Time :]1576337949.115981000 [Label :]Yes
[Protocol:] TCP [Source IP:] 11.56.3.224 [Destination IP:]192.168.78.132 [Length:] 60 [Time :]1576337949.127969000 [Label :]Yes
[Protocol:] TCP [Source IP:] 1.160.37.153 [Destination IP:]192.168.78.132 [Length:] 60 [Time :]1576337949.138159000 [Label :]Yes
[Protocol:] TCP [Source IP:] 151.105.119.85 [Destination IP:]192.168.78.132 [Length:] 60 [Time :]1576337949.150785000 [Label :]Yes
[Protocol:] TCP [Source IP:] 237.205.182.205 [Destination IP:]192.168.78.132 [Length:] 60 [Time :]1576337949.163046000 [Label :]Yes
[Protocol:] TCP [Source IP:] 211.213.162.109 [Destination IP:]192.168.78.132 [Length:] 60 [Time :]1576337949.175201000 [Label :]Yes
[Protocol:] TCP [Source IP:] 145.135.0.3 [Destination IP:]192.168.78.132 [Length:] 60 [Time :]1576337949.186277000 [Label :]Yes
[Protocol:] TCP [Source IP:] 198.16.212.92 [Destination IP:]192.168.78.132 [Length:] 60 [Time :]1576337949.196690000 [Label :]Yes
[Protocol:] TCP [Source IP:] 44.13.122.119 [Destination IP:]192.168.78.132 [Length:] 60 [Time :]1576337949.208527000 [Label :]Yes
[Protocol:] TCP [Source IP:] 13.229.91.143 [Destination IP:]192.168.78.132 [Length:] 60 [Time :]1576337949.221381000 [Label :]Yes
[Protocol:] TCP [Source IP:] 135.135.62.62 [Destination IP:]192.168.78.132 [Length:] 60 [Time :]1576337949.233221000 [Label :]Yes
[Protocol:] TCP [Source IP:] 236.126.19.214 [Destination IP:]192.168.78.132 [Length:] 60 [Time :]1576337949.243508000 [Label :]Yes
[Protocol:] TCP [Source IP:] 170.154.146.45 [Destination IP:]192.168.78.132 [Length:] 60 [Time :]1576337949.255709000 [Label :]Yes
[Protocol:] TCP [Source IP:] 110.210.20.222 [Destination IP:]192.168.78.132 [Length:] 60 [Time :]1576337949.268397000 [Label :]Yes
[Protocol:] TCP [Source IP:] 160.68.227.73 [Destination IP:]192.168.78.132 [Length:] 60 [Time :]1576337949.279295000 [Label :]Yes
[Protocol:] TCP [Source IP:] 118.218.30.238 [Destination IP:]192.168.78.132 [Length:] 60 [Time :]1576337949.292994000 [Label :]Yes
[Protocol:] TCP [Source IP:] 197.232.135.254 [Destination IP:]192.168.78.132 [Length:] 60 [Time :]1576337949.306196000 [Label :]Yes
```

This model takes the data packets Figure 3 from the network as input and labels them after going through the algorithm and gives a label to each and every data packet. These labeled data packets are then stored in a table which is to be displayed in the output. System model displays the data being monitored and their flags are displayed simultaneously. Figure 4 shows the packet classification based on prediction results. If any of the data packets are marked as DDoS during the process, then the system

Figure 4. Prediction classification

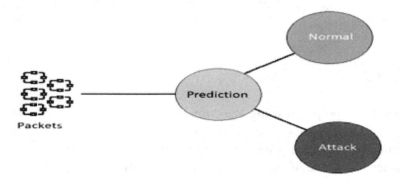

user is alerted using a prompt in the web application displaying that an attack is happening. Then all these data are saved in a database as a log for future reference. The accuracy in classification is shown in Figure. 5 for different machine learning techniques in detecting the DDoS attack.

Figure 5. Classification accuracy of ML techniques

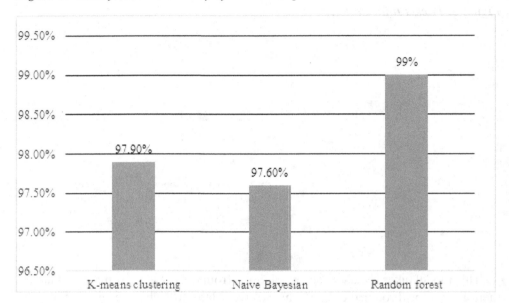

Results of Random Forest model ensembles decision tree vote for the final output. The parameters of random forest is analyzed from its different combinations which is used to find optimal response. Gini impurity and the entropy are the decision tree output criteria with different values of estimator parameters is applied. Grid search technique is used to systematize the process of obtaining the best combinations of parameters. Gini impurity measures the misclassification frequency element of the dataset received.

CONCLUSION

A new model is proposed using Random Forest, a machine learning algorithm to detect the DDoS attack in the network flow with 99% accuracy. The results of detecting DDoS attack shows there is a significant reduction of feature. The performance of the classification results are nominally optimized. This algorithm requires or consumes less resource power. Thus flagging the packets which one has some suspicious characteristics and label them as suspicious. There are several other attacks are to be considered in future to substantiate the creditability of machine learning techniques. In future, supervised, semi supervised and unsupervised models of machine learning algorithms are to be experimented across multiple DDoS datasets. A hybrid method of selecting features using various statistical approaches and meta heuristic genetic algorithm is planned for feature selection in DDoS attack detection, which is a wide open area research.

REFERENCES

Aamir, M., & Syed, M. A. Z. (2019). DDoS attack detection with feature engineering and machine learning: The framework and performance evaluation. *International Journal of Information Security*, *18*(6), 761–785. doi:10.100710207-019-00434-1

Bindra, N., & Sood, M. (2019). Detecting DDoS attacks using machine learning techniques and contemporary intrusion detection dataset. *Automatic Control and Computer Sciences*, *53*(5), 419–428. doi:10.3103/S0146411619050043

Çakmakç, S. D., Kemmerich, T., Ahmed, T., & Baykal, N. (2020). Online DDoS attack detection using Mahalanobis distance and Kernel-based learning algorithm. *Journal of Network and Computer Applications*.

Doshi, R., Apthorpe, N., & Feamster, N. (2018, May). Machine learning ddos detection for consumer internet of things devices. In *2018 IEEE Security and Privacy Workshops (SPW)* (pp. 29-35). IEEE. doi:10.1109/MILCOM.2018.8599738

Goparaju, B., & Bandla, S. R. (2020). *Distributed Denial of Service Attack Classification Using Artificial Neural Networks (No. 3201)*. EasyChair.

He, Z., Zhang, T., & Lee, R. B. (2017, June). Machine learning based DDoS attack detection from source side in cloud. In *2017 IEEE 4th International Conference on Cyber Security and Cloud Computing (CSCloud)* (pp. 114-120). IEEE. 10.1109/CSCloud.2017.58

Hou, J., Fu, P., Cao, Z., & Xu, A. (2018, October). Machine learning based DDoS detection through netflow analysis. In MILCOM 2018-2018 IEEE Military Communications Conference (MILCOM) (pp. 1-6). IEEE.

Kushwah, G. S., & Ranga, V. (2020). Voting extreme learning machine based distributed denial of service attack detection in cloud computing. *Journal of Information Security and Applications*, *53*, 102532. doi:10.1016/j.jisa.2020.102532

Obeidat, I. (2019). *Intensive pre-processing of kdd cup 99 for network intrusion classification using machine learning techniques.* Academic Press.

Polat, H., Polat, O., & Cetin, A. (2020). Detecting DDoS Attacks in Software-Defined Networks Through Feature Selection Methods and Machine Learning Models. *Sustainability*, *12*(3), 1035. doi:10.3390u12031035

Sahoo, K. S., Tripathy, B. K., Naik, K., Ramasubbareddy, S., Balusamy, B., Khari, M., & Burgos, D. (2020). An Evolutionary SVM Model for DDOS Attack Detection in Software Defined Networks. *IEEE Access: Practical Innovations, Open Solutions*, *8*, 132502–132513. doi:10.1109/ACCESS.2020.3009733

Thomas, T., Vijayaraghavan, A. P., & Emmanuel, S. (2020). *Machine Learning Approaches in Cyber Security Analytics.* Springer. doi:10.1007/978-981-15-1706-8

Tuan, N. N., Hung, P. H., Nghia, N. D., Tho, N. V., Phan, T. V., & Thanh, N. H. (2020). A DDoS Attack Mitigation Scheme in ISP Networks Using Machine Learning Based on SDN. *Electronics (Basel)*, *9*(3), 413. doi:10.3390/electronics9030413

Tuan, T. A., Long, H. V., Kumar, R., Priyadarshini, I., & Son, N. T. K. (2019). Performance evaluation of Botnet DDoS attack detection using machine learning. *Evolutionary Intelligence*, 1–12.

Wang, M., Lu, Y., & Qin, J. (2020). A dynamic MLP-based DDoS attack detection method using feature selection and feedback. *Computers & Security*, *88*, 101645.

Chapter 5
A Novel Ensemble Learning for Defect Detection Method With Uncertain Data

Sreedevi E.
Koneru Lakshamiah Education Foundation, India

PremaLatha V.
Koneru Lakshamiah Education Foundation, India

Prasanth Y.
Koneru Lakshamiah Education Foundation, India

Sivakumar S.
ⓘ https://orcid.org/0000-0003-3076-0900
Koneru Lakshmaiah Education Foundation, India

ABSTRACT

Data which contains noise is termed as uncertain data, and the presence of noise makes a deviation in the correct, intended, or original values. Size and complexity of the software products are the two main reasons for uncertain data set that identifying defective modules in uncertain datasets has become a challenging issue. In this chapter, the authors implemented a multi-learner ensemble model for uncertain datasets for defect detection. In this model, different weak classifiers are optimized to improve the classification rate on uncertain data. They have implemented their proposed model on NASA(PROMISE) metric data program repository. Accuracy is used as performance evaluation metric for our multi-learner ensemble defect detection model and ensemble model outcome achieved higher accuracy rate of 97% and when compared to another classification model.

DOI: 10.4018/978-1-7998-3335-2.ch005

INTRODUCTION

The defects in the software which is developed, is the origin of lacking software to achieve its functions. Different vulnerabilities produced at different SDLC phases these occur due to the manual or automatic errors and these vulnerabilities can be found with the help of defect detection models, an optimized way to find defects in software.

Analysing defects is an average research problem in NDE. The data procured from ECT measure is going to enhance two specifications quality and quantity, for example in railway track review, oil or gas pipeline detection etc. Li et.al. (2015), Dorazio et. Al. (2008) & Mohamed et.at. (2015). When data set contains huge number of features to analysis these features is problematic issue and Big data facing various challenges to increase the performance and accuracy of defect detection algorithms. This issue can be solved by applying Machine learning data analysis tool Bishop (2006) and this tool has been successfully used to diagnosis basic health structure based on ECT method Behmann et.al (2015) & Xie (2008).

Numerous Machine learning classification algorithms available and these algorithms provide various techniques using which we can improve defect detection efficiency of data sets which contains huge amount features, of data processing in ECT system. Principle Component Analysis (PCA) Sophian et. Al (2003) & Marinetti et. al. (2004) and Independent Component Analysis (ICA) sivakumar et. al (2017) & sreedevi et. al. (2019) performs effective functions in abstracting defective features from huge data dimensions. Andrea Bernieri et al. applied Support Vector Machine (SVM) and Artificial Neural Network (ANN) to evaluate crack structure and dimensions by studying from a great deal of conductive materials established on ECT Bernieri (2005) & Gaanesan et al. (2015) has been established a support metric based on Bayesian posterior probability to calculate the determination for tubes signal classification results in ECT. For all that, big data in coming of time, ML with easy forms has finite capabilities to model complicated data types in ECT.

Data analysis is a complicated issue in huge data sets, and in recent times deep leaning has advanced a research on tremendous presentation on data investigation task for example, face appreciation and object detection Lecun (2015). In deep learning back propagation algorithm can be applied to find complex structure in huge data sets and this procedure is termed as representation learning methods. Without adding any artificial interpretation these methods can get features from raw data. In, Convolutional neural network (CNN) is one of the most desirable algorithms for its attractive work on generic visual recognition task. Currently, many bests in class CNNs have been commonly utilized in classification Bishop (2006) & Behmann et. al (2015), detection (Xie, 2008), (Sophian et al., 2003), and segmentation (Marinetti et al., 2004). It has been successfully applied to different defect detection situation and it is showing better execution compared to earlier techniques, in spite of their good progress in defect detection accuracy.

In present times the quality of the software which is developed is having more and more important, as the dependency of software programs are growing. If software contains defects, the customer may fit into disappointment for these defects such as failures and faults which may in turn affect the quality of the software. The evaluation of the software project or process can be performed by picking up the continuous or minimal features they include the tools or procedures of Software metrics and Computations (Ramuhalli et al., 2002). To find the internal performance of the metrics, implementation, quality, and reliability, most of the software metrics commonly use correlations or similarity measures. Due to the growing of software constraints and complexity metrics it is too difficult to generate a quality product.

RELATED WORK

To search the stochastic process regarding the defect factors and discover the interval between the variable level the defect prediction models are calculated (Zimmermann & Nagappan, 2009), (Ceylan et al., 2006). To calculate the total amount of defects that appear during the defect dependency test they are calculated by utilizing non-homogeneous poisson process. Search the poisson process P (t) for each one defect, the probability of obtaining k defects at the time and it is declared in time of the Poisson distribution with mean m(t) as

$$Prob(P(t) = k) = m(t)n.e^{-ml}/n!$$

To search the defect distribution in the analysis an exponential model is applied in the SDLC mainly in the segments of regression testing and integrated testing. Defect can appear at any time during the testing phase or failure mode, this is the fundamental assumption and it is the best sign of dependability of its software (Liu et al., 2010), (Drown et al., 2009).

To predict the occurrence of defects found that are on the training data in Nave Bayes is a very efficient classification technique. The basic concept used in Naïve Bayes is bayes theorem and Naïve Bayes classifier is one of the probabilistic Machine Learning technique used for classification.

Bayes theorem is applied with an independence assumption among predictors. In the above expression B is the evidence and A is the hypothesis. The hypothesis composed here is that the predictor features are independent. This in turn means that availability of one feature doesnt affect the other and this is called Naïve.

Neural Network Framework

To predict attacks from defect database the poposed model is feed forward neural network. This model is fixed in three levels, that is an input level, a non-linear hidden level, and the linear output level. Let the arrangement of training defect data instances are represented as $X = \{ins1, ins2, ins3, \ldots, insm\}$ and the defect prediction is $Y = \{atk1, atk2, atk3, \ldots, atkn\}$ as appeared in Fig. 1. The Gaussian function is implementing the Gaussian Naïve Bayes theorem for supervised learning algorithm. The probability of the features is accepted on basis of Gaussian function as

$$P\left(x_i / y\right) = \frac{1}{\sqrt{2\pi\sigma_y^2}} \exp\left(-\frac{\left(x_i \mu_y\right)^2}{2\sigma_y^2}\right)$$

Multinomial Naive Bayes

Figure 1. Nonlinear Neural Network Structure

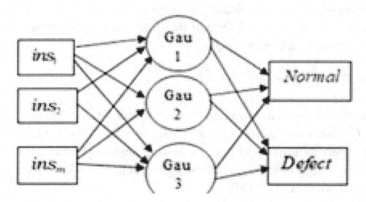

For discrete features (for example word counts for text min-ing classification) Multinomial Nave Bayes classifier can be applied as classification technique. The multinomial classifier generally requires integer features. Naïve Bayes algorithm is applied to multinomial distributed data set and is one of the binary classifier applied in text mining classification where the data are generally defined as word counts.

For every class y the distribution is characterized by vectors $\theta y_= (\theta y1 \ldots, \theta yn)_w$ here n represents the entire number of features in text classification (the size of the vocabulary) and θ_{yi} represents the likelihood $P\left(\dfrac{x_i}{y}\right)$ of feature i to be found in a example belonging to class y. The parameters θ_y is predicted by a curved version of maximum possibility, i.e. relative occurrence as well as:

$$\hat{\theta}_{yi} = \frac{N_{yi} + \alpha}{N_y + \alpha n}$$

Complement Naive Bayes

The ComplementNB is a deviation of the basic multinomial Naïve Bayes (MNB) technique which is actually applicable for unbalanced data base. In order to calculate model weights CNB utilizes statistics from the complement of every class. The author of the ComplementNB proved analytically that the parameters of CompelementNB are more secure than the MNB. On text classification CNB systematically achieves than MNB (generally by a sizable margin). The weights are computed as follows:

$$\hat{\theta}_{ci} = \frac{\alpha_i + \sum_{j:y_j \neq c} d_{ij}}{\alpha + \sum_{j:y_j \neq c} \sum_k d_{ij}}$$

$$w_{ci = log\,\hat{\theta}_{ci}}$$

$$w_{ci} = \frac{w_{ci}}{\sum_j |w_{cj}|}$$

Metric Selection Measures

A notable measure in information theory, i.e. entropy is utilized to discover the contamination of the random tests in order to handle the uncertain data efficiently applying the information gain accurately (Dorazio et al., 2008). Entropy calculates the impurity level in a gathering of tests. The calculation of information gain and gain ratio can be obtained as follows:

$$Entropy = \sum_{i=0}^{c} - p_i \, log(p_i)$$

The trained occurrence is subdivided properly to evaluate metrics in order to define the performance of split up metric in decision tree structure that utilizes to gain information. The gain measure of an attribute A, comparative to a group of instances I, is well-defined as,

$$Gain(I, A) = Entropy(I) - \sum_{v \in A} \frac{|I_v|}{|I|} Entropy(S_v)$$

The information gain condition, $G(I, A)$ is biased in the direction of attributes that have a huge amount of values over attributes that have a lesser number of values. These Super Attributes will effectively be chosen as the root, followed in a large tree that classifies completely but works poorly on unseen occurrences. We can penalize attributes with huge amount of values by applying an alternative method for attribute selection, referred to as Gain Ratio. Set of each different value for an metric is specified by value *(A)*, and *Iv* is the subset of *I* for which the metric a has instance value *v*. The gain ratio of a metric *A* is given as:

$$Gain\ Ratio = \frac{Gain(I, A)}{SplitInfo(I, A)}$$

Pruning technique is utilized to improve the metric relation-ships efficiency in order to defeat the uncertain challenge, particularly in noisy or uncertain data. Not many of the blocking conditions that are utilized in the literature are:

1. Horizon the class homogeneity
2. Horizon the smallest number of occurrences for a non-terminal node. Ex: Range [2,230] occurrences
3. Horizon a determined tree depth. Ex: Range: [2,9] levels.
4. Horizon the predictive accuracy threshold within a node. Range: {75%,89%}.

Decision tree models that are ensembled namely C4.5, CART, random forest, and Bayesian tree for defect analysis are established that are classification models using Nave Bayes

Defect prediction with huge amount of attributes set are determined to handle uncertainty there exists no single traditional model.

For finding the defected features which are of the software product, a machine learning or statistical methodology can be applied to work for the software defect prediction. Random Forest, Naïve Bayesian, Decision Tree, SVM with logistic regression etc of software defect detection are utilizing a huge amount of statistical models and machine learning that can be utilize in many recent studies where SVM that includes RBF, Chi-square and log polynomial functions using non-linear kernel (Bishop, 2006),

SELECTION BASED ENSEMBLE MODEL FEATURE

To address the problem of class inequality and software defect prediction are proposed classifiers which is an organized in this paper. feature selection and probability estimation tasks are the fundamental features of this model. a gathering of trained classifiers are generated which is the way, towards the learning models in Ensemble learning.

High true positive rate and data inequality problem elimanation are applied to the two phases of predict that are utilized in learn-ing model various learners are trained which are Ensemble learning to explain the unbalanced problem. Heterogeneous and homogeneous methods are the two types of Ensemble learners that are classified algorithm another way developed by each base learner model. The multi-learning ensemble model fundamental framework is shown in

Figure 2. Ensemble Model

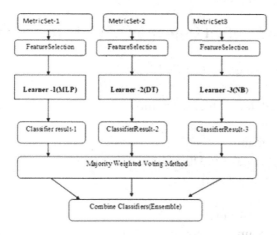

Figure 2. Model learning are applying for the two phases of basic framework. Ensemble E as well as base classifiers is achieved in the learning part. Entire training data is split up into subsets and then to develop one base classifier to every one of

them in the process of ensemble. The class defect predicators of the base classifiers are incorporated utilizing H in the utilizing phase to form the final classifier of the ensemble model. An Ensemble fit in to be a more effective than any of the base classifiers for defect prediction.

*=F(h$_1$,h$_2$,...,h$_s$) or

$$H\left(x_i\right) = sign\left(\sum_{i=1}^{N} w_i h_i\left(x_{ij}\right)\right)$$

Where w_i is the weight of the selected classifier h_i.

Selection Feature Function

Feature selection module can be used for defect class distribution, Chi-square statistic is computed that can evaluate the defect for Chi-square based defects selection. To improve the prediction accuracy rate and to increase their performance on very high dimensional datasets the Chi-square feature selection module is utilized on sample data. And also, this is and also this improves the performance of the overall software detection model. Many feature selection techniques like Bayesian probabilistic, Decision induction tree, correlation-based classifier are available and can be used for dimensionality reduction.

Ensemble Based Defect Detection Model Algorithm:

Input: Defect detection datasets as D List.

Output: Classified defect detection results.
Procedure:
Ensemble Selection feature
For every metric set Data[i] in Dlist Do
For every attribute A_j in Data[i]
Do
For every occurrence $I(A_j)$ in A_j do
If(Typeof (I(A$_j$)) == Numerical && Aj == Null) then I(A$_j$) = (Max(D1(A$_j$), D2(Aj))/
(m S.D(D1, D2));
Endif
If(*Typeof (I(Aj) == Nominal &&Aj = Null*) then
To find a novelty conditional of posterior probability estimation as

74

$P(vi) = \log(Prob(vi/Cm)) + \log(Prob(Cm))$

$P2(vj) = \log(P\ rob(vj/Cm)) + \log(Prob(Cm))$

P1(Vj) is combined along with classifier-1 and *P2(Vj)* is combined along with classifier-2.

$A_j = maxprob(\{P1(Vi)\}, \{P2(Vj)\});$

Value = (Chi-Square)$\chi 2$

$$= \sum_{k=1}^{n} (obser_k - Expect_k)^2$$

if (max *prob*∈$P1(vi)$ && *Value > threshold*) then

else

$I(A_j) = V_j$

End if

Done

Done

Ensemble Implementing

Input: Classified Features Data set in the same way as FData;

Output: Defect Detection and Model Learning

Procedure: To read defect data feature set in the same way as FData

For all Feature FData[i] in FData Do

For all occurrence of *I(Ai)* in *Ai* do Do

Subdivide the data instances of *FA(Di)* into *k* independent sets. Select classifier $C_{i=i=1m}$

While i < k

Do

if(C_i *is M LP*) Then

$I_j = \Sigma iw_{ij}O_i + \theta j$

else if *(C_i is NB)* then

else if *(C_i is Decision tree)*

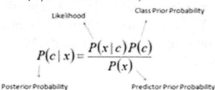

$P(c \mid X) = P(x_1 \mid c) \times P(x_2 \mid c) \times \cdots \times P(x_n \mid c) \times P(c)$

end if

end while

Compute the misclassified error rate and statistical true positive rate.
Done
Done

At the initial stage the data sets contain missing values both in continuous and nominal features, so these defect datasets are taken as the same way and applied the above algorithm. Extract phase established decision models for decision making an ensemble classifier is applied to Filtered phase database are that are handled. Training dataset are established on reality of defects to predict the supervised learning algorithm that is very active in Naïve bayes. The two classifier is considered as bug prediction in naïve Bayes model by evaluating historical metric data, that is trained and predicted in this model. It is challenging to predict the defects expected to missing values or uncertain data if there are attributes of metric data that are mixed type.

When Decision Tree algorithm is used for classification over fitting problem occurs and this can solve by using Decision tree pruning. Pre-pruning and post-pruning are the two types of Decision tree pruning techniques. While constructing a decision tree, the decision tree construction is stopped at a leaf node. The contamination level produced by the separation by one node decreases less than α, we can get this node as a leaf node, and stop the construction of the tree. It is very essential on how to decide the value of, attributes at the same time precise will be not so high, if α is too big, this will cause the stop of dividing and the constructed decision tree has no large distinction from the original one if α is too small.

EXPERIMENTAL RESULTS AND DISCUSSIONS

Datasets

The software metrics data set has been collected for the NASA (PROMISE) metrics data program repository. Eight types of defect datasets contain in PROMISE repository. Which includes at least 45 software metrics, including 25 product metrics, 15 process metrics and 5 execution metrics. We studied four different ensembles of feature selection func-tions with different ranking functions such as IG, MI, and Chi-square in our experiment. Refer the Table II.

Execution Result

Randomized Rules: 339, Time taken to run Proposed method: 0.31 seconds Table II, explains the classification models in terms of the true positive rate and comparison of accuracy with ensemble model. From the table it is observed that the ensemble

Table 1. Accuracy of proposed method

ACCURACY BY CLASS			
	TP Rate	FP Rate	Class
Accuracy By Class	0.970	0.085	Y
	0.970	0.579	N
	0.970	0.332	

Table 2. Accuracy comparison of ensemble model with other classification models

Algorithm	Ensemble Model	SVM	DT	Naive Bayes
KC1	0.96	0.91	0.86	0.910
CM1	0.93	0.917	0.8056	0.886
JM1	0.95	0.932	0.889	0.879
MC2	0.969	0.960	0.900	0.8449
PC4	0.959	0.923	0.869	0.830
MW1	0.959	0.929	0.929	0.939
PC1	0.969	0.959	0.849	0.9100
PC3	0.959	0.589	0.880	0.900

model outcome achieved higher accuracy rate of 97% and compared to another classification model. Figure 3, explains the accuracy comparison of the ensemble model with the other classification models in terms of true positive rate.

Figure 3. Accuracy comparison of ensemble model with other classification models

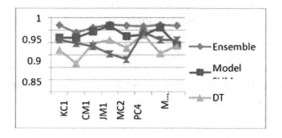

CONCLUSION

Several defect detection models are proposed by using machine learning algorithms like SVM, NB, MLP and Decision Tree. But sometimes the performance of these models is degraded due to the presence of uncertain data. In order to improve the accuracy of the defect detection model we im-plemented our model by using multi-learner ensemble model in which set of learners are combined. This model effectively predicts and classifies the defects on the PROMISE defect data sets and ensemble model outcome achieved higher accuracy rate of 97% and compared to another classification model. In forthcoming this work can be extended to optimize the defect detection process using the dynamic optimization ensemble model and dynamically produced prediction rule in real time could be applied to achieve better results.

REFERENCES

Behmann, J., Mahlein, A., Rumpf, T., Romer, C., & Plumer, L. (2015). A review of advanced machine learning methods for the detection of biotic stress in precision crop protection. *Precision Agriculture, 16*(3), 239–260.

Bishop, C. (2006). *Pattern recognition and machine learning*. Springer.

Ceylan, E., Kutlubay, F., & Bener, A. (2006). Software defect identification using machine learning techniques. *Software Engineering and Advanced Applications. SEAA '06. 32nd EUROMICRO Conference on*, 240-247.

Dorazio, T., Distante, A., Pianese, V., Cavaccini, G., Leo, M., & Guarag-nella, C. (2008). Automatic ultrasonic inspection for internal defect detection in composite materials. *NDT & E International, 41*(2), 145–154.

Drown, D. J., Khoshgoftaar, T. M., & Seliya, N. (2009). Evolutionary sam-pling and software quality modeling of high-assurance systems. *IEEE Transactions on Systems, Man, and Cybernetics. Part A, Systems and Humans, 39*(5), 1097–1107.

Li, Q., Zhong, Z., Liang, Z., & Liang, Y. (2015). Rail inspection meets big data: Methods and trends. *International Conference on Network-Based Information Systems*, 302–308.

Liu, Y., Khoshgoftaar, T. N., & Seliya, N. (2010). Evolutionary optimization of software quality modelling with multiple repositories. *IEEE Transactions on Software Engineering, 36*(6), 852–864.

Marinetti, S., Grinzato, E., Bison, P., Bozzi, E., Chimenti, M., Pieri, G., & Salvetti, O. (2004). Statistical analysis of ir thermographic sequences by pca. *Infrared Physics & Technology*, *46*(1-2), 85–91.

Mohamed, A., Hamdi, M. S., & Tahar, S. (2015). A machine learning approach for big data in oil and gas pipelines. *International Conference on Future Internet of Things and Cloud*, 585-590.

Ramuhalli, P., Udpa, L., & Udpa, S. (2002). Electromagnetic nde signal inversion by function approximation neural networks. *IEEE Transactions on Magnetics*, *38*, 3633–3642.

Sophian, A., Tian, G., Taylor, D., & Rudlin, J. (2003). A feature extraction technique based on principal component analysis for pulsed eddy current ndt. *NDT & E International*, *36*(1), 37–41.

Xie, X. (2008). A review of recent advances in surface defect detection using texture analysis techniques. *ELCVIA. Electronic Letters on Computer Vision and Image Analysis*, *7*(3).

Zimmermann, T., & Nagappan, N. (2009). Predicting defects with program dependencies, in Empirical Software Engineering and Measurement. *ESEM 2009. 3ʳd International Symposium on*, 435-438.

Chapter 6
A Trustworthy Convolutional Neural Network– Based Malware Variant Detector in Python

Lavanya K. Sendhilvel
Vellore Institute of Technology, Vellore, India

Anushka Sutreja
Vellore Institute of Technology, Vellore, India

Aritro Paul
Vellore Institute of Technology, Vellore, India

Japneet Kaur Saluja
Vellore Institute of Technology, Vellore, India

ABSTRACT

Malware attacks are broadly disguised as useful applications. Many android apps, downloaded to perform crucial tasks or play games (take one's pick), seem to do completely different tasks, which are potentially harmful and invasive in nature. This could include sending text messages to random users, exporting the phone's contacts, etc. There exist some algorithms in place that can detect these malwares, but so far, it has been observed that many of these algorithms suffer from false negatives, which grossly reduced the effectiveness of said algorithms. The aim of this chapter is to introduce a flexible method to detect if a certain application is malware or not. The working can be loosely defined as the source of a set of applications is detected and the list of permissions is studied. The set of relevant and highly close applications is selected, and from the most relevant category, the permissions are checked for overlap to see if it can be stated as a possible anomalous application.

DOI: 10.4018/978-1-7998-3335-2.ch006

INTRODUCTION

With the technology rising every day and becoming more advanced, malware stands as a big issue. Malware is having a tremendous impact on the world with a number of computer incidents are rising day by day. Thus, it has become very important to understand what exactly a malware is and how we can detect and remove it. We all use applications for a variety of purposes from reminding us of our tasks or to play games or to make notes, we all are intimately familiar with the importance of apps in our lives and how dependent we are on them. It makes sense that an attack on our devices via apps would be a very effective and quick way to gain access to some of the most sensitive details we keep in our phone and laptops.. Malware hidden in apps is one of the most common ways of invading a user's privacy. The unsuspecting user downloads the app, believing it do the work it advertises to do, not knowing that while they use the app, in the back, the malware is at work, carrying out tasks that can be defined as invasive and unethical. These may include going through the user's contacts, exporting them to primary users, or sending messages to random people, or monitoring conversations. A malware is a software that is designed to cause damage or harm a computer system.(Landage & Wankhade, 2013) Most of the malware have the ability to spread on their own, remain undetectable and also cause changes to the network or system. They can cause a destruction of network and also hold the ability to bring down the performance of the machine. Viruses, worms, trojan horses, spam, adware, ransomware, rootkits are all some examples of malware. While the methods of attacking and specific functionalities are different for each malware, they all ultimately aim to damage the system in a certain way. (Idika & Mathur, 2007) Knowing what malwares are capable of, their detection is an area of major concern for both, the research community and also the general public. There are many ways through which a malware can be detected from a system.

Malware detection techniques can be used to malware from the system and prevent it from being infected, thus, protecting it from a possible information loss and compromise.(Tahir, 2018) Malware detection techniques can be broadly classified into signature based, behavior/anomaly based and specification based.

While these are the broad aspects of malware detection, there are many specific detection techniques that are already into existence. Some of them being: Data Mining approach for malware detection, using computer forensics, FSA for detecting anomalous programs, ACT (Attachment Chain Tracing), using deep learning for malware detection etc.(Gibert, 2016) To avoid the invasion of privacy, several algorithms exist to detect the presence of malware. But the current algorithms are prone to a lot of instances of false negatives, which is why it is imperative that we find an algorithm that correctively detects the presence of malware and protects the user from attacks. In this paper, our attempt to is to propose an algorithm that

Figure 1. Classification of malware detection techniques

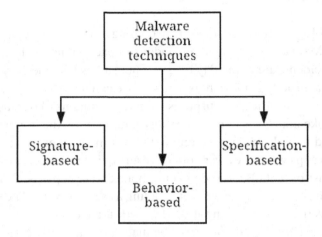

can effectively detect the presence of malware by black boxing only a very limited number of apps. In the longer run, this algorithm is intended to serve as a Cyber Security algorithm which is capable of giving positive and correct results majority of the times. One such possible approach is to use Neural Networks, specifically DenseNet, which are Densely Connected Convolutional Networks for malware detection. In this paper, we are using this particular technique of using neural networks for malware detection.

RELATED WORK

There have been many detection techniques proposed such as signature based or machine learning approaches. One such proposed method is malware detection system using deep neural network, developed by Invincea. The outline of the methodology used consists of feature extraction: which extracts four types of features from the static beign and malicious binaries; deep neural network classifier: consisting of input, hidden and output layers; and lastly score calibration: which carries out non-parametric score distribution estimation that can be interpreted through Bayesian estimation of a malware. This method is able to achieve a detection rate of 95% with a false positive rate of 0.1% over a dataset of 400,000 software binaries. It requires moderate computation and is able to achieve a good amount of accuracy. (Saxe & Berlin, 2015) Automatically generated malware poses as a significant issue for computer users. Feature selection for malware classification prevails but the number of features is still too large for neural networks which are much complex algorithms. Thus, to reduce this, an approach using random projection to even reduce dimensionality of input space further is proposed. To achieve this, firstly, a dataset is constructed. Then, to reduce dimensionality of the input space, initial feature selection is carried out. Next, random projections are used to further reduce the dimensionality, while still maintaining the highly important information. Finally, several models such as non-linear neural networks and linear logistic regression classifiers are trained to classify the files as malwares. This resulted in a 43% reduction in error rate compared to using all the features. For one-layer neural networks with random projections, the two-class error rate came out to be 0.49% and for a group of neural networks, it came out to be 0.42% which proves great performance. (Dahl, 2013) Neural Networks and AIS have been used in many areas for anomaly activity recognition and detection. But the existing methods were quite static and thus posed a problem for detection new viruses and malwares. Thus, an approach using various intelligent techniques such as fusion of neural networks and AIS was posed which proved to have better potential to recognize novel viruses. Integrating neural networks and AIS increases the performance of security system.(Golovko, 2010) . DBSCAN that was developed by Ester et al. (Ester et al., 1996) is one among the distance-based approaches that has been wide used for locating anomaly detection problems. The outline of the methodology used by (Saxe & Berlin, 2015) consists of feature extraction: which extracts four types of features from the static benign and malicious binaries; deep neural network classifier: consisting of input, hidden and output layers; and lastly score calibration: which carries out non-parametric score distribution estimation that can be interpreted through Bayesian estimation of a malware. This method is able to achieve a detection rate of 95% with a false positive rate of 0.1% over a dataset of 400,000 software binaries. It requires moderate computation and is able to achieve a good amount of accuracy. (Dahl, 2013) states that automatically generated malware poses as a significant issue for computer users. Feature selection for malware classification prevails but the number of features is still too large for neural networks which are much complex algorithms. Thus, to reduce this, an approach using random projection to even reduce dimensionality of input space further is proposed. To achieve this, firstly, a dataset is constructed. Then, to reduce dimensionality of the input space, initial feature selection is carried out. Next, random projections are used to further reduce the dimensionality, while still maintaining the highly important information. Thus, an approach using convolutional neural proved to have better potential to recognize novel viruses.

PROPOSED METHODOLOGY

The proposed Malware Detection System (Fig. 2) is based in the Python Programming Language and uses the concept of Neural Networks in order to classify an application

Figure 2. Framework of proposed methodology

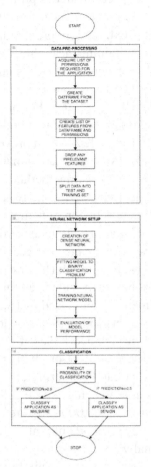

on the basis of their permissions that it requests for in the due course of its running. The idea behind this detection system is to know whether or not an application can turn out to be malware, and hence protect potential users from using software applications with harmful ramifications. Major concepts used in the proposed system:

- **Neural Networks:** It is a network that is composed of artificial neutrons or nodes and is used to perform certain kinds of processing and solving problems connected to artificial intelligence. All connections have a certain weight, which can be positive or negative, attached to them. The output in the output layer is a function of the inputs that are given in the input layer or the results from the layers in the middle of the input and the output layer, which are known as the Hidden Layers. These networks are modelled after and take inspiration from the neurons in the human brain.

- **DenseNet:** Densely Connected Convolutional Networks or commonly known as a DenseNet is a type of Neural Network. The main characteristic of this neural network is that they have shorter connections between those layers that are close to the input and those layers that are close to the output. This makes these networks not only considerably deeper but significantly more accurate as well as extremely efficient in terms of training. In this kind of network each layer is connected to every other layer in a manner of forward propagation. This also leads to a considerable reduction in the number of parameters that need to be used for the application as there is no compelling reason to relearn feature maps that are redundant.

The System is divided mainly into three different subsystems for clarity of purpose. These subsystems are:

Data Pre-Processing

In this module the data that is required for the classification of an application into 'Malware' or into 'Benign' is obtained and made ready for usage in the code. The data needs to be made usable and in a format that is efficient for the neural network. Thus, to achieve this aim, the following steps are taken:

1. Primarily the list of permissions that an application requires in order to function is to be identified .Then there is a need to filter all of these for commonly found permissions to determine viable permissions to be used for the determination of Malware.
2. A dataset is taken with information regarding the features of permissions of applications that malware applications usually request for and the permission that other harmless applications request for. A data frame is made from the acquired dataset.
3. Next, application features need to be matched with the dataset features and all relevant features that can be viable for the detection of malware need to be picked out and appended to this list of features.
4. Any features from the previous step that are seen to be useless or seen to not affect the predictions as much are dropped. These are unwanted parameters and after the removal of these parameters, the parameters that need to be used in the neural network model are finally obtained.

5. Finally, data is split in the ratio of 75 percent: 25 percent as the training data: testing data ratio and can be taken up further for the training, evaluation and working of the neural network model.

Dense Neural Network Setup

The Neural Network is the key to getting the classifier right thus, the most accurate form of data, as obtained in the data pre- processing must be used to train and test it once the model has been setup. The task at hand is to perform Binary Classification with the help of a Densely Connected Convolutional Neural Network and to that end, the following actions have been followed: i.) The dense net is created. The Model is created as a sequence of layers. This paper uses Sequential models that add one layer at a time. The Function is of the form: Dense (number of neurons, input_dim, activation function). The rectifier that has been used in this paper is Rectified Linear Unit ('relu') activation function on the first two layers and the sigmoid function has been made use of in the output layer. Better performance is achieved using the rectifier activation function. The ReLU is the most used activation function in all of the world. Usually all deep learning or convolutional neural networks use the Rectified Linear Unit. However, the usage of the sigmoid function on the output layer is necessary as on the output layer it is extremely important to ensure that the network output is between 0 and 1 and easy to map to either a probability of class 1 or a probability of the other class. The entire system is pieced together by adding each layer. The first layer has 12 neurons and expects 10 input variables. The second hidden layer has 8 neurons and finally, the output layer has 1 neuron to predict the class of the particular application and classify whether it is 'Malware' or 'Benign'. ii.) After creation, the model is fit to solve a binary classification problem. This is done by using logarithmic loss, which for a binary classification problem is defined in the python Keras library as "binary_crossentropy". The efficient gradient descent algorithm "adam" has been used in order to perform the operations because it is an efficient default. It is an optimizer that normally has shown best performance as compared to other alternatives thus has been the choice of optimal in this paper. iii.) The neural network has now been set up and requires training for efficient prediction of classes. The training process will run for a fixed number of iterations through the dataset called epochs that must be specified using the nepochs argument. The number of instances that are evaluated before a weight update in the network is performed can also be manually set up, called the batch size and set using the batch_size argument. The training for this model has been done with 150 epochs i.e. iterations on the entire dataset with keeping the batch size as 10. iv.) After training the evaluation is performed on the test set and the performance parameters like accuracy are calculated in order to determine how well the model has fit the data

Figure 3. Output depicting the given application as malware

and what is the level of accuracy f the predictions that the model is making. This outcome of this step determines whether any specific changes need to be made in the model on the basis of its performance.

The job of the classification subsystem is to determine finally, whether or not the application can be classified as Malware or whether it is not Malware. To do this, the classification system has been implemented as a simple module that finds the probability of an application to be malware within a range of 0 to 1(this is achieved by the sigmoidal function in the output layer that maps the input range to a range of 0 to 1 on the basis of this probability:

1. If the probability of application to be Malware is greater than 0.5 then the application is classified as 'Malware'.

Figure 4. Output depicting the results of various performance parameters

2. Otherwise the application which has probability less than or equal to 0.5 is classified as 'Benign'. Thus, in this way the final outcome of the Binary Classification into 'Malware' and 'Benign' is achieved.

OUTPUT AND PERFORMANCE PARAMETERS

We executed the Dense Neural Network to get malware classification on the given android app, which determines if it's a Malware or not. We used performance measures such as accuracy, loss, root mean squared error and mean absolute error. The Neural Network runs for 150 epochs, with a training accuracy of 91.35% and a validation accuracy of 87.85%. We added the 'Swiggy' Application as an example and on the basis of the permissions it asks for, the program declares it as malware(Fig.3).

Fig. 5 consists of a graph which has the X-axis as epochs and Y-axis as the percentage. It illustrates the accuracy and loss of the experiment. Orange line represents accuracy whereas the blue line represents loss for the particular setup.

Figure 5. Graph depicting accuracy and loss for the particular experiment

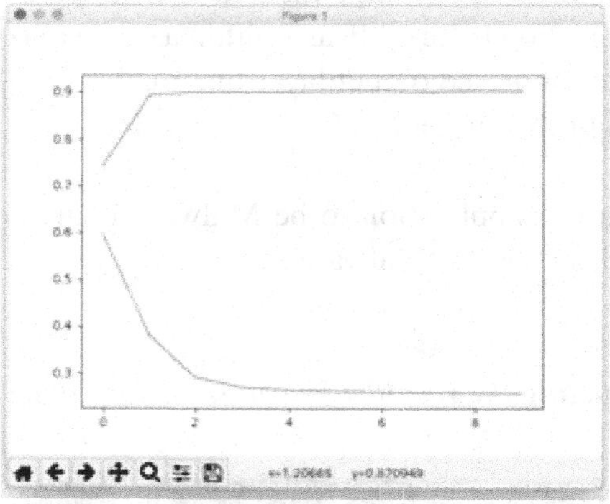

CONCLUSION AND FUTURE WORK

This paper proposed a novel approach to spotify and diagnose unusual Android applications in a way by identifying the most precise and significant permissions to match from and then approving behaviors. The significant category is recognized using Dense Neural Networks that has the latent to explore new deviating applications. In our evaluation of proposed methodology initial results show that our approach is more accurate to detect malware applications. Our future work would include evaluation of various applications and query types, and application of the approach to address even other security vulnerabilities.

REFERENCES

Dahl, G. E. (2013). Large-scale malware classification using random projections and neural networks. In *2013 IEEE International Conference on Acoustics, Speech and Signal Processing*. IEEE. 10.1109/ICASSP.2013.6638293

Ester, M., Kriegel, H.-P., Sander, J., & Xu, X. (1996). A density-based algorithm for discovering clusters in large spatial databases with noise. *KDD-96 Proceedings*, 226-231.

Gibert, D. (2016). *Convolutional neural networks for malware classification*. University Rovira i Virgili.

Golovko, V. (2010). Neural network and artificial immune systems for malware and network intrusion detection. In *Advances in machine learning II* (pp. 485–513). Springer. doi:10.1007/978-3-642-05179-1_23

Idika & Mathur. (2007). *A survey of malware detection techniques*. Purdue University.

Landage, J., & Wankhade, M. P. (2013). Malware and malware detection techniques: A survey. *International Journal of Engineering Research & Technology (Ahmedabad)*, 2(12).

Saxe, J., & Berlin, K. (2015). Deep neural network based malware detection using two dimensional binary program features. In *2015 10th International Conference on Malicious and Unwanted Software (MALWARE)*. IEEE. 10.1109/MALWARE.2015.7413680

Tahir, R. (2018). A Study on Malware and Malware Detection Techniques. *International Journal of Education and Management Engineering, 8*(2).

Chapter 7

Security and Privacy for Electronic Healthcare Records Using AI in Blockchain

Ramani Selvanambi
Vellore Institute of Technology, Vellore, India

Samarth Bhutani
Vellore Institute of Technology, Vellore, India

Komal Veauli
Vellore Institute of Technology, Vellore, India

ABSTRACT

In yesteryears, the healthcare data related to each patient was limited. It was stored and controlled by the hospital authorities and was seldom regulated. With the increase in awareness and technology, the amount of medical data per person has increased exponentially. All this data is essential for the correct diagnosis of the patient. The patients also want access to their data to seek medical advice from different doctors. This raises several challenges like security, privacy, data regulation, etc. As health-related data are privacy-sensitive, the increase in data stored increases the risk of data exposure. Data availability and privacy are essential in healthcare. The availability of correct information is critical for the treatment of the patient. Information not easily accessed by the patients also complicates seeking medical advice from different hospitals. However, if data is easily accessible to everyone, it makes privacy and security difficult. Blockchains to store and secure data will not only ensure data privacy but will also provide a common method of data regulation.

DOI: 10.4018/978-1-7998-3335-2.ch007

INTRODUCTION

Blockchain technology began from Bitcoin, giving stability against failure and cyber assaults. It utilizes technologies, for example, hash chains, digital signatures, and consensus mechanism to record bitcoin exchanges by building dispersed, shared database in decentralized way. Such technologies make interactions secure by providing services like distributed storage, non-repudiation, time-based traceability for exchange substance, which frame a vital framework. Albeit, at first developed for bitcoin, it was later understood that this innovation could also profit in different fields. It was then implemented in different fields, for example, healthcare, fintech, computational law, review, notarization, et cetera by outlining different keen contracts in view of blockchain. This paper includes the way in which blockchain can be used to solve the above-mentioned problem and make electronic healthcare data storage easier and more secure.

As to Bitcoin, (Nakamoto, 2008) Pierro depicts each Bitcoin as a number, and that these numbers are the response for a condition. Each new response for the condition makes another bitcoin and the exhibition of creating an answer is assigned "mining." Once mined, a bitcoin can be traded or exchanged, and each trade produces a segment into the blockchain's activity log. This is regularly suggested as a "record." What makes the blockchain champion is that the record isn't guaranteed or taken care of by one association, yet rather every trade drove has a copy of the focal points of that trade set aside on every PC that was a piece of the trade.

(Ekblaw et. al., 2016) study shows that clinical data is not, at this point restricted to compose news, study of images, and testing blood sample. Genomic information and to facilitate gathered by wearable gadgets, for example, arm bands and watches installed with sensors, are progressively aggregated. Whenever abused viably, the accessibility of the new types of information may prompt superior healing choices and results and might likewise be analyzed by medical coverage organizations offer limits designed for "solid" conduct. Further advantages emerge in the domain of computerized reasoning. (Zhang et. al., 2017) at the point when given the suitable information, this can gather patterns from the information that are then used to produce populace level knowledge, thus accomplish populace wellbeing overall. These new information designs, nonetheless, will require cautious combination to permit suitable examination while keeping up quiet protection and protection from programmers.

(Crosby, 2016) identifies that despite the fact that digitization of wellbeing records has been set up in the overall specialist (GP) area for more than 30 years (though inadequate with regards to fundamental information sharing and trading capacities), optional consideration has not yet effectively accomplished this true norm. Appropriated record innovation, started and exemplified by the bitcoin blockchain, is growingly affecting IT conditions in which compliance to authoritative guidelines and support of open trust is progressively foremost, and it might be utilized in acknowledging digital objective. The point of this survey be to sum up the proof identifying with the execution of blockchain to oversee electronic wellbeing records (EHRs) in addition to examine whether this might get better productivity of record the executives.

(Danbar, 2012) said it is additionally significant that the target of this survey isn't simply to distinguish the utilization or the instances of blockchain based application in medical services, yet in addition to comprehend the constraints and difficulties for the blockchain-based medical care applications just as the momentum patterns regarding the specialized methodologies, strategies, and ideas utilized in building up these applications (defeating the restrictions) in a vision to unwind the territories for prospect examination. Also, this audit covers numerous new equipment that has not been distributed by the hour of the past surveys. As eminent before, the utilization of blockchain in medical care is a generally new worldview which is developing quickly.

The remainder of the paper discusses the vulnerabilities in present healthcare data storage system and how these can be overcome using blockchain. Each vulnerability is discussed along with how it affects the security and access of data in section 3. Centralized data has been a popular data storing approach in healthcare; however, alternative approaches have not been explored. Further, section 4 explains the basic working of blockchain. Terminologies such as "distributed ledger technology" and "SSL certificate" are explained. It also explains the decentralized storage and traceability of blockchain. Section 5, the final section, discusses the integration of blockchain in healthcare and how its use can transition the healthcare storage for the better.

Inspiration and Contribution

As opposed to the referenced documents, this proposed work depicts an orderly audit plus investigation of the cutting edge blockchain investigation in the ground of medical care. The aim of this work is likewise to show the expected use of block chain in medical care and to give you an idea about the difficulties and likely bearings of research in blockchain. This orderly audit just incorporates research that presents another arrangement, calculation, strategy, philosophy, or design in the ground of medical services. Audit form research, conversations of potential use as well as utilizations of blockchain, and various not significant distributions are avoided.

LITERATURE REVIEW

Few education institutes, organizations have linked blockchain technologies into teaching, and largely universities and organizations use it to help managers learn and learn the summative assessment of outcomes. This technology is able to calculate the entire transcription. In official learning environment, these include learning content and results, as well as academic performance and academic statements. In these areas, in the leisure learning environment, data on research engagement, competence, web-based learning, and additional single premiums are included. This information can be securely placed and arranged in a blockchain in a fitting manner.

Decentralization points to procedures for the identification, storage, support and dissemination of information on blockchains, which depend on the framework of the dissemination. In this arrangement, the faith flanked by the communicating hubs is achieved through science and technology to a certain extent than the gathering of associations.

Traceability includes that every exchanges on the blockchain are planned in sequential requests, while squares identify two consecutive squares by cryptographic hashing. In this way, each exchange can be identified by looking at the square data connected by the hash key. Blockchain technology is permanent for two reasons. From one point of view, all exchanges are placed in a square where one hash key joins the past square and a hash key indicates the square behind. Chaos of any exchange produces various hashes and is therefore recognized by the various centres that run similar approval calculations. Then, the blockchain is a shareable open record, placed on many hubs, and all records are constantly being adjusted. Effective changes require changes to more than 51% of system records.

(Mettler M, 2016) Blockchain technology and encryption funds cannot distinguish any blockchain organization with digital currency attributes. The essence of blockchain technology is peer-to-peer exchange, which does not include outsiders, which means that all exchanges do not require the cooperation of outsiders. The dissemination of advanced funds that rely on blockchain technology has been resolved. In the Bitcoin the age of advanced cash is achieved through the use of explicit mining calculations and is limited by pre-characterized formulations. Therefore, problems such as swelling or falling do not occur. In the Blockchain version 2.0 and version 3.0 applications, a mix of different exercises, like management exercises, teaching exercises, plus money-related exercises, can make these non-currency practice cash assets.

VULNERABILITIES IN HEALTH CARE DATA STORAGE

Current Infrastructure

Currently, there are a number of different health data frameworks that store individual patient information in a large health data warehouse. These data systems are ordered in a variety of ways. In order to solve the problem of connecting a unique health information storage system, various standards have emerged. In the current agreement, to hand is no extensively recognized agreement, the issue of information trading is again a real problem.

Centralized Data Storage

A centralized framework can provide the information you need in a fairly smooth way, with a focus on centralization itself. Excessive authorization in the hands of the central government has led to a complex licensing system that includes the possibility of data breaches and information disclosure.

Multiple Devices

Medical institutions are equipped with a variety of gadgets. As healthcare workers use their gadgets for expert purposes, it becomes more and more complex. Customers, IT increases the risk of security, which is now diverse and difficult to explain.

Embedded Devices

Even if the problem is solved, the connection is prone to problems. The same seamless connection enables tracking and logging to easily open healthcare IT networks to various forms of cyber threats, including viruses.

Patient data availability

Information is one of the most significant resources in the creation of medical care frameworks. Getting to this advantage makes a great deal of issues. Members inspired by this information are basically patients, care suppliers and outsiders who can utilize this information for various interests. Locale ought to give clear rules with regards to which outsiders, under what conditions and for what reason. Currently, the regulations are unclear and inconsistent, so if the healthcare system even contains any solutions, it usually contains inconsistent solutions.

Interoperability

Wellbeing information is dynamic and broad, and consistent trade of wellbeing information across wellbeing data frameworks would be invaluable. As it would not be reasonable regarding speed, stockpiling limit, or supportability to repeat all wellbeing records on each PC in the blockchain organize, rather activist blockchain as a strategy in the direction of oversee right of entry control (savvy indenture the board) by efficiently putting away a list of all clients' wellbeing accounts and connected metadata. Every occasion information is put to the EHR by a specialist (portable application), a metadata pointer to this be further added to the blockchain, whilst the information are put away safely resting on cloud. A complete file of a specific patient's accounts is put away in a solitary area alongside related metadata, paying little heed to the whereabouts of the clinical information. The blockchain, with this made sure about file of records, at that point guides approved people to the cloud-based information, along these lines permitting the prompt trade of data between endorsed experts, while likewise keeping an unchanging record of those pursuers.

(Ivan D, 2016) described the method that blockchain relies upon open source programming moreover has potential focal points, as prosperity trust can use the open application programming border to fuse data, give them ideal induction to correct information in a setup which can be used by them. Trying interoperability is moreover a key part of the Health Information Technology for Economic and Clinical Health Act, inferred 2011; American clinical consideration providers have been known cash related spurring powers to display critical usage of EHRs.

Health

Quick admittance to a far reaching group of patient information permit specialists to get patients devoid of the necessitate hang tight for the appearance of past outcomes. The accessibility of brief as well as more continuous information would permit doctors to make specific treatment plans based on results and treatment adequacy. Day by day wellbeing information would likewise draw in a patient added in their medical services, and get better quiet consistence a notable test in the domain. The capacity of customized medication, consequently, is better with this interoperability, as a solitary passageway for every one constant wellbeing information is made for every patient. Information accumulated from handheld sensors and portable applications would add data on the dangers and advantages of medicines, in addition to persistent announced result process.

Reliability

The unchanging nature of a blockchain that comes as of connecting the hash of resulting squares conveys by means of characteristic trustworthiness because squares can't be revised devoid of the coordinated effort of a larger part of hubs. This is critical to keeping up a genuine documentation of patient supplier communications just as information starting from gadgets, the two of which could impact clinical choices as well as those including protection. A framework that permits patients to maintain ownership of their clinical pictures, alongside a permanent chain of guardianship. Impermanent tokens are able to be made by blockchain clients and voted for onto those, for example, medical concern suppliers, life insurance provider agencies, giving brief access to patients.

The voucher is free of the information, contain just approval orders, and is checked and approved previous to the necessary information are sent. Respectability may likewise be kept up by the utilization of outside evaluators, who may confirm framework exactness continuously and reflectively. Expected approaches to improve the respectability are to utilize daze marks, which fortify assurance from altering just as affirming the sender's and watcher's characters, or to utilize marks from different specialists.

Security

(Guo, 2018) explained touchy information must be remained careful from spies and interlopers. Penetrates negatively affect the open view of the medical services field and take steps to obstruct future exploration through more tough administrative limitations. The WannaCry assault of May 2017 contaminated a large number of PCs around the world. One prior assault in US States focused on electronic health records specifically, requesting a huge number of dollars in recover. A blockchain is safer than heritage techniques, which give patients with qualifications. It accomplishes these belongings by the utilization of open key cryptography. This includes creating an open and private key for every client utilizing a single direction encryption work, known as a hash. It's absolutely impossible for anybody yet the beneficiary to observe data conveyed over the blockchain, as it is made sure about by their secret key.

WORKING OF BLOCKCHAIN

The blockchain is essentially a decentralized, digitized, open record that includes all the cryptocurrency exchanges and uses known to distributed ledger technology. (Underwood, 2016) mentioned the use of a centralized architecture and simple login is an important part of a regular system. There is not much money available for investment security, and all of these efforts can be made if employees and customers can use it to modify or destroy it. Blockchain offers powerful opportunities and solves a single point at a certain time. With the help of blocking, the security system used in the organization can provide users with useful devices and distributed public key information structures. This security system provides a specific SSL certificate for each device. The production of the certificate was carried out on the blockade, which made it impossible for the manufacturer to use the fake certificate.

Decentralized Storage

Blockchains prevent users from placing their computers on their computers in their network. Still, they can be sure that this product will not collide. In the real world, if someone who is not the owner of a component (such as a component) tries to block the component, the entire system excludes a block that can prevent it from being distinguished from other components. If this type of block is located by the system, it simply excludes the block from the block and identifies it as valid.

Traceability

Every task performed on a private or public block is done in a time and digitally signed manner. This way you can complete each task in a public place and then find the corresponding features on the block. This situation relies on non-repudiation: some people have not proved that their signal is the authenticity of the document. This blocking feature increases the reliability of the system and encrypts the user with each check.

BLOCKCHAIN IN HEALTHCARE

The constantly updated distributed database brings much reward to healthcare industry. The reward is more than ever exciting as multiple parties want to access the same data. For example, medical treatment in areas of aged care or chronic disease is a predetermined field of application in which blockchain technology can create added value. (Broderson et. al., 2016) the number of media disruptions involved in the treatment of patients involved in various mediators, media changes, numerous clinical health facts and incompatible IT interfaces may result in prolonged with supply wide correlations Certification and information flow for medicinal stakeholders.

(Yue et. al., 2016) the implementation of blockchain in healthcare will work similarly to how a bitcoin transaction takes place. The patient and the doctor will be the two parties involved in the transaction and all the medical data of the patient will be stored in the form of chains with hash functions for extraction of data. This will enable the patient or the doctor to extract data whenever necessary. Blockchain will also provide data security as the medical information is only accessible by the parties involved and does not require authorization by a third party. Since it is decentralized, it also prevents access of data by any third party. All the information is traceable and is time-stamped for ease of availability of healthcare information.

A US company is effectively engaged with this region and, accordingly, delivered the Gem Health network dependent on the Ethereum technology. This mutual organization foundation; diverse medical services specialists can get to similar records. These likewise allow the making of another polish of Blockchain based applications in medical care that would open squandered assets and healing issues. (Peterson et. al., 2016) Consequently, the Gem wellness network speaks to medical services environmental factors that consolidate the two organizations, people and specialists and which, simultaneously, upgrade understanding focused on care while tending to operational execution issues. This organization is a case of a Blockchain approach that offers all pertinent clinical partners straightforward and clear admittance to bleeding edge treatment data. Additionally, the Swiss computerized wellbeing, fire up, adopts a drastically new strategy with regards to the treatment of information exchanges and the sharing of individual wellbeing information. This start company offers its clients a stage on which they can store and deal with their wellbeing data in a safe situation.

(Banerjee et. al., 2018), the Blockchain library model sponsorships the ability to create and change essentially all through the blockchain lifetime by including new individuals with varying legitimate connections. Its advancement is particularly useful for recording the steady and predictable improvement of trades. EHR structure, there is an upper bound on the quantity of records, which is the quantity of occupants it serves. People improvement is by and large more slow than the advancement of the quantity of monetary trades, for the model, in the Bitcoin technology. Chain structure in blockchain also maintains the ever-creating clinical files by keeping up a reliably creating associated summary of clinical records; in which each square contain a details of timestamp and an association with a past square.

(Mannaro et. al., 2018) an elective arrangement would be a Blockchain containing pointers to off-chain information; the metadata which are related with the pointers be able to incorporate data requisite for following interoperability. With this methodology, paper information, counting imaging test outcome, might be put away off-chain. With regards to the sharing of imaging test result, a couple of creators proposed putting away encoded wellbeing data legitimately on the Blockchain; in any case, putting away the scrambled imaging investigations of all patients would bring about a tremendous Block chain, that is excessively huge for a hub which is running on a cell phone or an advanced computer unit to extract, store up, approve.

(Kleinaki et. al., 2016) the size of the blockchain is difficult which is under dynamic investigation and it is demonstrated to be a restricting element in any event, for chains that store basic conditional information, considerably less the monstrous hinders that might be required to put away clinical studies. When blockchain keeps on developing, the versatility of the framework might be undermined in light of the fact that just clients who have enormous extra rooms and high computational force will have the option to participate in Blockchain as diggers or complete hubs. To defeat this subject, this technology commonly bolsters 3 kinds of hubs: Complete hubs, light hubs, and document hubs:

Complete Hubs: It is the measure of each exchange and stores each square in the Blockchain.

Light Hubs: It is possible to ensure trades instead of running a full framework centre. Customers should simply maintain a copy of the square headers of the best confirmation of work chain, which can be acquired by addressing framework centre points till they obtain the best lengthy chain. By taking care of the square header, a light centre can watch that a trade is not adjusted devoid of submitting colossal fragments of blockchain memory. Light centres can in like manner contact the data they want.

Document Hubs: It stores each exchange with square on the technology blockchain. Likewise, they store up exchange receipts and the whole position tree.

CONCLUSION

This paper has shown how the use of blockchain in the healthcare industry for the use of storing data can help solve the various problems. Although this technology has been around for a few years, it has still not been utilized to its full potential. Integrating blockchain with healthcare information storage will not only provide the much-needed security but will also enable patients to access their data without the presence of a middle man. This omission of a middle party prevents many errors and security faults which are otherwise common. Migrating the existing network to blockchain could initially be expensive. However, as shown above, the overall advantages of this outweigh the limitations by a large degree. This technology opens new doors to the working and management of the healthcare industry.

Today, some of the people own belongings but can't establish possession or rights, like intellectual property disputes. It might cause clashes with others. Some business information, for example, auxiliary outlines, corporate plans, perhaps taken. The innovation of blockchain can be utilized to secure these asset benefits by putting away information in a block chain network. Blockchain innovation shields instructors' encouraging plans from being usurped, along these lines improving the security of protected innovation insurance. Security implies that every center keeps the whole record, including all information aside from the genuine element. So as to secure protection, the client's particular distinguishing proof is totally demonstrated by the ID number. This implies blockchain innovation can ensure the protection of brokers as just they will have the private key.

REFERENCES

Banerjee, M., Lee, J., & Choo, K. K. R. (2018). A blockchain future for internet of things security: A position paper. *Digital Communications and Networks*, *4*(3), 149–160. doi:10.1016/j.dcan.2017.10.006

Brodersen, C., Kalis, B., Leong, C., Mitchell, E., Pupo, E., Truscott, A., & Accenture, L. (2016). *Blockchain: Securing a new health interoperability experience*. Accenture LLP.

Crosby, M., Pattanayak, P., Verma, S., & Kalyanaraman, V. (2016). Blockchain technology: Beyond bitcoin. *Applied Innovation*, *2*(6-10), 71.

Dankar, F. K., & El Emam, K. (2012, March). The application of differential privacy to health data. In *Proceedings of the 2012 Joint EDBT/ICDT Workshops* (pp. 158-166). 10.1145/2320765.2320816

Ekblaw, A., Azaria, A., Halamka, J. D., & Lippman, A. (2016). A Case Study for Blockchain in Healthcare:"MedRec" prototype for electronic health records and medical research data. Proceedings of IEEE open & big data conference, 13.

Fan, K., Ren, Y., Wang, Y., Li, H., & Yang, Y. (2017). Blockchain-based efficient privacy preserving and data sharing scheme of content-centric network in 5G. *IET Communications*, *12*(5), 527–532. doi:10.1049/iet-com.2017.0619

Gordon, W. J., & Catalini, C. (2018). Blockchain technology for healthcare: Facilitating the transition to patient-driven interoperability. *Computational and Structural Biotechnology Journal*, *16*, 224–230. doi:10.1016/j.csbj.2018.06.003 PMID:30069284

Guo, R., Shi, H., Zhao, Q., & Zheng, D. (2018). Secure attribute-based signature scheme with multiple authorities for blockchain in electronic health records systems. *IEEE Access: Practical Innovations, Open Solutions*, *6*, 11676–11686. doi:10.1109/ACCESS.2018.2801266

Ivan, D. (2016, August). Moving toward a blockchain-based method for the secure storage of patient records. In *ONC/NIST Use of Blockchain for Healthcare and Research Workshop. Gaithersburg, Maryland, United States: ONC/NIST* (pp. 1-11). Academic Press.

Kleinaki, A. S., Mytis-Gkometh, P., Drosatos, G., Efraimidis, P. S., & Kaldoudi, E. (2018). A blockchain-based notarization service for biomedical knowledge retrieval. *Computational and Structural Biotechnology Journal, 16*, 288–297. doi:10.1016/j. csbj.2018.08.002 PMID:30181840

Kuo, T. T., Kim, H. E., & Ohno-Machado, L. (2017). Blockchain distributed ledger technologies for biomedical and health care applications. *Journal of the American Medical Informatics Association, 24*(6), 1211–1220. doi:10.1093/jamia/ocx068 PMID:29016974

Lohr, K. N., & Donaldson, M. S. (Eds.). (1994). *Health data in the information age: use, disclosure, and privacy*. National Academies Press.

Mannaro, K., Baralla, G., Pinna, A., & Ibba, S. (2018). A blockchain approach applied to a teledermatology platform in the Sardinian region (Italy). *Information, 9*(2), 44. doi:10.3390/info9020044

Mettler, M. (2016, September). Blockchain technology in healthcare: The revolution starts here. In *2016 IEEE 18th international conference on e-health networking, applications and services (Healthcom)* (pp. 1-3). IEEE.

Nakamoto, S. (2008). *Bitcoin: A peer-to-peer electronic cash system.* Retrieved from https://bitcoin.org/ bitcoin.pdf

Peterson, K., Deeduvanu, R., Kanjamala, P., & Boles, K. (2016, September). A blockchain-based approach to health information exchange networks. In *Proc. NIST Workshop Blockchain Healthcare* (*Vol. 1*, No. 1, pp. 1-10). Academic Press.

Pilkington, M. (2016). Blockchain technology: principles and applications. In *Research handbook on digital transformations*. Edward Elgar Publishing. doi:10.4337/9781784717766.00019

Wang, H., & Song, Y. (2018). Secure cloud-based EHR system using attribute-based cryptosystem and blockchain. *Journal of Medical Systems, 42*(8), 152. doi:10.100710916-018-0994-6 PMID:29974270

Yue, X., Wang, H., Jin, D., Li, M., & Jiang, W. (2016). Healthcare data gateways: Found healthcare intelligence on blockchain with novel privacy risk control. *Journal of Medical Systems, 40*(10), 218. doi:10.100710916-016-0574-6 PMID:27565509

Zhang, P., White, J., Schmidt, D. C., & Lenz, G. (2017). *Applying software patterns to address interoperability in blockchain-based healthcare apps.* arXiv preprint arXiv:1706.03700

Zyskind, G., & Nathan, O. (2015). Decentralizing privacy: Using blockchain to protect personal data. In 2015 IEEE Security and Privacy Workshops (pp. 180-184). IEEE.

Chapter 8

Hyperspectral Image Classification Through Machine Learning and Deep Learning Techniques

Tamilarasi R.
Vellore Institute of Technology, Vellore, India

Prabu Sevugan
Vellore Institute of Technology, Vellore, India

ABSTRACT

Dimensionality reduction for hyperspectral imagery plays a major role in different scientific and technical applications. It enables the identification of multiple urban-related features on the surface of the earth, such as building, highway (road), and other natural and man-made structures. Since manual road detection and satellite imagery extraction is time-consuming and costly, data time and cost-effective solution with limited user interaction will emerge with road and building extraction techniques. Therefore, the need to focus on a deep survey for improving ML techniques for dimensionality reduction (DR) and automated building and road extraction using hyperspectral imagery. The main purpose of this chapter is to identify the state-of-the-art and trends of hyperspectral imaging theories, methodologies, techniques, and applications for dimensional reduction. A different type of ML technique is included such as SVM, ANN, etc. These algorithms can handle high dimensionality and classification data.

DOI: 10.4018/978-1-7998-3335-2.ch008

INTRODUCTION

Remote hyperspectral detection also referred as to spectroscopy, reflects a full use of field-vegetation, resources, and land use/terror monitoring by scientists and researchers. While this information has been available since 1983 in various fields of engineering and science, it is primarily used by many complicated factors. For many years' scientists, in particular, physicists have used spectroscopy for the identification of material composition. In the field of analytical chemistry, many techniques used for reflectance spectrum analysis have been developed. Identify the characteristics of the individual absorption by using solid/liquid chemical gassing bonds. Technological progress made it possible to extend image spectroscopy to satellite applications outside laboratory conditions to concentrate their applicants globally (Volchok, B. A., and Chernyak, M. M 1968). Figure 1 displays the schemes used in our research of the hyperspectral imaging system. The following components are typically included in a standard hyperspectral imaging device: a light source (illumination), a wavelength distributor (spectrometer), and a zone detector (camera), a transportation system (Qin, J., et.al., 2013). The light source can usually be divided into two groups for spectral imaging application: illumination and excitation source. Broadband lights are typically used as sources of illumination for reflection and transmitting images, whereas narrowband lights are widely used as sources of excitation. Illumination is therefore a key aspect of the hyperspectral imaging system. Compared to naked eyes, vision systems are influenced by the intensity and consistency of lighting. Illumination devices produce light that illuminates the image features evaluated; thus, the output of the illumination system can significantly affect the quality of the images and play an important role in the overall efficiency and accuracy of the system (Liu, D.et.al., 2015). Effective lighting can help enhance image processing and analysis performance by minimizing noise, shadow, reflection, and improving contrast image (Zhang, B., et.al., 2014). Furthermore, the locations, types of lamps, and color quality of the lighting are all considered when selecting the most effective lighting. The widely used sources of light are incandescent lamps, fluorescent lamps, lasers, and infrared lamps (Kodagali, J. A., and Balaji, S 2012).

Hyperspectral was used synonymously with the spectrometer for imagery in some books. Not all the spectral bands can be used in the electromagnetic spectrum for remote sensing purposes. The consuming bands appear to be isolated where remote sensing is possible by atmospheric windows or areas. In these atmospheric windows, hyperspectral images are measurements. The remote sensing technology combines the imaging and spectroscopy of the hyperspectral in one system, which produces large groups of data requiring complex handling procedures. In general, data set hyperspectral consist of around 100 to 200 spectral bands which, in contrast to the multi-spectral data sets, possess only five to ten bands with relatively large

Figure 1. A hyperspectral imagery schematics system

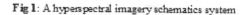

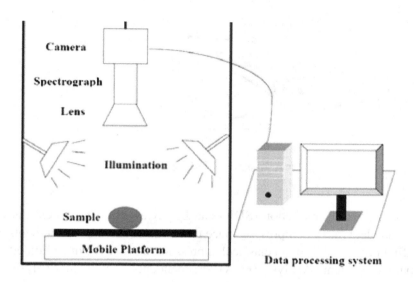

bandwidths that are relatively small. The Hymap or hyperspectral mapper used for airborne and visible / IRS imagery (AVIRIS) is an example of a hyperspectral device. NASA was first used in the early 1980s.

Hyperspectral remote sensor system records hundreds of relatively small bandwidth spectral bands (5 to 10nm) together with these details; it is greatly improved that unique tends have been detected and identified on the ground and atmosphere. It makes it possible to analyze land cover by far more specific. The emissivity levels of each band can be combined to form a spectral reflectance curve. Hyperspectral data may produce higher accuracy of the classification and a more detailed taxonomy. But it is also a unique challenge to classify hyperspectral data (Wilheit, T. T., et.al., 1977).

DIMENSIONALITY REDUCTION

Dimensionality reduction (DR) methods keep hyperspectral image interpretation thoroughly studied and appropriate Commonly, a set of the preprocessing method, dimensional reduction processes is sufficient to overcome very high-dimensional data to the availability of the low-dimensional distance, where the information search can be made in a larger efficient and strong way. Two main classifications, such as transformation-based dimensionality reduction (TDR) and band selection-

Figure 2. Concept of an imaging spectrometer

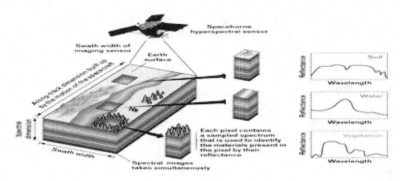

Fig 2: Concept of an Imaging Spectrometer

based dimensionality reduction (SDR) can be reviewed in the article discussed. The original data into a compressed space takes into account basic elements which are the first process. The main classical approaches include the main Folded- PCA, Principal Components Analysis (PCA), Independent Component Analysis (IPA), Orthogonal Subspace Projections (OSP), Minimum Noise Fraction (MNF), The applications for hyperspectral images (HIS) were fully united (Liu, D.,. et.al., 2015).

Feature Selection

The selection of feature is a significant step in analyzing the high-spectral image needed for a small number of examples compared to numerous characteristics which cause the harsh phenomenon. We can divide three categories of feature selection algorithms such as filtration, wrapper, and embedded techniques, in a variety of highly correlated and immaterial features (Archibald, R., and Fann, G 2007).

Feature Extraction

Feature extraction has primarily been investigated by a data mapping technique that establishes a subspace of suitable dimensionality M from the actual dimensionality space N (M £ N) the characteristic extraction can be linear or non-linear. Must be designed the feature extraction algorithm to keep interesting data on a certain issue such as de-noise or compression and classification. For example, the classification of the hyperspectral image is better because the separation of the processing class is more efficient. In feature extraction, a main component process technology has been commonly used (Hsu, P. 2004).

Figure 3. Feature selection algorithm

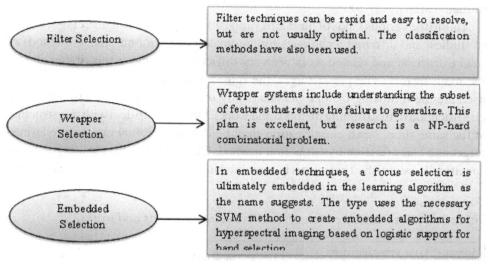

Fig 3: Feature Selection Algorithm

Principal Component Analysis (PCA)

The standard main principal components analysis is used to decrease dimensionality. The method of dimension reduction was usually implemented by the PCA. The PCAs converts the presented attribute space (here: the hyperspectral bands have all spanned feature space) to different feature space crossed by linear meta-features. The PCA showing the variability of the data displayed, including a specific dimension. The greatest variation is, therefore, the meta-functions of the various related data are processed In the case of a PCA-based feature ranking, the sorting-meta, the sorting meta-feature of the data variability, a subset of the PCA collection characteristic, apply a set of several important meta-features, containing 99.9% of the data variance, and suppose no significant decrease is achieved in imports. It is also assumed that the number of important data is not significantly reduced (Bradley, P., et.al., 2018).

METHODS FOR ROAD EXTRACTION: GENERAL CLASSIFICATION

A review of state-of-the-art automated road extraction has been submitted. This research can be used to collaborate on this subject as a detailed summary. Several methods and suggestions have been considered, including a comment on a number of them (Mena, J. B 2003).

Due to the various kinds of literature, proposals already in existence, classification of studies, and different techniques for automated and semi-automatic methods of road extraction and related work are very difficult. To achieve this, it can choose the main factors. The preset target, the removal method, and the type of sensor used are the following factors. Schematically in table 1 is presented the proposed classification of road mining methods and works. Obviously to deal with this structure at the same time. Next, classification shall be drawn up following the predefined target and classification by extraction method. Classification by sensor type is not specifically established because it is contained implicitly in the other two categories.

Table 1. General classification of road extraction methods and works

According to the preset objective:
 · Road extraction, general methods
 · Road network reconstruction methods
 · Segmentation general methods
 · Vectorization methods
 · Optimization methods
   o Neural networks
   o Genetic algorithms
   o Other optimization methods
 · Evaluation methods
 · Other objectives
	Low and medium level techniques have been used according to the extraction method.
	 · Road tracking methods
	 · Morphology and filtrate
	 · Dynamic programming and snakes
	 · Segmentation and classification
	 · Multi-scale and multi-resolution
	 · Stereoscopic analysis
	 · Multi-temporal analysis
	 · Other techniques

According to the type of sensor utilized
 · Another type of sensor
 · Monochromatic imagery
 · Infrared band
 · Color imagery (RGB)
 · Multi-and hyperspectral imagery (HYDICE)
 · Synthetic aperture radar imagery (SAR)
	Mid and high methods
	 Knowledge representation and fuzzy modeling
	   o Logic systems
	   o Rules-based systems
	   o Blackboard systems
	   o Frames based systems
	   o Semantic networks
	   o Fuzzy logic-based systems
	 Other methods of spatial reasoning

Various earth remote sensing problems that can be used to address health information receive data to a hyperspectral imaging spectrometer. The hyperspectral imagery requires preparing the classifications for many applications which perform two basic objects 1) identify also analyze each component substance to every pixel within each image; 2) minimize that information amount dimensionality, out a loss about censorious data, so which can be executed systematically including confirmed on a human investigator. The small list of applications involves geological study, wetlands mapping, plant and mineral recognition, also wealth opinion, environmental mapping, global change research, bathymetry, and crop analysis. The general aim in each from some applications implies essentially for every classification about every pixel within that image also decreases in the input amount to the manageable size. The demerits are covered the high-resolution aerial images and, are extremely complex in context. So need to reduce the time-consuming and costly and improvising the classification accuracy using hyperspectral imagery (Liu, P. et.al., 2019).

Proposed an unsupervised technique for hyperspectral image band selection that takes to reduce data dimensions, spectral and spatial information are taken into account. This method takes advantage of the concepts of super pixels and chuckles to identify the spectral channels best suited for classification in the discriminating classes of land over (Yang, C., et.al., 2018). Submitted a 3DCNN classification approach based upon parameter optimization and in conjunction with transfers and virtual samples is proposed to solve insufficient samples and improve the classification of HSIs. First, the 3D-CNN parameters can be adjusted by the variable principle. Second, initial weights can be converted from another well-trained 3D-CNN with source data from the parameter optimized bottom 3D-CNN layers of the specific data (Liu, X., et.al., 2018). Proposed Dimensionality reduction and deep learning techniques were used to reduce the computational burden and improve classification accuracy. The most reliable measures for the reduction of dimensionality and also the proposed neural network shall be analyzed with precision success (ORTAÇ, G., and ÖZCAN, G 2018). Using image processing to described deep learning methods and as well as features extracted from video, text, audio, and images. The method of deep learning is very advanced to predict the accuracy of the high classification (Shamila. S. N. S et.al., 2019). Presented the support vector machine (SVM) by integrating Principal Components Analysis (PCA) to accomplish classification tasks. PCA integrated feature reduction dimensionality to reduce the classification complexity of multi-class SVM (Vishwakarma, G., and Thakur, G. S 2019).

APPLICATIONS OF HYPERSPECTRAL

Land Use Applications

Generally, the processing of digital images (for example, controlled and unattended classification) is used in remote sensing images. The possibility of land use classification is increasing the availability of enhanced spatial and spectral resolution hyperspectral information. This data collected in specific spectral bands complement existing information from typical remote sensed images. The vegetation mapping should be mentioned especially because, in its different stages of growth, it has

Figure 4. Applications of hyperspectral

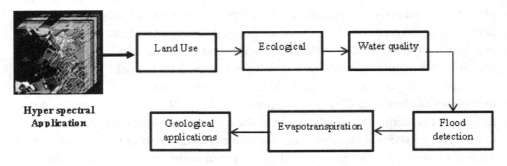

Fig 4: Hyperspectral applications

unique spectral signatures of a variable species. The hyperspectral imagery ensures improved classification due to the improvement in quality in the reference spectrum.

Ecological Applications

A vegetation indicator derived from hyperspectral sensors is more sensitive and better than that obtained from optical images. For many applications, knowledge of the vegetation reflection spectrum is crucial. The biophysical factor which affects the spectrum of activity vegetation is leaf chemistry which is accountable for leaf spectrum absorption features in the visible waveband and different vegetation has different curves of spectrum reflection characterized by vegetation indices. These indicators are primary relations that do not measure the steepness of the spectral reflecting curve in the red infrared area. With the help of hyperspectral sensor data, this steep increase in the reflection curve can be characterized by a single wavelength.

Water Quality

Implicit use of the hyperspectral image was the classification of lake trophic status, the classification of algal blooms and the estimation of complete ammonia levels for monitoring changes in wetland most open water marine habitats have water quality. The content of chlorophyll is usually assessed with a remote sensor image which can then be used to track the content of algal and, hence, the water quality. The hyperspectral image improves chlorophyll and algal sensing in the small adjacent ranges.

Flood Detection

Although the sensing remote satellite allowed in inundated areas to be monitored during floods or any other natural disaster, it was impossible to detect floods almost in real-time. To provide information about natural disasters such as flooding in real-time, sufficient space and temporal resolutions need prompt information on water conditions. This is possible with the use of sensors like Hyperion on the EO-1 satellite. Many USGS and NASA studies have been performing early warning systems for satellite-based precipitation observations, topography, soil humidity, evapotranspiration. In research on the development of a flood wave in a synthetic river channel, it can be used hydraulic information is obtained through remotely controlled images. There's also a research project to calculate river leakage with microwave, satellite sensors to enhance altering systems.

Evapotranspiration (ET)

The different applications including irrigation, reservoir loss study, runoff prediction, climatic science, ect., information regarding Evapotranspiration is essential. Although it cannot be measured directly, hyperspectral sensors provide a way of estimating energy balance components for ET mapping spatially. AVHRR and MODIS data are typically used in the estimation of the evaporative fraction, which is an ET ratio with the radiant energy available. Further details could be found in the study of hyperspectral objects that can encourage the quality of spectral information by detecting the earth's surface properties. The analysis of large volumes of hyperspectral images is currently underway. This is important, as mentioned previously, in different applications such as aerosol verification, gas plumes, etc.

Geological Applications

The remote sensing of hyperspectral is very likely to identify not only, but also to particular chemical and geometrical land patterns, which can be connected to the identities of precious mineral /oil deposits (Mather, P. M., and Koch, M 2004).

MACHINE LEARNING CLASSIFICATION FOR HYPERSPECTRAL ANALYSIS

Classification is the method used to identify actual-world objects/land cover in remotely sensed images. Consider a multi-spectral image that has m bands. If the pixel is simplest, its features are expressed as a vector, where the vector elements represent the pixel's spectral features, these m bands are captured. Using certain indices or with prior can be determined by the number of classes. The pixels are classified in water bodies, forests, grasslands, agriculture, metropolitan areas, and other landforms. Classification identifies each pixel's land cover based on its spectral reflection value (or digit number). The method also consists of labeling a numeric value on a classification rule or a decision-making rule for each class entity. In this respect, the clustering method includes an exploratory process aiming to assess and attribution of the pixels to these groups of various soils covering classes in a region. The classification of images can be different. The two main types of classification are supervised and unsupervised. These two pixels labeling techniques can also be used to segment an image with similar attributes into regions. The spectral data currently in the bands can be used to define features/models.

Supervised Classification

The location of types of land cover should be known a priori in a supervised classification technique. Training sites are known as areas in every land cover type. To produce multivariate statistical parameters for each of the locations, spectral features of pixel images within each land-covering type can be used. Since these techniques of controlled classification are based on statistical ideas, they are also referred to as a per-point and per-pixel grade. The generation of a scatter plot was the first technique utilized to visualize the distribution of spectral values measured against two features (for example, water body and farmland). Two different kinds of land use will be shown during a visual inspection. This illuminates two basic classification thoughts. The first thing which represents the selected features is using Euclidean space. The supervised classifiers require the number of classes in advance and the prior knowledge of certain statistical features of each class (Cao, X., et.al., 2016).

Unsupervised Classification

Unsupervised classification needs minimal original input from the analyst compared to the supervised classification method. In multi-spectral feature space, the nature, grouping of spectral information present in pixels emerged. Unsupervised classification allows the computer to select the mean and covariance class matrices, which are further utilized for classification, instead of allowing the user to collect the training data. The system is left entirely to the automatic process of classification, so the name is not controlled. The client selects the number of clusters to be created. After classification, the analyst will assign these spectral groups to the valuable knowledge categories. For the clusters, they can be labeled as containing useful information or meaningless, the analyst should understand clearly the spectral characteristics of the terrain. For identifying the spectral classes created by an unsupervised classifier, the analysis relies on whatever reference information (surface truth) about the classified surface. For this reason, sometimes the term exploratory is used instead of unsupervised classification. In recent years, numerous clustering algorithms have been developed which different terms of clustering reliability and classification rules. All these algorithms require a certain type of iterative estimates to achieve optimal decisions for the information set (Liu, S., et.al., 2012). In this section to examine the new techniques of hyperspectral image analysis and machine learning. In every section, techniques are discussed and using a specific type of machine learning algorithm.

Logistic Regression

Logistic regression is a hierarchical method used mainly to characterize the soil cover of remote sensing. The distribution of class probability is modeled as the weighted sum of the input function 'logistical function. Logistic regression was used mainly for pixel-specific classification and is the building block of more advanced algorithms that use ensemble, random fields, and deep learning.

K-Nearest Neighbors (KNN)

K Classification methods for nearest neighbors (KNN) are classifications for every unlabeled case: K-nearest neighbors are split by training in the multidimensional function examples and are class methods that are designated in a particular neighborhood for the majority of a specific class. The nearest K neighbors are on the list to determine the distance to be examined between the un-labeling example, vectors, and the set of training instances provided to the classificatory. The nearest neighbors are listed; the forecasts are based on the most or weighted lengths.

Support Vector Machine (SVM)

In a classification of the support vector machine, which discovers the theory of mathematical learning, Vladimir Vapnik has individually introduced it. For example, the standard pixel classification process is a pixel classification by using conventional classifiers, generally accepted, for example, Random Forest (RT) or Support Vector Machine (SVM) (Hsu, P 2004). The SVM is a supervised learning technique based on the analytic theory. A good generalization and handling of non-linear grading kernels benefit SVM over other approaches to machine learning. A kernel function is used for designing non-linear splitting classes to provide an outstanding dimension of the original space where classes are not linearly divided by the original linear space (Wieland, M., and Pittore, M 2014).

Deep Learning

Deep learning techniques are based on information that produces an abstract and valuable representation through the hierarchy of non-linear transformations. Increasing the development of graphical processing units (GPUs), the availability of large-scale data sets, and innovations in the field of deep network training such as dropping out, correcting linear units, residual learning, batch normalization, and thick connections have resulted in cutting-edge machine learning, voice recognition, and machine learning achievements.

Furthermore, researchers in the remote sensing industry have developed numerous methods of high-quality, remote sensing data analysis based on the learning. The focus is currently on the classification task on land cover, but we can also expect profound training for further tasks in the future. A common, visionary architecture of deep learning is CNN (Convolution Neural Network). Inspired by the visual mammal scheme, these neural networks have a variety of convolution layers, non-linear layers, and layer bodies to learn low to high-level tasks. Each hidden layer unit in the convolution layers is connected to the local receiver filed around the entry via share weight (pixels in the neighborhood for images) rather than fully connected to the input. Layer with non-linearity does not perform the activation of the input. In the pooling layers, answers to input translation invariance are the max operations are summarized at several input sites.

RECENT ADVANCES REVIEW OF HYPERSPECTRAL IMAGERY

PROPOSED FLOW OF RESEARCH AND DISCUSSION

To make the satellite image processing more efficient, fully automated analysis methods are more important and crucial. Most of the time, when remote sensing satellite records data of the earth's surface, it records multi-spectral or hyperspectral data. Each of the records would have many variables/features. We need to reduce the number of variables/features to view the information more meaningfully. Principal Component Analysis is a statistical method for the extraction of features. Machine learning enables the ability to classify spatial imagery effectively and usefully. Machine learning involves multiple algorithms along with Artificial Neural Networks, Support

Table 2. Advantages of hyperspectral imagery

Year's	Author's	Methods/Algorithms	Advantages
2019	(Hong Huang, Zhengying Li, and Yinsong Pan 2019).	Manifold discriminant analysis (MFMDA), multi-feature classification.	The proposed MFMDA technique can enhance classification efficiency considerably and lead to smoother classification maps, respectively 95.43%, 97.19%, and 96.60%, as compared to some state-of-the-art techniques and less training samples.
2019	(Lan Zhang, Hongjun Su and Jingwei Shen 2019).	Super-pixel Segmentation, Kernel Principal Component Analysis (KPCA).	In most cases, the proposed method performs better than SuperPCA (by performing PCA on each Superpixel) based on single-scale segmentation or multi-scale segmentation.
2019	(Weijia Li, Conghui He, Jiarui Fang, Juepeng Zheng, Haohuan Fu and Le Yu 2019).	Deep Learning, U-Net-based Semantic Segmentation method.	The experimental results show that our proposed method increases the overall F1 score by 1.1%, 6.1%, and 12.5% compared to the top three approaches in the Space Net building detection competition.
2019	(K. Dijkstra, J. van de Loosdrecht, L. R. B. Schomaker, M. A. Wiering 2019).	Convolutional neural networks and end-to-end trainable method	All tests were carried out with a 4×4 image mosaic, but it can easily modify our similarity to integrate larger sensor mosaics. The method generates an image cube hyperspectral 16 times the current cube spatial resolution while maintaining a 0.85 median structure similarity (SSIM) index (compared to a 0.55 SSIM when using bilinear interpolation).
2019	(K. S. Charmisha, V. Sowmya, and K.P. Soman 2019).	Vectorized convolution neural networks (VCNNs)	The experiment results show that although there is a reduction in dimensions, a VCNN can achieve nearly the same accuracy in classification as that of raw hyperspectral image data.
2019	(Tao Li, Jiabing Leng, Lingyan Kong, Song Guo, Gang Bai1 & Kai Wang 2019).	Deep cube Convolutional neural network model	The number of well-designed studies tests the DCNR system. The results show that the high classification of the CNN cube with neighboring pixel spectral-spatial information can be achieved and that RF outperforms other models like RF (Random forest) and SVM indicating the DNCR model's performance.
2019	(Ugur Ergul and Gokhan Bilgin 2019).	Multiple kernel learning, Composite kernels.	The results show MCK-ELM's advantage in terms of accuracy as compared with others. It is also an effective solution because complex optimization tasks are not needed. Unlike classical CK methods, it is longer necessary to manually arrange the spectral and spatial parts.
2019	(Utsav B. Gewali, Sildomar T. Monteiro and Eli Saber 2019).	Machine learning techniques.	It provides the two-way map of the tasks of the analytical image and the various types of algorithms that can be used.

Vector Machine, Self-Organizing Maps, and DT. Such algorithms are capable of managing large-scale data and mapping properties of different components. Machine learning has become a major priority in remote sensing Literature over the last few years. Artificial Intelligence - Machine learning concentrates on automatic data extraction using computational and mathematical mechanisms.

In figure 5 the ML-based approach for several earth sciences applications was also significantly improved. The main challenge for these regarding apply Machine Learning methods is data models. The main objectives of this research are, Dimensionality Reduction of Hyperspectral Imagery with Machine learning techniques, Automated Building Footprint Detection from Hyperspectral Imagery by Artificial Neural Networks, Automated Road Detection from Hyperspectral Imagery using Support Vector Machine/Relevance Vector machine, and Exploring the possibilities of applying Deep learning in geospatial data in smart city development.

The flow of research shows the overall proposed framework for building footprint and road detection. It consists of various phases, such as data collection, pre-processing portion, dimensionality reduction, and classification. The first phase is designed for pre-processing hyperspectral data. Generally pre-processing precedes data analysis. The second phase is the dimensionality reduction using Principal Component Analysis (PCA) techniques. The results of machine learning methods are compared with a classical approach. After reducing the bands required to process for classification part using Support Vector (SVM) and Convolution Neural Network (CNN). The hyperspectral image is used for automated building footprint extraction using advanced machine learning techniques which extracts the boundary of the building. This result would be used for smart city development and reconstructing the building. The fourth phase: the dimensional reduced hyperspectral image is used for automated road detection. For doing this, machine learning algorithms will be proposed for road detection.

Building Extraction (BE)

Building footprint (boundary) provides primary information about a building structure since a footprint shows the exact position and the potential shape of a building. Different data sources are would be used for building footprint extraction includes such are aerial images, interferometry synthetic aperture radar (InSAR), recent high-resolution satellite imagery, and light detection and ranging (LiDAR). The study focuses on the extraction of a building footprint using a hyperspectral image. Automatic building footprint extraction from remote sensing information is a requirement for many applications of GIS (Geographic Information System) applications, such as urban planning and disaster management. A building footprint is a digital form of the actual building boundary.

116

Figure 5. Proposing Flow of Research

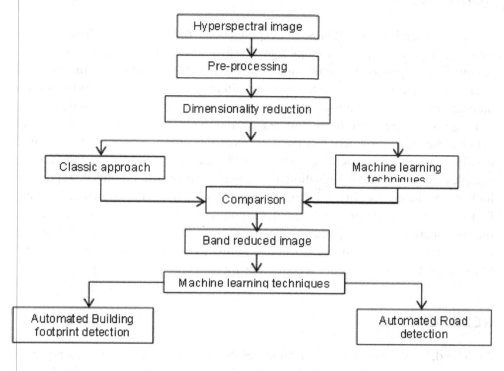

Fig 5: Proposing Flow of Research

Road Detection (RD)

Detecting the road network without remote sensing data is time and cost consuming. So, this research proposes a novel technique to detect the road network from hyperspectral images. Roads are the backbone and vital of transport, supplying human civilization with many distinct supports. For traffic management, city planning, road track tracking, navigation, and map updates, work into path extraction of great importance. Even though, different remote sensing data available, mainly this research is concentrating on the hyperspectral image. Because the need to be extracted after dimensionality reduction.

CONCLUSION

In various scientific and technological applications, the reduction of dimension for hyperspectral imagery plays a major role. The Principal Component Analysis (PCA) is a numerical method of feature extraction. Machine learning provides the potential to efficiently classify spatial images. The main purpose of this review is to identify the state-of-the-art and trends of hyperspectral imaging theories, methodologies, techniques, and applications for dimensional reduction. An overview of the concept of deep learning is provided in different types of algorithms, such as artificial neural networks and support vector machine (SVM), etc. these algorithms may handle complex characteristics of high dimensional data map classes. Finally, it proposes to look for the dimensionality reduction of hyperspectral imagery, automated building footprint detection, automated road detection, and smart city enhancement using machine learning and deep learning techniques. In the feature, we are planning to find out the best algorithms of machine learning techniques, classic approach, and implement the dimensionality reduction using hyperspectral imagery.

REFERENCES

Archibald, R., & Fann, G. (2007). Feature selection and classification of hyperspectral images with support vector machines. *IEEE Geoscience and Remote Sensing Letters*, *4*(4), 674–677. doi:10.1109/LGRS.2007.905116

Bradley, P., Keller, S., & Weinmann, M. (2018). Unsupervised feature selection based on ultrametricity and sparse training data: A case study for the classification of high-dimensional hyperspectral data. *Remote Sensing*, *10*(10), 1564. doi:10.3390/rs10101564

Cao, X., Xiong, T., & Jiao, L. (2016). Supervised band selection using local spatial information for hyperspectral image. *IEEE Geoscience and Remote Sensing Letters*, *13*(3), 329–333.

Charmisha, K. S., Sowmya, V., & Soman, K. P. (2018). Dimensionally reduced features for hyperspectral image classification using deep learning. In *International Conference on Communications and Cyber Physical Engineering 2018* (pp. 171-179). Springer.

Dijkstra, K., van de Loosdrecht, J., Schomaker, L. R. B., & Wiering, M. A. (2019). Hyperspectral demosaicking and crosstalk correction using deep learning. *Machine Vision and Applications*, *30*(1), 1–21. doi:10.100700138-018-0965-4

Ergul, U., & Bilgin, G. (2019). MCK-ELM: Multiple composite kernel extreme learning machine for hyperspectral images. *Neural Computing & Applications*, 1–11.

Gewali, U. B., Monteiro, S. T., & Saber, E. (2018). *Machine learning based hyperspectral image analysis: a survey.* arXiv preprint arXiv:1802.08701

Hsu, P. (2004). Feature extraction of hyperspectral images using matching pursuit. *Proc. Of the XXth ISPRS Congress.*

Hsu, P. (2004). Feature extraction of hyperspectral images using matching pursuit. *Proc. of the XXth ISPRS Congress.*

Huang, H., Li, Z., & Pan, Y. (2019). Multi-Feature Manifold Discriminant Analysis for Hyperspectral Image Classification. *Remote Sensing*, *11*(6), 651. doi:10.3390/rs11060651

Kodagali, J. A., & Balaji, S. (2012). Computer vision and image analysis based techniques for automatic characterization of fruits-a review. *International Journal of Computers and Applications*, *50*(6).

Li, T., Leng, J., Kong, L., Guo, S., Bai, G., & Wang, K. (2019). DCNR: Deep cube CNN with random forest for hyperspectral image classification. *Multimedia Tools and Applications*, *78*(3), 3411–3433. doi:10.100711042-018-5986-5

Li, W., He, C., Fang, J., Zheng, J., Fu, H., & Yu, L. (2019). Semantic Segmentation-Based Building Footprint Extraction Using Very High-Resolution Satellite Images and Multi-Source GIS Data. *Remote Sensing*, *11*(4), 403. doi:10.3390/rs11040403

Liu, D., Zeng, X. A., & Sun, D. W. (2015). Recent developments and applications of hyperspectral imaging for quality evaluation of agricultural products: A review. *Critical Reviews in Food Science and Nutrition*, *55*(12), 1744–1757. doi:10.1080/10408398.2013.777020 PMID:24915395

Liu, P., Liu, X., Liu, M., Shi, Q., Yang, J., Xu, X., & Zhang, Y. (2019). Building Footprint Extraction from High-Resolution Images via Spatial Residual Inception Convolutional Neural Network. *Remote Sensing*, *11*(7), 830. doi:10.3390/rs11070830

Liu, S., Bruzzone, L., Bovolo, F., & Du, P. (June 2012). Unsupervised hierarchical spectral analysis for change detection in hyperspectral images. In *2012 4th Workshop on Hyperspectral Image and Signal Processing: Evolution in Remote Sensing (WHISPERS)* (pp. 1-4). IEEE. 10.1109/WHISPERS.2012.6874245

Liu, X., Sun, Q., Meng, Y., Fu, M., & Bourennane, S. (2018). Hyperspectral image classification is based on parameter-optimized 3D-CNNs combined with transfer learning and virtual samples. *Remote Sensing*, *10*(9), 1425. doi:10.3390/rs10091425

Mather, P. M., & Koch, M. (2004). *Computer processing of remotely-sensed images: an introduction*. John Wiley & Sons.

Mena, J. B. (2003). State of the art on automatic road extraction for GIS update: A novel classification. *Pattern Recognition Letters*, *24*(16), 3037–3058. doi:10.1016/S0167-8655(03)00164-8

Ortaç, G., & Özcan, G. (2018, October). A Comparative Study for Hyperspectral Data Classification with Deep Learning and Dimensionality Reduction Techniques. *Uludağ University Journal of The Faculty of Engineering*, *23*(3), 73–90.

Qin, J., Chao, K., Kim, M. S., Lu, R., & Burks, T. F. (2013). Hyperspectral and multispectral imaging for evaluating food safety and quality. *Journal of Food Engineering*, *118*(2), 157–171. doi:10.1016/j.jfoodeng.2013.04.001

Shamila, S. N. S., Mahendran, D. S., & Sathik, M. M. (2019). Image and Video Frame Extraction System Based on Improved Deep Learning Technique. *International Journal on Emerging Technologies*, *10*(3), 384–390.

Vishwakarma, G., & Thakur, G. S. (2019). Comparative Performance Analysis of Combined SVM-PCA for Content-based Video Classification by Utilizing Inception V3. *International Journal on Emerging Technologies*, *10*(3), 397–403.

Volchok, B. A., & Chernyak, M. M. (1968). Transfer of microwave radiation in clouds and precipitation. *Transfer of Microwave Radiation in the Atmosphere, NASA TT, F-590*, 90–97.

Wieland, M., & Pittore, M. (2014). Performance evaluation of machine learning algorithms for urban pattern recognition from multi-spectral satellite images. *Remote Sensing*, *6*(4), 2912–2939. doi:10.3390/rs6042912

Wilheit, T. T., Chang, A. T. C., & Rao, V., M. S., Rodgers, E. B., & Theon, J. S. (1977). A satellite technique for quantitatively mapping rainfall rates over the oceans. *Journal of Applied Meteorology*, *16*(5), 551–560. doi:10.1175/1520-0450(1977)016<0551:ASTFQM>2.0.CO;2

Yang, C., Bruzzone, L., Zhao, H., Tan, Y., & Guan, R. (2018). Superpixel-based unsupervised band selection for classification of hyperspectral images. *IEEE Transactions on Geoscience and Remote Sensing*, *56*(12), 7230–7245. doi:10.1109/TGRS.2018.2849443

Zhang, B., Huang, W., Li, J., Zhao, C., Fan, S., Wu, J., & Liu, C. (2014). Principles, developments, and applications of computer vision for external quality inspection of fruits and vegetables: A review. *Food Research International, 62*, 326–343. doi:10.1016/j.foodres.2014.03.012

Zhang, L., Su, H., & Shen, J. (2019). Hyperspectral Dimensionality Reduction Based on Multiscale Superpixelwise Kernel Principal Component Analysis. *Remote Sensing, 11*(10), 1219. doi:10.3390/rs11101219

Chapter 9
Review on Sparse Matrix Storage Formats With Space Complexity Analysis

Saira Banu Jamalmohammed
Vellore Institute of Technology, Vellore, India

Lavanya K.
Vellore Institute of Technology, Vellore, India

Sumaiya Thaseen I.
Vellore Institute of Technology, Vellore, India

Biju V.
Jubail University College, Saudi Arabia

ABSTRACT

Sparse matrix-vector multiplication (SpMV) is a challenging computational kernel in linear algebra applications, like data mining, image processing, and machine learning. The performance of this kernel is greatly dependent on the size of the input matrix and the underlying hardware features. Various sparse matrix storage formats referred to commonly as sparse formats have been proposed in the literature to reduce the size of the matrix. In modern multi-core and many-core architectures, the performance of the kernel is mainly dependent on memory wall and power wall problem. Normally review on sparse formats is done with specific architecture or with specific application. This chapter presents a comparative study on various sparse formats in cross platform architecture like CPU, graphics processor unit (GPU), and single instruction multiple data stream (SIMD) registers. Space complexity analysis of various formats with its representation is discussed. Finally, the merits and demerits of each format have been summarized into a table.

DOI: 10.4018/978-1-7998-3335-2.ch009

INTRODUCTION

SpMV forms a basic computational kernel in many scientific, industrial and general purpose applications (Mukaddes et al., 2014)(Goharian et al., 2001)(Chen et al., 2012) (Wang et al., 2011). Modern High Performance Computer systems (HPC) accelerates SpMV computation for numerous tasks with the help of multi-cores (Yang et al., 2015)(Zhang, 2012), GPU (Li et al., 2015)(Tang, Tan, Goh et al, 2015)(Guo et al., 2014), SIMD computation using coprocessor and special XMM registers (Yavits et al., 2015)(Liu & Vinter, 2015). SpMV is usually represented as $Z = A \times X$ where A represents a sparse matrix and Z and X represents a vector each. Sparse matrix is a matrix which has more number of zero values than the non-zero values. Storing a sparse matrix as it is in a memory is a space overhead and in some applications it doesn't fit into the available memory.

To effectively reduce the storage space of sparse matrix many data structures have been proposed in the literature. These data structure reduces the storage space by storing only the non-zero values of the matrix and thereby it reduces the computation of SpMV algorithm. This is important in HPC community since all modern computer system is equipped with small storage devices. The compression of sparse matrix using efficient storage format influence the performance of SpMV operation. There are also other criteria considered in the literature for evaluating the performance of sparse formats (Langr & Tvrdik, 2015). From 1970 onwards there are many formats evolved to reduce the storage space of the sparse matrix which has been specified in the paper given by (Bell & Garland, 2008). Among these, most of the formats are customized for specific cases. CSR, COO, ELLPACK and Diagonal are the four basic formats from which the other formats have been evolved. All these formats behave differently in different computing platforms.

Greathouse and Daga (Greathouse & Daga, 2014) proved CSR format is best suited for the systems having deep cache memory hierarchy but it fails in GPU with coalesced memory and it fails to provide parallelism. ELLPACK format compared to CSR outperforms in GPU environment by providing coalesced memory and by providing instruction level parallelism as specified by Bustamam et al. (Bustamam et al., 2012). ELLPACK format is formed by adding zeros in each row to have uniform row length. This increases the storage overhead and can be eliminated with the advanced format such as sliced ELLPACK format given by Kreutzer et al. (Kreutzer et al., 2014). In this format, the given sparse matrix is divided into blocks and the individual block is stored in an ELLPACK format. This is known as sliced ELLPACK format. As CSR format doesn't perform well with GPU environment, variations of CSR format such as adaptive CSR and Compressed Multi-Row Storage (CMRS) format are proposed by Greathouse and Daga (Greathouse & Daga, 2014) and Koza et al. (Koza et al., 2014) in the literature.

In the literature, review on sparse formats are done with respect to the language used (Luján et al., 2005)(Gundersen & Steihaug, 2004)(Shahnaz et al., 2005), specific application based (Yang et al., 2011), and the implementation hardware based like multi- cores (Williams et al., 2009), GPU (Wu et al., 2010)(Hugues & Petiton, 2010)(Su & Keutzer, 2012), Coprocessor (Bernabeu et al., 2015)(Saule et al., 2014)(Tang, Zhao, Lu et al, 2015), and FPGA(Zou et al., 2013) (Umuroglu & Jahre, 2014).

This chapter deals with various storage formats used in literature and its adaptivity to the current generation processor to provide performance improvement in SpMV operation. Here, the representation of various formats and its occupancy of storage space are presented.

This chapter is organized such as Section 2 deals with the basic storage formats, Section 3 describes the block based sparse matrix storage formats, Section 4 gives the vectorizable format, Section 5 summarizes all storage formats with its advantages and disadvantages and Section 6 provides the conclusion.

BASIC STORAGE FORMATS

Diagonal Format

This format is appropriate for the matrices where the non-zero values are concentrated on the diagonal of the matrix (Bell & Garland, 2008). Figure 1 shows the diagonal format representation for the sample sparse matrix considered. This format is both space and time efficient but it is not suitable for all types of matrices. These types of matrices arise from applications such as stencil to regular grids. It is implemented with two arrays, one 2- dimensional data array that holds the non-zero values in which the diagonal elements are placed in column wise and another one is the offset array which stores the offset of the sub diagonal from the main diagonal. Diagonal format shows performance gain in SpMV operation by reducing the number of memory accesses of the data array, and X, Z vectors since they are stored in adjacent memory locations. However this format shows storage overhead since it stores explicitly the zero values occupied in the diagonal of the matrix. This format shows performance gain only for the specific application.

There are also other versions of diagonal format evolved in the literature like Compressed Row Segment with Diagonal-pattern (CRSD)(Sun et al., 2011), Diagonal Register Blocking (DRB) format (Tvrdík & Šimeče, 2006), Hierarchical Diagonal Blocking (HDB)(Blelloch et al., 2010), Sparse Quasi-Diagonal Matrix-Vector(SQDMV) multiplication (Yang et al., 2014), Jagged Diagonal Storage (JDS) format and Transpose Jagged Diagonal Storage(TJDS) format (Montagne &

Ekambaram, 2004) for improving the performance of SpMV in various applications and in various implementation platforms

Figure 1. Diagonal format with data and offset field

$$A_{mxn} = \begin{bmatrix} 0 & 4 & 0 & 7 & 0 \\ 2 & 0 & 3 & 0 & 6 \\ 0 & 5 & 0 & 0 & 0 \\ 0 & 0 & 0 & 0 & 2 \\ 1 & 0 & 0 & 6 & 0 \end{bmatrix}$$

$$Data = \begin{bmatrix} * & 2 & 4 & 7 \\ * & 5 & 3 & 6 \\ * & 0 & 0 & * \\ 1 & 6 & 2 & * \end{bmatrix} \qquad Offset = \begin{bmatrix} -4 & -1 & 1 & 3 \end{bmatrix}$$

Storage space occupied by diagonal format is given in equation (1)

$$Diagonal_{storage} = N_{dia} + N_{lz} \times N_{dia} \quad (1)$$

Where N_{lz} specifies the length of the largest non-zero diagonal and N_{dia} specifies the number of non-zero diagonal offsets.

ELLPACK Format

This format is well suited for semi-structured and unstructured meshes and adapts well for vector architecture(Bell & Garland, 2008). It is similar to that of diagonal format and the only difference is the column indices are specified explicitly as shown in Figure 2. But in diagonal, it is implicit in the offset array. It is formed by two 2-dimensional matrix one to store the data values in row wise and the other to store the column indices. If the matrix size is m x n with N_{mnzr} representing maximum number of non-zero values per row, the column indices array are specified with the size of m x N_{mnzr}. ELLPACK is suited for the matrices in which the maximum number of non-zero values does not differ more with the average. The storage space occupied by ELLPACK format is given in equation (2)

In recent years there has been a large variant of ELLPACK format progressed in the literature. Formats like Sliced ELLPACK format (Kreutzer et al., 2014), BELLPACK (Choi et al., 2010), ELLPACK-R and ELLR-T (Vázquez et al., 2010), ELLPACK Sparse Block (ESB) for Knights Corner coprocessor (Liu et al., 2013),

Figure 2. ELLPACK format with data and column indices field

$$A_{mxn} = \begin{bmatrix} 0 & 4 & 0 & 7 & 0 \\ 2 & 0 & 3 & 0 & 6 \\ 0 & 5 & 0 & 0 & 0 \\ 0 & 0 & 0 & 0 & 2 \\ 1 & 0 & 0 & 6 & 0 \end{bmatrix}$$

$$Data = \begin{bmatrix} 4 & 7 & * \\ 2 & 3 & 6 \\ 5 & * & * \\ 2 & * & * \\ 1 & 6 & * \end{bmatrix} \qquad Colum\_indices = \begin{bmatrix} 1 & 3 & * \\ 0 & 2 & 4 \\ 1 & * & * \\ 4 & * & * \\ 0 & 3 & * \end{bmatrix}$$

Sliced ELLR-T (Dziekonski et al., 2011), ELLPACK-RP format which is a combination of ELLPACK-R and JAD format(Cao et al., 2010), Bisection ELLPACK (BiELL) format (Zheng et al., 2014) has been proposed to accelerate SpMV operation in GPU environment. Various applications like support vector machines and Markov clustering in bioinformatics use ELLPACK-R format to improve their performance (Bustamam et al., 2012)(Lin & Chien, 2010).

Coordinate (COO) Format

It is one of the most general purpose formats described for storing the sparse matrices in terms of coordinates of the non-zero values (Dongarraxz et al., 1994). It can be implemented in any platform without the fear of losing any data. This format stores the row index, column index along with the non-zero values. It is simple and for any pattern of sparsity the storage required is dependent on the number of non-zero values. It is implemented with three 1-dimensional arrays, one to store the non-zero values and the other two to hold the row and column index of the corresponding non-zero values as depicted in Figure 3. To improve the readability, the row array or the column array is sorted. To ensure the elements in the same row are stored contiguously the row array is sorted.

Storage space occupied by this format is given in equation (3)

$$COO_{storage} = 3 \times NZV \qquad\qquad (3)$$

where *NZV* represents the number of non-zero values in the matrix of size *m* x *n*.

Figure 3 COO format with data, row and column indices field

$$A_{mxn}=\begin{bmatrix} 0 & 4 & 0 & 7 & 0 \\ 2 & 0 & 3 & 0 & 6 \\ 0 & 5 & 0 & 0 & 0 \\ 0 & 0 & 0 & 0 & 2 \\ 1 & 0 & 0 & 6 & 0 \end{bmatrix}$$

$$Data = \begin{bmatrix} 4 & 7 & 2 & 3 & 6 & 5 & 2 & 1 & 6 \end{bmatrix}$$

$$Row\_indices = \begin{bmatrix} 0 & 0 & 1 & 1 & 1 & 2 & 3 & 4 & 4 \end{bmatrix}$$

$$Column\_indices = \begin{bmatrix} 1 & 3 & 0 & 2 & 4 & 1 & 4 & 0 & 3 \end{bmatrix}$$

Compressed Sparse Row (CSR) Format

CSR is the most popular and general format that provides excellent compression for both structured and unstructured sparse matrices in high performance architecture (Dongarraxz et al., 1994). SpMV with CSR format shows good performance improvement when implemented on CPUs and all algorithms like BLAS, LAPACK and CUSparse supports this format only. It uses three 1-dimensional arrays, one to hold the non-zero values, the second one holds the number of non-zero values per row and the third one holds the column index of the non-zero values as seen in Figure 4. The size of this format is mainly dependent on the number of non-zero values in the matrix. CSR shows good performance for the matrices having more number of non-zero values and it is affected by the distribution of non-zero values per row.

Figure 4. CSR format with data, column and ptr indices field

$$A_{mxn}=\begin{bmatrix} 0 & 4 & 0 & 7 & 0 \\ 2 & 0 & 3 & 0 & 6 \\ 0 & 5 & 0 & 0 & 0 \\ 0 & 0 & 0 & 0 & 2 \\ 1 & 0 & 0 & 6 & 0 \end{bmatrix}$$

$$Data = \begin{bmatrix} 4 & 7 & 2 & 3 & 6 & 5 & 2 & 1 & 6 \end{bmatrix}$$

$$Column\_indices = \begin{bmatrix} 1 & 3 & 0 & 2 & 4 & 1 & 4 & 0 & 3 \end{bmatrix}$$

$$Ptr = \begin{bmatrix} 0 & 2 & 5 & 6 & 7 & 9 \end{bmatrix}$$

Storage space occupied by this format is given in equation (4).

$$CSR_{storage} = 2 \times NZV + m + 1 \qquad (4)$$

Compressed Column Storage (CSC) Format

CSC format is similar to CSR format in which the non-zero values in the column are stored contiguously in the memory (Duff et al., 1989). CSC format of matrix is equivalent to the CSR format's transpose This format came into existence because of some programming languages such as FORTRAN which stores the matrix in column wise rather than row wise in the memory. This is also known Harwell-Boeing sparse matrix format. It is shown in the Figure 5. Storage space occupied by this format is given in equation (5).

$$CSC_{storage} = 2 \times NZV + n + 1 \qquad (5)$$

BLOCK BASED FORMATS

Blocked CSR Format

In certain real time applications the occurrence of zero in sparse matrix shows regularity in their structure such as zero occurring in the blocks of size r. To

Figure 5. CSC format with data, row and column ptr indices field

$$A_{mxn}=\begin{bmatrix} 0 & 4 & 0 & 7 & 0 \\ 2 & 0 & 3 & 0 & 6 \\ 0 & 5 & 0 & 0 & 0 \\ 0 & 0 & 0 & 0 & 2 \\ 1 & 0 & 0 & 6 & 0 \end{bmatrix}$$

$$Data = \begin{bmatrix} 2 & 1 & 4 & 5 & 3 & 7 & 6 & 6 & 2 \end{bmatrix}$$

$$Row\_indices = \begin{bmatrix} 1 & 4 & 0 & 2 & 1 & 0 & 4 & 1 & 3 \end{bmatrix}$$

$$Column\_ptr = \begin{bmatrix} 0 & 2 & 4 & 5 & 7 & 9 \end{bmatrix}$$

improve the performance of SpMV kernel special block based formats evolved in the literature (Karakasis et al., 2009).This format performs better than CSR for the matrix showing this kind of substructure (Im & Yelick, 2001). Here, the matrix is splitted into blocks of size *r*. This format is shown in Figure 6 for the sample matrix. It consists of three arrays such as data array to store the data values of the non-zero block in row wise, column indices array to store the block column indices and the row pointer to store the starting of the block in each row. In the following example a block size of 2 is considered.

Figure 6. Blocked CSR format with data, row pointer and column indices field

$$A_{m \times n} = \begin{bmatrix} 0 & 4 & 0 & 7 & 0 & 0 \\ 2 & 0 & 3 & 0 & 0 & 0 \\ 0 & 5 & 0 & 0 & 0 & 0 \\ 0 & 0 & 0 & 0 & 2 & 0 \\ 1 & 0 & 0 & 0 & 0 & 0 \\ 0 & 0 & 0 & 0 & 0 & 0 \end{bmatrix}$$

$$Data = \begin{bmatrix} 0 & 4 & 2 & 0 & 0 & 7 & 3 & 0 & 0 & 5 & 0 & 0 & 0 & 0 & 2 & 0 & 1 & 0 & 0 & 0 \end{bmatrix}$$

$$Bcolumn\_indices = \begin{bmatrix} 0 & 1 & 0 & 2 & 0 \end{bmatrix} \qquad Row\_ptr = \begin{bmatrix} 0 & 2 & 4 & 5 \end{bmatrix}$$

The main drawback of this format is the added number of zero elements if there are insufficient numbers of non-zero values in the block size considered. Alternative formats to overcome this drawback are evolved in the literature. Block size is an important parameter to determine the efficiency of this format and increase in block size reduces the efficiency of this format.

Storage space required by BCSR format is given in equation (6).

$$BCSR_{storage} = (N_{nzb} \times 2r) + N_{nzb} + m/r + 1 \tag{6}$$

where N_{nzb} represents the number of non-zero blocks of a given matrix and *r* represents the block size.

Row-Grouped CSR format

This is an extension of CSR format where the matrix is decomposed into sections by row-wise (Oberhuber et al., 2010). Each section consists of group of rows. It has four 1-D arrays. The data array is used to store the first occurrence of non-zero values in each row then the second and so on… within a group and then continues for the same way in the second group. The padding of zero occurs if the number of non-zero values in each row is less than the maximum value. This causes an overhead when compared to the CSR format. The column array holds the column indices of the data values. Row length array shows the number of non-zero values in each row and the group pointer holds the offset of group beginning. This format shown in Figure 7 utilizes the cache better compared to the other format.

Figure 7. Row grouped CSR format with data, column indices, row length and group pointers field

$$A_{mxn} = \begin{bmatrix} 0 & 4 & 0 & 7 & 0 \\ 2 & 0 & 3 & 0 & 6 \\ 0 & 5 & 0 & 0 & 0 \\ 0 & 0 & 0 & 0 & 2 \\ 1 & 0 & 0 & 6 & 0 \\ 0 & 0 & 4 & 0 & 0 \end{bmatrix}$$

$$Data = [4 \quad 2 \quad 5 \quad 7 \quad 3 \quad 0 \quad 0 \quad 6 \quad 0 \quad 2 \quad 1 \quad 4 \quad 0 \quad 6 \quad 0]$$

$$Column\_indices = [1 \quad 0 \quad 1 \quad 3 \quad 2 \quad * \quad * \quad 4 \quad * \quad 4 \quad 0 \quad 2 \quad * \quad 3 \quad *]$$

$$Row\_length = [2 \quad 3 \quad 1 \quad 1 \quad 2 \quad 1] \qquad Group\_pointer = [0 \quad 9]$$

Storage space required by RCSR format is given in equation (7).

$$RCSR_{storage} = 2X + m + N_g \tag{7}$$

Where $X = \sum_{i=1}^{N_g} (N_{mnzr}g(i)) \times G_{size}$, $N_{mnzpr}g(i)$ represents the maximum number of non-zero elements per row in each group, G_{size} represents the number of rows clumped together to form a group, here we consider the G_{size} as 3, m represents the number of rows and N_g represents the number of groups.

Quad Tree CSR Format

It is a combination of CSR and Quad tree format where the given matrix divided into four quadrants recursively until the node size is equal to the density size(Zhang et al., 2013). These nodes can be of three types such as empty nodes where the entire node has zero values, mixed node where there are combination of zero and non-zero values and the full node which entirely consists of non-zero values only. Mixed and full nodes in turn are stored using CSR format and the empty node is ignored. This format is advantageous due to easy conversion from popular formats, easy modifications to the data and better cache utilization due to recursive programming style.This format shown in Figure 8 is not space efficient since it has to store the node information along with the non-zero values but the implementation of SpMV using this format is faster than the CSR format.

Figure 8. Quad tree CSR format

$$A_{mxn}=\begin{bmatrix} 0 & 4 & 0 & 7 \\ 2 & 0 & 3 & 0 \\ 0 & 5 & 0 & 0 \\ 0 & 0 & 0 & 0 \end{bmatrix}$$

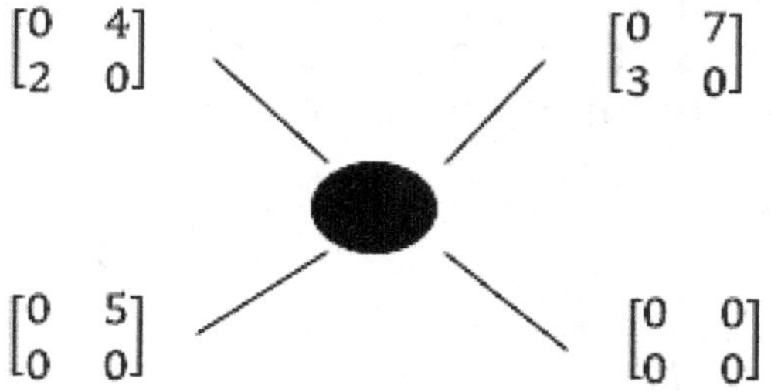

In Figure 8, the fourth node is an empty node and it is ignored. The other nodes are mixed nodes and they are stored using normal CSR format with three 1-dimensional array. The performance of this format is mainly dependent on the density size and loading of the data into the cache which increases the data locality and increases the speedup.

Storage space required by QCSR format is given in equation (8).

$$QCSR_{storage} = N_q \times CSR_{storage} \tag{8}$$

where N_q represents the number of quadrants and $CSR_{storage}$ represents the storage space required for CSR.

Minimal Quad Tree (MQT) Format

This is a new storage format known as Minimal Quad tree which is efficiently used in I/O operations (Simecek et al., 2012). It is an extension of quad tree format and overcomes the drawback of quad tree format such as space overhead in storing the pointers. This format focuses on compressing the structure of the sparse matrix where the non-zero values are implicit. An application such as storing the incident matrix of unweighted graphs shows space efficiency with this format. Similar to quad tree format the given matrix is recursively divided into blocks and the blocks are represented with a bit value of 0 if the elements are all zero and by a value of

Figure 9. MinQuad tree format

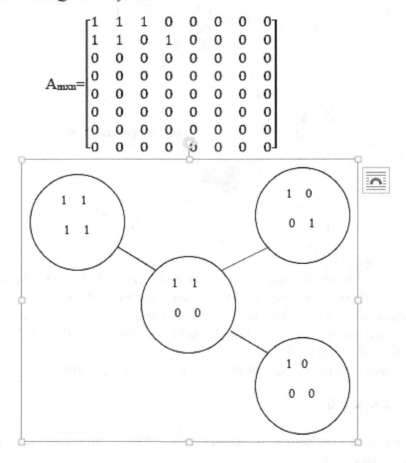

$$A_{mxn}=\begin{bmatrix} 1 & 1 & 1 & 0 & 0 & 0 & 0 & 0 \\ 1 & 1 & 0 & 1 & 0 & 0 & 0 & 0 \\ 0 & 0 & 0 & 0 & 0 & 0 & 0 & 0 \\ 0 & 0 & 0 & 0 & 0 & 0 & 0 & 0 \\ 0 & 0 & 0 & 0 & 0 & 0 & 0 & 0 \\ 0 & 0 & 0 & 0 & 0 & 0 & 0 & 0 \\ 0 & 0 & 0 & 0 & 0 & 0 & 0 & 0 \\ 0 & 0 & 0 & 0 & 0 & 0 & 0 & 0 \end{bmatrix}$$

$bitstream = \begin{bmatrix} 1 & 0 & 0 & 0 & 1 & 1 & 0 & 0 & 1 & 1 & 1 & 1 & 1 & 0 & 0 & 1 \end{bmatrix}$

one if there are non-zero values in the block. This format uses the stream of bits to represent the structure of the matrix and not the information about the non-zero values. For the above example, the matrix is divided into blocks with the density two and it is represented as bit stream as shown in Figure 9.

The minimum size of the MQT format is given in equation (9).

$$Min(MQT)_{storage} = 4 \times (N/3 + \log_4(n^2/N)) \tag{9}$$

The maximum size of the MQT format is given in equation (10).

$$Max(MQT_{storage}) = 4 \times N(1/3 + \log_4(n^2/N)) \tag{10}$$

Where N equal to the number of nonzero elements and n represents the order of the matrix.

VECTORIZABLE FORMAT

Compressed Multi-Row Storage (CMRS) Format

CMRS is a new format proposed specifically for GPU's (Koza et al., 2014). It is an extension of CSR format and can be converted to and from this format efficiently without any memory overhead. This format is advantageous when compared to other format since it does not require any zero padding and row or column reordering. This format shows good speedup in GPU and it scales well with the future GPU and in other throughput oriented architecture. This format consists of four 1-dimensional array and one integer element to keep track of the height parameter as seen in Figure 10. The data and column indices array are same as that of CSR format. The array string pointer is used to hold the number of non-zero values in each strip and the row in strip array holds the row number of individual strip.

Number of strips (N_s) = Number of rows/ Strip height = 5/2 = 3,

Storage space required by CMRS format is given in equation (11).

$$CMRS_{storage} = (3 \times NZV) + N_s + 1 \tag{11}$$

Figure 10. Compressed Multi row storage with data, column indices, row strip and strip pointer

$$A_{mxn} = \begin{bmatrix} 4 & 5 & 0 & 1 & 0 \\ 0 & 7 & 8 & 0 & 0 \\ 0 & 9 & 2 & 3 & 0 \\ 0 & 0 & 0 & 6 & 0 \\ 0 & 0 & 0 & 10 & 11 \end{bmatrix}$$

$$Data = \begin{bmatrix} 4 & 5 & 1 & 7 & 8 & 9 & 2 & 3 & 6 & 10 & 11 \end{bmatrix}$$

$$Column\_indices = \begin{bmatrix} 0 & 1 & 3 & 1 & 2 & 1 & 2 & 3 & 3 & 3 & 4 \end{bmatrix}$$

$$Row\_strip = \begin{bmatrix} 0 & 0 & 0 & 1 & 1 & 0 & 0 & 0 & 1 & 0 & 0 \end{bmatrix}$$

$$Strip\_ptr = \begin{bmatrix} 0 & 5 & 9 & 11 \end{bmatrix}$$

Adaptive CSR Format

Normal CSR format performs poor in the GPU environment. This is due to load imbalance, reduced parallelism and irregular memory access patterns. To overcome this problem GPU specific formats have been evolved. The drawback here is the transformation overhead from CSR to these format which poses storage and runtime overhead. To overcome this drawback, a novel algorithm known as CSR-adaptive is proposed by Great house and Daga (Greathouse & Daga, 2014) and shown in Figure. 11. Depending on the number of non-zero values in a row, the matrix is classified as a long row and short row. This algorithm dynamically switches between CSR stream algorithm and CSR vector algorithm for short and long rows.

Threshold =4
Block 1 = Row 1 and 2 [short rows]
Block 2 = Row 3 [long row]
Block 3 = Row 4 and 5 [short rows]

Multiplication of different threading blocks:
Storage space required by Adaptive CSR format is given in equation (12).

$$AdaptiveCSR_{storage} = 2 \times NZV + m + 1 \tag{12}$$

Figure 11. Adaptive CSR format

$$\begin{bmatrix} 4 & 5 & 0 & 1 & 0 \\ 0 & 7 & 8 & 0 & 0 \\ 0 & 9 & 2 & 3 & 0 \\ 0 & 0 & 0 & 6 & 0 \\ 0 & 0 & 0 & 10 & 11 \end{bmatrix}$$

	T1	T2	T3	T4
Block1	4	5	1	7
Block2	9	2	3	0
Block3	6	8	10	11

Streamed Storage Formats

The key parameter that determines the performance of SpMV kernel is the memory bandwidth. Prefetch stream component in IBM power processor increases the memory bandwidth. A new streaming format to exploit this hardware component and to increase the performance of SpMV is proposed by Guo and Gropp (Guo & Gropp, 2011). These format show performance improvement of SpMV kernel than CSR and BCSR format in X86 processor. There are two formats evolved under streaming such as Streamed CSR and Streamed Block CSR.

Streamed CSR Format

This format is an extension of CSR format suitable for vectorization. Here the number of stream groups is defined and the row assigned to the group stream is found out by row number mod number of streams. For example if the number of stream is assumed to be 4 then the 0th row, 4th row are assigned to the stream 0, similarly other row elements are assigned accordingly. Zeros are padded into the streams such that the size of all stream are same. Column indices array holds the respective column ids. For the added zeros the column indices hold the same index of the non-zero value in that row. The ptr array holds the offset in column indices of the first element of each block row. Comparing to BCSR format, this format adds less number of non-zero values which improves the computation speed as shown in Figure 12.

Storage space required by streamed CSR format is given in equation (13).

Figure 12. Streamed CSR format

$$A_{mxn} = \begin{bmatrix} 4 & 5 & 0 & 1 & 0 & 0 & 0 & 0 \\ 0 & 7 & 8 & 0 & 0 & 0 & 0 & 0 \\ 0 & 9 & 2 & 3 & 0 & 0 & 0 & 0 \\ 0 & 0 & 0 & 6 & 0 & 0 & 0 & 0 \\ 0 & 0 & 0 & 10 & 11 & 0 & 0 & 0 \\ 0 & 0 & 0 & 0 & 0 & 0 & 0 & 0 \\ 0 & 0 & 0 & 0 & 0 & 0 & 0 & 0 \\ 0 & 0 & 0 & 0 & 0 & 0 & 0 & 0 \end{bmatrix}$$

Column indices arrays

$Column\_R = \begin{bmatrix} 0 & 1 & 3 & 3 & 4 \end{bmatrix}$ $Column\_G = \begin{bmatrix} 1 & 2 & 2 & * & * \end{bmatrix}$

$Column\_B = \begin{bmatrix} 1 & 2 & 3 & * & * \end{bmatrix}$ $Column\_P = \begin{bmatrix} 3 & 3 & 3 & * & * \end{bmatrix}$

Number of streams = 4

Data arrays

$R = \begin{bmatrix} 4 & 5 & 1 & 10 & 11 \end{bmatrix}$ $G = \begin{bmatrix} 7 & 8 & 0 & 0 & 0 \end{bmatrix}$

$B = \begin{bmatrix} 9 & 2 & 3 & 0 & 0 \end{bmatrix}$ $P = \begin{bmatrix} 6 & 0 & 0 & 0 & 0 \end{bmatrix}$

$ptr = \begin{bmatrix} 0 & 3 & 5 \end{bmatrix}$

$$StreamedCSR_{storage} = 2(Ns \times \max(NZS)) + S_r + 1 \tag{13}$$

where Ns represent the number of streams, NZS gives the number of non-zero values per stream and S_r gives the number of rows per stream.

Streamed BCSR Format

In certain applications where the non-zero values are concentrated in a particular block, then block CSR format is efficient. Streaming format can be adopted for this kind of matrix also. In Figure 13 the given matrix is divided into 4 x 4 blocks. In this format, the first rows of all blocks are stored first, then the second row and simultaneously. The column indices keeps track of the column index for each block and the ptr array holds the offset in the column indices array of the first block in each block row. Streamed BCSR format with block size of 4 shows better speedup than

BCSR format for the matrices having large number of non-zero values and when the sparse matrix could not fit into the cache. Streamed BCSR format shows performance improvements with the SIMD instruction available in the current processor.

Figure 13. Streamed BCSR format

$$|A_{mxn}| = \begin{bmatrix} 4 & 5 & 0 & 1 & 0 & 0 & 0 & 0 \\ 0 & 7 & 8 & 0 & 0 & 0 & 0 & 0 \\ 0 & 9 & 2 & 3 & 0 & 0 & 0 & 0 \\ 0 & 0 & 0 & 6 & 0 & 0 & 0 & 0 \\ 0 & 0 & 0 & 10 & 11 & 0 & 0 & 0 \\ 0 & 0 & 0 & 0 & 0 & 0 & 0 & 0 \\ 0 & 0 & 0 & 0 & 0 & 0 & 0 & 0 \\ 0 & 0 & 0 & 0 & 0 & 0 & 0 & 0 \end{bmatrix}$$

$$R = \begin{bmatrix} 4 & 5 & 0 & 1 & 0 & 0 & 0 & 10 & 11 & 0 & 0 & 0 \end{bmatrix}$$

$$G = \begin{bmatrix} 0 & 7 & 8 & 0 & 0 & 0 & 0 & 0 & 0 & 0 & 0 & 0 \end{bmatrix}$$

$$B = \begin{bmatrix} 0 & 9 & 2 & 3 & 0 & 0 & 0 & 0 & 0 & 0 & 0 & 0 \end{bmatrix}$$

$$P = \begin{bmatrix} 0 & 0 & 0 & 6 & 0 & 0 & 0 & 0 & 0 & 0 & 0 & 0 \end{bmatrix}$$

$$Ind = \begin{bmatrix} 0 & 0 & 1 \end{bmatrix}$$

$$Ptr = \begin{bmatrix} 0 & 1 & 3 \end{bmatrix}$$

Storage space required by streamed BCSR format is given in equation (14).

$$StreamedBCSR_{storage} = Ns \times (N_{nzb} \times b_{size}) + 2(N_{nzb}) \tag{14}$$

where N_{nzb} represents number of non-zero blocks in the matrix and b_{size} represents the block size.

Sliced ELLPACK-C-Sigma Format

Normal ELLPACK format performs well with the streaming processor by padding zeros and by providing coalesced memory access and instruction level parallelism. Based on the matrix characteristic this format outperforms CSR format. To overcome the storage overhead of ELLPACK due to zero padding, sliced ELLPACK format came into existence (Kreutzer et al., 2014) shown in Figure 14. In this, the given matrix is splitted into blocks of sizes and each slice is stored using ELLPACK format. It is also known as SELLPACK-C. Here C denotes the block size. The block size of 1 result in CSR format and block size equal to matrix dimensions results in ELLPACK format. This format overcomes the disadvantage of zero padding in ELLPACK format if all the rows in the chunk have equal number of non-zero values. But in the other cases there will be space overhead in this format by adding less number of zeros than in ELLPACK format. This drawback can be overcome by sorting the rows in descending order of non-zero values and grouping them into chunks. By this method the rows having equal length of non-zero values will be clumped together. However sorting globally will reduce the spatial and temporal locality of SpMV operation which will further reduce the performance of the kernel.

Figure 14. Sliced ELLPACK format

$$A_{mxn} = \begin{bmatrix} 0 & 4 & 0 & 7 & 0 \\ 2 & 0 & 3 & 0 & 6 \\ 0 & 5 & 0 & 0 & 0 \\ 0 & 0 & 0 & 0 & 2 \\ 1 & 0 & 0 & 6 & 0 \\ 2 & 4 & 0 & 0 & 5 \end{bmatrix}$$

$$Slice\_ptr = \begin{bmatrix} 0 & 6 & 9 & 15 \end{bmatrix}$$

$$Value = \begin{bmatrix} 4 & 2 & 7 & 3 & 0 & 6 & 5 & 2 & 1 & 2 & 6 & 4 & 0 & 5 \end{bmatrix}$$
$$Column = \begin{bmatrix} 1 & 0 & 3 & 2 & * & 4 & 1 & 4 & 0 & 0 & 3 & 1 & * & 4 \end{bmatrix}$$

Storage space required by Sliced ELLPACK format is given in equation (15).

$$SlicedELLPACK_{storage} = N_s + 1 + 4 \times \left(\sum_{i=1}^{N_s} N_{nzv}(i) \right) \tag{15}$$

Where N_s is the number of slices and N_{nzv} represents the maximum number of nonzero elements in a row of each slice. In the above matrix the chunk size is considered as 2 so the σ size is considered as multiple of chunk size such as 4, 8, 12 etc. Here we consider the value of σ as 4 consecutive rows and the elements are sorted in descending order and it is stored. It is best suited for the current generation processors

Table 1. Comparison of various sparse formats

Categories	Number of matrices required	Usage	Advantage	Disadvantage
Coordinate form (COO) (Bell & Garland, 2008)	Three -1D arrays	General purpose format	It is suitable for any random sparse matrix.	It occupies a lot of space.
CSR/Compressed Sparse Column (CSC) (Bell & Garland, 2008) (Duff et al., 1989)	Three -1D arrays	General purpose format	They reduce storage. Row pointers facilitate fast multiplication. The code need not be changed for SpMV implementation.	Not suitable for GPU due to load imbalance, reduced parallelism and irregular memory access patterns.
Blocked compressed row storage (BCSR) (Im & Yelick, 2001)	Four - 1D arrays	General purpose format	Reduces the number of load operations.	It requires an extra loop in the sparse matrix vector multiplication and suffers from additional loop overhead.
Diagonal Matrix (Bell & Garland, 2008)	One- 2D and one 1D array	Not a general purpose format	It is very effective for a matrix with non-zero elements occupied only in the diagonal.	It can be applicable only for matrices that have non-zero elements only in its diagonals and not a general purpose format.
ELLPACK format (Bell & Garland, 2008)	Two- 2D arrays	Not a general purpose format	Suitable for matrices obtained from semi-structured meshes, and well behaved unstructured meshes.	We need to know the maximum number of non-zero elements present in the matrix.
Quad tree (Simecek, 2009)	Structure of three 1-D arrays	General purpose format	SpMV implementation using this format is faster.	Space overhead.
Minimal Quad Tree (Zhang et al., 2013)	Three-1D arrays	Not a general purpose format	Suitable to store only the structure of distribution of non-zero values.	Not suitable for SpMV implementation.
Quadtree CSR (Zhang et al., 2013)	Structure of three 1-D arrays	General purpose format	SpMV implementation using this format is faster.	Space overhead.
Row-grouped CSR (Oberhuber et al., 2010)	Four-1D arrays	General purpose format	Allocates less artificial zeros, number of allocated elements per row vary from one group to another.	It is a very time consuming process and it requires 4 arrays.
Compressed Multirow Storage (Koza et al., 2014)	Four-1D arrays	General format	Does not require any zero padding and row or column reordering	This format is suitable for GPU architecture only.
Streamed CSR (Guo & Gropp, 2011)	Nine-1D arrays	General format	Comparing to BCSR format, this format adds less number of non-zero values which improves the computation speed	This format is suitable for coprocessor SIMD architecture only.
Streamed BCSR (Guo & Gropp, 2011)	Six-1D arrays	General format	Streamed BCSR format with block size of 4 shows better speedup than BCSR format for the matrices having large number of non-zero values and when the sparse matrix could not fit into the cache	This format is suitable for coprocessor SIMD architecture only.
Sliced ELLPACK-C-Sigma (Kreutzer et al., 2014)	Three-1D arrays	Not a general purpose format	It reduces the number of zero padded in ELLPACK format	The average number of Non-zero values per row should be greater than the SIMD width.

with SIMD capability such as Sandy Bridge, Xeon Phi and Nvidia Tesla K20. In order to have good performance improvement of SpMV in these architectures the average number of non-zero values per row should be greater than the SIMD width. This format shows better performance on a large range of computer devices. This format can be vectorised by using a compiler or by using C intrinsic.

COMPARATIVE STUDY

Table 1 gives the summary of various storage formats with the number of arrays used for implementation, the platform it is suitable for and its advantage and disadvantage.

CONCLUSION

In this paper, we made a detailed study on various sparse matrix storage formats used for effective implementation of SpMV kernel. We have categorised the formats as basic, blocked and vectorizable format. For each format, we have derived the storage space occupied and discussed their qualities with the example matrix. This paper will be useful for the researchers to select an appropriate format for optimizing the SpMV kernel based on the hardware accelerators used.

REFERENCES

Bell, N., & Garland, M. (2008). *Efficient sparse matrix-vector multiplication on CUDA*. Nvidia Technical Report NVR-2008-004, Nvidia Corporation.

Bernabeu, S. R., Puzyrev, V., Hanzich, M., & Fernandez, S. (2015). Efficient Sparse Matrix-vector Multiplication for Geophysical Electromagnetic Codes on Xeon Phi Coprocessors. *Second EAGE Workshop on High Performance Computing for Upstream*. 10.3997/2214-4609.201414033

Blelloch, G. E., Koutis, I., Miller, G. L., & Tangwongsan, K. (2010). Hierarchical diagonal blocking and precision reduction applied to combinatorial multigrid. In *IEEE conference on High Performance Computing* (pp. 1–12). Networking, Storage and Analysis. doi:10.1109/SC.2010.29

Bustamam, A., Burrage, K., & Hamilton, N. A. (2012). Fast parallel Markov clustering in bioinformatics using massively parallel computing on GPU with CUDA and ELLPACK-R sparse format. *IEEE/ACM Transactions on Computational Biology and Bioinformatics*, *9*(3), 679–692. doi:10.1109/TCBB.2011.68 PMID:21483031

Cao, W., Yao, L., Li, Z., Wang, Y., & Wang, Z. (2010). Implementing sparse matrix-vector multiplication using CUDA based on a hybrid sparse matrix format. *IEEE International Conference on Computer Application and System Modeling (ICCASM)*, 11, V11-16.

Chen, S., Cheng, X., & Xu, J. (2012). Research on image compression algorithm based on Rectangle Segmentation and storage with sparse matrix. *Proc. 9th IEEE International Conference on Fuzzy Systems and Knowledge Discovery (FSKD)*, 1904-1908. 10.1109/FSKD.2012.6233969

Choi, J. W., Singh, A., & Vuduc, R. W. (2010). Model-driven autotuning of sparse matrix-vector multiply on GPUs. *ACM SIGPLAN Notices, 45*(5), 115–126. doi:10.1145/1837853.1693471

Dongarraxz, J., Lumsdaine, A., Niu, X., Pozoz, R., & Remingtonx, K. (1994). A sparse matrix library in C++ for high performance architectures. Academic Press.

Duff, I. S., Grimes, R. G., & Lewis, J. G. (1989). Sparse matrix test problems. *ACM Transactions on Mathematical Software, 15*(1), 1–14. doi:10.1145/62038.62043

Dziekonski, A., Lamecki, A., & Mrozowski, M. (2011). A memory efficient and fast sparse matrix vector product on a GPU. *Progress in Electromagnetics Research, 116*, 49–63. doi:10.2528/PIER11031607

Goharian, N., El-Ghazawi, T., & Grossman, D. (2001). Enterprise text processing: a sparse matrix approach. *Proc. of IEEE International Conference on Information Technology: Coding and Computing*, 71-75. 10.1109/ITCC.2001.918768

Greathouse, J. L., & Daga, M. (2014). Efficient sparse matrix-vector multiplication on GPUs using the CSR storage format. *Proc. IEEE International Conference on High Performance Computing, Networking, Storage and Analysis*, 769-780. 10.1109/SC.2014.68

Gundersen, G., & Steihaug, T. (2004). Data structures in Java for matrix computations. *Concurrency and Computation, 16*(8), 799–815. doi:10.1002/cpe.793

Guo, D., & Gropp, W. (2011). Optimizing sparse data structures for matrix-vector multiply. *International Journal of High Performance Computing Applications, 25*(1), 115–131. doi:10.1177/1094342010374847

Guo, P., Wang, L., & Chen, P. (2014). A performance modeling and optimization analysis tool for sparse matrix-vector multiplication on GPU's. *IEEE Transactions on Parallel and Distributed Systems, 25*(5), 1112–1123. doi:10.1109/TPDS.2013.123

Hugues, M. R., & Petiton, S. G. (2010). Sparse matrix formats evaluation and optimization on a GPU. In *High Performance Computing and Communications (HPCC), 2010 12th IEEE International Conference on* (pp. 122-129). IEEE. 10.1109/HPCC.2010.85

Im, E. J., & Yelick, K. (2001). Optimizing sparse matrix computations for register reuse in SPARSITY. *Proc. Conference on Computational Science (ICCS)*, 2073, 127-136. 10.1007/3-540-45545-0_22

Karakasis, V., Goumas, G., & Koziris, N. (2009). A comparative study of blocking storage methods for sparse matrices on multicore architectures. *Proc. of IEEE International Conference in Computational Science and Engineering*, 1, 247-256. 10.1109/CSE.2009.223

Koza, Z., Matyka, M., Szkoda, S., & Miroslaw, L. (2014). Compressed multirow storage format for sparse matrices on graphics processing units. *SIAM Journal on Scientific Computing*, 36(2), 19–39. doi:10.1137/120900216

Kreutzer, M., Hager, G., Wellein, G., Fehske, H., & Bishop, A. R. (2014). A unified sparse matrix data format for efficient general sparse matrix-vector multiplication on modern processors with wide SIMD units. *SIAM Journal on Scientific Computing*, 36(5), 401–423. doi:10.1137/130930352

Langr & Tvrdik. (2015). Evaluation Criteria for Sparse Matrix Storage Formats. *IEEE Transaction on Parallel and Distributed Systems*, 1-14.

Li, K., Yang, W., & Li, K. (2015). Performance analysis and optimization for SpMV on GPU using probabilistic modelling. *IEEE Transactions on Parallel and Distributed Systems*, 26(1), 196–205. doi:10.1109/TPDS.2014.2308221

Lin, T. K., & Chien, S. Y. (2010). Support vector machines on gpu with sparse matrix format. *IEEE Ninth International Conference on Machine Learning and Applications*, 313-318. 10.1109/ICMLA.2010.53

Liu, W., & Vinter, B. (2015). CSR5: An Efficient Storage Format for Cross-Platform Sparse Matrix-Vector Multiplication. *Proc. of the 29th ACM International Conference on Supercomputing*, 339-350. 10.1145/2751205.2751209

Liu, X., Smelyanskiy, M., Chow, E., & Dubey, P. (2013). Efficient sparse matrix-vector multiplication on x86-based many-core processors. *Proceedings of the 27th international ACM conference on International conference on supercomputing*, 273-282. 10.1145/2464996.2465013

Luján, M., Usman, A., Hardie, P., Freeman, T. L., & Gurd, J. R. (2005). Storage formats for sparse matrices in Java. In *Computational Science–ICCS 2005* (pp. 364–371). Springer Berlin Heidelberg. doi:10.1007/11428831_45

Montagne, E., & Ekambaram, A. (2004). An optimal storage format for sparse matrices. *Information Processing Letters*, 90(2), 87–92. doi:10.1016/j.ipl.2004.01.014

Mukaddes, A. M., Shioya, R., & Ogino, M. (2014). Comparative Study of Sparse Matrix Storage Format in the Finite Element Analysis of Thermal-Structure Coupling Problem. *Proc. International conference on computational methods*, 1-9.

Oberhuber, T., Suzuki, A., & Vacata, J. (2010). New row-grouped CSR format for storing the sparse matrices on GPU with implementation in CUDA. Acta Technica Journal, 436-440.

Saule, E., Kaya, K., & Çatalyürek, U. V. (2014). Performance evaluation of sparse matrix multiplication kernels on intel xeon phi. In *Parallel Processing and Applied Mathematics* (pp. 559–570). Springer Berlin Heidelberg. doi:10.1007/978-3-642-55224-3_52

Shahnaz, R., Usman, A., & Chughtai, I. R. (2005). Review of storage techniques for sparse matrices. In *9th International Multitopic Conference, IEEE INMIC 2005* (pp. 1-7). IEEE. 10.1109/INMIC.2005.334453

Simecek, I. (2009). Sparse matrix computations using the quad tree storage format. *Proc. 11th International Symposium on Symbolic and Numeric Algorithms for Scientific Computing (SYNASC)*, 168-17.

Simecek, I., Langr, D., & Tvrdík, P. (2012). Space-efficient sparse matrix storage formats for massively parallel systems. *Proc. IEEE International Conference on Embedded Software and Systems*, 54-60.

Su, B. Y., & Keutzer, K. (2012). clSpMV: A cross-platform OpenCL SpMV framework on GPUs. In *Proceedings of the 26th ACM international conference on Supercomputing* (pp. 353-364). ACM. 10.1145/2304576.2304624

Sun, X., Zhang, Y., Wang, T., Long, G., Zhang, X., & Li, Y. (2011). CRSD: application specific auto-tuning of SpMV for diagonal sparse matrices. InEuro-Par 2011 Parallel Processing, 316-327.

Tang, W., Tan, W., Goh, R. S. M., Turner, S., & Wong, W. K. (2015). A Family of Bit-Representation-Optimized Formats for Fast Sparse Matrix-Vector Multiplication on the GPU. *IEEE Transactions on Parallel and Distributed Systems*, 26(9), 2373–2385. doi:10.1109/TPDS.2014.2357437

Tang, W. T., Zhao, R., Lu, M., Liang, Y., Huyng, H. P., Li, X., & Goh, R. S. M. (2015). Optimizing and auto-tuning scale-free sparse matrix-vector multiplication on Intel Xeon Phi. *International Symposium on Code Generation and Optimization (CGO)*, 136-145. 10.1109/CGO.2015.7054194

Tvrdík, P., & Šimeče, I. (2006). A new diagonal blocking format and model of cache behavior for sparse matrices. Parallel Processing and Applied Mathematics, 164-171. doi:10.1007/11752578_21

Umuroglu, Y., & Jahre, M. (2014). An energy efficient column-major backend for FPGA SpMV accelerators. In *Computer Design (ICCD), 2014 32nd IEEE International Conference on* (pp. 432-439). IEEE. 10.1109/ICCD.2014.6974716

Vázquez, F., Ortega, G., Fernández, J. J., & Garzón, E. M. (2010). Improving the performance of the sparse matrix vector product with GPUs. *IEEE 10th International Conference on Computer and Information Technology (CIT)*, 1146-1151. 10.1109/CIT.2010.208

Wang, Y., Yan, H., Pan, C., & Xiang, S. (2011). Image editing based on sparse matrix-vector multiplication. *Proc. IEEE International Conference on Acoustics, Speech and Signal Processing (ICASSP)*, 1317-1320. 10.1109/ICASSP.2011.5946654

Williams, S., Oliker, L., Vuduc, R., Shalf, J., Yelick, K., & Demmel, J. (2009). Optimization of sparse matrix–vector multiplication on emerging multicore platforms. *Parallel Computing*, *35*(3), 178–194. doi:10.1016/j.parco.2008.12.006

Wu, T., Wang, B., Shan, Y., Yan, F., Wang, Y., & Xu, N. (2010). Efficient pagerank and spmv computation on amd gpus. In *Parallel Processing (ICPP), 2010 39th International Conference on* (pp. 81-89). IEEE. 10.1109/ICPP.2010.17

Yang, W., Li, K., Liu, Y., Shi, L., & Wan, L. (2014). Optimization of quasi-diagonal matrix–vector multiplication on GPU. *International Journal of High Performance Computing Applications*, *28*(2), 183–195. doi:10.1177/1094342013501126

Yang, W., Li, K., Mo, Z., & Li, K. (2015). Performance Optimization Using Partitioned SpMV on GPUs and Multicore CPUs. *IEEE Transactions on Computers*, *64*(9), 2623–2636. doi:10.1109/TC.2014.2366731

Yang, X., Parthasarathy, S., & Sadayappan, P. (2011). Fast sparse matrix-vector multiplication on GPUs: Implications for graph mining. *Proceedings of the VLDB Endowment International Conference on Very Large Data Bases*, *4*(4), 231–242. doi:10.14778/1938545.1938548

Yavits, L., Morad, A., & Ginosar, R. (2015). Sparse matrix multiplication on an associative processor. *IEEE Transactions on Parallel and Distributed Systems*, *26*(11), 3175–3183. doi:10.1109/TPDS.2014.2370055

Zhang, J., Liu, E., Wan, J., Ren, Y., Yue, M., & Wang, J. (2013). Implementing Sparse Matrix-Vector Multiplication with QCSR on GPU. *International Journal of Applied Mathematics and Information Sciences*, *7*(2), 473–482. doi:10.12785/amis/070207

Zhang, N. (2012). A Novel Parallel Scan for Multicore Processors and Its Application in Sparse Matrix-Vector Multiplication. *IEEE Transactions on Parallel and Distributed Systems*, *23*(3), 397–404. doi:10.1109/TPDS.2011.174

Zheng, C., Gu, S., Gu, T. X., Yang, B., & Liu, X.-P. (2014). BiELL: A bisection ELLPACK-based storage format for optimizing SpMV on GPUs. *Journal of Parallel and Distributed Computing*, *74*(7), 2639–2647. doi:10.1016/j.jpdc.2014.03.002

Zou, D., Dou, Y., Guo, S., & Ni, S. (2013). High performance sparse matrix-vector multiplication on FPGA. *IEICE Electronics Express*, *10*(17), 20130529–20130529. doi:10.1587/elex.10.20130529

Chapter 10
Parallel Defect Detection Model on Uncertain Data for GPUs Computing by a Novel Ensemble Learning

Sivakumar S.

(iD) https://orcid.org/0000-0003-3076-0900
Koneru Lakshmaiah Education Foundation, India

Sreedevi E.
Koneru Lakshamiah Education Foundation, India

PremaLatha V.
Koneru Lakshamiah Education Foundation, India

Haritha D.
Koneru Lakshamiah Education Foundation, India

ABSTRACT

To detect defect is an important concept in machine leaning techniques and ambiguous dataset which develops into a challenging issue, as the software product expands in terms of size and its complexity. This chapter reveals an applied novel multi-learner model which is ensembled to predict software metrics using classification algorithms and propose algorithm applied in parallel method for detection on ambiguous data using density sampling and develop an implementation running on both GPUs and multi-core CPUs. The defect on the NASA PROMISE defect dataset is adequately predicted and classified using these models and implementing GPU computing. The performance compared to the traditional learning models improved algorithm and parallel implementation on GPUs shows less processing time in ensemble model compared to decision tree algorithm and effectively optimizes the true positive rate.
DOI: 10.4018/978-1-7998-3335-2.ch010

INTRODUCTION

Every day in the world, millions and millions of data are being produced and accumulated in various areas. These data's has to be processed and a specific pattern of how it is behaving must be discovered in order to process the newly incoming data. This is where the use of classification method in data mining comes into picture.

A simple example of this kind of process is a grocery shop which is giving you preferences or a discount on the prices based on your previous purchases. In this thesis, a decision tree based, predictive classifier called ensemble to predict software metrics here after, has been taken into consideration and is implemented in central processing unit (CPU) computation and Compute Unified Device Architecture (CUDA) for Graphical Processing Unit (GPU) computation.

In this paper it implements the algorithm which presents ensemble model with the help of GPU computing thereby reducing the time taken for classification and comparing it with the time taken for implementing the algorithm in CPU computing. To record the difference in its behaviour when we increase the amount of data on it. This is the first step of our future work where the goal is to generalize the idea of applying GPU computing in each and every area of computation wherever it is needed. To display the images as an output for the generated images that are available in frame buffer we use an (GPU)Graphics processing Unit which is an electronic circuit specially designed for it, which is also known as (VPU) Visual Processing Unit. In blown 80's and early 90's, GPUs were used for better visualization in video games.

In late 90's, GPUs become more programmable. Not only the game developers but also the researchers started using GPUs because of its excellent floating point performance. From that instance, General Purpose GPU (GPGPU) came into existence.

In the beginning, GPGPU programming was not so easy even for programmers who were expert in graphics programming languages like OpenGL. It was practically off-limits to those who didn't have knowledge about latest graphics like Application Programming Interfaces (APIs). A picture showing Intel mother-board with dedicated graphic card is shown in the figure below Sanders et.al (2010).

In early 2000's, A programming model, which is an extension of C programming language with data-parallel constructs was developed in NVIDIA lab. They named this new programming model as Compute Unified Device Architecture. It uses the concepts such as streams, kernels and reduction operators. GPU is needed to make parallel computing possible. A diagrammatic comparison between GPU and CPU architecture is given in the figure below.

CPU architecture has few computing cores optimised for sequential serial processing, while a GPU architecture consist of thousands of smaller computing cores to handle multi-tasks parallelly. GPU uses these massively parallel cores to provide high memory bandwidth for high performance computing. Even though

Figure 1. An Intel motherboard with dedicated graphic card slot

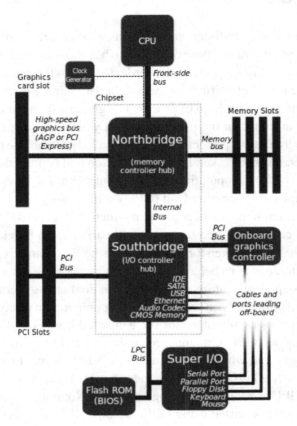

GPU has lot of computing cores, its architecture is simple as that of a CPU. There are many architectures available namely Tesla, Fermi and Kepler. Out of these, latest is the GPU architecture of NVIDIA which is Kepler sivakumar s & et.al (2017) & Musthafa Baig et.al (2020).

Compute Unified Device Architecture, in short form CUDA is a C/C++ SDK evolved by NVIDIA, first released in 2006 to use the GPU architecture produced by them effectively. C programming language which extends to be a CUDA which consists of library functions to access GPU. It contains directives and functions that call GPU device and CPU device whenever it is necessary. It grants for smooth accessing of multi - threading and execution in parallel on all the processors that leads to thread on the GPU device Sanders et.al (2010). A diagrammatic representation of the process flow on GPU using CUDA is given in the figure below.

GPU does not contain functions to access main memory directly. Likewise, CPU cannot access GPU memory directly. So all the data which is needed has to

Figure 2. Comparisons of CPU and GPU Architectures

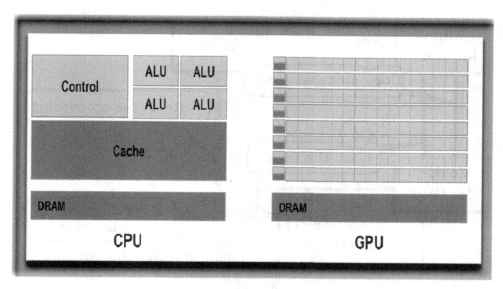

be copied to the device explicitly. This is done by a function called Cudamemcpy. CUDA kernels are subdivided into grids. The grids are then divided into blocks and then into threads. Each thread in a block executes the code independently and stores the result. Each thread can be accessed by indexing the block and grid of the kernel Sanders et.al (2010).

Programming in CUDA

CUDA programming is an objective of parallel computing design consists of a novel parallel programming design and an instruction regular architecture Nasridinov et.al(2014) & Nguyen (2007).

Before starting to write programs in CUDA, we need a basic understanding of C or C++ programming. Few things which we need to keep in mind while programming in CUDA are listed below.

1. CUDA produce function type qualifiers that aren't in C/C++ to allow the programmer to describe where a function would run.
2. The key words __host__ if the function statement contains this qualifier then it specifies that the program must run on the host CPU (it is the default) Nickolls et.al(2010) & NVIDIA(2010).

Figure 3. Process flow in CUDA

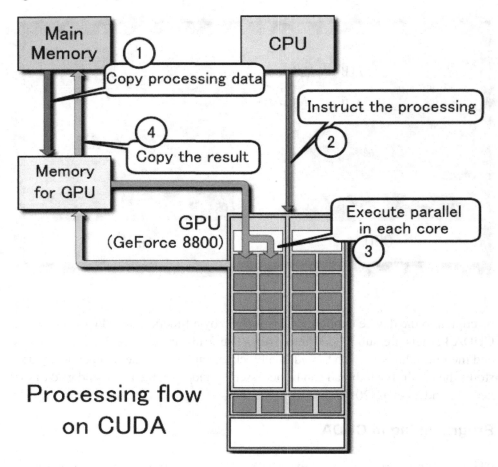

3. __device__ if the function declaration contains this qualifier then it specifies that the program ought to run on the GPU and the purpose can only be called by program consecutively on the GPU.
4. __global__ if the function statement contains this qualifier then it specifies that the program ought to run on the GPU but have to be named from the host (CPU) - this is the entrée point to start multi-threaded programmes consecutively on the GPU NVIDIA (2014).
5. Inside the <<< >>> syntax, we need at least two arguments to be present for calling any global or device function, one for blockgrid and another for number of thread blocks. A typical function call looks like function name <<<bg; tb>>>, bg identifies the dimensions of the block grid and tb identifies the dimensions of each thread block Munshi (2008).

6. __host__: if the function declaration contains this qualifier then it requires the code must run on the host CPU (it is the default).
7. GPU device could not execute code on the CPU host.
8. CUDA imposes a few limitations, for example, the only GPU code is C (CPU code can be C++), GPU code can't be called recursively.
9. All calls to a global function must specify how many threaded copies are to launched and in what configuration.
10. Call for any global or device function is defined by a specific syntax<<< >>> Sanders et.al(2011).
11. The keywords __device__ in the event that the variable presentation contains this qualifier, at that point it determines that the variable resides in the GPU global memory and is described while the code runs.
12. The __constant__ in the event that the variable announcement contains this qualifier, at that point it determines that the variable resides in the constant memory space of the device (GPU) and is characterized while the code runs.
13. The __shared__ if the variable declaration contains this qualifier at that point it indicates that the variable resides in the shared memory of the thread block and has the similar life expectancy as the block Munshi (2008).
14. A typical function call looks like function name <<< bg; tb >>>.
15. bg requires the dimensions of the block grid and tb requires the dimensions of every thread block.
16. A new datatype called dim3 has been defined by CUDA in which three unsigned integer components defaults to 1.
17. dim3 has struct-like access - members are x, y and z.
18. For the program running on the GPU (device and global), certain variables are predefined, which permit threads to be located inside their blocks and grids.
19. dim3 gridDim which specifies the dimensions of the grid.
20. uint3 blockIdx an unsigned integer which refers to the position of the block in the grid.
21. dim3 blockDim which specifies the dimensions of the block.
22. uint3 threadIdx an unsigned integer which refers to the position of the thread in the block.

RELATED WORK

In this paper, we list out all the existing techniques of classification and a brief description of those techniques. Classification is the process of applying the known structures that are discovered from clustering of the data. A simple example is a process of classifying a living thing which is having wings into the category of birds.

An algorithm or a program which implements classification is called a classifier. In Classification, we are provided with a training database with which we have to apply the known structures discovered during the clustering phase of data mining and categorizing the data's in the training database Ramuhalli et.al(2002). When a new observation or data record enters the database, we will be able to detect to which class this record belongs to Sreedevi E et.al(2019) Siva Kumar P et.al(2019).

In data mining, the learning approaches are of three kinds' viz., supervised learning, Unsupervised learning and Semi-Supervised learning. All the algorithms in data mining pursue the learning approaches in a different way Drown et.al(2009). Classification follows supervised learning approach, whereas Clustering follows unsupervised learning. There are many classification techniques available for classification. Few of them are listed below.

Regression Analysis

Regression Analysis is nothing but the process of finding a method which fits the given data with less error or no error. The goal of regression analysis lies in determining the value of parameters that makes a function to fits perfectly in a set of observations. The different kinds of regression are linear regression, non-linear regression, and multi-variate regression. Regression modelling is often utilized in business planning, financial forecasting, trend analysis, marketing and bio-medical.

Linear regression analysis is based on six fundamental norms:

1. The independent and dependent variables demonstration a linear association among the slope and the intercept.
2. The variable that is independent does not occur randomly.
3. The zero value should be considered for residual (error).
4. The residual (error) value is observed as constant through all observations.
5. The residual (error) value is observed as not correlated through all observations.
6. The distribution followed by residual (error) values is normal.

Simple Linear Regression

Simple linear regression analysis is a measures the connection among an independent variable and dependent variable. The simple linear analysis is declared applying the below equation:

$Y = a + bX + \epsilon$

where: a – Intercept, b – Slope, Y – Dependent variable, X – Independent variable, ϵ – Residual (error)

Multiple Linear Regression

Multiple linear regression is fundamentally like to the simple linear analysis, by the exclusion that multiple linear independent variables are utilized in the analysis. The scientific notation of multiple linear regressions is:

$Y = a + bX1 + cX2 + dX3 + \epsilon$

where: a-Intercept, b,c,d- Slope, Y – Dependent variable, X1, X2, X3- Independent variable, ϵ-Residual (error)

Bayesian Networks

Bayesian Network is nothing but a directed, cyclic graph with a probability distribution for every individual node depicted in that graph Cooper et.al (2010) & Rajesh Kumar et.al(2020). "A Bayes Network classifier is implemented on a Bayesian network which represents a joint probability distribution over a set of categorical attributes". The task for learning Bayesian network can be divided into two parts. The learning of the graph structure with nodes and arcs and the determination of its parameter. The nodes in the graph represent attributes and arc represents the relation between them Ganesn et.al(2015).

$$p(\mathrm{x}) = \prod_{i=1}^{n} p(x_i \mid pa_i)$$

Rule Based Classifiers

Rule Based Classifier has rule in the way of if - then. Rules has two parts the if part is called an antecedent and the then part is called consequent Rajesh Kumar (2019). When a data satisfies the set of conditions listed in the antecedent then the data will be assigned the class specified by the consequent . A rule-based classifier procedure a set of IF-THEN rules for classification Prasanth, Y et.al(2017) & Pradeepini et.al(2018). An IF-THEN rule is an expression of the general form

IF condition THEN conclusion.

Artificial Neural Network (ANN)

ANN is an inspiration from the biological concept, neurons which are the functioning elements of the brain. Likewise, ANN consists of a interconnected processing element which are referred to us as neurons. The neurons of ANN work together to produce the output. Since the computation is performed by connected set of neurons, ANN can produce a better result even if some of the individual neurons are not functioning.

Each neuron of the ANN is assigned an activation number and also joining between two neurons has a weight connected with it. The activation number of the neuron depends on the activation numbers of other neurons and the weights of the edges which connect it with the other neurons.

When the size of the network is decided, ANN is tested with a training data. ANN performs an iterative process with the training data in order to adjust the weights of the network, so that all the future predictions are optimal. Neural Networks often produce very accurate results. They follow a specific technique called "black box" testing Singh (2005).

Decision Tree

Decision Trees are considered as a powerful tool for classification. They are powerful because they represent rules that can be easily understood by anyone. Decision tree is a classifier that can be depicted in form of a binary tree, in which each node is either a leaf node, that decides the class (or) category of the record or a non-leaf (or) decision node which has the split point of an attribute. A decision tree follows a "Divide and conquer" rule in processing the data and classifies it. It divides the database into two at every non leaf node based on the condition specified. A decision tree classifies the record by starting at the root and passing through one specific path till it reaches a leaf node Sreedevi (2017) &Prasanth Y et.al(2019) .

A decision tree has to be transformed into rules which are required for classifying any record. A decision tree has to pass until there exist no more division of the record possible or all the taken attributes have been processed.

The advantage of decision tree is that it can generate rules which can easily understand. Decision tree does not require much computation. it can handle both numerical and categorical data's.

The disadvantage of decision tree is that it produces less appropriate results in estimating tasks. They are prone to errors when experimented with many classes Garofalakis (200). A typical decision tree with two levels is shown below.

In the above diagram, Nodes 1,2,3 represent some attributes for classification and Nodes 4,5,6,7 represents the leaf nodes or the category to which the data belongs. The algorithm of a decision tree based classifier is given as,

Figure 4. Decision tree algorithm

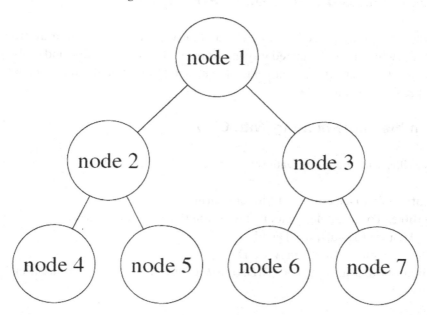

1. Generate a node N
2. If entire data are of similar category, say X at that time return node N as a terminal node considered with category X.
3. If attribute list is empty, at that time return node N as a terminal node labelled with furthermost existing category in the data's
4. If attribute list is non empty, select attribute from attribute list.
5. Label node N with this attribute.
6. Develop branch from node N with the data that satisfies the condition of the attribute.
7. Repeat the process until we get a database with pure data.

Association Rule Learning

Association Rule Learning, which is also called as dependency modelling is the process of identifying relationship between variables. A simple example of Association Rule Learning lies in identifying the purchasing habit of a customer in a super market where a customer who purchases toothbrush will also purchase toothpaste or a customer who purchase a television will also purchase a stabilizer.

Ensemble Implementing With CPU and GPU

To address the problem of class inequality and software defect prediction are proposed classifiers which is an organized way in this paper. Feature selection and probability estimation tasks are the fundamental features for this model Zimmermann et.al (2009) & Ceylan et.al(2006).

Ensemble Implementing With CPU

Input: Classified Features Data set in the same way as FData;

Output: Defect Detection and Model Learning

Procedure: To read defect data feature set in the same way as FData

For all Feature FData[i] in FData Do

For all occurrence of *I(Ai)* in *Ai* do Do

Subdivide the data instances of *FA(Di)* into *k* independent sets. Select classifier $C_{i=i=1m}$

While i < k

Do

if(C_i is *M LP*) Then

$I_j = \Sigma iw_{ij}O_i + \theta$j

else if *(C_i is NB)* then

else if *(C_i is Decision tree)*

Likelihood   Class Prior Probability

$$P(c\mid x) = \frac{P(x\mid c)P(c)}{P(x)}$$

Posterior Probability   Predictor Prior Probability

$P(c\mid X) = P(x_1\mid c) \times P(x_2\mid c) \times \cdots \times P(x_n\mid c) \times P(c)$

end if

end while

Compute the misclassified error rate and statistical true positive rate.

Done

Done

Ensemble Implementing With GPU

FData: Data value were generate randomly in database

$I(A_i)$: Instances

A_i: 'is an attribute having *n* attributes' A= {a_1, a2... an} in similarity, C_i: i[th] classifier (MLP,NB,DT)

Input: Classified features data set FData

Output: Defect detection and Model learning

Step1: Read defect data features set FData

Step2: For all features FData[i] in FData do

Step3: For all occurrence if $I(A_i)$ in A_i Do

Step4: Sub divide the data instances of $FA(D_i)$ in to k independent sets

Step5: select classifier C_i (for i=1 to n)

    Step 6:   while(i<n) do

```
        if (C_i  is MLP) then
        weights are adjusted in such a way that its
output would approximates the values in the data set
            else if (C_i is NB) then
                for every instance the probability of
defective and probability of non-defective is calculated.
            else if(C_i is DT) then
                Decision tree developed form training samples
```

Step7: Compute the misclassified error rate and statistical true positive rate.

Defect data set is divided into k independent sets. Each set is supplied to the each and every classifier. If classifier is MLP the attributes in the instances are supplied as input and weights are adjusted in such a way that its output would approximate the values in the data set. This learning knowledge is used to classify the new instances are defective or non-defective. If the classifier is NB then probability of defect class and non-defect class is calculated and if the probability of defect is more than the non-defect then the instance is classified as defect otherwise non-defect. If classifier is DT decision tree is developed from training samples. In tree growing phase for each and every node k attributes are selected randomly and best split computed. At the end misclassified error rate and statistical true positive rate is computed

Datasets Sketch

To simplify the similarity of data and to confirm our observations, four benchmark datasets that belong to Liu et.al(2010) which were taken from 'PROMISE Repository1' were utilized. "These datasets were collected from real scenario software projects provided by NASA that was created in C/C++ for the sake of instrumentation belonging to spacecraft (CM1 dataset), scientific data processing (JM1 dataset), storage management of ground data (dataset of KCI), and satellite flight control (PC3 dataset)". A detailed definition of the datasets is provided below Table 1.

Table 1. Datasets description

Data set	Language	Description	#Attributes	#Modules	#Non-defects	#Defects	%Non-defects	%Defects
CM1	C	NASA spacecraft instrument	22	498	449	49	90.16	9.83
KC1	C++	System implement ting storage mana gement for receiving and processing ground data	22	2019	1783	326	84.54	15.45
JM1	C	'Real-time predict ive ground system: Uses simulations to generate predicttions	22	10885	8779	2106	80.65	19.35
PC3	C	'Flight software for earth orbiting satellite metadata'	38	1563	1403	160	89.7	10.23

EXPERIMENTS AND RESULTS

The implementation of the ensemble and decision tree algorithm is done in both CPU computation and CUDA, the programming model developed by NVIDIA, to show that GPU computing is faster than CPU computing. To check the effectiveness of the algorithm, we are going to apply the algorithm to a randomly generated NASA Database is based on the classification done in the random database. Since there is no connection possible between the database and CUDA, the data for classification has to be generated randomly. The implementation involves in generating random data, this can be done in CUDA by using a built-in function called curand Sanders et.al (2010). Generation of random data is so much fast in CUDA. A picture depicting the time taken for generating lakhs of data is shown in Figure 5.

The sample data was generated randomly based on NASA data set used in this work lies between the sizes of 2, 6 to500 MB and the range of the total count depicts from 100000 to 5000000 (>50 million); the residing data is present in the host machine's in the external memory. In this paper, we use multiples threads that are supporting each block are utilized to improve the overall productivity of the system, the threads are locked to 128 for every block that is utilized and also the grids and blocks are considered as variables as to adjust among themselves depending on the requirement of algorithmic needs. Refer the table-2

In Table 2, an ensemble method implements into CPU and GPU and the total count of records in the file were increased upto 50 million. 'The result represents that the difference in the running time between the CPU and GPU'.

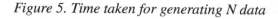

Figure 5. Time taken for generating N data

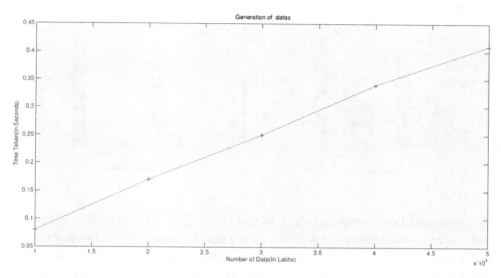

The result depicts the difference for the running time among the two algorithms. From this analysis, we have observed that kmp in GPU is 18 times swiftlier than the kmp in CPU from capturing the average of all the pattern sizes and keeping the thread count in each lock to its maximum available which is 128 as shown in Figure 6.

CONCLUSION

Classification is one of the main tasks in data mining. A new proposed Ensemble and Decision tree has been executed in host (CPU) computing and has been tried utilizing NASA dataset and furthermore same two methods have been programmed in GPU computing. In this paper, implementations that are in parallel were preformed using

Table 2. Depicts time of processing for ensemble and decision tree method implementing on CPU and GPU

Size of file (MB)	No.of records in the file	Running time (s)		Running time (s)	
		Ensemble (CPU)	DT (CPU)	Ensemble (GPU)	DT (GPU)
2.5	256076	6.54	7.52	0.006927	0.007224
4.95	552151	8.94	10.02	0.009180	0.009572
67.00	10434401	10.52	12.89	0.12945	0.14825
256	52403201	13.64	15.60	0.877660	0.95500

Figure 6. Processing time for Ensemble and Decision tree method implementing on CPU and GPU

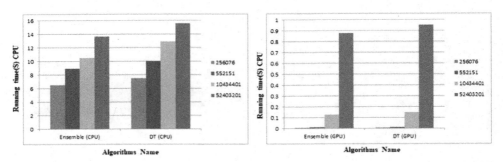

Ensemble and Decision tree algorithms and utilizing the CUDA toolkit. Ensemble method was compared in terms of processing time to decision tree algorithm while holding the thread size up to high. It was indicated that the implementations which are in parallel for algorithms was up to 24× faster than to CPU. The proposed Ensemble method was achieving peak performance on a GPU. The hardware needs to be utilized as possible and the size of thread for each block should be kept up to high levels that are supporting for each block. The depicted summarization of GPU characteristic using NVIDIA GT950M card is exhibited in Table 3.

Table 3. Characteristic of geforce gt525m card

Property	Value
CUDA Core	96
Graphics clock	475 MHz
Process clock	950 MHz
Memory clock	900 MHz
Memory Interface	128- it
Total available graphics	4095 MB
Dedicated video memory	2048 MB DDR3
Shared system memory	2047 MB

REFERENCES

Baig, Sivakumar, & Nayak. (2020). Optimizing Performance of Text Searching Using CPU and GPUs, Progress in Computing, Analytics and Networking. *Advances in Intelligent Systems and Computing, 1119*, 141-150.

Ceylan, E., Kutlubay, F., & Bener, A. (2006). Software defect identification using machine learning techniques. *Software Engineering and Advanced Applications. SEAA '06. 32nd EUROMICRO Conference on*, 240-247.

Cooper, G. F., Hennings-Yeomans, P., Visweswaran, S., & Barmada, M. (2010). An efficient bayesian method for predicting clinical outcomes from genome-wide data. *AMIA 2010 Symposium Proceedings*, 127 – 131.

Drown, D. J., Khoshgoftaar, T. M., & Seliya, N. (2009). Evolutionary sam-pling and software quality modeling of high-assurance systems. *IEEE Transactions on Systems, Man, and Cybernetics. Part A, Systems and Humans, 39*(5), 1097–1107. doi:10.1109/TSMCA.2009.2020804

Ganesan, P., Sivakumar, S., & Sundar, S. (2015). An Experimental Analysis of Classification Mining Algorithm For Coronary Artery Disease. *International Journal of Applied Engineering Research, 10*(6), 14467–14477.

Garofalakis, M., Hyun, D., Rastogi, R., & Shim, K. (2003). Building decision trees with constraints. *Data Mining and Knowledge Discovery, 7*(2), 187–214. doi:10.1023/A:1022445500761

Kumar, Anbazhaghan, Razia, Sivani, Pravalika, & Harshini. (n.d.). Prediction of cardiovascular disease using classification techniques with high accuracy. *JARDC, 12*(2), 1134-1139.

Kumar, R. (2020). Suicidal ideation prediction in twitter data using machine learning techniques. *Journal of Interdisciplinary Mathematics, 23*(1), 117–125. doi:10.108 0/09720502.2020.1721674

Kumar, R. E., & Rao. (2020). Suicide Prediction in Twitter Data using Mining Techniques: A Survey. *International Conference on Intelligent Sustainable Systems (ICISS 2019)*, 122-131.

Liu, Y., Khoshgoftaar, T. N., & Seliya, N. (2010). Evolutionary optimization of software quality modelling with multiple repositories. *IEEE Transactions on Software Engineering, 36*(6), 852–864. doi:10.1109/TSE.2010.51

Munshi, A. (2008). OpenCL: Parallel Computing on the GPU and CPU. *Proceeding of 35st International Conference and Exhibition on Computer Graphics and Interactive Techniques.*

Nasridinov, A., Lee, Y., & Park, Y. (2014). Decision Tree Construction on GPU: Ubiquitous Parallel Computing Approach. *Computing, 96*(5), 403–413. doi:10.100700607-013-0343-z

Nguyen, H. (2007). *GPU Gems 3*. Addison-Wesley Professional.

Nickolls, J., Buck, I., Garland, M., & Skadron, K. (2010). Scalable Parallel Programming with CUDA. *ACM Queue; Tomorrow's Computing Today, 6*(2), 40–53. doi:10.1145/1365490.1365500

NVIDIA Corporation. (2010). *CUDA Best Practices Guide*. NVIDIA Corporation.

NVIDIA Corporation. (2014). *CUDA C Programming Guide*. NVIDIA Corporation.

Pathuri. (2019). Feature-Based Opinion Mining for Amazon Product's using MLT. *International Journal of Innovative Technology and Exploring Engineering, 8*(11), 4105–4109. doi:10.35940/ijitee.K1837.0981119

Pradeepini, G., Pradeepa, G., Tejanagasri, B., & Gorrepati, S. H. (2018). Data classification and personal care management system by machine learning approach. *IACSIT International Journal of Engineering and Technology, 7*(32), 219–223. doi:10.14419/ijet.v7i2.32.15571

Prasanth, Y., Sreedevi, E., Gayathri, N., & Rahul, A. S. (2017). Analysis and implementation of ensemble feature selection to improve accuracy of software defect detection model. *Journal of Advanced Research in Dynamical and Control Systems, 9*(18), 601–613.

Ramuhalli, P., Udpa, L., & Udpa, S. (2002). Electromagnetic nde signal inversion by function approximation neural networks. *IEEE Transactions on Magnetics, 38*(6), 3633–3642. doi:10.1109/TMAG.2002.804817

Sanders, J., & Kandrot, E. (2010). *CUDA by Example: An Introduction to General Purpose GPU Programming*. Addison - Wesley.

Sanders, J., & Kandrot, E. (2011). CUDA by Example: An Introduction to General-Purpose GPU Programming. Addison-Wesley.

Singh, Y., & Chauhan, A. (2005). Neural networks in data mining. *Journal of Theoretical and Applied Information Technology*, 37-42.

Sivakumar, S., Ganesan, P., & Sundar, S. (2017). A MMDBM Classifier with CPU and CUDA GPU computing in various sorting procedures. *The International Arab Journal of Information Technology, 14*(7), 897–906.

Sreedevi, E., & Prasanth, Y. (2017). A novel class balance ensemble classification model for application and object oriented defect database. *Journal of Advanced Research in Dynamical and Control Systems, 9*, 702–726.

Sreedevi, E., PremaLatha, V., & Sivakumar, S. (2019). A Comparative Study on New Classification Algorithm using NASA MDP Datasets for Software Defect Detection. *2ⁿᵈInternational Conference on Intelligent Sustainable Systems (ICISS 2019),* 312-317.

Yalla, P., Mandhala, V. N., Abhishiktha, V., Saisree, C., & Manogna, K. (2019). Machine Learning Techniques to Predict Defects by using Testing Parameters. *International Journal of Recent Technology and Engineering, 8*(4), 7829–7834. doi:10.35940/ijrte.D5396.118419

Zimmermann, T., & Nagappan, N. (2009). Predicting defects with program dependencies, in Empirical Software Engineering and Measurement. *ESEM 2009. 3ʳd International Symposium on,* 435-438.

Chapter 11

Sentiment Analysis and Sarcasm Detection (Using Emoticons)

Vibhu Dagar
Vellore Institute of Technology, Vellore, India

Amber Verma
Vellore Institute of Technology, Vellore, India

Govardhan K.
Vellore Institute of Technology, Vellore, India

ABSTRACT

Sentiment analysis is contextual mining of text which identifies and extracts subjective information in source material and helps a business to understand the social sentiment of their brand, product, or service while monitoring online conversations. However, analysis of social media streams is usually restricted to just basic sentiment analysis and count-based metrics. This is akin to just scratching the surface and missing out on those high value insights that are waiting to be discovered. Twitter is an online person-to-person communication administration where overall clients distribute their suppositions on an assortment of themes, talk about current issues, grumble, and express positive or on the other hand negative notions for items they use in life. Hence, Twitter is a rich source of information for supposition mining and estimation investigation.

DOI: 10.4018/978-1-7998-3335-2.ch011

INTRODUCTION

Internet based Social Media websites, for example, Twitter enable clients to post short and casual messages, communicate their suppositions on a wide assortment of points and express their feelings. Clients express their assessments on the world of politics, strict convictions, purchaser items what's more, individual issues in a couple of words. Twitter is a rich asset from which you can pick up bits of knowledge by performing assessment examination. Supposition investigation is significant as it has some genuine applications. Corporate associations need to reveal bits of knowledge for better client the board. They need to hold old clients and pull in new ones.

Supposition investigation enables organizations to perform statistical surveying to assess client input, without having to convey polls or overviews. Political decision gatherings need to contemplate the move in popular conclusion about their up-and-comers. Notwithstanding, any standard calculation may neglect to catch genuine estimations covered up in the printed piece of tweets. There is the test of discovery of mockery or incongruity in the writings and it can prompt wrong classification of tweets.

With various settings they can mean various things. Incorrectly spelled words and linguistic mistakes can include to the clamor in the informational collection. Tweets containing a blend of positive and negative words can be wrongly classified as nonpartisan conclusion. Subsequently, recognizable proof of genuine feelings dependent on just literary piece of tweets isn't adequate as it is essential to comprehend the real plan of the creator of the tweet. Estimation examination, otherwise called Opinion mining, can be improved a lot further by utilizing emoticons. Emoticons were included to web based life destinations to speak to facial highlights of a creator and to zest up enthusiastic signs to instant messages. Numerous mind boggling thoughts can be passed on through basic emoticons. While customary notion investigation decides if a book is certain or negative (extremity), an additional layer of emoticons investigation can help in arranging messages into further classifications like love, happiness, shock, outrage, misery, dread, and so on. emoticons can likewise help in better characterization in instance of wry writings.

This examination expects to research the assumptions of tweets utilizing emoticons. By performing emoticons investigation, this examination fills a hole between the territory where most research has been centered distinctly around the literary piece of tweets. These emoticons can also be used to identify sarcasm in some cases. Sarcasm is in the tone of a person but sometimes its the emoticons that bring it out. Tweets with text portraying certain meaning can mean different altogether when seen in contrast with the emoticons. We have tried to capture this aspect of tweets in our research.

Figure 1.

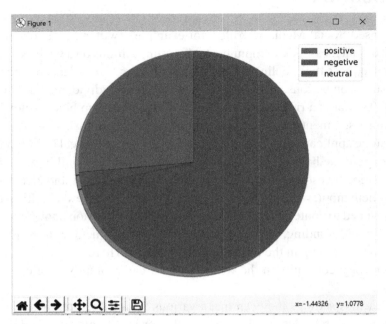

ML-Based: Classifies the content as certain, uncertain or impartial utilizing Machine Learning grouping calculations and etymological highlights.

Vocabulary Based: Makes utilization of opinion dictionaries, assessment vocabularies are assortments of clarified and preprocessed assumption terms. Conclusion esteems are alloted to words that portray the positive, negative and impartial demeanor of the speaker. It is additionally named:

Word Reference Based Strategy: It utilizes a little arrangement of seed words and an online word reference. The procedure here is beginning seed set of words with their realized directions are gathered and afterward online word references are looked to locate their plausible equivalents and antonyms. The example is arranged dependent on the presence of such flagging opinion words.

Corpus-Based Technique: Uses corpus information to distinguish notion words. Despite the fact that it isn't as successful as word reference based plan, it is useful in finding the area and setting of explicit opinion words against the corpus information. The calculation will approach not exclusively to estimation names, yet in addition to a unique situation.

Hybrid: It is a blend of both Machine Learning and dictionary based methodologies.

In view of an investigation of online message sheets, Russell S, Norvig P. (2003) proposes that females utilize less emoticons than guys, and use them in progressively shifted settings, with guys generally utilizing them for mockery and prodding. In any case, these discoveries ought to be seen circumspectly, since the impacts are probably going to have been vigorously affected by the themes of the message sheets analyzed. While the male commanded message board was about football, the theme of the female overwhelmed message board was "dietary issue support," a region probably not going to be related with mockery or emoticons use in general.Our point is to uncover how emoticons are utilized in explaining wry versus exacting plan. Mockery (and incongruity all in all) is particularly liable to be misconstrued in composed correspondence, as it includes unraveling an implying that is regularly something contrary to what is said. According to Manning, Surdeanu, Bauer, Finkel, Bethard, and McClosky (2014) rather than rating explicit emoticons or looking over a set, the two examinations talked about here enable members to openly create emoticons. This will empower us to see which emoticons are favored when expressly stamping wry and exacting analysis and snide and strict applause, just as the scope of emoticons utilized by members. We expect members will utilize a wide scope of emoticons, with a smaller subset being used most frequently.

LITERATURE SURVEY

Emojis were initially utilized in Japanese electronic messages and spreading outside in various other areas of Japan. According to Baccianella, Esuli, and Sebastiani (2010) the characters are utilized a lot of like emojis, albeit a more extensive territory is given. The ascent of prominence of emojis is because of its being joined into sets of characters accessible in cell phones. Apple, Android and other portable working frameworks incorporated a few emojis character sets. emojis characters are likewise remembered for the Unicode standard. According to Novak, Smailović, Sluban and Mozetič (2015) the fundamental issue is the way to extricate the rich data that is accessible on Twitter and how might it be utilized to draw significant bits of knowledge. To accomplish this, first we have to manufacture an exact estimation analyzer for tweets, which is the thing that this arrangement expects to accomplish. As a product to information dissect can be utilized SAS Text Miner, SAS Visual Analysis or different devices. The test stays to get modified Tweets and clean information before any content or image mining. SAS Visual Analysis permits direct import of Twitter information, yet to utilize SAS Text Miner and different devices, information must be downloaded and converted.

Various people have proposed Characteristic Language Processing (NLP) systems to address this test and concentrate low-level syntactic highlights from the content of tweets, for example, the nearness of explicit sorts of words and grammatical forms, to build up a classifier to recognize tweets which add to situation mindfulness and tweets which don't. Consequently separating such tweets from those that reflect feeling or on the other hand assumption is a non-inconsequential test, for the most part due to the very little size of tweets and the casual manner by which tweets are composed, with a great deal of emoticons, contractions, etc.

Examinations over tweets identified with four various calamity occasions demonstrate that the proposed highlights distinguish situation mindfulness tweets with fundamentally higher precision than classifiers dependent on standard pack of-words models alone. Sen, Rudra, and Ghosh (2015) proposed a similar examination of Fuzzy C-Means versus K-Means on the Iris data set. They play out a period multifaceted nature correlation between the calculations for modest number of highlights. The outcomes demonstrate that FCM works better than K-implies for modest number of highlights.

Stoyanov, Cardie, and Wiebe (2005) present a similar investigation of K- implies and Soft K-Means(Fuzzy) on the BIRCH and Wine dataset from UCI, which contains 100 and 3 bunches individually.

Vibhu Dagar and Amber Verma, students of Vellore Institute of technology, along with Prof. K Govardhan have worked on this topic to come up with an efficient solution to solve the complicated sentimental analysis problem with the help of emoticons and almost exactly segregate tweets on the basis of exact sentiment score.

PROPOSED WORK

With the help of a python library (tweepy), we gathered the latest 93124 tweets from the twitter stream, sifting the tweets based on the language, the emoticons present and whether they were retweets. Twitter uncovered a stream API to gather such information with channel parameters, for example, language and question. We gathered tweets with around 20 chose emoticons. From these we evacuated all tweets which are retweets or were rehashed. We at that point expelled all tweets with under 5 words to guarantee an exact extremity score. We were left with around 15652 tweets coordinating the above determinations. In these lone 6 emoticons were available, in numbers surpassing an edge of around 2000 tweets.

Along these lines, we chose to diminish the quantity of emoticons to 6 and evacuate all tweets with different emoticons. A sum of 1621 tweets were left, where every emoticon has around 3000 tweets each except for affection, which had around 2400 tweets. Hyperlinks, user names and prevent words were expelled from each tweet, and every one of the characters were changed over to lowercase. Hashtags and emoticons in each tweet were isolated. On the off chance that hashtags were found in camel cased structure, each word will be treated as a different hashtag.

In addition to the above information, we utilized extremity scores from the site which contained a rundown of 8221 positive and negative words. This was to check our tweets for precision. The stop-words in each tweet were distinguished by utilizing the Stanford NLP site, which has around 257 stop-words. We additionally utilize the Snowball stemmer from nltk if there should arise an occurrence of action words, to search for positive or negative words.

EMOTICON BASED METHOD

Previous studies have shown that maostly the distribution of scores primarily based on the intensity of the emotions being analyzed as an integer polarity. We select 6 of the most commonly used emoticons from a list of 751 emoticons with respect to their frequency and distinction in the emoticons scores. These researched scores are the basis of our approach. The scores are mentioned below:

Figure 2.

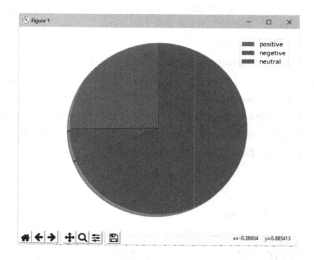

SENTIMENT SCORE

Scoring Parameters and Logic

1. Since soft-clustering doesn't need extensive training and works on-the-go, we had to ensure that we cover all features of tweets/text. Apart from the general text pre-processing and considering emoticons and hashtags together, we are focusing on patterns in parts-of-speech(POS), rather than merely judging on

the basis of the tag. We check for noun-adjective pairs, and stemmed verbs for helpful understanding of the potential subjectivity of the tweet.

2. Since all noisy parts of data have been removed in pre-processing, we are left with emoticons, hashtags and list of keywords in each twee

3. We had to decide on the amount of data to be shifted for positive or negative words encountered. Rather than using integer polarity to express intensity of words, we use emoticon scores. Since we are using emoticons Sentiment Ranking as our basis, we take average of all the emoticons scores to get 0.124833. We refer to this value as Change In Sentiment. This will be the value used for increasing or decreasing sentiment score

Scoring Components

(1) Emoticons - For each emoticon, assign the sentiment score corresponding to its value in the emoticons ranking site.

(2) Hashtags - If a hashtag is encountered, if its a positive word, increment by 2*averageChangeInSentiment and by - 2*averageChangeInSentiment for a negative word.

(3) POS tags(nltk POS tagger) -
   a)If a noun is encountered - if its preceded by an adjective, then we increment or decrement by 2*averageChangeInSentiment depending on polarity of the word, else we add or subtract the value of averageChangeInSentiment
   (b) If a verb is encountered, stem it and check for positive or negative polarity and assign 2*averageChangeInSentiment. Repeat the same for adjective without the stemming.

Table 1. Emoticon based scores

EMOTICON	SYMBOL	SCORE
laughing emoji	😄	0.221
wink emoji	😉	0.445
heart emoji	💜	0.746
crying emoji	😢	-0.093
angry emoji	😠	-0.173
confused emoji	😕	-0.397

METHODOLOGY

Firstly we have segregated all of the tweets from twitter and stored them into a text file. Then we read all these tweets one by one form the text file and removed any mentions or hyperlinks to any websites from the tweets. After lemmatization of these tweets was done. Stop words were removed to make the processing easy. Nltk library is used for lemmatization.

Two methods are used to calculate the score of the tweets. The first one is done using the library TextBlob. This library can classify text into positive, negative or neutral form and display it in the form of scores ranging from -1 to 1, below 0 for negative and above 0 for positive.The second method is the one in which each word is compared to a list of positive and negative words, and then the respective scores are updated for each sentence.

After calculating the scores from both the methods, they are analyzed to accurately predict the final scores. The scores are also analyzed using pie charts. After this the same file containing the tweets are opened in Unicode 16 format so as to make the emoticons readable rather than Unicode 8. Then the emoticons are read one by one for each tweet and converted into text using the emoticons library. Then these specific texts are analyzed to calculate the final score and are combined with the text scores of each tweet with lesser weight.

Figure 3. Pie chart is constructed using positive and negative word search method

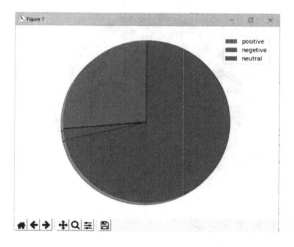

RESULT ANALYSIS

Final Analysis was made using the final scores obtained from both the methods and analyzing the pie chart along with sentiment percentages.
   Percentages for both the methods are given below.

```
Percentages Score 1 :
   Positive :   26.400000000000002
   Negetive :   2.1
   Neutral :   71.5
Percentages Score 2 : (TextBlob)
   Positive :   25.2
   Negetive :   5.800000000000001
   Neutral :   69.0
```

Final scores and sarcasm values.

Figure 4. Pie chart is constructed using the TextBlob library.sdd

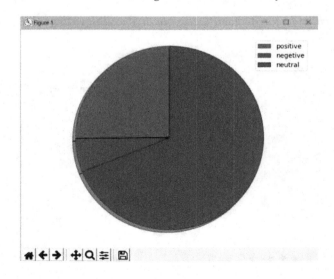

```
[0.0, 0.05, 0.C8000000000000002, -0.05, 0.0,
[-0.093, 0.221, -0.093, 0.445, 0.746, 0.001,
[-1.0, 1.0, -1.0, 1.0, 1.0, 1.0, -1.0]
['yes', 'no', 'yes', 'yes', 'yes', 'yes', 'nc
>>> |
```

CHALLENGES

Sentiment analysis may not be all that swish in the end. There are many problems associated with Sentiment analysis that could result in the loss of recognition of the technique. It tends to be difficult to comprehend for a machine as well as for a human. The consistent variety in the words utilized in mocking sentences makes it hard to effectively prepare assumption investigation models. Basic points, interests, and chronicled data must be shared between two individuals to make mockery accessible.

- Opinion spam: Sentiment analysis are often employed by competitors to portray negative image of a corporation. Once sentiment analysis gains quality as a metric to measure performance and complete image of a corporation, such mal- practices could become quite common which can result in weakened quality.
- Result measure: The outputs of Sentiment analysis are helpful as a reactive measure. It can't be accustomed to predict the performance of a corporation or alternative metrics. In some cases, Sentiment analysis are often redundant and might be solely a coverage live once the harm has been done.
- Biased results supported the sources: The sources of extracting info are often a serious roadblock in sentiment analysis. Analysis of a state of affairs on incomplete info will result in inclined results. Sources like Twitter, Facebook are often strip- mined to urge complete info.
- Negation Detection: There is no fixed size for the extent of influenced words. For instance, in the sentence "The amazing show was not extremely fascinating," the extension is just the following word after the invalidation word. Be that as it may, for sentences as "I don't consider this film a satire film," the impact of the nullification word "not" is until the finish of the sentence. The first importance of the words changes if a positive or negative word falls inside the extent of nullification—all things considered, inverse extremity will be generated.

- Word ambiguity: Word vagueness is another entanglement you'll confront dealing with a conclusion examination issue. The issue of word vagueness is the inconceivability to characterize extremity ahead of time on the grounds that the extremity for certain words is emphatically reliant on the sentence setting.
- Multiple polarity: Once in a while, a given sentence or report or whatever unit of text we might want to examine, this will show various extremity. In these cases, having just the all out consequence of the investigation can be deceiving, especially like how a normal can once in a while conceal important data pretty much all the numbers that went into it.

But, alternative sources like blogs, posts, forums etc are often tough to retrieve info from that may result in a biased result-set.

CONCLUSION

We are getting high accuracy on maximum occasions when comparing to the TextBlob to our code. That by no means, concludes that we have solved the Sentiment Analysis problem. There are multiple reasons for this result:

(1) Heavy text pre-processing - Out of around a million tweets, we only chose the ones which had the emoticons with clear distinction on the emoticons ranking website

(2) Emoticons - All the tweets included the emoticons, so it is bound to converge to all the clusters. Also, we couldn't impose heavy penalty on positive or negative words or that would change the whole context of sentences.

If we could add subjectivity pre-processing before feeding it to clustering algorithms, it is possible to use these techniques on a much more diverse dataset and get more realistic results. TextBlob algorithms can be very effective if proper structured dataset is fed to them, and in many cases, they can be faster than Machine Learning techniques like Neural Networks etc. without the pains of tuning required.

FUTURE WORK

In future, there can be some changes and modifications done. There can be specific sets of emoticons to judge different type of texts or tweets based on the maximum used emoticons. Also the possibility for adding new emoticons is endless. By collecting more and more data we can correctly predict the scores for each newer emoticon and run it with the adjusted scores of other emoticons to get more efficient results

The work done in this exploration is just identified with order opinion into two of the classes (double grouping) that is a positive class and negative class. Later on advancement, a multiclass of assessment grouping, for example, positive, negative, nonpartisan, etc may be mulled over. In this work, the emphasis is on discovering highlights that show up expressly as things or thing phrases in the surveys. The finding of certain highlights is left to future work. As gathering learning strategies need a great deal of figuring time, parallel processing procedures ought to be investigated to handle this issue. A significant impediment of group learning strategies is the absence of interpret ability of the outcomes and the information learned by outfits is hard for people to get it.

In this way improving the interpretability of gatherings is another significant research course. Future conclusion mining frameworks need more extensive and more profound normal and realistic learning bases. This will prompt a superior comprehension of regular language conclusions and will all the more proficiently overcome any issues between multimodal data and machine processable information. Mixing logical speculations of feeling with the commonsense building objectives of investigating slants in characteristic language content will prompt more bio-enlivened ways to deal with the structure of clever supposition mining frameworks equipped for taking care of semantic information, making analogies, adapting new full of feeling learning, and identifying, seeing, and "feeling" feelings.

REFERENCES

Baccianella, S., Esuli, A., & Sebastiani, F. (2010). *SentiWordNet 3.0: An enhanced lexical resource for sentiment analysis and opinion mining* (Vol. 10). LREC.

Dagar, V., Verma, A., Govardhan, K. (2019). *Sentiment analysis and sarcasm detection (using emoticons)*. Academic Press.

Kolchyna, O., Souza, T. T. P., Treleaven, P. C., & Aste, T. (2015). *Twitter Sentiment Analysis: Lexicon Method, Machine Learning Method and Their Combination*. arXiv preprint arXiv:150700955

Manning, Surdeanu, Bauer, Finkel, Bethard, & McClosky. (2014). The Stanford CoreNLP Natural Language Processing Toolkit. Association for Computational Linguistics (ACL).

Novak, P. K., Smailović, J., Sluban, B., & Mozetič, I. (2015). Sentiment of emoticons. *PLoS One*, *10*, 12.

Russell, S., & Norvig, P. (2003). *Artificial Intelligence: A Modern Approach* (2nd ed.). Prentice Hall.

Sen, A., Rudra, K., & Ghosh, S. (2015). Extracting situational awareness from microblogs during disaster events. *2015 7th International Conference on Communication Systems and Networks (COMSNETS)*. 10.1109/COMSNETS.2015.7098720

Stoyanov, Cardie, & Wiebe. (2005). *Multi-perspective Question Answering Using the OpQA Corpus.* doi:10.3115/1220575.122069

Chapter 12
Smart Sensing Network for Smart Technologies

Francina Sophiya D.
Vellore Institute of Technology, Vellore, India

Swarnalatha P.
Vellore Institute of Technology, Vellore, India

Prabu Sevugan
Vellore Institute of Technology, Vellore, India

T. D. K Upeksha Chathurani
Sri Lanka Technological Campus, Sri Lanka

R. Magesh Babu
Sri Sakthi Amma Institute of Biomedical Research, India

ABSTRACT

Smart environments based on wireless sensor networks represent the next evolutionary development step in engineering, such as industrial automation, video surveillance, traffic monitoring, and robot control. Sensory data come from multiple networks of interconnected sensors with complex distributed locations. The recent development of communication and sensor technology results in the growth of a new attractive and challenging area: wireless sensor networks (WSNs). A wireless sensor network which consists of a large number of sensor nodes is deployed in environmental fields to serve various applications. Facilitated with the ability of wireless communication and intelligent computation, these nodes become smart sensors that do not only perceive ambient physical parameters but also are able to process information, cooperate with each other, and self-organize into the network. These new features assist the sensor nodes as well as the network to operate more efficiently in terms of both data acquisition and energy consumption.

DOI: 10.4018/978-1-7998-3335-2.ch012

INTRODUCTION

Smart environment dependent on Wireless Sensor Networks speak to the following transformative improvement step in building, for example, mechanical computerization, video reconnaissance, traffic observing, and robot control. Tactile information originate from different organizations of interconnected sensors with complex appropriated areas. The ongoing improvement of correspondence and sensor innovation brings about the development of another appealing and testing zone - remote sensor organizations (WSNs). A remote sensor network which comprises of an enormous number of sensor hubs is sent in natural fields to serve different applications. Encouraged with the capacity of remote correspondence and insightful calculation, these hubs become brilliant sensors that don't just see encompassing physical boundaries yet in addition have the option to handle data, help out one another and self-arrange into the organization. These new highlights help the sensor hubs just as the organization to work all the more effectively as far as both information securing and vitality utilization. Particular reasons for the applications require plan and activity of WSNs unique in relation to ordinary organizations, for example, the web. The organization configuration must assess the destinations of explicit applications. The idea of sent condition must be thought of. The restricted of sensor hubs assets, for example, memory, computational capacity, correspondence transfer speed and vitality source are the difficulties in network plan. A shrewd remote sensor network must have the option to manage these requirements just as

Figure 1. Wireless sensor Network

to ensure the availability, inclusion, dependability and security of organization's activity for a boosted lifetime.(M.A. Matin and M.M. Islam 2012)

GOALS OF SMART SENSING NETWORK

The essential objectives of a smart sensor network by and large rely on the application, yet the accompanying undertakings are basic to numerous organizations.

1. **Determine the Estimation of Some Boundary at a Given Area:** In a natural organization, one may one to know the temperature, environmental weight, measure of daylight, and the overall mugginess at various areas. This model shows that a given sensor hub might be associated with various sorts of sensors, each with an alternate inspecting rate and scope of permitted esteems. (Buratti, Conti, Dardari &Verdone,2009)
2. **Detect the Event of Occasions of Intrigue and Gauge Boundaries of the Distinguished Event(s):** In the rush hour gridlock sensor organization, one might want to recognize a vehicle traveling through a crossing point and gauge the speed and heading of the vehicle.
3. **Classify a Recognized Item:** Is a vehicle in a rush hour gridlock sensor network a vehicle, a scaled down van, a light truck, a transport, and so forth.
4. **Track an Item:** In a military sensor organization, track a foe tank as it travels through the organization.

In these four undertakings, a significant necessity of the sensor network is that the necessary information be dispersed to the best possible end clients. Sometimes, there are genuinely severe time necessities on this correspondence. For instance, the location of an interloper in a reconnaissance organization ought to be promptly conveyed to the police so move can be made.

Sensor network prerequisites incorporate the accompanying:

1. **Large Number of (Generally Fixed) Sensors**: Networks of 10,000 or even 100,000 hubs are imagined, so versatility is a significant issue.
2. **Low Vitality Use:** Since in numerous applications the sensor hubs will be set in a far off region, administration of a hub may not be conceivable. For this situation, the lifetime of a hub might be dictated by the battery life, along these lines requiring the minimization of vitality consumption. (Buratti, Conti, Dardari &Verdone,2009)
3. **Network Self-Association:** Given the enormous number of hubs and their possible position in antagonistic areas, it is fundamental that the organization

have the option to self-compose; manual setup isn't attainable. Also, hubs may fizzle (either from absence of vitality or from physical demolition), and new hubs may join the organization. Accordingly, the organization must have the option to intermittently reconfigure itself so it can keep on working.

4. **Collaborative Sign Preparing:** To improve the location execution, it is regularly very helpful to meld information from numerous sensors. This information combination requires the transmission of information and control messages so it might put limitations on the organization design.

5. **Querying Capacity:** A client might need to question an individual hub or a gathering of hubs for data gathered in the locale. Contingent upon the measure of information combination performed, it may not be plausible to send a lot of the information over the organization. Rather, different nearby sink hubs will gather the information from a given region and make outline messages. A question will be coordinated to the sink hub closest to the ideal area.

WSN are a gathering of specific gadgets or sensorsnodes which are utilized to screen diverse ecological conditions and to gather and sort out that information at some specific focal area. It identifies and gauges various states of being, for example, stickiness, temperature, sound, weight, speed and heading, compound fixations, vibrations, toxin levels and numerous other places. It has numerous application with micro controlling ventures.

SYSTEM ARCHITECTURE

With the coming accessibility of minimal effort, short range radios alongside progresses in remote systems administration, it is normal that savvy sensor organizations will turn out to be regularly sent. In these organizations, every hub will be furnished with an assortment of sensors, for example, acoustic, seismic, infrared, actually/movement camcorder, and so forth. These hubs might be composed in groups with the end goal that a locally happening occasion can be recognized by the vast majority of, if not every one of, the hubs in a bunch.

Every hub will have adequate handling capacity to settle on a choice, and it will have the option to communicate this choice to different hubs in the group. One hub may go about as the bunch ace, and it might likewise contain a more extended territory radio utilizing a convention, for example, IEEE 802.11, Bluetooth, or use Bluetronix exclusive steering calculations. (Buratti, Conti, Dardari &Verdone, 2009)

Figure 2. WSN Architecture

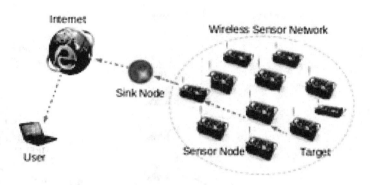

Types of WSN

Based on the surroundings it's been deployed, sorts area unit determined in order that those is used underground, underwater, on ground, and so on. Various kind of WSNs are:

Terrestrial WSN

In this type of WSN area unit capable of communicating effectively, and comprises 100 to 1000s of wireless detector nodes deployed either in unstructured or organized way. IN unstructured the sensors are not in structure pre-planned, it is randomly placed. Where as in 2nd category structured, the nodes are arranged in pre-planned structured. Structured architecture is placed in 2Dimentional or in 3Dimentional planes. (Swetha, Santhosh & Sofia, 2018).

In this type, power is restricted; the power supply is also supported with solar power in cases needy. Energy management is practiced by lowduty cycle

Underground WSN

Underground WSN territory unit prepared for impartation base stations successfully, and contain huge amounts of to a huge number of far off locator center points sent either in unstructured (exceptionally selected) or sorted out (Preplanned) implies. In Associate in Nursing unstructured mode, the detector hubs area unit haphazardly circulated within the target territory that's born from a set plane.

This type of wsn sent into the bottom area unit arduous to revive. The power units power supply is hard to regenerate/charge battery outfitted with a restricted battery power area unit arduous to revive. what is additional, the underground condition

Figure 3. Underground WSN

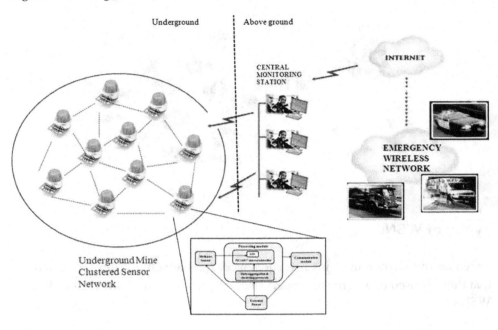

makes communication difficult because of expected /weakening and signal loss. (Swetha, Santhosh & Sofia, 2018).

Underwater WSN

This type of wsn is used under the water, major of earth space is occupied with water, so it requires more technology for efficient energy and network maintenance under water. Here sensors transmit data under water which can get loss because of signal weakening or network failure. Under water data are usually collected using self-operated vehicles with is deployed with sensor nodes.Energy management is the bigger constraint in this type,since battery is hard to get recharged or changed.

Multimedia System WSN

Multimedia wsn is formed to transmit multimedia data's such as image, video, audio. This type of WSN is constructed with low-cost sensors. This uses high bandwidth and power to transmit data. This is constructed with cameras, microphones and sensors. This can have problem in data compression, data correlation and data retrieval

Disadvantage of this is high bandwidth and power usage, correlation algorithm,Data compression technique.

Figure 4. Under Water WSN

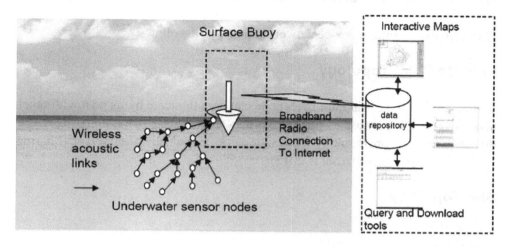

Mobile WSN

This type of WSN is movable, smart, and self-operatable. This connects with the nearer physical component by itself. This can process and communicate by itself. This is different and effective than static WSN. Its major advantage is high channel capacity,good coverage and long battery life

Figure 5. Multimedia WSNs

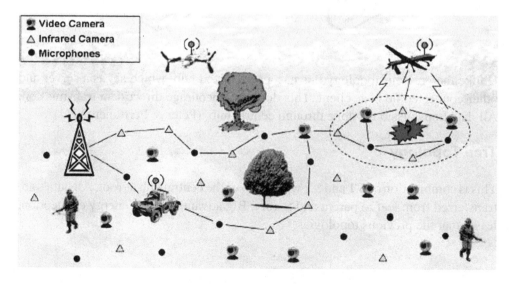

Wireless Sensor Networks Topologies

There are four common device network topologies as follows:

Point to Point Topology

In this, there's no central hub. Each node can communicate by its own with other nodes.it is most widely used topology, this uses single data transmission path, where this act as more secure topology. Each node can be as both client and server. (Sharma D,Verma, Sandeep & Sharma K.2013)

Star Topology

Figure 6. Point to point N/W

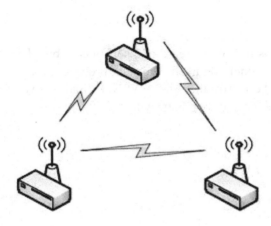

Unlike the previous topology this has a centralized hub, which act as a server and other connected node as client. This does not encourage direct data transmission. All data transmission is done through central hub. (Peter & Perttunen 2014)

Tree Topology

This is combination of 5.1 and 5.2 which makes the central hub as root. All data's are transferred from leaf to parent and to root. Big advantage is its energy conception, lesser that the previous topologies.

Figure 7. Star N/W

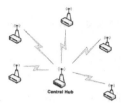

Figure 8. Tree N/W

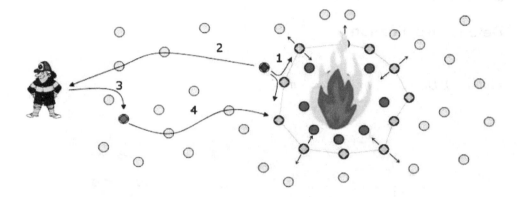

Mesh Topology

Most complex topology which doesn't have single node failure since all nodes are connected by themselves.no centralized hub. Requires more power. Data can be transferred from one node to other without depending on any central hub.

Figure 9. Mesh N/W

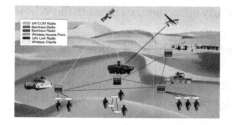

Applications of WSN for Smart Technologies

There are many applications of WSN in real world, few are discussed here

Disaster Help

In the place/ zone is accounted for to possess been blasted from a sort of cataclysm, as an example, fierce blaze, at that time drop the detector hubs on the Screen the knowledge of each hub and build a temperature guide to plan legitimate ways that and procedures to beat the hearth (Sharma D,Verma, Sandeep & Sharma K. 2013)

Defence Application

Figure 10. Disaster help application

WSNs can be used rapidly and are self-form subsequently, they can be significant used in defence exercises. Can be used in identifying & watching considerate / opposing developments. In bleeding edge observation ought to be conceivable through the sensor centers to keep a brain everything if more prominent apparatus, Human resources are required in the combat area. Many nuclear, substance, and natural attacks can similarly be recognized through the Wireless sensing center points.

Example: Sniper Detection Application. (Brassard & Siu 2005).

This is used in, detection of fire using sensors, even shooter position and location can also be identified by the use of sensors and microphone.

Applications on Environment

Figure 11. Defence applications

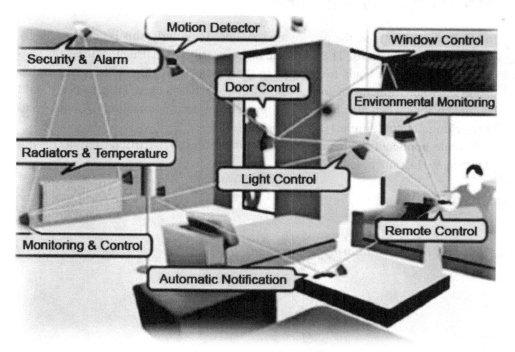

Sensor networks has endless applications for environment. They can be used to follow advancement of animals, winged creatures and save/store them nature data. Ecording the data of environment such as ground/soil, humidity,rain,fire,wind and PA ought to be conceivable through these sensors. These application can be used wisely for detection in the area in fire, flood, quakes, engineered/common scene, etc.

Figure 12. Environmental Applications

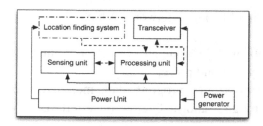

A typical model is of 'Zebra Net'. (Prabhu, Boselin, Sudhir, Sophia, S.Maheswaran,& M.Navaneethakrishnan,2013)

Health Monitoring Applications

In Medical applications, the patient are monitored regularly, this is conceivable by using sensor applications. The medicine that prescribed and drug that used can also be monitored which leads for growth in the medical industry. Things happening inside and improvements of animals health can also be checked. Diagnostics should be conceivable. They also help in keeping a brain drug association in centers and in watching patients similarly as authorities.

Sample application which used in medical industry: Artificial retina.(Elsaid, Shaimaa & Hassanien, Ella, 2013)

Smart Home

Figure 13. Health monitoring Applications

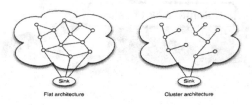

As technology develops, home is be sophisticated with the things with has life using sensors. Home is transformed into smart home as sensors control our devices using internet. Normally things that deploy sensors are washing machine, ACs, Smart TV, Refrigerator, Oven, Water heater, LPG leakage detection system. All the devices form a smart network that controls the devices/nodes.

Sensor Node Structure

Nodes are the building blocks of network. Which consist of Sensing, processing, Communication.

Main components of WSN node are controller, communicating device, sensor or actuators, memory unit and power supply.

The processing subsystem is program, data, memory which communicate with sensor subsystem through Analog to Digital converter(ADC)(M.A. Matin and M.M.

Figure 14. Node architecture

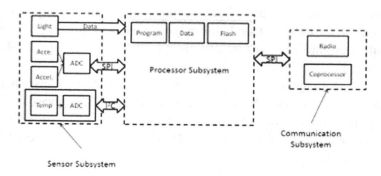

Islam 2012) for sensor data.it transfer these data to communicating subsystem, which has RFID and coprocessor .All these unit gets energy from power unit. The Power unit uses stored or solar power. Major constrain is power balancing, which makes sensor node to live long. When power supply is loss whole node fails, so major concern is there while developing power unit. Usually data's are transferred bidirectional in nodes, unless unidirectional is required. Node location can be identified, for efficient dynamic WSN construction. This would help much when particular node fail. This makes the nearer node to connect automatically.

The Energy unit and the energy generator are important in the sensor structure. Savvy power units are additionally proficient to give data on the remaining accessible vitality, so as to apply vitality mindful choices and assent the handling unit to finish the main job. Since the force generator as a rule comprises of batteries, such gadgets have restricted measure of vitality accessible, consequently restricting the lifetime of the hub. In ongoing year there has been a major exertion in discovering elective answer for force such hubs utilizing the vitality accessible on the hub condition with great outcomes.

Figure 15. Sensor node architecture

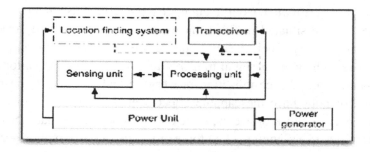

While a few off-the-rack WSN stages are accessible available, nobody of them is considered as a standard true. Each examination gathering or industry will in general understand its own foundation relying upon the goal. This is generally because of the significant expense of existing arrangements contrasted with the expenses of the parts.

Besides, WSNs major drawback is low computational ability, since smart system uses 32/64 bit processors, which cannot be used for WSN processing. Regular working frameworks run on large memory and speedy processor. WSNs can be utilized to screen strategic frameworks, a Real-Time Operating System (RTOS) is frequently needed.

Network Architecture

Wireless sensor network architecture is the representation/construction/design of WSN. Wireless sensor network is formed in raw field, the sensors are places either in structured or unstructured. These uses a particular design in forming a network. The network is constructed to collect, process and transfer data. The sensors collects the data and send to sink node, this transfers to external nodes to access over internet. Sink collect and process sensor data that should be available to users. This act as a gateway. Sensor node can communicate sink through 2 ways single hop and multihop. Single hop is direct data transmission, requires high signal and bandwidth. Next is multihop which uses neighbour to transfer data to sink, which increase network lifespan. Multihop transmission requires perfect network architecture, which is divided into two, flat and hierarchical (M.A. Matin and M.M. Islam 2012).

In flat network architecture all nodes play same work, but in hierarchical node cluster is formed and cluster head is represented based on high battery life or location. Cluster head is selected dynamically by the network. There can be different cluster heads for different cluster.

Energy Consumption

A WSN comprises of numerous sensor hubs which sense physical marvels or gather information from a situation. Contingent upon a predefined use of an organization, sensor hubs can be situated in fixed places or conveyed arbitrarily over a huge topographical territory. Their correspondence with one another happens remote and they share a channel for signal transmission. A few boundaries, for example, position, separation, and force utilization for every hub and correspondence innovation between sensor hubs have inescapable effect over the organization's exhibition. Despite an enormous turn of events, there are still constraints that WSNs endure. A few difficulties like planning a low force organization, information security and engineering of organization have taken the most consideration of specialists in the most recent years. The vitality utilization is one of the most well-known issues in the remote sensor network that doesn't show up in more customary wired sensor organization. Every sensor hub is battery worked and it makes a remote sensor network profoundly relied upon every hub battery. It is essential to anticipate the lifetime of a remote sensor network before network establishment.

REFERENCES

Brassard & Siu. (2005). *Sniper Detection Using Wireless Sensor Networks EE-194WIR*. Wireless Sensor Networks Tufts University.

Buratti, C., Conti, A., Dardari, D., & Verdone, R. (2009). An Overview on Wireless Sensor Networks Technology and Evolution. *Sensors (Basel)*, *9*(9), 6869–6896. doi:10.339090906869 PMID:22423202

Carlos-Mancilla, López-Mellado, & Siller. (2016). Wireless Sensor Networks Formation: Approaches and Techniques. *Journal of Sensors*. doi:10.1155/2016/2081902

El-Said, S. A., & Hassanien, A. E. (2019). Artificial Eye Vision Using Wireless Sensor Networks. In Wireless Sensor Networks: Theory and Applications. CRC Press, Taylor and Francis Group.

Matin & Islam. (2012). Overview of Wireless Sensor Network. In *Wireless Sensor Networks - Technology and Protocols*. IntechOpen. Doi:10.5772/49376

Peter & Perttunen. (2014). *Network Topologies*. https://www.stl.tech/sterlite-live/application_notes/1/original/Network_Topologies.pdf?1499156038

Prabhu, B., Sudhir, S., Maheswaran, S., & Navaneethakrishnan, M. (2013). Real-World Applications of Distributed Clustering Mechanism in Dense Wireless Sensor Networks. International Journal of Computing. *Communications and Networking.*, *2*, 99–105.

Sharma, Verma, Sandeep, & Sharma. (2013). Network topologies in wireless sensor networks: A review. *Int. J. Electron. Commun. Technol.*, *4*, 93–97.

Swetha, Santhosh, & Sofia. (2018). Wireless Sensor Network: A Survey. *IJARCCE*, *7*, 114-117. doi:10.17148/IJARCCE.2018.71124

Chapter 13
IoT in the Education Sector:
Applications and Challenges

Brijendra Singh
Vellore Institute of Technology, Vellore, India

Anbarasi Masilamani
Vellore Institute of Technology, Vellore, India

ABSTRACT

Smart education derived from information communication technologies (ICT) has attracted various academicians towards it. The growth of multiple sensor devices and wireless networks has brought drastic changes in IoT in the education sector. Applications of IoT in the education sector can improve academicians' and learners' considerable skills. Therefore, this chapter analyses various applications, advantages, and challenges of IoT in the education sector. The multiple applications of IoT in the education sector are identified in terms of smart classroom management, student tracking and monitoring, campus energy management, and intelligent learning. IoT in education's significant advantages are an innovative teaching and learning process, cost reduction, and smart infrastructure development. Various challenges in developing IoT-based applications identify as designing a secure learning environment, efficient resource tracking, efficient access to information, and intellectual plan development.

DOI: 10.4018/978-1-7998-3335-2.ch013

INTRODUCTION

The rapid growth of various technologies like wearable sensors, information communication technologies, smart devices, cloud computing, fog computing, big data analytics, and machine learning has brought a drastic revolution in IoT in the education sector. The use of information communication technologies by the students are always studied by potential researches (Magesh, G., Muthuswamy, P., & Singh, B. 2015). The development of IoT (Ning, H., & Hu, S, 2012) in the education sector throughout the developing countries is booming faster. The various aspects (Mrabet, H. E., & Moussa, A. A, 2017) of intelligent learning and management are smart libraries, classrooms, webinars, and learning labs. The journey of education from traditional learning to pedagogical learning through e-learning, there is now a trend to introduce IoT in academia to make smart learning. It will attract new approaches to make the academic environment more flexible, safe, and secure.

IoT in education (Pai, S. S. 2017, Marquez, J., Villanueva, J., Solarte, Z., & Garcia, A, 2016) aims to improve learners' lifelong learning skills through a smart learning environment. IoT enabled education environment provides more flexibility to students to learn from any place at any time. It also allows educational institutions to track and monitor students' performance and attendance using different sensor technologies to provide them with a safe and healthy learning environment.

The need for IoT for smart campus development is analyzed (Veeramanickam, M. R. M., & Mohanapriya, M, 2016). It shows that IoT devices are embedded with a microchip playing an essential role in converting technical classrooms to smart classrooms. Smart classrooms' various requirements are identified as intelligent whiteboards, standard communication methods, intelligent monitoring of classroom, efficient energy devices, e-notes management and sharing, data traffic, and interoperability in IoT. IoT connects all teaching-learning objects and enables them to communicate with the internet. It collects essential academic data and processes it to obtain crucial information shared with different academicians through cloud technologies. Hence, it makes teaching-learning more effective by smart decision-making tasks.

Various educational institutions have taken the transformation from paper-based study to tablets/PCs/mobiles place (Pervez, S., UR Rehman, S., & Alandjani, G, 2018). Various IoT tools in the education sector are massive open online courses (MOOC), virtual reality, RFID, e-books, tablets and gadgets, smart boards, biometric attendance trackers, and augmented reality. All these tools are beneficial for academicians to improve the learning environment with real-time exposure. The importance of IoT is more if it comes to fulfill the need of learners with disabilities. Educational sectors must realize the importance of incorporating various new technologies like green IoT to empower academicians and researchers. One of the IoT trends in the education sector is exposure to computational thinking to students, which helps solve complex problems in a new way. The integration of engineering curricula with IoT is essential by the academic institutions to enhance digital literacy and innovative skills.

Education institutions benefited by IoT ecosystems in the past few years. The development of various advanced technologies like wireless sensors, body area networks, cloud computing, big data analytics, and pervasive computing has brought drastic changes in the education sector. IoT makes the academic environment to make smarter by connecting various objects. The integration of IoT in education sectors facilitates two central communities' students and teachers. An intelligent environment enables students to provide excellent learning opportunities and develop interpersonal and intrapersonal skills among them. IoT helps students communicate and discuss various academic activities like projects, assignments with their classmates, and access to virtual labs and learning materials remotely. IoT ecosystem allows parents and teachers to track their ward performance like their mark's history, attendance, pick-up, and drop details with smart cameras installed on campus premises. IoT helps instructors to handle classes and examination remotely. Apart from all these, academicians can organize various programs like annual day, sports day with the IoT ecosystem's help.

IoT plays an essential role in converting traditional teaching-learning process to IoT enabled smart teaching-learning process. There exists a broad spectrum of various IoT applications in the education sector. Multiple applications exist like remote health monitoring, energy-efficient campuses, interactive learning, and secure classrooms. With various sensor devices, we can monitor students' health conditions to provide a rich learning environment. Further, this information can be forwarded to parents and teachers to take the necessary steps to improve their health. Various sensors can be installed in water and lights around the campus for providing energy-efficient services to the campus management. Thus, IoT helps campus to save energy and water to make a healthier environment around. Interactive learning makes students learn even they are sick using various powerful IoT tools and applications. One of the main goals for education institutions is to provide a healthy and safe environment with IoT ecosystems. Different embedded technologies help in tracking student location and other activities to make a safe academic environment.

There is no doubt that education institutions have realized the benefits of the IoT ecosystem. However, the development and integration of IoT enabled applications in the education sector is not an easy task. Simultaneously, academicians must identify and address various implementations challenges to successfully integrate IoT in the education sector. For the simplicity of readers, this chapter is organized in different sections. The second section talks about the literature review. In the third section, we described potential applications related to IoT in the education sector. The fourth chapter depicts various advantages of IoT in the education field.

Different implementation challenges in integrating IoT with the education sector are identified in the fifth chapter, followed by a conclusion.

APPLICATIONS OF IOT IN EDUCATION

The application of IoT in education (Bagheri, M., & Movahed, S. H, 2016) have been divided into various categories like campus energy management and ecosystem monitoring, secure campus and classroom access control, student's health monitoring, and improving teaching and learning. Campus energy management system allows universities and colleges to save energy to reduce the power consumption by using special sensors and actuators and various energy management techniques. Secure campus and access control allow making the educational environment safer by using different RFID technologies and near future communication. For example, RFID can be used to track student location by embedding it into their ID cards. Student's health is vital for a healthy learning process. Student health monitoring can be done using wearable technology. Smartwatches and health monitoring bands are a few examples of wearable technology that help students monitor and motivate them. Teaching and learning processes can be improved by monitoring some environmental factors like the temperature of the classroom. Additionally, various sensors can be used to monitor the teaching-learning processes.

A new model (Marquez, J., Villanueva, J., Solarte, Z., & Garcia, A. 2016) is developed, connecting various objects to virtual academic communities (VAC). This model consists of four layers, namely, communication, service, message, and application layers. Objects in the proposed model are divided into two categories, like physical and virtual. Physical objects compromise classrooms, laboratory, auditorium, and other physical resources while facilitating the teacher to share and interact. On the other hand, virtual objects allow information to store, process, and exchange through e-mail, social networks, and discussion forums. Interactions of these objects with VAC results in more dynamic interactions and generates more data for academicians. Further, the impact of IoT in the higher education field based on various parameters is predicted after theoretical analysis (Abbasy, M. B., & Quesada, E. V, 2017). Analysis results show that hyper-connectivity is an essential property of IoT to glue both physical and virtual objects in a higher educational environment.

An approach of green IoT (Maksimović, M, 2017) towards educational environment transformation is proposed. Authors (Zhu, Z. T., Yu, M. H., & Riezebos, P. 2016) proposed a smart education framework, shown in Figure 1 highlighting essential features in a digital environment for effective learning. There is no doubt that information communication technology with IoT brings a massive change in the education sector with quality education. But at the same time, one must remember to utilize energy and resources. Green IoT can bring a drastic change to make a learning environment. Overall, all these lead to the sustainable development of IoT in the educational sector.

Figure 1.

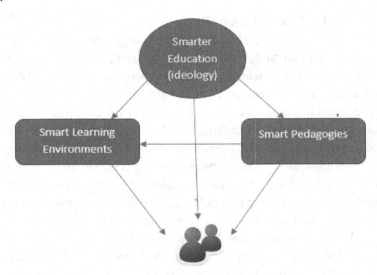

Two models for future IoT are proposed (Ning, H., & Hu, S, 2012) to successfully implement IoT in the education sector. A reorganized U_2IoT model for future IoT is proposed, which combines ubiquitous and unit IoT. A dimensional model based on U_2IoT is proposed, which compromises of four dimensions called the body, processing, intelligence, and sociality. A four-layer architecture model based on U_2IoT is proposed, which is an advancement of the three-layered model by adding an extra layer called the social layer. Other layers are perception, network, and application layer. Further, new approaches should be adopted by different countries to set their IoT majors according to the requirements.

An IoT based flipped learning platform (Ali, M., Bilal, H. S. M., Razzaq, M. A., Khan, J., Lee, S., Idris, M., & Kang, B. H, 2017). is proposed using cloud-based technology with an improved state of the art privacy and security measures. The proposed model's working is tested on medical students to collect real data from the gadgets to produce a real-world case using an interactive case-based flipped learning tool. This architecture is not only useful to the medical field but in another domain too.

An optimal technical oriented, IoT based platform (Banica, L., Burtescu, E., & Enescu, F, 2017) with the incorporation of real-time information facilitated by cloud services is proposed. This model aims to collect vast amounts of data and analyze it to obtain useful information for academia. It also introduces a secure platform for the interaction of all essential components like hardware and software. Various companies like IBM and SMART came further to excel in teaching IoT in academia by developing "smart university" projects. There is a need to establish a well-defined, IoT based educational model for smart universities to realize the benefits of IoT. Various applications are developed by Google to support academia to be considered as "things" to facilitate the teaching and learning process. For example, teachers and students can use "Google Apps" to prepare and share online documents.

An IoT based smart education service business model (Gandhi, S. L, 2017, April). is proposed. M2M connectivity was found to be more demanding. The role of social media is found to be more prominent for teaching learning and development tasks. Analysis of smart education can be done by student feedback about faculties and learning process.

Figure 2 illustrates the activities in the smart classrooms (Aldowah, H., Rehman, S. U., Ghazal, S., & Umar, I. N, 2017). It involves an intelligent system designed with advanced learning aids on the latest technology or smart things. These creative things can work out with the cameras, microphones, and lots of other sensors that can be used to gauge student satisfaction learning, or any other items associated. The smart artifact provides class control with ease and convenience.

Figure 2.

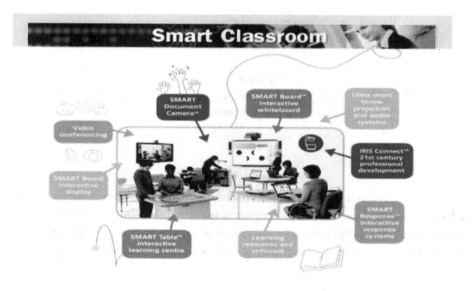

An IoT based learning framework (He, J. S., Ji, S., & Bobbie, P. O, 2017, April) is proposed for science, engineering, technology, and mathematics (STEM) students. This framework incorporates IoT with hardware and software to promote a learning environment. This learning approach helps students to learn better and gain knowledge efficiently. Incorporating IoT in STEM curriculum allows students to fulfill their academic needs with an enhanced, innovative learning environment. An IoT infrastructure for agriculture education with diverse applications and less technical skills is proposed (Gunasekera, K., Borrero, A. N., Vasuian, F., & Bryceson, K. P, 2018). The proposed architecture can use a variety of sensor devices and the capacity to incorporate multiple sensors.

Marzano, G., Martinovs, A., & Usca, S. (2019) highlighted the smart teaching-learning framework in Figure 3 that should support the current curriculum in mechatronics. The authors highlighted the smart teaching-learning framework that should support the current curriculum in mechatronics. Authors (Veeramanickam, M. R. M., & Mohanapriya, M 2016) specified that IoT had been rapidly evolving developments in computing. In the modern world, campus required IoT technology to access quality environments successful E-lessons. IoT's effectiveness and importance on campus at smart college will hit the market very soon in the education field. This conveys the dramatic changes for the students soon with IoT highly enabled: i-Campus environments.

Figure 3.

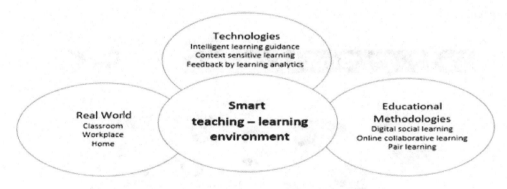

IoT can address many universities' problems, such as; improving access to knowledge, creating smarter plans, keeping track of vital resources, and designing safer campuses. IoT programs have enormous potential to add positive values to higher education by engaging and inspiring students and staff and increasing learning speed. They aimed to ascertain the potential of IoT in higher education and optimize its benefits while resolving its challenges and reducing its risks.

ADVANTAGES OF IOT IN EDUCATION

The advantages of incorporating IoT in the education sector (Bhatt, J., & Bhatt, A, 2017) are more than the traditional education sector. It increases reach and access to education with the help of digital resources. False proxies are prohibited due to the automation process. Students have more flexibility to repeat lectures from any place with more accessibility to educational material, resulting in better academic performance. A model is developed (Marquez, J., Villanueva, J., Solarte, Z., & Garcia, A, 2016) and tested with the help of a case study and shows that the integration of IoT in education gives both students and teachers great opportunities for learning. It helps them to get rid of learning difficulties using more interactions with real-world objects. Smart learning through IoT (Mrabet, H. E., & Moussa, A. A, 2017) has more involvement, motivation, interactivity, creativity, reflection, and teamwork than online and traditional learning. Smart education's various advantages through IoT are learning outside the classrooms, more actionable learning, an efficient search of information, time flexibility, innovative approach development, and better speaking capabilities.

IoT has great potential (Abbasy, M. B., & Quesada, E. V, 2017) to form an extensive, intelligent network of schools, educational institutions, and groups through the internet. Further, the IoT platform facilitates them to collaborate and interact with the vast connectivity of physical and virtual objects in academic communities. Introduction to IoT in the educational field eliminates instructors' physical presence by providing a real-time teaching-learning environment and access teaching-learning material. It would also be helpful to provide international exposure to students. Finally, analysis shows that the importance of IoT in academia is predictable and should not be ignored.

A study (Zhamanov, A., Sakhiyeva, Z., Suliyev, R., & Kaldykulova, Z, 2017) describes the benefits of implementing IoT applications in smart universities like IoT-based entrance examinations, classroom and feedback systems. Implementation of IoT with a flipped classroom is demonstrated. The flipped classroom is an educational learning model where an instructor prepares a video or content lecture and shares it with students in advance. Before participating in the class, students watch the lectures or read the content and do the class assignment or task based on the watched video or contents. IoT enabled flipped classroom allows students to learn from anywhere at any time. This model has been implemented and found that 27.5 percent of students strongly agreed on the best learning approach than traditional techniques. The purpose of incorporation of smart IoT system for universities is to facilitate them to automate the teaching-learning process. IoT based flipped classrooms are one of the best examples of it.

A study (Aldowah, H., Rehman, S. U., Ghazal, S., & Umar, I. N, 2017) has conducted to realize the potential of IoT in higher education with maximized profit and minimizing the risk involved. A positive impact of IoT in higher education is projected if it is well planned and implemented with students' and teachers' full potential with leadership. Students, researchers, and academicians play an essential role in the development of IoT based model.

IoT and flipped classrooms (Ali, M., Bilal, H. S. M., Razzaq, M. A., Khan, J., Lee, S., Idris, M., & Kang, B. H, 2017) have brought significant changes in the education sector in recent years. The integration of these in case-based learning can bring innovative improvement to the performance of medical students. It facilitates students to provide real exposure to different medical cases with improved knowledge and the best decision-making process. Evidence of the internet (Pervez, S., UR Rehman, S., & Alandjani, G, 2018) in education is there for a long time in e-learning to enhance academic performance. However, the IoT applications in the education field have a significant impact, which helps academicians prepare smart lesson plans and other activities like student monitoring and tracking.

IoT has the potential (Abdel-Basset, M., Manogaran, G., Mohamed, M., & Rushdy, E, 2019) to transform the traditional education system to a smart system by integrating different information communication technology to enhance the learning process according to academicians' needs. The vast development of various sensing devices and information processing platforms helps the academic institute vastly monitor and track students' performance by getting feedback about their learning strategies. Quality of education improves with the introduction of IoT by fast learning to make academicians more efficient.

We have seen that the advantages of IoT in the education sector can be viewed with three main perspectives instructors, students, and management. With the instructor's perspective, the IoT ecosystem facilitates them in tracking students' attendance, performance, and monitoring their health smartly. On the other hand, with the student perspective, they benefit from flexible learning, which helps them attend the online classes according to their convenience. Additionally, they get benefited from flipped classrooms, smart software for education, and interactive learning. From the management perspective, IoT allows them for intelligent building management, develop advanced learning management system, efficient tracking of staff performance, and provide a safe and hygienic environment.

CHALLENGES IN IoT EDUCATION

Key factors (Bhatt, J., & Bhatt, A, 2017) for the successful implementation of IoT in the education sector are discussed. Four pillars people, process, data, and IoT are essential to bringing changes in the teaching and learning process. People are important because they must be well trained to use this virtual and physical environment of learning. Quality of data is essential as it can be utilized for research development and teaching process. IoT-driven approaches with automated processes use different sensors and a cloud platform to bring drastic changes in the teaching-learning process. Various elements like people, data, and IoT, connect and collaborate to form a strong network is a part of the teaching-learning process. IoT in the education sector (Pai, S. S, 2017), which combines people, processes, data, and devices resulting in massive data collection, allows educational institutions to extract meaningful information to bring innovative teaching-learning changes.

A solution integration approach is proposed (Mathews, S. P., & Gondkar, D. R, 2017) for IoT based educational system by integrating various technologies to the cloud platform to provide a centralized system which can act as a central hub for student tracking, secure student management, and give an e-learning environment. Various challenges are identified in the research. Different devices and gadgets use heterogeneous technologies. Current solutions are isolated, and they impose restrictions in terms of scalability and reliability. Providing a standard flexible system to integrate all these technologies is still a challenge. Research challenges identified are the incorporation and adaptability of various technologies in an IoT based educational based environment. An approach is needed to architect different cloud and gateways to improve the communications between educational clients and remote devices over the cloud.

Challenges identified IoT in education (Pai, S. S, 2017) are the difficulties of integrating various technologies to embedded devices and gadgets. The requirement of the best educational quality of services arises from the vast development of multiple sensors and actuator devices with improved capabilities. Further, the challenges (Aldowah, H., Rehman, S. U., Ghazal, S., & Umar, I. N, 2017) for future IoT in higher education are analyzed. Challenges identified are designing a secure learning environment, efficient resource tracking, efficient access to information, and smart plan development. Some of the other challenges (Mrabet, H. E., & Moussa, A. A, 2017) of IoT in teaching and research are pedagogical approaches, confidentiality, and data availability. Challenges for the integration of IoT (Burd, B., Barker, L., Divitini, M., Perez, F. A. F., Russell, I., Siever, B., & Tudor, L, 2018, He, J. S., Ji, S., & Bobbie, P. O, 2017) in the education sector are identified as hardware and software integration, the preparedness of instructors and up to date infrastructure, cost, reliability, management, security, and privacy. However, other challenges are security, privacy, authentication, scalability, flexibility, and communication.

CONCLUSION

This book chapter has enlightened the various applications, advantages, and challenges associated with IoT in the education field. Advancements of IoT in the education sector have increased rapidly after developing sensors and wireless network technologies. There is no doubt that the integration of IoT in the education sector can enhance learner's lifelong skills by providing them real-world exposure, expertise, and knowledge. Smart education employing IoT enabled technologies to provide campuses to manage and monitor smart classes and academic activities. The different IoT applications in education are identified as intelligent campus monitoring, energy-efficient campuses, student activities tracking, development of education models, and learning framework. We recommend that academic authorities implement some of these applications on their campuses to realize the actual benefits.

IoT in the education sector has realized different benefits from various perspectives of teachers, learners, and management. IoT facilitates technology-enabled innovative teaching processes as compared to traditional teaching-learning practices. There is more transparency between parents and teachers to discuss and monitor students' classroom performances. On the other hand, learners are facilitated in terms of more flexibility in attending their classes and discuss academic activities with teachers and friends. Also, learners realized that they have a broad spectrum of their career development through efficient communication with various academic communities worldwide. Individuals in the educational sector must understand the applicability and usefulness of IoT applications in the education sector.

It is clear that academic communities get benefited and realized the importance of IoT in the education sector. However, various implementation challenges are existing and need to be addressed. Challenges in implementing IoT in the education sector are identified as designing a secure learning environment, efficient resource tracking, efficient access to information, intellectual plan development, hardware and software integration, infrastructure development, integration of various devices, cost-effectiveness, and reliability. Further, these challenges can be addressed to realize the actual benefits comes out after integrating IoT in the education sector. In the future, the development of innovative approaches and rectifying the issues and challenges in implementing IoT in the education sector is recommended.

REFERENCES

Abbasy, M. B., & Quesada, E. V. (2017). Predictable influence of IoT (Internet of Things) in the higher education. *International Journal of Information and Education Technology (IJIET)*, *7*(12), 914–920. doi:10.18178/ijiet.2017.7.12.995

Abdel-Basset, M., Manogaran, G., Mohamed, M., & Rushdy, E. (2019). Internet of things in smart education environment: Supportive framework in the decision-making process. *Concurrency and Computation*, *31*(10), e4515. doi:10.1002/cpe.4515

Aldowah, H., Rehman, S. U., Ghazal, S., & Umar, I. N. (2017, January). Internet of Things in higher education: a study on future learning. Journal of Physics: Conference Series, 892(1). doi:10.1088/1742-6596/892/1/012017

Ali, M., Bilal, H. S. M., Razzaq, M. A., Khan, J., Lee, S., Idris, M., Aazam, M., Choi, T., Han, S. C., & Kang, B. H. (2017). IoTFLiP: IoT-based flipped learning platform for medical education. *Digital Communications and Networks*, *3*(3), 188–194. doi:10.1016/j.dcan.2017.03.002

Bagheri, M., & Movahed, S. H. (2016, November). The effect of the Internet of Things (IoT) on education business model. In *2016 12th International Conference on Signal-Image Technology & Internet-Based Systems (SITIS)* (pp. 435-441). IEEE.

Banica, L., Burtescu, E., & Enescu, F. (2017). The impact of internet-of-things in higher education. *Scientific Bulletin-Economic Sciences*, *16*(1), 53–59.

Bhatt, J., & Bhatt, A. (2017). IoT techniques to nurture education industry: scope & opportunities. *International Journal on Emerging Technologies*, 128-132.

Burd, B., Barker, L., Divitini, M., Perez, F. A. F., Russell, I., Siever, B., & Tudor, L. (2018, January). Courses, content, and tools for internet of things in computer science education. In *Proceedings of the 2017 ITiCSE Conference on Working Group Reports* (pp. 125-139). Academic Press.

Gandhi, S. L. (2017, April). Smart education service model based on IOT technology. *International Interdisciplinary Conference on Science Technology Engineering Management Pharmacy and Humanities.*

Gunasekera, K., Borrero, A. N., Vasuian, F., & Bryceson, K. P. (2018). Experiences in building an IoT infrastructure for agriculture education. *Procedia Computer Science*, *135*, 155–162. doi:10.1016/j.procs.2018.08.161

He, J. S., Ji, S., & Bobbie, P. O. (2017, April). Internet of things (iot)-based learning framework to facilitate stem undergraduate education. In *Proceedings of the SouthEast Conference* (pp. 88-94). 10.1145/3077286.3077321

Magesh, G., Muthuswamy, P., & Singh, B. (2015). Use of Information Technology among school students in the State of Tamil Nadu, India. *International Journal of Applied Engineering Research, 10*(1), 2201–2209.

Maksimović, M. (2017). Transforming educational environment through Green Internet of Things (G-IoT). *Trend, 23*, 32–35.

Marquez, J., Villanueva, J., Solarte, Z., & Garcia, A. (2016). IoT in education: Integration of objects with virtual academic communities. In *New Advances in Information Systems and Technologies* (pp. 201–212). Springer. doi:10.1007/978-3-319-31232-3_19

Marzano, G., Martinovs, A., & Usca, S. (2019). Mechatronics Education: Needs and Challenges. In *Proceedings of the 12th International Scientific and Practical Conference*. Volume II (Vol. 214, p. 217).

Mathews, S. P., & Gondkar, D. R. (2017). Solution Integration Approach using IoT in Education System. *International Journal of Computer Trends and Technology, 45*(1), 45–49. doi:10.14445/22312803/IJCTT-V45P109

Mrabet, H. E., & Moussa, A. A. (2017). Smart Classroom Environment Via IoT in Basic and Secondary Education. *Transactions on Machine Learning and Artificial Intelligence, 5*(4).

Ning, H., & Hu, S. (2012). Technology classification, industry, and education for Future Internet of Things. *International Journal of Communication Systems, 25*(9), 1230–1241. doi:10.1002/dac.2373

Pai, S. S. (2017). IOT Application in Education. *International Journal for Advance Research and Development, 2*(6), 20–24.

Pervez, S., ur Rehman, S., & Alandjani, G. (2018). Role of Internet of Things (IOT) in Higher Education. In *4th International Conference on Advances in Education and Social Sciences* (pp. 792-800). Academic Press.

Veeramanickam, M. R. M., & Mohanapriya, M. (2016). Iot enabled futurus smart campus with effective e-learning: i-campus. *GSTF Journal of Engineering Technology (JET), 3*(4), 8-87.

Zhamanov, A., Sakhiyeva, Z., Suliyev, R., & Kaldykulova, Z. (2017, November). IoT smart campus review and implementation of IoT applications into education process of university. In *2017 13th International Conference on Electronics, Computer and Computation (ICECCO)* (pp. 1-4). IEEE. 10.1109/ICECCO.2017.8333334

Zhu, Z. T., Yu, M. H., & Riezebos, P. (2016). A research framework of smart education. Smart learning environments, 3(1), 4.

Chapter 14
A Proficient Hybrid Framework for Image Retrieval

Rajkumar Soundrapandiyan
Vellore Institute of Technology, Vellore, India

Ramani Selvanambi
Vellore Institute of Technology, Vellore, India

ABSTRACT

In this work, an image retrieval system based on three main factors is constructed. The proposed system at first chooses relevant pictures from an enormous information base utilizing colour moment data. Accordingly, canny edge recognition and local binary pattern and strategies are utilized to remove the texture plus edge separately, as of the uncertainty and resultant pictures of the underlying phase of the system. Afterward, the chi-square distance between the red-green and the blue colour channels of the query and the main image are calculated. Then these two (the LBP pattern and the edge feature extracted from the canny edge detection and by chi-square method) data about these two highlights compared to the uncertainty and chosen pictures are determined and consolidated, are then arranged and the nearest 'n' images are presented. Two datasets, Wang and the Corel databases, are used in this work. The results shown herein are obtained using the Wang dataset. The Wang dataset contains 1,000 images and Corel contains 10,000 images.

DOI: 10.4018/978-1-7998-3335-2.ch014

INTRODUCTION

Computerized imaging is an imperative fragment in a large number of utilizations, for example, biomedical imaging, distant sensors, wrongdoing location, training, sight and sound, information mining, and so forth. Those application need computerized pictures as a hotspot for different cycles similar to division, entity acknowledgment, following, and others. To list and search appropriate pictures from the quickly expanding computerized picture assortments, a picture recovery framework is utilized. In picture information bases, for quick and proficient recovery, pictures are filed and looked in two different ways, to be specific, utilizing catchphrases and utilizing visual substance of a picture. The conventional technique, for example, the text based image retrieval (TBIR) framework utilizes watchwords for semantic picture recovery. Be that as it may, this framework neglects to deal with huge information base in view of its non-programmed watchword age plan and it completely depends on the impression of human specialists who are utilized in the catchphrase age task. This regularly prompts improper catchphrase age for a picture.

In this work, the Content-Based Image Retrieval (CBIR) structure, the illustration substance i.e., shading, surface, shape, and so forth, of a picture are used to give conceivable outcomes from the enormous information base. Among the visual substance, shading assumes an imperative part in person discernment by displaying a lovely perspective on the earth. It is able to likewise be utilized to recognize an entity and recognize one item from another. Henceforth, in CBIR, shading can be measured as the main descriptor because of its straightforwardness in the computation and invariant conduct towards interpretation, turn, and adjust in the review point.

LITERATURE REVIEW

Yue et al. (2011) uses Color histogram and Gray Level Co-occurrence Matrix highlights to give more precise recovery brings about the CBIR framework. Worldwide and nearby histograms are assessed over the HSV shading space picture. The nearby histogram gives preferred execution over a worldwide histogram and afterward GLCM is utilized to separate the surface component of a dim level picture. Neighborhood histogram and GLCM highlights are melded by equivalent load toward shading with surface highlights.

Color Co-occurrence Matrix, Difference between Pixels of Scan Pattern and Color Histogram K-Mean (CHKM) picture highlights are intertwined to obtain the exceptionally comparative picture outcome. Amongst the three highlights, two highlights are utilized to remove the surface data and the final component (CHKM) is utilized to separate just the shading data.

The multi-scale edge field technique for interactive media recovery utilizes canny edge extraction as some portion of cycle to acquire the article limits in various scales.

Agarwal et al. (2014) include vigilant edge recognition on the luminance channel of the YCbCr shading picture so as to improve the exhibition of the picture recovery framework.

Liu and Yang (2013) had projected Color Difference Histogram (CDH) on laboratory shading room which is totally not quite the same as since quite a while ago settled shading histogram technique. Lab shading space is favored for assessing CDH on the grounds that it utilizes the shading contrast among shading and edge direction surface subtleties of the picture. Along these lines, Canberra separation metric is utilized to quantify the comparability among inquiry and information base pictures. Besides, surface and shading highlights based recovery is acquired by neighborhood extrema top valley example and RGB shading histogram. Surface and shape highlights are examined utilizing Local Ternary Pattern (LTP) and mathematical minutes to draw enormous number of significant pictures.

The neural system structure is anticipated to decrease the semantic hole in picture recovery. The system is prepared starting the baggage of images which have the third level deteriorated wavelet bundle hierarchy data and the eigen vector mean of every Gabor channel reaction picture. At that point, the Pearson connection coefficient is utilized to discover the comparability between the component vectors. At last, the yields are refined with the assistance of a significance input component. However, the preparation stage multifaceted nature and assembly season of this methodology are high.

Wang et al. (2011) integrates Color, texture and shape highlights to give effective recovery by CBIR framework. The shading highlight is determined by means of a marginally altered prevailing color descriptor. The picture is sectioned into 8 coarse parts, and afterward the mean estimation of each fragment goes about as its quantized shading. Afterward, the bunching is utilized to consolidate the closest hues. At last, five predominant hues and their rates are gotten. The surface element is extricated by taking a convolution among picture and bandpass channel with four bearings.

Wang et al. (2017) introduced a novel shape based descriptor called nearby chordiogram descriptor which is extricated from the neighborhood edges and rather than picture powers it catches neighborhood mathematical highlights and it is utilized with the halfway whole of the request insights of the fix shrewd separations to deal with the commotion and lighting varieties in the scenes, and it fundamentally beats SURF, GIST, SIFT What's more, MROG descriptors for place acknowledgment particularly at the point when the enlightenment varieties are extreme.

The novel chart structure is portrayed and it recovers comparable clinical pictures dependent on tumor area by obliging tumors to its related anatomical structures and is accomplished by utilizing a chart in which the edges are associated with tumor vertices dependent on the spatial closeness of tumors and organs

METHODOLOGY

Color Descriptor

Our first step in this work is to extract the color features of the images in Wang dataset or any dataset that is used. The query image also needs the color features extracted from it and then calculating the mean and the standard deviation we set a threshold for a high and low to segregate images from the wang dataset.

Here, color moments (statistical compute) are picked to speak to the shading subtleties of the picture. It shows the pixel conveyance data of the picture in two minimized structures. The principal request second provides normal data for the circulation of pixel of a given picture. The propinquity of the pixel appropriation about mean shading is assessed by second-request second.

In initial retrieval process stage, normal shading data (mean) in addition to amount of the quantity of pixels to facilitate varies from the mean (standard deviation) of the inquiry picture are assessed worldwide starting the 3 shading channels of the RGB shading area as follows.

$$Mean(Ic) = \frac{1}{M \times N} \sum_{i=1}^{M} \sum_{j=1}^{N} P_{cij}, \ c = \{R, G, B\}$$

and

$$Std(Ic) = \left(\frac{1}{M \times N} \sum_{i=1}^{M} \sum_{j=1}^{N} \left(P_{cij} - Mean(Ic) \right)^2 \right)^{\frac{1}{2}}, \ c = \{R, G, B\}$$

Color images Mean value gives the normal shading data of the picture. The SD of the picture is likewise critical to offer insights concerning the dispersion of picture pixel just about the normal data.

The code snippet for the same is shown in Figure 1.

Figure 1. Sample Code for Mean and Standard Deviation Calculation

```
11 -    meanEachImage=arrayfun(@(x) mean(reshape(imread(cell2mat(fullfile('wangsame',F1(x)))),[],n)
12 -    query = imread('query.jpg');
13 -    meanofquery =int16(mean2(query));
14 -    sdofquery = int16(std2(query));
15      %lc and hc
16 -    lowrange=meanofquery-sdofquery;
17 -    highrange=meanofquery+sdofquery;
18 -    array1=int16([]);
19
20
21
22 -    ☐for i=1:1000
23 -        if(lowrange<cell2mat(meanEachImage(i)) && cell2mat(meanEachImage(i))<highrange)
24 -            array1=[array1,meanEachImage(i),i];
```

Texture Descriptor

Texture formally has no definition. Intuitively texture measures the smoothness, coarseness, regularity. The local binary pattern (LBP) surface examination administrator is characterized as a dim scale invariant surface measure, gotten from an overall meaning of surface in a neighborhood. The current type of the LBP administrator is very not quite the same as its essential form: the first definition is stretched out to discretionary round neighborhoods, and various expansions have been created. The fundamental thought is anyway the equivalent: a paired code that portrays the nearby surface example is worked by thresholding an area by the dark estimation of its middle.

Texture is the significant descriptor in a CBIR framework. Because of its straightforwardness of implementation and productive execution LBP based surface extraction is widely utilized in the proposed framework. This mining calculation is applied above the division of pictures chose from the principal juncture of the recovery cycle.

$$LBP_N = \sum_{i=0}^{N-1} f(P_i - CP)2^i; \quad f(p) = \begin{cases} 1; P \geq 0 \\ 0; P < 0 \end{cases}$$

210

Code Snippets

Figure 2. LBP Feature Extraction

```
query1=imread('querygray.jpg');
lbpFeatures = extractLBPFeatures(query1)

array2=[];
FileList2 = dir(fullfile('wangselectgray', '*.jpg'));
F2 = natsortfiles({FileList2.name});

]for iFile = 1:numel(F2)
    File2 = fullfile('wangselectgray', F2(iFile));
    Img2  = imread(cell2mat(File2));
    lbpFeatures1 = extractLBPFeatures(Img2);
    A=abs(lbpFeatures-lbpFeatures1)
    B=sum(A);
    array2=[array2,B];
```

Vector Result

Figure 3. LBP Vector Values

	1	2	3	4	5	6	7	8	9	10	
1	1.4418	2.0343	2.9845	2.1859	3.3051	3.0978	2.4987	1.7402	2.8793	2.1951	^
2											
3											
4											
5											

ans
1x883 single

Edge Descriptor

For edge description we use canny edge detection method. The method works as follows. From the wang dataset the images (RGB) are converted to HSV as canny edge detection is applied on top of the Value channel of the HSV. After which the HSV is combined back and converted to the RGB. Thus, here we obtain the edges RGB which can be operated on to identify the edges similarity.

In RGB shading space, every shading canal is exceptionally connected with further shading channels to such an extent that the parting of chrominance and luminance data is unthinkable and is perceptually questionable to person discernment. Grayscale

Figure 4. Canny Edge Extraction

```
1    function cannyedge()
2 -    FileList3 = dir(fullfile('wangselect', '*.jpg'));
3 -    F3 = natsortfiles({FileList3.name});
4 -  for iFile = 1:numel(F3)
5 -      File3 = fullfile('wangselect', F3(iFile));
6 -      Img3  = imread(cell2mat(File3));
7 -      [H S V]=rgb2hsv(Img3);
8 -      a=edge(V,'Canny');
9 -      b=hsv2rgb(H,S,a);
10 -     filename3=sprintf('wangselectedge/myimage%02d.jpg',iFile);
11 -     imwrite(b,filename3);
```

Figure 5. Sample code of Query Image

```
3 -   query2=imread('queryedge.jpg');
4 -   Red = query2(:,:,1);
5 -   Green = query2(:,:,2);
6 -   Blue = query2(:,:,3);
```

data is sufficient to check edges in pictures yet dim to RGB transformation is absurd to expect to deliver a shading picture.

To vanquish this concealing space change is executed to gain the edge nuances as of the power plane of an image. We call this as the underlying stage in edge feature extraction measure. Hue and Saturation pass on the chrominance nuances of the given picture. Value channel hold the force image scattering. Insightful edge area count is lope over the Value channel. Edge eliminated Value channel is gotten

Figure 6. Comparing R, G, B Values

```
-    File3 = fullfile('wangselectedge', F3(iFile));
-    Img3  = imread(cell2mat(File3));
-    Red1 = Img3(:,:,1);
- Green1 = Img3(:,:,2);
- Blue1 - Img3(:,:,3);
```

together with an un-adjusted Hue and Saturation channel and changed back to Red, Green, and Blue concealing space.

Code Snippets

And finally we save the sum of the three into one array as their sum. It gives RGB edge images as the output as the following.

Figure 7. Sample Code to convert R, G, B values to Image

```
C=abs(Red-Red1);          G=abs(Green-Green1);
D=Red+Red1;               H=Green+Green1;
E=C.^2 ./D;               I=G.^2 ./H;
F=E./2                    J=I./2
fmat=reshape(F,1,256*256); jmat=reshape(J,1,256*256);

K=abs(Blue-Blue1);
L=Blue+Blue1;
M=L.^2 ./L;
N=M./2
nmat=reshape(N,1,256*256);
```

Figure 8. Sample Output of RGB edge images

Similarity Measure

We get two feature arrays one from the LBP and the second one from the comparing the edges extracted from the Canny edge detection. After which we combine them both by taking their average.

Before that we normalize them, by using Figure 9.

Figure 9. Similarity Measure of features

```
normarray2=[];
normarray2=(array2 - min(array2))./(max(array2)-min(array2))

normarray3=[];
normarray3=(array3 - min(array3))./(max(array3)-min(array3))


array4=[];
array4 = normarray2./2 + normarray3./2

array5=[];
array5=sort(array4)
```

A similitude measure is compulsory in a wide range of the recovery framework as it explains the proportion of the separation linking the lower or bottom level visual substances of 2 pictures. Separation data is the central aspect of the comparability computation. The low resulting worth demonstrates to the comparing information base picture is exceptionally near the given question picture. LBP and edge highlights likeness are assessed through the Chi-square separation measure which is given by the two conditions beneath.

$$LBP\_SM(QLBP_{IMAGE}. NewDBLBP_{COUNTIMAGES}) = \sum_{i=1}^{N} |f_{QLBP_{IMAGE}}(i) - f_{NewDBLBP_{COUNTIMAGES}}(i)|$$

and

Figure 10. Algorithm for Extraction of Color, Texture, and Edge features.

Algorithm

CTEBIR (*QIMAGE, DBNIMAGES*) – Color, Texture and Edge Based Image Retrieval.

Input: Query image from the user is denoted by *QIMAGE*. Image Database (DB) contains N number of images denoted by *DBNIMAGES*. N denotes the total number of images.

Output:

K number of images IM_1, IM_2.....$IM_K \in DB_{NIMAGES}$ retrieved as similar images for the given query image QIMAGE

1. Separate the R, G and B shading channel data from QIMAGE and DBNIMAGES.
2. Calculate the 1st and 2nd order color moments for the QIMAGE and form low and high threshold.
3. Calculate the 1st order color moment for images ? DBNIMAGES
4. Count=0;
5. for i=1 to N do
    a. if the 1st order CM of $DB_{iIMAGES}$ lies between the low and high threshold of the QIMAGE then select the particular image (IM) and store that in New Database (NewDB)
    b. Count=Count+1;
6. C. NewDBCOUNTIMAGES =IM;
7. d. end if end
8. Calculate LBP texture feature for QIMAGE and NewDBCOUNTIMAGES
9. Calculate Canny edge feature for QIMAGE and NewDBCOUNTIMAGES
10. for each image in NewDBCOUNTIMAGESdo
    a. Measure the similarity metric between QIMAGE and NewDBCOUNTIMAGES using normalized texture and edge feature
    b. Combine the calculated similarity metric of the texture and edge feature of the images ? NewDBCOUNTIMAGES end
11. Bubble sorting is performed on NewDBCOUNTIMAGES according to the value of each image which is obtained from step 8(b)
12. return K number of similar images IM_1,IM_2.....IM_K

Figure 13

$$EDGE\_SM(QEDGE_{IMAGE}.\ NewDBEDGE_{COUNTIMAGES}) = \sum_{i=1}^{\cdot\cdot} |f_{QEDGE\_R_{IMAGE}}(i) - f_{NewDBEDGE\_R_{COUNTIMAGES}}(i)|$$
$$+ \sum_{i=1}^{N} |f_{QEDGE\_G_{IMAGE}}(i) - f_{NewDBEDGE\_G_{COUNTIMAGES}}(i)|$$
$$+ \sum_{i=1}^{N} |f_{QEDGE\_B_{IMAGE}}(i) - f_{NewDBEDGE\_B_{COUNTIMAGES}}(i)|$$

In the assessed standardized element esteems are consolidated utilizing equivalent loads and are composed in rising request utilizing bubble sort to accomplish identical pictures at the high degree of the recovery. Moreover, the proposed CBIR framework is tested with the normalized exhibition trial above the diverse amount of recovery outcome.

RESULT

>> projectmain

Figure 11. Query image 1

Figure 12. Query image 2

What dataset u want to choose? – (enter core110k OR core15k OR wang) wang

Figure 13. Flow image result

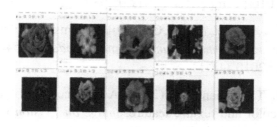

Figure 14. Human image result

REFERENCES

Pavithra, L. K., & Sharmila, T. S. (2018). An efficient framework for image retrieval using color, texture and edge features. *Computers & Electrical Engineering*, *70*, 580–593. doi:10.1016/j.compeleceng.2017.08.030

Yue, J., Li, Z., Liu, L., & Fu, Z. (2011). Content-based image retrieval using color and texture fused features. *Mathematical and Computer Modelling*, *54*(3-4), 1121–1127. doi:10.1016/j.mcm.2010.11.044

Lin, C. H., Chen, R. T., & Chan, Y. K. (2009). A smart content-based image retrieval system based on color and texture feature. *Image and Vision Computing*, *27*(6), 658–665. doi:10.1016/j.imavis.2008.07.004

Kiranyaz, S., Ferreira, M., & Gabbouj, M. (2006). Automatic object extraction over multiscale edge field for multimedia retrieval. *IEEE Transactions on Image Processing*, *15*(12), 3759–3772. doi:10.1109/TIP.2006.881966 PMID:17153949

Agarwal, S., Verma, A. K., & Dixit, N. (2014). Content based image retrieval using color edge detection and discrete wavelet transform. In *2014 International Conference on Issues and Challenges in Intelligent Computing Techniques* (pp. 368-372). IEEE. 10.1109/ICICICT.2014.6781310

Liu, G. H., & Yang, J. Y. (2013). Content-based image retrieval using color difference histogram. *Pattern Recognition, 46*(1), 188–198. doi:10.1016/j.patcog.2012.06.001

Dey, M., Raman, B., & Verma, M. (2016). A novel colour-and texture-based image retrieval technique using multi-resolution local extrema peak valley pattern and RGB colour histogram. *Pattern Analysis & Applications, 19*(4), 1159–1179. doi:10.100710044-015-0522-y

Srivastava, P., Binh, N. T., & Khare, A. (2014). Content-based image retrieval using moments of local ternary pattern. *Mobile Networks and Applications, 19*(5), 618–625. doi:10.100711036-014-0526-7

Irtaza, A., Jaffar, M. A., Aleisa, E., & Choi, T. S. (2014). Embedding neural networks for semantic association in content based image retrieval. *Multimedia Tools and Applications, 72*(2), 1911–1931. doi:10.100711042-013-1489-6

Wang, X. Y., Yu, Y. J., & Yang, H. Y. (2011). An effective image retrieval scheme using color, texture and shape features. *Computer Standards & Interfaces, 33*(1), 59–68. doi:10.1016/j.csi.2010.03.004

Wang, X., Zhang, H., & Peng, G. (2017). A chordiogram image descriptor using local edgels. *Journal of Visual Communication and Image Representation, 49*, 129–140. doi:10.1016/j.jvcir.2017.09.005

Kumar, A., Kim, J., Wen, L., Fulham, M., & Feng, D. (2014). A graph-based approach for the retrieval of multi-modality medical images. *Medical Image Analysis, 18*(2), 330–342. doi:10.1016/j.media.2013.11.003 PMID:24378541

Chapter 15
A Study and Analysis of Trust Management System in Cloud Technologies

Lahari Anne
School of Computer Science and Engineering, Vellore Institute of Technology, Vellore, India

S. Anandakumar
School of Computer Science and Engineering, Vellore Institute of Technology, Vellore, India

Anand Mahendran
School of Computer Science and Engineering, Vellore Institute of Technology, Vellore, India

Muhammad Rukunuddin Ghalib
School of Computer Science and Engineering, Vellore Institute of Technology, Vellore, India

Uttam Ghosh
Vanderbilt University, USA

ABSTRACT

Cloud computing is a technology that has enabled individual users and organizations alike to implement such functionality. Currently, a large percentage of the data being generated is stored on clouds, and the number of organizations opting for cloud-based technologies is continuously on the rise. With such growing numbers

DOI: 10.4018/978-1-7998-3335-2.ch015

accessing and utilizing cloud resources, data security has become a significant cause of concern. Traditional methods of cloud computing are becoming obsolete and ineffective with each technological breakthrough, and data is thus highly subjected to getting corrupted or hacked. This chapter provides a survey on various trust management techniques used in cloud technology to protect the data with multiple security features.

INTRODUCTION

In information system and technology, trust management is an abstract system that processes symbolic representations of social trust, usually to aid the automated decision-making process. Such representations, e.g. in the form of cryptographic credentials, can link the abstract system of trust management with results of trust assessment. Trust management is widespread in implementing information security, specifically access control policies. The concept of trust management has been introduced by Matt Blaze to aid the automated verification of actions against security policies. In this concept, activities are allowed if they demonstrate sufficient credentials, irrespective of their actual identity, separating symbolic representation of trust from the real person. Trust management can be best illustrated through the everyday experience of tickets. One can buy a ticket that entitles him, e.g. to enter the stadium. The ticket acts as a symbol of trust, stating that the bearer of the ticket has paid for his seat and is entitled to enter. However, once bought, the ticket can be transferred to someone else, thus symbolically transferring such trust. At the gate, only the ticket will be checked, not the identity of a bearer. Cloud computing is the technology that provides different types of services as a useful resource on the Internet.

Resource trust value will help the cloud users to select the services of a cloud provider for processing and storing their essential information. Also, service providers can give access to users based on trust value to secure cloud resources from malicious users. This chapter provides the various trust models in Cloud Computing, which comes under the subjective trust model based on the behaviour of user and service provider to calculate the trust values. The trust is fuzzy, which motivated us to apply fuzzy logic for calculating the trust values of the cloud users and service providers in the cloud environment. Mamdani fuzzy method uses gauss membership function for fuzzification and triangular membership function for defuzzification. Parameters such as performance and elasticity are taken for trust evaluation of the resource.

The attributes for calculating performance are workload and response time. And for calculating elasticity, we have taken scalability, availability, security, and usability. The fuzzy C-means clustering is applied to parameters for evaluating the trust value of users such as bad requests, bogus requests, unauthorized requests, and total requests.

ANALYSIS OF TRUST MANAGEMENT SYSTEM IN CLOUD TECHNOLOGIES

Cloud provides services in the form of a platform, infrastructure, and software and storage. However, for a real-time business application, the cloud provider is to be selected based on trustworthiness. Thus, in this chapter, the authors proposed a trust model to facilitate the process of choosing the right and trusted cloud service provider(CSP). This model is based on previous research publications on SLA based trust framework. The proposed model uses an SLA agent to perform the tasks such as grouping cloud consumers, designing and drawing SLA metrics, determining the negotiation terms with the cloud providers etc. The model comprises of four steps. Firstly, an SLA agent monitors business activities, trust parameters and business reports. Secondly, consumers are classified based on a cloud consumer model. This also deals with the price models and charges for services. Thirdly, the cloud directory lists the existing providers based on required service parameters. Lastly, the selected cloud providers own the cloud infrastructures and provide services to the consumers. The model is developed, keeping a protocol in mind. The protocol involves steps of determining the trusted Cloud service provider based on advertising, discovery and analysis by the SLA agent. The future scope of this model includes the evaluation in a simulated environment with effective experimentations. Theoretically, the model proved to be a novel approach to trust management in cloud technologies (Alhamad et al., 2010).

Cloud computing is being accepted as a new-age technology, but one of the major problems with it is the trust management. This issue of managing trust feedbacks mainly arises due to unexpected and unpredictable consumers at a given time and dynamic nature of Cloud. "Trust as a Service" TaaS is proposed in this chapter as a method that can be adapted to enhance trust management in cloud services. It can essentially be used to filter credible and malicious trust feedbacks based on consumer's capability and their feedback consensus. They proposed an architecture, which is developed using SOA (Service Oriented Architecture). Their experimentation is developed on NetLogo platform. This platform stimulates cloud environments. Additionally, the platform also supports multi-cloud environments. A real-life dataset is used to test the developed credibility model.

Both empirical and analytical analysis is performed on the data. The analytical study aimed at finding the trusted accuracy, whereas the empirical analysis is to determine the credibility of selected factors. Both the analysis are weighted equally to determine the final trust value for a Cloud Service Provider. The Trust Management Service ensures that though the cloud system receives inaccurate trust feedbacks, they cannot manipulate the trust results. This TMS distinguishes between experienced and inexperienced consumers. This Trust Management System assesses the trust feedback assessment, and it allows storage management in a distributed manner. The future scope of their proposed Trust management system includes dealing with real-life problems like Sybil attacks, Whitewashing attacks etc. Performance optimization is also a significant focus area. The advantage of this model is that it uses a simple mathematical model and direct trust model, thus directly determining the trusted Cloud service providers. However, it does not consider turn around efficiency as a parameter, thus reducing the performance of the cloud system (Noor & Sheng, 2011a).

Cloud computing includes a trust relationship establishment phase which is highly dependent on Cloud Service Provider(CSP) services, requirements dependencies and trust models. The Cloud Service Users declare the trust levels they require from each service provider. The authors of this chapter have suggested a model based on fuzzy set theory to identify the Cloud Service Providers that perfectly match the requirements of the particular users. The model considers trust similarity, trust chain, and nodes behaviour, unlike conventional trust management systems, which consider feedbacks and reputation. The model uses time decaying function, interactive feedback factors, membership function etc. The model evaluates the trust values of Cloud Service Providers and establishes a trust relationship between customers and Cloud Service Providers. This relationship is essentially dependent on the requirements determined by the users primarily. Before the primary model, a prototype was proposed with the name TMFC. In this, trust assessment attribute differences lead to two types of direct trust. This model is developed based on various trust definitions and evaluation of trust similarity as revealed by a few malicious nodes. This prototype had led to an increase in fault tolerance of the cloud system. However, the major drawback of the system is that trust accuracy depends on the trust results of the previous analysis. An error in one stage drastically affects the next step as it uses fuzzy networks. The future scope of this model is the deployment and testing of the model on established platforms like Oracle-Sun and Mars Information Open source Center. The prototype gave good accuracy, but when deployed on real-time platforms, the accuracy might vary positively or negatively. The advantage of this model is that it does not depend on feedback or reputation like other Trust management system. It depends on trust similarity. However, the fuzzy network leads to dependence of trust accuracy of one stage on the previous step. If anyone step leads to erroneous trust values for cloud service providers, the errors are carried forward in the fuzzy network (Sun et al., 2011).

Cloud computing is emerging as a technology that is offering various services like virtual computing, storage, bandwidth etc. It is accessible, dynamic and often virtualized. Despite this, security remains the paramount concern. A data colouring method is proposed in this chapter, which is based on Cloud watermarking. These watermarks identify and recognize consumer reputations. Besides, cloud robustness ensures the embedded, unique reputation identifiers for each consumer. Watermarking adds tiny bits of specific data to actual data without creating visible changes. In colour marking, each user is given a colour, which protects the copyrights of that user on any data. A cloud watermark is a logo that everyone accessing the Cloud recognize as belonging to a user. This watermark can be any image pattern or a series of characters. The location and embedding algorithm for the watermark depends on security parameters chosen by the user. The final step in this process is the watermark detection. This is done based on the identification of the keys. However, the leak of crucial data is enough for attackers to manipulate the watermark. Cloud watermarks are visible watermarks and thus offer security only until the private information is secret. Therefore, these watermarks provide trust management to the cloud systems only until the critical data is secure and offer no security when the vital information is compromised. However, the experiments conducted by the authors revealed that the process of colour watermarking is uncertain and irreversible. The robustness of reverse cloud generator ensures the social reputation identification with high accuracy (Liu et al., 2011).

Cloud service providers provide technical and functional descriptions in a Service Level Agreement. These descriptions vary from one provider to another, although they offer the same functionality. Problems arise when these cloud providers are not consistent with their specifications. Dissimilarities in actual functionalities and those mentioned in agreements give way to trust issues amongst the cloud users. Costumers face it difficult to choose a trusted cloud provider. Hence, in this chapter, a Trust Management system architecture is proposed, especially for the market. The proposed system identifies trustworthy providers based on factors like security, compliance, overload etc. This system comprises of a Registration Manager, CQIA (Consensus Assessments Initiative Questionnaire), Trust manager, Trust Semantics Engine, Trust computation engine and Trust update Engine. The model starts by validating and monitoring the SLAs and standardizes them. The model takes general security test parameters like Audit results from known auditing tools like Google Lists SASA 70II etc., ratings, measurements and self-assessment questionnaire results etc. Thus the proposed system increases trust by enhancing the transparency between provider and user (Habib et al., 2011).

The critical issues of a trust management system are robustness, availability and trust feedback assessment and storage. This chapter marks a proposal for a credibility model that distinguishes feedback from validated and new customers. It is based on a service-oriented architecture (SOA). Along with this, it also detects negative feedback. The proposed model also includes a Replication determination model that dynamically determines the replicas optimal number. The automatic determination of acceptable replica value ensures the availability of the trust management model. Besides, a Distributed trust feedback assessment and storage facility is incorporated, which overcomes the problems of the centralized architecture of the model as a whole. The proposed framework has a layered architecture dividing the service request layer from the service's trust validation layer. Like most other trust management systems, it uses service advertisements, service discoveries and trust validation parameters and analysis. Also, the model is tested against man-in-the-middle attacks, slandering attacks, self-promoting attacks etc. The authors introduced two new factors to evaluate trust. They are Majority Consensus and Feedback Density. The future scope of this model includes dealing with Sybil and Whitewashing attacks (Noor & Sheng, 2011b).

Cloud computing facilities are used considering the load on the intermediary nodes. However, the need for data integrity demands that trust values should be considered before dispatching work to Cloud Service Providers. Compromising a single node leads to an attack on the entire distributed system. In a nutshell, the chapter is an evaluation of an existing Trust Management System called Hatman. Hatman is a data-centric, full-scale reputation based Trust Management System. It assesses node integrity, and this gives trust feedback based on EigenTrust values. The model is built on a Hadoop cluster structure, and stimulation is done by implementing the vector logic. The simulation is done on a Penta IV Ubuntu system that supports Hadoop clustering technique. The model simultaneously formulates both consistency and trust management. Hatman on an average attains an accuracy of 90% in a situation where the Cloud is 25% malicious. Thus in times where cloud accuracy is high as 25%, the trust management system still stays stable and provides a reliable outcome of trust values for Cloud Service Providers. The authors claim that the model is a full-scale system, but their analysis is preliminary. They plan to investigate more on data integrity attacks to increase the consistency of the system. The advantage is that the Hadoop clustering technique allows distributed architecture and provides higher accuracy. However, the model does not directly determine the Cloud Service Providers suitable for the system. The relevant providers are determined from consistency values (Khan & Hamlen, 2012).

Cloud computing provides several new technologies like rapid elasticity, dynamic infrastructure, charging per use etc. To deal with security concerns, a trust management system is proposed in this chapter. This system includes a Cloud service Registry and

Discovery. This is a registry or list of all service providers categorized based on their trust feedbacks values. It also consists of a trust calculator that calculates trust values based on two parameters, namely Service Level Agreement and Quality of Service (QoS). The proposed system also includes a trusted monitor for monitoring trust values. Monitoring is done from time to time and is triggered with each transaction. The proposed registry differentiates cloud service providers(CSPs) based on three types of services, namely SaaS, PaaS and IaaS. The future scope of this work is to incorporate third party providers, which are common in real-time, and to evaluate the system on proper stimulation (Muchahari, & Sinha, 2012).

Wireless Sensor networks are highly useful to sense information from controlled and hostile environments. A broad range of applications uses Wireless Sensor Networks, whereas data accumulation and computation are growing to be a significant concern. Data is available from various sources, but the credibility of data has to be validated, and its credibility shall be found. On the other hand, cloud computing provides data-intensive storage and computation services. Cloud technologies provide memory storage for data from various locations. Thus, integrating cloud computing and Wireless Sensor Networks is an adaptable solution for better usage of Wireless Sensor Networks and Cloud technologies together. However, security is again the main concern here. The balance between data security and performance optimization is essential for any application. Wireless Sensor networks in hostile environments often lead to unsatisfactory performance. Cloud services deal with data, and often data integrity is a crucial requirement. Thus, the chapter reflects on the architecture of most Wireless Sensor Networks, identify security challenges and propose trust management systems that can be incorporated. Cloud integrated Wireless Sensor Network architecture has four phases, namely, sensing and generation of data at remote nodes, processing at intermediate nodes, transmission through the Cloud and analysis at the data servers.

In the first phase, data is acquired from all possible and reliable sources. In the second phase, data is converted from one format to another compatible format and processed. In the third phase, the information is transmitted through the Cloud to store at places and determine accessibility factors, security parameters, confidentiality standards etc. In the fourth phase data from cloud servers in analyzed at servers using new-age machine learning techniques to obtain outcomes for applications. For example, Weather Monitoring System. Security issues arise at all four of these phases. Trust Management System ideally aims to combat these issues at all four stages by generating trust values for each Cloud Service Provider and nodes. At each stage and at each intermediate node, Cloud Service providers are given a trust value by the proposed trust management system. Each Cloud Service Provider is marked as trusted or untrusted or no-decision. No decision arises when the trust value of that node is not in the range determined in the system. Thus, traffic from trusted sources is only allowed by established firewall systems. This proposed model is robust to the inconsistent behaviour of the nodes (Savas et al., 2013).

Cloud computing is raising issues in design, implementation and architecture, especially for smart devices like mobile phones. This is mainly due to storage and computation restrictions. This chapter marks the proposal of a trust management system based on human behavioural patterns, primarily focusing on reliable mobile cloud computing. This model involves the analysis of telephone call data of mobile devices. This analysis is done to quantify 1-dimensional trust relation between clients and server. The model also includes inter-user trust relationship analysis. The model aims to increase trustworthiness in data sensing, generation and management. The call logs are analyzed to establish a cognitive, social network entirely based o behaviour. This later leads to a global social trust model. The future scope of this work is to determine social influence models, environmental influence models, and community influenced models (Kimv& Park, 2013).

This chapter proposes a TMS in multi-cloud environments. This model is based on distributed Trust Service Providers (TSP). These Trust Service Providers are third-party trust providers. These are highly trusted by Cloud Service Providers and users and cloud participants. The model considers Service Level Agreements (SLAs) and feedback from users to determine the trustworthiness of the Cloud Service Provider. The Cloud Service Providers perform intercommunication using trust propagation network. Also, these networks obtain trust information from Trust Service Providers. The overall framework includes Cloud Service Providers, Service Level Agreements Management agents, Cloud Service Users (CSUs), and Trust Service Providers. The methodologies used are SLA based trust evaluation models, Local objective trust evaluation model (LOT), Global Objective Trust Evaluation model (GOT). The model effectively distinguishes between trustworthy and untrustworthy Cloud Service Users and Cloud Service Providers. The future scope of this model is to completely mitigate the untrustworthy Cloud Service Providers and reduce relative errors. The filters can be enhanced to prevent negative feedback from Cloud Service Users. Further, the model can be evaluated on stimulated environments with actual subjective and objective use cases (Fan & Perros 2014).

Trust management system (TMS) in Cloud is essential for e-commerce trading partners. Potential cloud users find it challenging to identify the apt cloud service provider (CSP). In this chapter, the authors proposed a multi-faceted trust management model. This model rightly aims at marketplaces to facilitate the customers in identifying the Cloud Service Providers. The report also highlights the threats to the TMS and suggested methods for tracking them. The trust management system also helps in determining if making a transaction is trustworthy or not based on the trust values of Cloud Service Providers. Collusion and Sybil attacks were identified as significant threats to the system. The proposed framework mainly focusses on access control and trust evaluation. The developed model is run on stimulating environments, and satisfactory accuracy is obtained as a result. The main aim of this chapter was to filter malicious feedbacks to identify feedback related vulnerabilities. As future work, the authors aim to develop a complete framework for all e-commerce Trust Management Systems. However, the present system can be used in all electronic markets with high effectivity (Chong et al., 2014).

Trust management in Cloud is difficult due to the dynamic nature of cloud services. Trust Management systems proposed so far are vibrant but not automatic. This chapter marked a proposal for an automated Trust Management system for highly dynamic IoT systems. This system is based on the MAPE-K feedback control loop. The method, like other TMS systems, aims to determine the trust values for each Cloud Service Provider. The system is trained for risky and uncertain environments, trained to deal with prior experience and knowledge, personal opinions and behaviours of customers, day-to-day decisions, contextual information and timely changes. Just like a machine learning model, the system takes into account all the mentioned parameters to determine the trust value of a Cloud service provider. The technique was especially stimulated for smart home applications. The evaluation was done on four factors, namely, availability, response time, reliability, and capacity.

Moreover, availability is considered to check the system functionality in a remote location and remote nodes. Performance evaluation of the system depends on the response time. Also, reliability is supposed to validate the functioning of the system and to trust its automatically formulated decisions and trust values. While capacity is considered to check the measure of data load and several nodes the system can support. Yet, trust protocols were applied to determine the levels of trust. MAPE-K feedback loop is used to maintain the consistency of the level of trust. History of records was used to learn from previous decision mistakes and enhance the trust levels, and increase reliability. These records also make the system automatic, as the system is trained based on years of data. The four parameters have certain weightage in determining trust values. These weights are customizable, allowing the user to use the Trust Management System model as per his requirement. This makes the whole model flexible and automatic. The advantage of this model is that it Uses Neural networks for simulation providing automation. It also considers turn around efficiency as a parameter. However, it does not consider SLA(Service Level Agreements) as a parameter to determine CSPs (Namal et al., 2015).

Cloud is a dynamic and distributed service. Trust management is a significant issue in cloud computing. This is due to sensitive data exchange between the customers and Trust management systems. The availability of trust management is in question due to the dynamic nature of the Cloud. Thus, a CloudArmor is designed and developed, which is a reputation-based framework. This framework provides many functionalities that make "Trust as a Service" possible. The major functionalities of the proposed are proving credibility of trust feedbacks, robust and flexible credibility model and an availability model. The backbone of the framework is the Zero-Knowledge Credibility Proof protocol (ZKCP2). Misleading attacks like Sybil attack or collusion attack can be mitigated to an extent with this model. The proposed model is evaluated over a vast data set collected from real worlds trust feedbacks from various cloud providers. The future scope of this work is to combine different trust management techniques like reputation and recommendation, to increase accuracy (Noor et al., 2015).

Pointed out in many research articles, cloud computing demands a security check due to its highly dynamic and distributed architectures. Trust values are calculated using reliability(RE), availability(AV), turnaround efficiency(TE), and data integrity(DI). This chapter marks a model that considers the parameters as mentioned above to evaluate a node and determine its trust value. These four weightage parameters are given, say w1,w2,w3 and w4.

The trust value = w1*RE+ w2*AV + w3*TE + w4*DI.

The weightage is predetermined for a model but can be altered to meet the customer's requirements. Higher weightage is given to the parameter based on those requirements. For instance, for increased efficiency as a requirement, w3 is given high value. The metrics for this trust value consists of Quality of Service (QoS). Hence this model is called Quality Of Service trust model. The Quality Of Service deals with the following: Turnaround time, cost, computing power, and Networking speed. The results of the simulation show that the proposed QoS model is better than the conventional FIFO model (Manuel, 2015).

CONCLUSION

This chapter has attempted a comprehensive review of the various trust management techniques used in Cloud Technology to protect the data with multiple security features. The primary thrust in this work is the trust model to facilitate the process of choosing the right and trusted cloud service provider(CSP). The proposed model uses an SLA agent to perform the tasks such as grouping cloud consumers, designing and drawing SLA metrics, determining the negotiation terms with the cloud providers etc. In extension to this work, parameters like accountability, auditability, returns of investment, etc., can be used to calculate the trust values of CSPs.

Table 1. Analysis Table

Chapter	TMS based on	Approach model /Mathematical model	Trust Model	Parameters						Year
				Centralized/ Distributed	Automatic	Turn around Efficiency	CSP determination	SLA Based	Test Platform	
1	Credibility values	Protocols	Direct	Centralized	No	No	Yes	Yes	N/A	2010
2	Feedback	Parameter Normalization	Direct	Centralized	No	No	Yes	No	NetLogo	2011
3	Trust Similarity	Fuzzy Networks	Direct	Centralized	No	No	Yes	No	Oracle sun	2011
4	Reputation	Random realization using a normal distribution	Indirect	Centralized	No	No	No	No	Forward and Reverse cloud generator	2011
5	Reputation	CertainTrust Bayesian probability distribution	Direct	Centralized	No	Yes	Yes	Yes	Cloud Security Alliance	2011
6	Feedback	Slandered deviation and density collusion	Direct	Distributed	No	No	Yes	No	NetLogo	2011
7	Reputation	Vector logic	Indirect	Distributed	No	No	No	No	Hadoop clustering on Ubuntu	2012
8	Feedback	Median logic	Indirect	Centralized	No	No	No	Yes	N/A	2012
9	Reputation	Probabilistic and Eigenvalue logic	Indirect	Distributed	No	Yes	No	No	Sample WSN architecture	2013
10	Reliability	1-dimensional relation analysis	Indirect	Centralized	No	No	No	No	Android Studio	2013
11	Feedback	Propositional calculus and set theory	Direct	Distributed	No	Yes	Yes	Yes	Multi-cloud environment	2014
12	Feedback	N/A	Direct	Centralized	No	No	Yes	No	N/A	2014
13	Feedback	Neural Networks	Direct	Distributed	Yes	Yes	Yes	No	Matlab	2015
14	Reputation	Density Estimation	Indirect	Centralized	No	No	No	No	Cloud Armor	2015
15	Reliability	Weighted average	Direct	Centralized	No	Yes	Yes	No	CloudSim	2015

REFERENCES

Alhamad, M., Dillon, T., & Chang, E. (2010, September). The SLA-based trust model for cloud computing. In *2010 13th international conference on network-based information systems* (pp. 321-324). IEEE.

Chong, S. K., Abawajy, J., Ahmad, M., & Hamid, I. R. A. (2014). Enhancing trust management in a cloud environment. *Procedia: Social and Behavioral Sciences*, *129*, 314–321. doi:10.1016/j.sbspro.2014.03.682

Fan, W., & Perros, H. (2014). A novel trust management framework for multi-cloud environments based on trust service providers. *Knowledge-Based Systems*, *70*, 392–406. doi:10.1016/j.knosys.2014.07.018

Habib, S. M., Ries, S., & Muhlhauser, M. (2011, November). Towards a trust management system for cloud computing. In *2011 IEEE 10th International Conference on Trust, Security and Privacy in Computing and Communications* (pp. 933-939). IEEE. 10.1109/TrustCom.2011.129

Khan, S. M., & Hamlen, K. W. (2012, June). Hatman: Intra-cloud trust management for Hadoop. In *2012 IEEE Fifth International Conference on Cloud Computing* (pp. 494-501). IEEE. 10.1109/CLOUD.2012.64

Kim, M., & Park, S. O. (2013). Trust management on user behavioural patterns for mobile cloud computing. *Cluster Computing, 16*(4), 725–731. doi:10.100710586-013-0248-9

Liu, Y. C., Ma, Y. T., Zhang, H. S., Li, D. Y., & Chen, G. S. (2011). A method for trust management in cloud computing: Data colouring by Cloud watermarking. *International Journal of Automation and Computing, 8*(3), 280.

Manuel, P. (2015). A trust model of cloud computing based on Quality of Service. *Annals of Operations Research, 233*(1), 281–292. doi:10.100710479-013-1380-x

Muchahari, M. K., & Sinha, S. K. (2012, December). A new trust management architecture for a cloud computing environment. In *2012 International Symposium on Cloud and Services Computing* (pp. 136-140). IEEE. 10.1109/ISCOS.2012.30

Namal, S., Gamaarachchi, H., MyoungLee, G., & Um, T. W. (2015, December). Autonomic trust management in cloud-based and highly dynamic IoT applications. In 2015 ITU Kaleidoscope: Trust in the Information Society (K-2015) (pp. 1-8). IEEE.

Noor, T. H., & Sheng, Q. Z. (2011, October). Trust as a service: A framework for trust management in cloud environments. In *International Conference on Web Information Systems Engineering* (pp. 314-321). Springer. 10.1007/978-3-642-24434-6_27

Noor, T. H., & Sheng, Q. Z. (2011, December). Credibility-based trust management for services in cloud environments. In *International Conference on Service-Oriented Computing* (pp. 328-343). Springer. 10.1007/978-3-642-25535-9_22

Noor, T. H., Sheng, Q. Z., Yao, L., Dustdar, S., & Ngu, A. H. (2015). CloudArmor: Supporting reputation-based trust management for cloud services. *IEEE Transactions on Parallel and Distributed Systems, 27*(2), 367–380. doi:10.1109/TPDS.2015.2408613

Savas, O., Jin, G., & Deng, J. (2013, May). Trust management in cloud-integrated wireless sensor networks. In *2013 International Conference on Collaboration Technologies and Systems (CTS)* (pp. 334-341). IEEE. 10.1109/CTS.2013.6567251

Sun, X., Chang, G., & Li, F. (2011, September). A trust management model to enhance the security of cloud computing environments. In *2011 Second International Conference on Networking and Distributed Computing* (pp. 244-248). IEEE. 10.1109/ICNDC.2011.56

Chapter 16
Image Classification Using CNN With Multi-Core and Many-Core Architecture

Debajit Datta
Vellore Institute of Technology, Vellore, India

Saira Banu Jamalmohammed
Vellore Institute of Technology, Vellore, India

ABSTRACT

Image classification is a widely discussed topic in this era. It covers a vivid range of application domains like from garbage classification applications to advanced fields of medical sciences. There have been several research works that have been done in the past and are also currently under research for coming up with better-optimized image classification techniques. However, the process of image classification turns out to be time-consuming. This work deals with the widely accepted FashionMNIST (modified national institute of standards and technology database) dataset, having a set of sixty thousand images for training a model and another popular dataset of MNIST for handwritten numbers. The work compares several convolutional neural network (CNN) models and aims in parallelizing them using a distributed framework that is provided by the python library, RAY. The parallelization has been achieved over the multiple cores of CPU and many cores of GPU. The work also shows that the overall accuracy of the system is not affected by the parallelization.

DOI: 10.4018/978-1-7998-3335-2.ch016

INTRODUCTION AND OVERVIEW

A machine aided image classification application is an application that is used for training machines to learn the identification of different classes of images from a given dataset, which is known as the training dataset, and apply the knowledge to classify new images. Human beings may have enormous knowledge but at the same time, they are also prone to do silly mistakes, or they can overlook at times – for issues, as crucial as identifying brain tumors in the patient's brain, a small overlook can cost someone's life. On the other hand, machines after proper training can give high accuracy, but they are time-consuming or monotonous for a human, like the classification of garbage, and it is likely that some overlook from the human side can be there – the same task if given to a machine, the time consumption can be reduced and it is likely the classification can achieve accuracy close to cent percent. In recent years, parallel computing has become a rapidly evolving field of study. Over the years, there have been a lot of advancements in the field of image classification, namely, artificial neural networks, convolutional neural networks (CNN), fuzzy-sets, etc. In recent years, image classification approaches have started to use advanced CNN architecture which helps in securing accurate and precise results. CNN is used across a wide range of domains that deal with machine learning and deep learning. As inferred from extensive research, CNN gives noticeably better results than the previous methods. In order to overcome the problems, which are associated with choosing an ideal model, that are associated with regular neural networks, there has been the development of CNN for classification and identification of images. Several architectures are built on CNN in order to classify images with high accuracy; however, not all architectures can give high accuracy for all forms of the datasets (Deng, 2012). Different architectures are suitable for different image datasets, since, there can be problems associated with the training of a model.

In recent years, parallel computing and soft computing has become a rapidly evolving field of study. The demand for parallel processing is growing every day because the associated computations are increasing, but people want solutions to problems within less time. There are various software tools and libraries by which the programs can be parallelized – like, there is OpenMP for C and C++ (Liu, et al., 2015), multiprocessing library in python (Datta et al., 2020a). Parallelization within the unused cores of CPU, if done properly, decreases the overall time of execution, however, if parallelization is not proper or there are a greater number of parallel overheads, there can be adverse effects that will increase the time of execution. Though parallelizing of applications can be complicated and complex, but they need to be modified for coming up with the most optimal one. Multiprocessing library can be used for parallelization, but suffers from inconsistency while handling larger numeric data (Datta et al., 2020a) and it does not support the concept of shared variables. This issue has been addressed by Ray, a python library, which is open source library and provides a distributed framework. It's not widely used, although, with this work, it is shown that this library can be used for parallelizing several algorithms that are associated with Computer Science domains like Artificial Intelligence, Machine Learning, and even other associated fields dealing with Big Data, High-Performance Computing, Data Mining, etc. for coming up with better performance and attain an overall speedup of the system (Liu, et al., 2015; Hill & Marty, 2008). The distribution of workload over the available cores not only helps in the reduction of time, but rather it also provides better performance of the system and hence, better efficiency.

The result of these research can be fruitful for other future works, and the overall result of the output of parallelization over CPU cores can also be compared with the result of parallelizing within the many cores of a GPU that are available. This work analyzes the performance on the basis of speedup achieved based on Amdahl's law on both CPU and GPU in a distributed framework, Ray. The second section of this work deals with the literature review of the related works and applications that are related and are referred to while coming up with this work. The third part of this paper deals with the description of the proposed system along with the concepts that are referred. The fourth section discusses the implementation of the system followed by the results and its interpretation and analysis which are discussed in the fifth section. Finally, the sixth section concludes the work along with a brief insight into the possible future works.

RELATED WORK AND APPLICATION

Architecture of CPU and GPU

One should be familiar with the internal architecture of a CPU and a GPU, for avoiding problems that may arise while parallelizing the cores. The multiple cores of CPU have independent ALUs in them, but they share a single Control unit and Cache memory. The work of Reddy et al. (2017) deals with the internal architecture of a CPU and a GPU. CPUs and GPUs not only have differences in their architecture, but they are also different based on their performance as discussed by Syberfedt & Ekblom (2017). Parallelization requires knowledge of various other factors, namely decomposition, dependencies, interactions, concurrency, granularity, mapping. The decomposition of tasks can be recursive or based on the input or output or intermediate data or can be functional decomposition or explorative and speculative decomposition as discussed in the work of Kumar (2002). One must be aware of the task dependency graph and the task interaction graphs associated with their decomposition as shown in the work of Hwang & Faye (1984). According to the work of Simon (1991), the modules that interact a lot can be put under the same processor while the ones that do not interact much can be put under separate processors to have concurrent processing, which will save time and not have parallel overheads. The appropriate mapping techniques and procedures are determined by both the task dependency and task interaction graphs as expressed by Inchingolo & Stanfill (2008). As discussed by Stone (1971), the granularity of the processing can also be found out, whether the decomposition resulted in coarse grain or fine grain, which will give ideas about the locality and concurrency of the given code and will thus help in the parallelization.

The work of Blake et al. (2009) portrays a better performance speed within the processors since numerous cores run concurrently. It has also been inferred that the signals do not weaken, removing the need for reiterating signals and further, transmission o data is possible, as mentioned in the work of Zhuravlev et al. (2010). With single-core, in a CPU with multiple cores, the CPU utilization reduces and time consumption is also high, whereas, the other cores are just idle and not utilized at all. According to Jeffers & Reinders (2015) the parallelization of tasks is important for reducing the workload over the single core of CPU and further it reduces time consumption by parallelizing the task. This work is based on training a CNN model on a CPU without any parallelization and comparing it with the same by parallelizing the task over multiple cores of CPU as well as many-cores of GPU as shown by Markall et al. (2013), which provides a comparison of performance after parallelizing CNN algorithm within CPU and GPU cores.

PARALLELIZATION WITHIN CPU AND GPU CORES

The work of Liu et al. (2015) provides a parallelization of CNN with OpenMP on Intel® Xeon Phi™ Coprocessor, which has been used as their platform. The system proposed by O'Shea et al. (2015) deals with the increase of accuracy, precision, and total result after classification and detection of images, which are all totally built on numerous CNN methods. Parallel overheads and improper load balancing are some of the challenges that can be faced while parallelizing. There are several laws associated with performance analysis, like to analyze whether a program merits parallelization is portrayed by Amdahl's law (Hill & Marty, 2008). This law plays an important role in predicting the theoretical maximum speedup for program processing using multiple processors (Sun & Chen, 2010). There is another law that is used for evaluation of the performance after parallelization, called Gustafson-Barsis law, which allows solving larger problems by using more processors with a scaled speedup, ignoring the parallelization overheads (Karbowski, 2008). Unlike

Amdahl's law and Gustafson Barsis law, the Karp-Flatt metric takes the parallel overhead into consideration and decides whether the actual barrier to the attainable speedup is caused due to inherently sequential code or due to parallel overheads (Nunes & Almeida, 2010). The iso-efficiency metric evaluates the scalability of a parallel program executing on a parallel computer (Grama et al., 1993). The scalability of a parallel computer system is a measure of the system's ability to increase the performance with an increase in the number of processors.

IMAGE PROCESSING AND CLASSIFICATION

The image processing algorithms have developed with time, and now they require a high amount of processing especially in the neural networks to get high precision and accuracies. The paper provided by Marwa et al. (2014) gives a detailed explanation of all the methods and procedures involved in developing a model for creating a specific image processing application. The work of Wang et al. (2016) proposes a framework combined with the advantages of image embedding and label models by using CNN and RNN. Parallel processing as proposed by Saxena et al. (2017) helps reduce the execution time and provide high CPU utilization. Parallel processing can be applied to image processing algorithms too. The computing mechanism in GPU is done by Computer Unified Device Architecture (CUDA). One of the research works, by Perez & Wang (2017) shows various methods to increase the accuracy of classification tasks. It proposes the combination of traditional augmentation techniques followed by neural augmentation further improves the classification strengths.

PYTHON PARALLELIZATION LIBRARY, RAY

Studies of Zhai et al. (2018) come across various mockups of machine learning that are implemented to precisely feign the many-body postponement of the complete energy. The concurrency obtained by OpenMP and CUDA implementations, can clasp the CPU and GPU progressions correspondingly. Just like for concurrent computation in C or C++, there is OpenMP library, for Python, there is a module called Multiprocessing, a separate parallel processing module. This module also gives special permission to the programmer to completely control the computing power of multiple processors. But Multiprocessing fails to coordinate with all of the processes as well as the data with huge numeric data, moreover, it doesn't support shared variables. Thus, to handle those situations, There is further another framework for concurrent computing in Python, Ray which can be highly implemented for the applications based on Artificial Intelligence and Machine Learning, for parallelizing the task amongst the cores of CPU as well as GPU. A research work of Moritz et al. (2018) gives a piece of detailed information about the supplies and provisions that resulted in this parallel computing framework, Ray. This work provides execution of Ray in testing in 1.8 million tasks each second over all the parameters.

MNIST DATASETS

The datasets that are used in this work include the Fashion dataset and Handwritten Numbers dataset which are provided by the Modified National Institute of Standards and Technology (MNIST). The data has been used in the research of Zhou et al. (2017) where they have tried to parallelize the CNN. The selection of components for classification or prediction has to be up to the mark, because if a pattern exists and it is not determined, then it leads to underfitting as mentioned in the work of Lee et al. (2018), else, if unnecessarily patterns are formed that are forcefully created then, it leads to overfitting of data. The work of Datta et al. (2020a) deals with the parallelization of image classification algorithm based on only plant datasets in order to identify diseases that are present. Automation of CNN parallelization as discussed in the work of Guedria et al. (2019) states that parallelization can be obtained within the architecture of CNN. However, finer-grained parallelism leads to better performance of the system, as discussed by Dryden et al. (2019) in their work.

APPLICATIONS OF IMAGE CLASSIFICATION

The applications of image classifications are not limited to classifying handwritten numbers or identifying a dress, rather, it is a broad domain and can be included in several fields ranging from medicines to agriculture and astronomy, and many more.

According to the research work of Feng et al. (2019), image classification is used in astronomy for creating a feature that possess a multilayer spatial-spectral for fusion. Another work in the field of astronomy is proposed by Jiménez et al. (2020), where they have classified the images of the galaxies using CNN. Image classification can also be implemented in detecting Martian rock images as represented in the work of Li et al. (2020), using deep CNN techniques. The work of Kyrkou & Theocharides (2019) provides an application of image classification for creating an emergency response for unmanned aerial vehicles. Images of clouds can also be classified according to the work of Liu et al. (2019), using deep residual learning. The have used VGG-16, ResNet, MobileNet CNN models.

The work of Rasti et al. (2019) contributes in detecting weeds in the crop fields using image classification. According to the work of Datta et al. (2020a) and Too et al. (2019) image classification can be implemented for detecting plant diseases. This classification techniques can be applied in the domain of agriculture for identification of the diseases in plants at early stages, so that, they can be monitored and also track the fresh and healthy ones.

Image classification is also used in medical sciences, as shown in the work of Zhang et al. (2019), where they have used image classification for classifying histopathology cancer. They have used MobileNet CNN model for classification. The research proposed by Mallick et al. (2019) focuses on image classification of brain MRI images for detecting cancer. The work of Li et al. (2020) have used image classification for classifying Pseudoprogression and true tumor progression. Similar to their work, Yang et al. (2019) have also worked with image classification for feature extraction of tumor images. The work of Faes et al. (2019) deal with image classification of medical images by the health-care professionals, that is automated for catering the professionals who do not have previous exposure to computer science. Researches with image classification in the field of medical sciences are continuing. The works of Hassanien et al. (2020), Apostolopoulos et al. (2020) and Abbas et al. (2020) deal with image classification in classifying COVID-19 lung images and chest X-ray images. DeTraC deep CNN model has been used for classification of the images.

MATERIALS AND METHODS

Image Classification

In this era of smart computation, there is a big crave for multiprocessing. In order to achieve multiprocessing in image classification, this work has implemented python's ray library. The field of artificial intelligence is evolving every day and the scope of research and job opportunities have also increased over this decade. There has been an enormous growth in the field of Artificial Intelligence recently, which has helped in fixing the gaps between machine and human through basically four different methods, namely thinking humanly, acting humanly, thinking rationally and acting rationally. Computer vision is one of those domains that is getting a lot of popularity and attention and is emerging every single day.

A lot of researches are still going on, in the domain of computer vision and researchers are coming up with better algorithms with better accuracy and time complexity. The main focus and aim of these researchers are to enable several machines that can be used to imitate human beings in terms of visualizing the world and interpreting it. The focus can be broadly extended to various tasks that a normal human being does in everyday life, starting from classifying images, for example, while picking an apple from the refrigerator, they can be classified as fresh or rotten, just by looking at them; or looking at different handwritings, the comparison can be made to decide whether both the writings belong to a single person or multiple persons; or comparing two different images and concluding whether they are taken at the same place or not; etc. Most of the advancements in the computer vision branch, as well as that of the deep learning branch, are created and modified gradually, they are also a huge field of researches, and are carried out primarily over one of the most popular and widely used algorithms, CNN.

CONVOLUTIONAL NEURAL NETWORK

A CNN is an algorithm that is widely used in machine learning, artificial intelligence, deep learning and a lot of other fields. This algorithm processes an image like its input and provides them with corresponding weights to let the later part of the algorithm to understand the importance of various attributes or aspects of the image and be able to differentiate amongst themselves. One of the reasons that CNN are preferred over other algorithms that perform classifications, is that the CNN use very less amount of preprocessing. Most human beings are blessed with a functioning nervous system that can easily interpret the vivid colors and distinguish features, interpret distinct objects, and memorize them by storing it in their brains. They can recall their memories from their brains and use it for identifying and classifying objects they come across later if they have seen one before or store it if it is a new one. Humans also have imagination ability that helps them in connecting dots and finding relations amongst the different objects. Suppose a person visits the Himalayas, the person is likely to identify mountains, and terrain of it along with the wildlife that is present; the same person visiting Patagonia will be able to identify the mountains, and understand the difference in wildlife that is present, although the types of mountains are different and the wild lives are also different. For a computer system or any other electronic machine, an image is just a series of arranged pixels, that are placed in a specific order. Alteration of the pixels of an image will alter the image itself, and although the difference will be very evident to humans but not for the machines. After the machines are properly trained and tested, the machine can also perform same work as that of humans, and that is how Artificial Intelligence has been emerging since the time of Alan Turing.

A machine stores an image as a matrix of pixels in specific order and stores the value of code that is associated with the color for every pixel that is present in their specified locations. By convention, the lesser color code values are assigned to the lighter colors while higher color code values are assigned to the darker colors. A fully connected network converts the image, which is nothing but a matrix of ordered pixels, into an array, by performing a flattening function on it. The flattened form can neither be read by machines, nor they can be interpreted by a human. Thus, a fully connected network is not a good option for image classification. The Convolution layer is applied that, such that the pixel value of the output matrix are calculated with the formula given in equation (1) (Skalski, 2020), where f is taken as the input image and h is taken as filter and m and n are the dimensions of the resultant matrix. Let the input image matrix dimension be M x N and the dimension of the filter be A x B, the resultant matrix will have (M-A+1) x (N-B+1) as its dimensions if there is no stride.

$$G[m,n] = (f*h)[m,n] = \sum_j \sum_k h[j,k] f[m-j,n-k] \tag{1}$$

With CNN, the features within an image are extracted by simply defining a weight matrix that is convolved with the input image, without losing any information about how the pixels within the matrix are arranged within the space. However, multiple filters are applied onto an image, this, the resultant becomes multidimensional as shown in equation (2) (Skalski, 2020), where n is input image size, n_c is number of channels that are present in the image, f is filter size, p is the size of padding that is used, s is the stride size and n_f is number of filters that are present. The floor() function in the equation gives the greatest integer value which is less than or equal to the number. The number of filters that can be present must be equal to the number of channels of the image.

$$[n,n,n_c] * [f,f,n_c] = \left[floor\left(\frac{n+2p-f}{s}+1\right), floor\left(\frac{n+2p-f}{s}+1\right), n_f \right] \tag{2}$$

Image classification is performed with the CNN models. There are several approaches and models that are used for the classification of images. The MNIST datasets that have been used for the training CNN model are the Fashion dataset and the Handwritten Numbers dataset. Traditionally, the pre-existing model that have been used works only with one processor, that is, only one core of a multicore CPU, so the CPU utilization is not much. According to previous findings most human beings are able to clasp and observe an image like layers within the brain, the CNN is inspired from the same. The model takes covers from a picture within the convolution layer and performs several filter actions on it. Further, the output is fed into the pooling layer to reduce the image size. Similar processes are carried out for down-sampling the images to identify patterns within the information left.

In the end, the layers of nodes are fully connected. Finally, the model is trained with all the images in order to classify into the classes given.

VARIOUS ARCHITECTURES OF CNN

There are several architectures that belong to the CNN – GoogleNet, LeNet-5, AlexNet, VGG-16, Inception, Xception, ResNet, (Zhou et al.,2017) etc. Some features are common to all CNN architecture; however, the architectures differ in parameters like the size of filters, number of layers, and sequence of layers, etc. Some architectures are ideal for some datasets, but are not for other datasets as they can lead to underfitting or overfitting, hence choosing a particular architecture is a challenging task. The convolutional operation is basically a mathematical operation that is carried out on any two functions say, f and g, where f and g need not be different. These functions are operated as the integral product of each one after a reversal and shift of the other one. Apart from that, there are several hidden layers comprising of numerous convolutional operations that are enclosed with input and output layers. The basic convolution operations that are used for creating a model are the Convolution layer, Max Pooling, Flattening, Fully Connection layer. The main objective of the convolutional operation is to fetch and extract several features like edges from the input image. The CNN algorithm comprises of several layers in them, out of which, traditionally, the first convolution layer is held accountable for captivating the low-level attributes like color, etc. The features that have been convolved, are either reduced dimensionally with the help of valid padding or are increased, or kept equal using the same padding.

The pooling layer is used to reduce the overall size that is occupied by the space of the features and attributes that have been convolved already. This layer plays a very important role in decreasing the computational power that is needed by the system in order to process the data, and simultaneously have a reduction in dimensions. This layer is widely known for its astonishing method of extracting the features or attributes that are dominant in nature and are invariant on the basis of rotation and position. Pooling can be of two types, max-pooling, and average pooling. Match pooling returns the value which is maximum out of a portion of the image which is covered by the Kernel; Average pooling, unlike max-pooling returns the average of all the values from the part of the image. Max pooling is also a technique that can be used for de-noising the impure data. A general architecture of a CNN model, like the AlexNet architecture, is shown in Figure 1, however, there are several different architectures of CNN that are available.

The layer that moves the filter to all possible position within the image is called the convolution layer. In this layer, the data from images are collected from the filters

Figure 1. General convolutional neural network

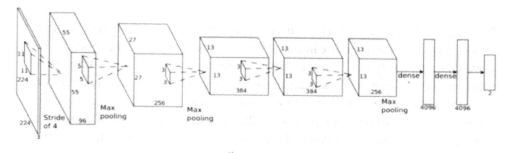

by organizing the pixels and average is taken to get the output for that particular patch. Different activation layers are used like tanh, sigmoid, Rectified Linear Unit (ReLU), etc., to arrange the output pixel values. Further, when entire image is covered, the output of the layer is fed into the pooling layer with a fixed window size, in order to pick the maximum value from that window. The reduced size of image is further fed to the dense layer that creates complete connection with the nodes, and some connections are dropped too. Further, the output is flattened from dimension size of two to one. There are numerous architectures of CNN like LeNet, AlexNet, GoogleNet, VGGNet, etc., further, new architectures can also be developed.

CONTRAST BETWEEN CPU AND GPU

The Central Processing Unit (CPU) and Graphics Processing Unit (GPU) have different architectures in terms of number of cores as well as other features like the Arithmetic-Logic Unit (ALU) and the Control Unit (CU) and cache. CPU is a multicore hardware that are used for general purpose applications whereas, GPU is many-core hardware which is mainly used for computations that require a high performance of the system. The cores of CPU share a single cache and a CU, but the ALUs are separate in the cores, whereas, the cores of GPU have distinct caches and CU along with distinct ALU for the systems. Latency is the time that is needed for undergoing a task, that is, some actions in order to fetch the solution or the output. Contrastingly, throughput refers to the total number of executed tasks or actions or number of outputs fetched per unit time. Ideally, a machine is required to have low latency and high throughput. However, the GPUs are well known for providing higher throughputs and the CPUs for lower latency. The CPUs are capable of processing only a few processes at a time but the GPUs are capable of processing several processes at a time compared to that of the CPUs.

DISTRIBUTED FRAMEWORK, RAY

The program for image classification can be parallelized using Python's Ray library. This library is instantiated for initializing the context using the method, ray.init() in which the quantity of CPUs and GPUs are passed as parameters, although, it is totally optional. The part of code that needs to be executed concurrently is converted into methods that are preceded with annotation @ray.remote() with the quantities of CPUs or GPUs as parameters. The method to be executed parallelly is, further, called by using another built in method of the library called 'get()' with the name of the function as the parameter. The other methods of the library that have been used include ray.put() and ray.get() – these are used for loading the object corresponding to its identification and returning the same, individually in a synchronous method.

IMPLEMENTATION

System Specification

In this study, an image classification process is performed using TensorFlow's Keras, which is an open-source library in python. It is a high-level API for building and training deep learning models. This work has implemented the image classification application in python environment and it is carried out on the Kaggle platform, which provides online notebooks to run python3 codes. It has all the libraries including TensorFlow and Keras pre-installed in it. Kaggle provides four central processing units (CPU) and one graphics processing unit (GPU). The provided GPU is NVIDIA Tesla K80, which has 2496 x2 cores, a GK210 x2 graphics processor, and 12GB x2 memory size. The configuration is good enough to execute code with high speed.

DATASET

In this work, the dataset that is used include the MNIST (Modified National Institute of Science and Technology) Number dataset and MNIST Fashion dataset. Both of them contain 60000 training images and 10000 testing images. It has an enormous dataset that is widely used for training various image processing systems. The MNIST dataset for both, fashion and handwritten dataset, includes images consist of small 28x28 pixels which are in grayscale. The classes of fashion dataset include t-shirts, trousers, pullover, dress, coat, sandal, shirt, sneaker, bags and ankle boot and the classes of handwritten dataset includes numbers from 0-9 that are handwritten.

ACHIEVING PARALLELIZATION

The parallelization of the CNN will decrease the execution time, which is generally high for sequential execution. In the convolution layer, a matrix is convolved with another smaller matrix with dimensions very small compared to that of the original image. The original image is padded with either 0 value, or using repetitive pixels at the edge, or are folded. When someone goes for multiple filters, the depth dimension of the filter is kept the same as that of the original image, but every filtering layer is stacked onto one another, resulting in a depth dimension the same as that of the number of filters.

Figure 2. Parallel convolutional neural network

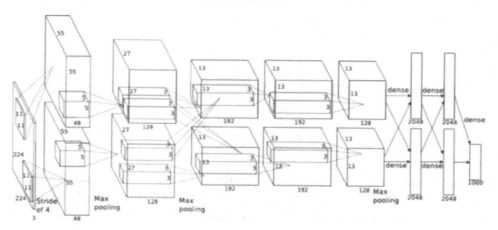

For instance, if the original image is of dimension 64*64*5 the filters must be of dimension x*x*5 where x<64, say 5*5*5, now say 15 filters are used, the resulting image will be 60*60*15. In the pooling layer, the dimensions are reduced, preferentially, max pooling is used the most, where small sub-matrices are selected from the convolved image and the maximum of it is taken for the next generated image. After several layers of convolution and pooling, the dense filter and drop filters are also used for getting an output image, which goes to one of the classes that are present in the dataset.

For parallelizing the Convolution Neural Network model as shown in Figure 2, within multiple cores of a CPU or with many cores of GPU, multiple images are taken and are set to execute all the layers of a CNN and classified at the same time, like the one as shown in Figure 2. Having multiple images to be used at the same time while training a model increases the speed of execution, and helps to balance

Figure 3. Flowchart for parallelization of Convolutional Neural Network

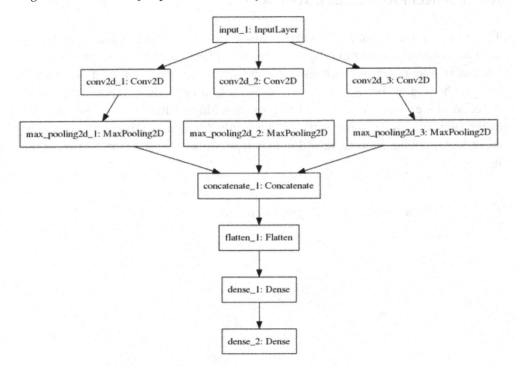

the load amongst the cores present, and increases CPU utilization and minimizes the idle time of CPU. But the parallelization of the particular part should be proper as displayed as a flowchart in the Figure 3, otherwise it can have adverse effect on the execution. Ultimately, all the images are collected at the end and are passed through the dense layer in order to complete the training of the model and help in the final classification. The multicores of CPU are used for increasing the performance parameters of CPU.

Ray library is used in order to execute the Convolution Neural Network concurrently, in this work. It is widely implemented for computing concurrently, and execute computation within a distributed environment, thus making it easier for the developers working with parallelization or for having a distributed computing. The initialization of the ray module context is carried out using *ray.init()* with the specification of the quantity of CPUs and GPUs. *@ray.remote()* is a class or function decorator used for specifying which class or which function is to be parallelized within the processes during execution with the parameters being the quantity of CPUs or GPUs. *ray.put()* and *ray.get()* are used for storing the object along with the ID that is specified and returning the object along with the ID that is specified, respectively in a synchronous way.

CALCULATING ACCURACY METRICS

The dataset is divided into training and testing dataset. The CNN model is created and trained using the training dataset, next, the model is validated by testing dataset. The models are tested on the basis of several accuracy metrics that are accepted worldwide as benchmark for checking the over accuracy of the model. The actual class labels of the system are used for validating the predicted class labels in order to test the model that is created. A confusion matrix is created based on the results; a better model will be most of its data marked the diagonal of the confusion matrix, however, a worse model will have data scattered throughout the matrix. On the basis of the confusion matrix, the True Positive, True Negative, False Positive and False Negative are calculated for each class label. For a particular class label, if an object belongs to the class label and the prediction also predicts the same class label, then it is True Positive, else False Negative; alternatively, if an object does not belong to the class label and the prediction also predicts a different class label, then it is True Negative, else False Positive.

After the True Positive (TP), True Negative (TN), False Positive (FP) and False Negative (FN) are calculated for the class labels, the other metrics are calculated – Precision score, Recall score, F1 score, Sensitivity and Specificity as shown in equations (3) to (7) (Datta et al., 2020b; Joshi, 2020).

$$Precision, P = \frac{TP}{TP + FP} \tag{3}$$

$$Recall, R = \frac{TP}{TP + FN} \tag{4}$$

$$F1\, Score = \frac{2 * P * R}{P + R} \tag{5}$$

$$Sensitivity = \frac{TP}{TP + FN} \qquad (6)$$

$$Specificity = \frac{TN}{TN + FP} \qquad (7)$$

An ideal model will have all these scores equal to 1, however, any model generating scores close to 1 are termed as nearly perfect models for the dataset. Models generating scores close to 0 are underfitted and are not properly trained for the dataset. These scores are separately for different class labels that are available within the dataset.

Apart from these metrics, based on the Receiver Operating Characteristics (ROC) curve and the Area Under the Curve (AUC) are studied for visualizing the performance of the classification (Narkhede, 2020; Ghoneim, 2020). This curve is plotted between the True Positive Rate (TPR) to False Positive Rate (FPR). TPR is basically the same as the Sensitivity score and FPR is (1-Specificity score). An ideal model has the AUC value equal to 1, however, models having AUC values close to 1 are considered to be almost perfect for the dataset. Models having AUC values close to 0 are yet to be trained more with the given dataset.

OBSERVATION AND ANALYSIS

Overview of the System

The execution the programs for classification of the images that are present in the MNIST datasets – the datasets used are fashion dataset with different kinds of clothing as their classes, and handwritten number dataset with classes consisting of all the single digits.

The Kaggle platform provides a CPU with the configuration of an i5 version of Intel Core which is of 7th generation, having a RAM that is of 16GB and a 2GB graphics card of Nvidia 940MX, and a GPU with the configuration of a Tesla P100 graphics card. The model is trained with a single core of CPU in sequential as well as multiple cores of CPU in parallel, the time and accuracy are also noted. The performance is then compared with that of GPU. The data are tabulated and are also plotted for easier visualization and comparison; the outputs of the model are also shown.

Observing the Outputs

The fashion dataset that is provided by MNIST contains a total of 60000 training images and 10000 testing images, consisting of several class labels including t-shirts, trousers, pullover, dress, coat, sandal, shirt, sneaker, bags and ankle boot.

Figure 4. The output of accuracy, where green shows correct classification and red denotes incorrect.

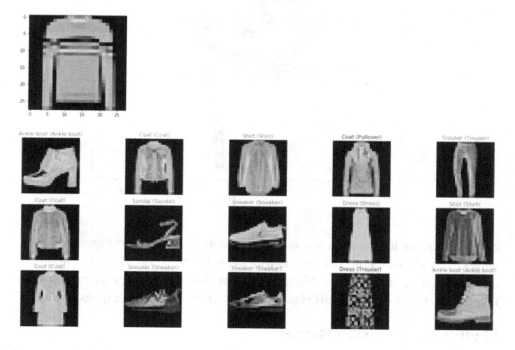

Visualizing the data collected for the fashion MNIST dataset.

After the training of the model, it is tested on the training set of the images in order to classify them and verify the correctness of it. The sample output of classification for fashion MNIST dataset is shown in Figure 4, where red denotes wrongly classified images and green denotes correctly classified images.

The handwritten number MNIST dataset also contains a total of 60000 training images and 10000 testing images, consisting of number 0 to number 9 as its class labels.

After the training of the CNN model, it is tested on the training set of the images in order to classify them and verify the correctness of it. A sample output of

Figure 5. The number 9 which is chosen and identified from the handwritten numbers MNIST dataset.

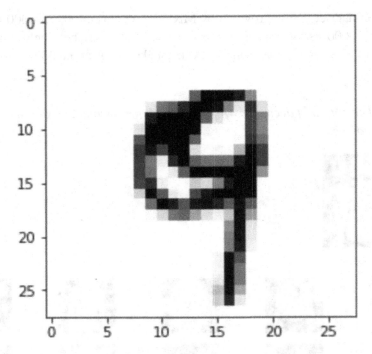

classification for handwritten number MNIST dataset is shown in Figure 5, where number 9 is identified by the machine with the help of CNN models. The numbers are identified by the different CNN architectures. The images are grayscale images thus consideration of red, green or blue value is not required for these types of images.

Finding the Accuracy Metrics

The CNN models are tested on the basis of several parameters and several accuracy metrics, for testing the overall accuracy of the model. The Receiver Operating Characteristic (ROC) curve is also plotted along with a heatmap representation of the confusion matrix. Sever other metrics are also calculated which are accepted worldwide, including Precision score, Recall score, F1 score, Sensitivity and the Specificity of the models.

The ROC curves of Fashion MNIST dataset are shown in Figure 6, the left image is the actual curve, and the right image shows a zoomed version of the same left image, zoomed into its left side.

Figure 6. ROC curves of Fashion MNIST dataset (l) actual curve (r) zoomed in curve.

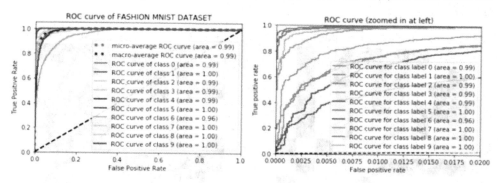

The ROC curves of Handwritten Numbers MNIST dataset are shown in Figure 7, the left image is the actual curve, and the right image shows a zoomed version of the same left image, zoomed into its left side.

Figure 7. ROC curves of Handwritten Numbers MNIST dataset (l) actual curve (r) zoomed in curve.

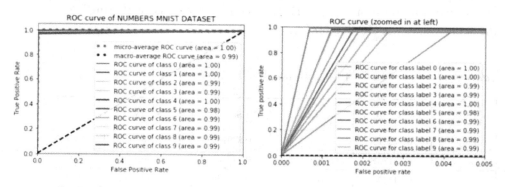

The heatmap representation for the confusion matrix of handwritten dataset and fashion MNIST dataset are shown in Figure 8, the left image shows the confusion matrix for fashion MNIST dataset, while the right image shows the confusion matrix for handwritten numbers MNIST dataset. The white colored boxes in the heatmaps represent 0, whereas, the other dark blue boxes represent lower values, and the greenish-yellow boxes denote higher values. The models that are made for the two datasets are nearly perfect as most of the higher values belong to the diagonal of the matrices, and the lower values belong to the other places within the matrices.

Figure 8. Confusion matrices as Heatmap for (l) Fashion MNIST dataset (r) Numbers MNIST dataset

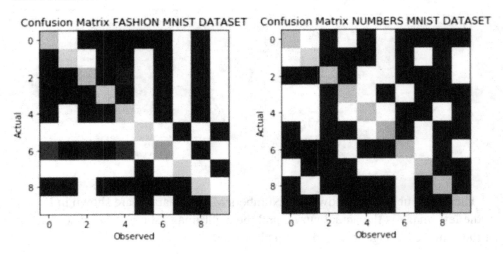

The accuracy metrics of Fashion MNIST dataset in terms of precision, recall, F1 score, sensitivity and specificity can be seen in Table 1. The values of the scores are close to 1 for most of the class labels except for the class label 'Shirt', for which, the score values are close to 60%.

Table 1. Accuracy metrics for Fashion MNIST dataset.

CLASS LABEL	PRECISION	RECALL	F1 SCORE	SENSITIVITY	SPECIFICITY
T-Shirt/Top	0.818613	0.862	0.839747	0.862	0.978778
Trouser	0.991761	0.963	0.977169	0.963	0.999111
Pullover	0.841734	0.835	0.838353	0.835	0.982556
Dress	0.853933	0.912	0.882012	0.912	0.982667
Coat	0.758148	0.884	0.816251	0.884	0.968667
Sandal	0.984631	0.961	0.972672	0.961	0.998333
Shirt	0.777181	0.579	0.663610	0.579	0.981556
Sneaker	0.926316	0.968	0.946699	0.968	0.991444
Bag	0.970942	0.969	0.969970	0.969	0.996778
Ankle boot	0.965517	0.952	0.958711	0.952	0.996222

The accuracy metrics of Handwritten Numbers MNIST dataset in terms of precision, recall, F1 score, sensitivity and specificity can be seen in Table 2. The values of the scores are close to 1 for all of the class labels.

Table 2. Accuracy metrics for Handwritten Numbers MNIST dataset

CLASS LABEL	PRECISION	RECALL	F1 SCORE	SENSITIVITY	SPECIFICITY
0	0.985801	0.991837	0.988810	0.991837	0.998448
1	0.994695	0.991189	0.992939	0.991189	0.999323
2	0.983479	0.980620	0.982048	0.980620	0.998104
3	0.976447	0.985149	0.980779	0.985149	0.997330
4	0.983887	0.994908	0.989367	0.994908	0.998226
5	0.993088	0.966368	0.979545	0.966368	0.999341
6	0.988458	0.983299	0.985871	0.983299	0.998783
7	0.980639	0.985409	0.983018	0.985409	0.997771
8	0.961771	0.981520	0.971545	0.981520	0.995790
9	0.988934	0.974232	0.981528	0.974232	0.998777

The accuracy metrics of both Fashion MNIST dataset and Handwritten Numbers MNIST dataset in terms of precision, recall, F1 score, sensitivity and specificity are visualized as line plots in Figure 9. The metrics score for numbers dataset is better than that of the fashion dataset, according to the graphs.

Figure 9. Accuracy metrics plot for (l) Fashion MNIST dataset (r) Numbers MNIST dataset.

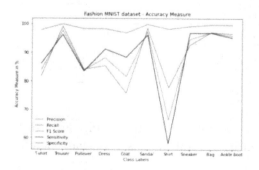
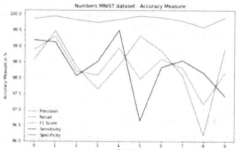

253

PARALLELIZING THE MODELS OVER CPU AND GPU

For the fashion MNIST dataset, the models that are used includes (I) Model 1: starts with convolution layer, which is followed by the max-pooling layer. Further there is a layer performing dropout, and again the convolution layer, followed by the layer executing max-pooling, then the dropout layer, then flattening layer, again dropout layer and finally the dense function (II) Model 2: AlexNet (III) Model 3: VGG-19. The data obtained after the implementation are shown in Table 3, Table 4 and Table 5 and contains information for both CPU and GPU respectively.

Table 3. Time-taken and accuracy obtained for fashion MNIST dataset with model 1

FASHION MNIST: Model 1 (10 EPOCHS)		
CPU (CORES) / GPU	TIME (s)	ACCURACY
CPU (1 CORE)	504.51	88.32%
CPU (2 CORES)	480.56	89%
CPU (3 CORES)	469.4	89.29%
CPU (4 CORES)	399.41	88.95%
GPU	280.65	88.98%

The visualization of the time taken for the fashion dataset for different models that are used are shown in Figure 10.

Table 4. Time-taken and accuracy obtained for fashion MNIST dataset with model 2, AlexNet

FASHION MNIST: AlexNet (10 EPOCHS)		
CPU (CORES) / GPU	TIME (s)	ACCURACY
CPU (1 CORE)	2324.68	60.14%
CPU (2 CORES)	2107.67	61.28%
CPU (3 CORES)	1989.13	60.12%
CPU (4 CORES)	1899.2	61.99%
GPU	1080.89	59.89%

The comparison of time taken and their accuracy are plotted in Figure 11 that shows the visualization of the time taken by several models with and without

Table 5. Time-taken and accuracy obtained for fashion MNIST dataset with model 3, VGG-19

FASHION MNIST: VGG-19 (10 EPOCHS)		
CPU (CORES) / GPU	TIME (s)	ACCURACY
CPU (1 CORE)	7571.19	49.92%
CPU (2 CORES)	7499.68	50.03%
CPU (3 CORES)	7128.35	50.94%
CPU (4 CORES)	7068.57	51.67%
GPU	4750.57	48.35%

Figure 10. The time taken plot for the fashion MNIST dataset.

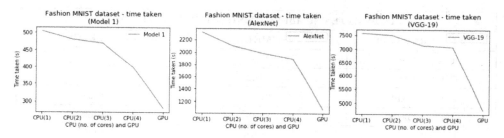

parallelization of the cores of CPU and that of the GPU. The accuracy is also plotted to visualize the proper fit model for the dataset.

For the handwritten number MNIST dataset, the models that are used includes (I) Model 4: starts with convolution layer, followed by max-pooling, then flatten,

Figure 11. The time-taken and accuracy plots and their comparison for the fashion MNIST dataset.

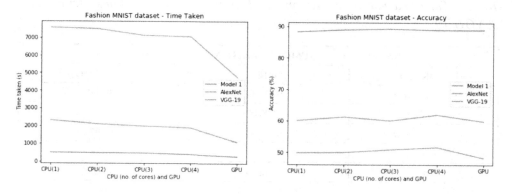

Table 6. Time-taken and accuracy obtained for numbers MNIST dataset with model 4

HANDWRITTEN NUMBERS MNIST: MODEL 1 (10 EPOCHS)		
CPU (CORES) / GPU	TIME (s)	ACCURACY
CPU (1 CORE)	284.91	98.50%
CPU (2 CORES)	281.59	98.54%
CPU (3 CORES)	273.99	98.51%
CPU (4 CORES)	263.82	98.60%
GPU	240.22	98.67%

Table 7. Time-taken and accuracy obtained for numbers MNIST dataset with model 2, AlexNet

HANDWRITTEN NUMBERS MNIST: ALEXNET (10 EPOCHS)		
CPU (CORES) / GPU	TIME (s)	ACCURACY
CPU (1 CORE)	972.13	68.97%
CPU (2 CORES)	969.42	69.47%
CPU (3 CORES)	897.27	69.20%
CPU (4 CORES)	857.46	68.36%
GPU	508.08	68.12%

then dense, dropout and dense function (II) Model 2: AlexNet (same model that is used in fashion MNIST dataset) (III) Model 3: VGG-19 (same model that is used in fashion MNIST dataset). The data obtained after the implementation are shown in Table 6, Table 7 and Table 8 and contains information for both CPU and GPU respectively. After tabulation of the data, for better understanding and proper

Table 8. Time-taken and accuracy obtained for numbers MNIST dataset with model 3, VGG-19

HANDWRITTEN NUMBERS MNIST: VGG-19 (10 EPOCHS)		
CPU (CORES) / GPU	TIME (s)	ACCURACY
CPU (1 CORE)	2003.31	39.87%
CPU (2 CORES)	1990.07	43.61%
CPU (3 CORES)	1977.02	41.97%
CPU (4 CORES)	1969.19	42.48%
GPU	1312.89	40.25%

visualization and comparison, the data points based on the observations are plotted using matplotlib library of python.

The visualization of the time taken for the handwritten numbers dataset for different models that are used are shown in Figure 12.

The comparison of time taken and their accuracy are plotted in Figure 13 that shows the visualization.

Figure 12. The time taken plot for the fashion MNIST dataset.

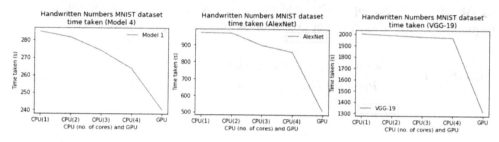

From the accuracies obtained, it can be noticed that the accuracy for AlexNet model and VGG-19 model results in poor accuracy for classification of the testing dataset. Thus, it can be concluded from the result and accuracy that these CNN models are not ideal for classification of MNIST dataset, however they are widely accepted

Figure 13. The time-taken and accuracy plots and their comparison for the fashion MNIST dataset.

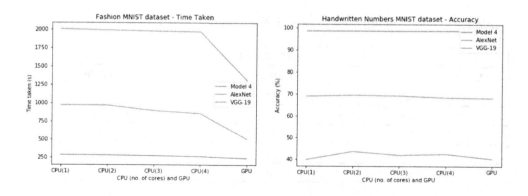

for providing accurate results. It is possible that the model is overfitted, since the training data is properly classified but the testing data is not accurately classified.

CALCULATING THE SPEEDUP

On parallelizing the CNN, there has been a substantial reduction in the time taken for execution of the codes that perform classification on the two different datasets present. According to the law corresponding to parallelization, that is proposed by Amdahl, the speedup is obtained by taking the ratio of the execution times in sequential to that of concurrent execution as shown in equation (8).

$$Speedup, \Psi_{n,p} = \frac{Sequential\ Execution\ Time}{Parallel\ Execution\ Time} = \frac{\sigma(n) + \varphi(n)}{\sigma(n) + \frac{\varphi(n)}{p}} \tag{8}$$

From equation 6, it can be observed that sequential time is calculated as the sum $\sigma(n)$ and $\varphi(n)$, where $\sigma(n)$ is the part of the program that is not parallelized during parallel execution and $\varphi(n)$ is the part of the program that is parallelized during parallel execution. The parallel execution is calculated as the sum of $\sigma(n)$ and $\frac{\varphi(n)}{p}$, where p is the number or processors or cores among which the parallel execution is carried out.

The tabulation of the speedup according to equation (6) are shown in Tables 9 – 14 for both Fashion MNIST dataset and Handwritten Numbers MNIST dataset based on the different CNN models that are used for training.

Table 9. Speedup obtained for fashion MNIST dataset with model 1

FASHION MNIST: Model 1 (10 EPOCHS)		
CPU (CORES) / GPU	**TIME (s)**	**SPEEDUP**
CPU (1 CORE)	504.51	-
CPU (2 CORES)	480.56	1.0498377
CPU (3 CORES)	469.4	1.0747976
CPU (4 CORES)	399.41	1.2631381
GPU	280.65	1.7976483

Table 10. Speedup obtained for fashion MNIST dataset with model 2, AlexNet

FASHION MNIST: AlexNet (10 EPOCHS)		
CPU (CORES) / GPU	**TIME (s)**	**SPEEDUP**
CPU (1 CORE)	2324.68	-
CPU (2 CORES)	2107.67	1.102962
CPU (3 CORES)	1989.13	1.1686918
CPU (4 CORES)	1899.2	1.2240312
GPU	1080.89	2.1507091

Table 11. Speedup obtained for fashion MNIST dataset with model 3, VGG-19

FASHION MNIST: VGG-19 (10 EPOCHS)		
CPU (CORES) / GPU	**TIME (s)**	**SPEEDUP**
CPU (1 CORE)	7571.19	-
CPU (2 CORES)	7499.68	1.0095351
CPU (3 CORES)	7128.35	1.0621238
CPU (4 CORES)	7068.57	1.0711063
GPU	4750.57	1.5937435

ANALYZING THE SPEEDUP

The CNN models are tested on the basis of several parameters and several accuracy metrics, for testing the overall The tables 9, 10 and 11 show the speedup obtained by parallelization for fashion MNIST dataset while, tables 12, 13 and 14 show the speedup that is obtained after parallelization using RAY framework for handwritten numbers dataset. It can be seen that the speedup is always more than 1, thus instead

Table 12. Speedup obtained for handwritten numbers MNIST dataset with model 4

HANDWRITTEN NUMBERS MNIST: MODEL 1 (10 EPOCHS)		
CPU (CORES) / GPU	**TIME (s)**	**SPEEDUP**
CPU (1 CORE)	284.91	-
CPU (2 CORES)	281.59	1.0117902
CPU (3 CORES)	273.99	1.0398555
CPU (4 CORES)	263.82	1.0799409
GPU	240.22	1.1860378

Table 13. Speedup obtained for handwritten numbers MNIST dataset with model 2, AlexNet

HANDWRITTEN NUMBERS MNIST: ALEXNET (10 EPOCHS)		
CPU (CORES) / GPU	TIME (s)	SPEEDUP
CPU (1 CORE)	972.13	-
CPU (2 CORES)	969.42	1.0027955
CPU (3 CORES)	897.27	1.0834309
CPU (4 CORES)	857.46	1.1337322
GPU	508.08	1.9133404

of 10 epochs, for higher number of epochs, the speedup will result in lesser time. Apart from this, the CPU or GPU utilization will also be high, resulting in low idle time for CPU or GPU and maximum throughput which is desirable from any process.

The parallelization needs to be carried out properly so that the parallel overheads are minimum, and inter-process communication is also low, otherwise, the overheads can adversely affect the efficiency and accuracy of the code, by increasing the total time for execution.

CONCLUSION

After parallelizing the program, the observation obtained was that the engagement of the system with respect to time is strikingly less for the execution that is carried out with multiple CPU cores, compared to that of the one where only one core of CPU is used. Further, the time taken by GPU is the least as compared to that of the CPUs. It is also observed that in terms of accuracies, the execution with greater

Table 14. Speedup obtained for handwritten numbers MNIST dataset with model 3, VGG-19

HANDWRITTEN NUMBERS MNIST: VGG-19 (10 EPOCHS)		
CPU (CORES) / GPU	TIME (s)	SPEEDUP
CPU (1 CORE)	2003.31	-
CPU (2 CORES)	1990.07	1.006653
CPU (3 CORES)	1977.02	1.0132978
CPU (4 CORES)	1969.19	1.0173269
GPU	1312.89	1.525878

quantity of CPUs have resulted into higher accuracy values. For GPU, the accuracy is kind of the same as that of mean accuracy of all the CPUs, thus it can be inferred that parallelization does not reduce the accuracy of a model, but it helps a lot in reducing the time taken by them for execution. The engagement of CPU is higher and the idle time is less, thus the CPU utilization is higher for the concurrently executed programs. Hence, in the terms of performance metrics, the throughput is higher for the concurrently executed programs, which is always desirable.

At the same time, GPU reduces the time of execution noticeably, and the accuracy is also quite the same as that of CPUs. For a matter of fact, it is necessary to have parallelization of the programs in an optimal manner for resulting in better utilization of the CPU as well as the GPU and simultaneously maintain a decent accuracy of the overall work. Two different image classification programs have been used in order to uplift the benefits of concurrent execution of the program, for improving the overall performance of the system.

The work also analyzes the parallelization of CNN models in a distributed framework under three distinct architectures of CNN. However, there is a scope of comparing the same amongst all the available architectures of CNN. The hardware can be improvised in order to compare and analyze the efficiency of parallelization over different hardware configuration. Further the scope of application, that is used to compare the performance after parallelization, can be broadened further to other applications that are based on neural networks, or other machine learning algorithms.

REFERENCES

Abbas, A., Abdelsamea, M. M., & Gaber, M. M. (2020). *Classification of COVID-19 in chest X-ray images using DeTraC deep convolutional neural network.* arXiv preprint arXiv:2003.13815

Apostolopoulos, I. D., & Mpesiana, T. A. (2020). Covid-19: automatic detection from x-ray images utilizing transfer learning with convolutional neural networks. *Physical and Engineering Sciences in Medicine, 1.*

Blake, G., Dreslinski, R. G., & Mudge, T. (2009). A survey of multicore processors. *IEEE Signal Processing Magazine, 26*(6), 26–37. doi:10.1109/MSP.2009.934110

Datta, D., David, P., Mittal, D., & Jain, A. (2020b). Neural Machine Translation using Recurrent Neural Network. *International Journal of Engineering and Advanced Technology, 9*(4), 1395–1400. doi:10.35940/ijeat.D7637.049420

Datta, D., Mittal, D., Mathew, N. P., & Sairabanu, J. (2020a, February). Comparison of Performance of Parallel Computation of CPU Cores on CNN model. In *2020 International Conference on Emerging Trends in Information Technology and Engineering (ic-ETITE)* (pp. 1-8). IEEE.

Deng, L. (2012). The MNIST database of handwritten digit images for machine learning research. *IEEE Signal Processing Magazine, 29*(6), 141–142. doi:10.1109/MSP.2012.2211477

Dryden, N., Maruyama, N., Benson, T., Moon, T., Snir, M., & Van Essen, B. (2019, May). Improving strong-scaling of CNN training by exploiting finer-grained parallelism. In *2019 IEEE International Parallel and Distributed Processing Symposium (IPDPS)* (pp. 210-220). IEEE. 10.1109/IPDPS.2019.00031

Faes, L., Wagner, S. K., Fu, D. J., Liu, X., Korot, E., Ledsam, J. R., ... Moraes, G. (2019). Automated deep learning design for medical image classification by health-care professionals with no coding experience: A feasibility study. *The Lancet Digital Health, 1*(5), e232–e242. doi:10.1016/S2589-7500(19)30108-6

Feng, J., Chen, J., Liu, L., Cao, X., Zhang, X., Jiao, L., & Yu, T. (2019). Cnn-based multilayer spatial–spectral feature fusion and sample augmentation with local and nonlocal constraints for hyperspectral image classification. *IEEE Journal of Selected Topics in Applied Earth Observations and Remote Sensing, 12*(4), 1299–1313. doi:10.1109/JSTARS.2019.2900705

Ghoneim, S. (2020). *Accuracy, Recall, Precision, F-Score & Specificity, Which To Optimize On?* Medium. Available at: https://towardsdatascience.com/accuracy-recall-precision-f-score-specificity-which-to-optimize-on-867d3f11124

Grama, A. Y., Gupta, A., & Kumar, V. (1993). Isoefficiency: Measuring the scalability of parallel algorithms and architectures. *IEEE Parallel & Distributed Technology Systems & Applications, 1*(3), 12–21. doi:10.1109/88.242438

Guedria, S., De Palma, N., Renard, F., & Vuillerme, N. (2019, December). Auto-CNNp: a component-based framework for automating CNN parallelism. In *2019 IEEE International Conference on Big Data (Big Data)* (pp. 3330-3339). IEEE. 10.1109/BigData47090.2019.9006175

Hassanien, A. E., Mahdy, L. N., Ezzat, K. A., Elmousalami, H. H., & Ella, H. A. (2020). *Automatic x-ray covid-19 lung image classification system based on multi-level thresholding and support vector machine.* medRxiv.

Hill, M. D., & Marty, M. R. (2008). Amdahl's law in the multicore era. *Computer, 41*(7), 33–38. doi:10.1109/MC.2008.209

Hwang, K., & Faye, A. (1984). *Computer architecture and parallel processing.* Academic Press.

Inchingolo, F., & Stanfill, C. W. (2008). *U.S. Patent No. 7,467,383.* Washington, DC: U.S. Patent and Trademark Office.

Jeffers, J., & Reinders, J. (2015). *High performance parallelism pearls volume two: multicore and many-core programming approaches.* Morgan Kaufmann.

Jiménez, M., Torres, M. T., John, R., & Triguero, I. (2020). Galaxy Image Classification Based on Citizen Science Data: A Comparative Study. *IEEE Access: Practical Innovations, Open Solutions, 8,* 47232–47246. doi:10.1109/ACCESS.2020.2978804

Joshi, R. (2020). *Accuracy, Precision, Recall & F1 Score: Interpretation Of Performance Measures - Exsilio Blog.* Exsilio Blog. Available at: https://blog.exsilio.com/all/accuracy-precision-recall-f1-score-interpretation-of-performance-measures/

Karbowski, A. (2008). A*mdahl's and Gustafson-Barsis laws revisited.* arXiv preprint arXiv:0809.1177

Kumar, V. (2002). *Introduction to parallel computing.* Addison-Wesley Longman Publishing Co., Inc.

Kyrkou, C., & Theocharides, T. (2019, June). Deep-Learning-Based Aerial Image Classification for Emergency Response Applications Using Unmanned Aerial Vehicles. doi:10.1109/CVPRW.2019.00077

Lee, S., Agrawal, A., Balaprakash, P., Choudhary, A., & Liao, W. K. (2018, November). Communication-Efficient Parallelization Strategy for Deep Convolutional Neural Network Training. In *2018 IEEE/ACM Machine Learning in HPC Environments (MLHPC)* (pp. 47-56). IEEE.

Li, J., Zhang, L., Wu, Z., Ling, Z., Cao, X., Guo, K., & Yan, F. (2020). Autonomous Martian rock image classification based on transfer deep learning methods. *Earth Science Informatics,* 1–13.

Li, M., Tang, H., Chan, M. D., Zhou, X., & Qian, X. (2020). DC-AL GAN: Pseudoprogression and true tumor progression of glioblastoma multiform image classification based on DCGAN and AlexNet. *Medical Physics, 47*(3), 1139–1150. doi:10.1002/mp.14003 PMID:31885094

Liu, C. C., Zhang, Y. C., Chen, P. Y., Lai, C. C., Chen, Y. H., Cheng, J. H., & Ko, M. H. (2019). Clouds classification from sentinel-2 imagery with deep residual learning and semantic image segmentation. *Remote Sensing, 11*(2), 119. doi:10.3390/rs11020119

Liu, J., Wang, H., Wang, D., Gao, Y., & Li, Z. (2015, March). Parallelizing Convolutional Neural Networks on Intel $$^{\textregistered}$$ Many Integrated Core Architecture. In *International Conference on Architecture of Computing Systems* (pp. 71-82). Springer. 10.1007/978-3-319-16086-3_6

Mallick, P. K., Ryu, S. H., Satapathy, S. K., Mishra, S., Nguyen, G. N., & Tiwari, P. (2019). Brain MRI image classification for cancer detection using deep wavelet autoencoder-based deep neural network. *IEEE Access: Practical Innovations, Open Solutions*, *7*, 46278–46287. doi:10.1109/ACCESS.2019.2902252

Markall, G. R., Slemmer, A., Ham, D. A., Kelly, P. H. J., Cantwell, C. D., & Sherwin, S. J. (2013). Finite element assembly strategies on multi-core and many-core architectures. *International Journal for Numerical Methods in Fluids*, *71*(1), 80–97. doi:10.1002/fld.3648

Marwa, C., Haythem, B., Ezahra, S. F., & Mohamed, A. (2014). Image processing application on graphics processors. *International Journal of Image Processing*, *8*(3), 66.

Moritz, P., Nishihara, R., Wang, S., Tumanov, A., Liaw, R., Liang, E., . . . Stoica, I. (2018). Ray: A distributed framework for emerging {AI} applications. In *13th {USENIX} Symposium on Operating Systems Design and Implementation ({OSDI} 18)* (pp. 561-577). Academic Press.

Narkhede, S. (2020). *Understanding AUC - ROC Curve*. Medium. Available at: https://towardsdatascience.com/understanding-auc-roc-curve-68b2303cc9c5

Nunes, R., & Almeida, J. A. (2010). Parallelization of sequential Gaussian, indicator and direct simulation algorithms. *Computers & Geosciences*, *36*(8), 1042–1052. doi:10.1016/j.cageo.2010.03.005

O'Shea, K., & Nash, R. (2015). *An introduction to convolutional neural networks*. arXiv preprint arXiv:1511.08458

Perez, L., & Wang, J. (2017). *The effectiveness of data augmentation in image classification using deep learning*. arXiv preprint arXiv:1712.04621

Rasti, P., Ahmad, A., Samiei, S., Belin, E., & Rousseau, D. (2019). Supervised image classification by scattering transform with application to weed detection in culture crops of high density. *Remote Sensing*, *11*(3), 249. doi:10.3390/rs11030249

Reddy, B. M., & Shanthala, S. (2017). *Performance Analysis of GPU V/S CPU for Image Processing Applications*. Issue II. *International Journal for Research in Applied Science and Engineering Technology*, *5*(II), 437–443. doi:10.22214/ijraset.2017.2061

Saxena, S., Sharma, S., & Sharma, N. (2017). Study of Parallel Image Processing with the Implementation of vHGW Algorithm using CUDA on NVIDIA'S GPU Framework. In *Proceedings of the World Congress on Engineering (Vol. 1)*. Academic Press.

Simon, H. D. (1991). Partitioning of unstructured problems for parallel processing. *Computing Systems in Engineering*, *2*(2-3), 135–148. doi:10.1016/0956-0521(91)90014-V

Skalski, P. (2020). *Gentle Dive Into Math Behind Convolutional Neural Networks*. Medium. Available at: https://towardsdatascience.com/gentle-dive-into-math-behind-convolutional-neural-networks-79a07dd44cf9

Stone, H. S. (1971). Parallel processing with the perfect shuffle. *IEEE Transactions on Computers*, *100*(2), 153–161. doi:10.1109/T-C.1971.223205

Sun, X. H., & Chen, Y. (2010). Reevaluating Amdahl's law in the multicore era. *Journal of Parallel and Distributed Computing*, *70*(2), 183–188. doi:10.1016/j.jpdc.2009.05.002

Syberfeldt, A., & Ekblom, T. (2017). A comparative evaluation of the GPU vs. the CPU for parallelization of evolutionary algorithms through multiple independent runs. *International Journal of Computer Science & Information Technology*, *9*(3), 1–14. doi:10.5121/ijcsit.2017.9301

Too, E. C., Yujian, L., Njuki, S., & Yingchun, L. (2019). A comparative study of fine-tuning deep learning models for plant disease identification. *Computers and Electronics in Agriculture*, *161*, 272–279. doi:10.1016/j.compag.2018.03.032

Wang, J., Yang, Y., Mao, J., Huang, Z., Huang, C., & Xu, W. (2016). Cnn-rnn: A unified framework for multi-label image classification. In *Proceedings of the IEEE conference on computer vision and pattern recognition* (pp. 2285-2294). 10.1109/CVPR.2016.251

Yang, A., Yang, X., Wu, W., Liu, H., & Zhuansun, Y. (2019). Research on feature extraction of tumor image based on convolutional neural network. *IEEE Access: Practical Innovations, Open Solutions*, *7*, 24204–24213. doi:10.1109/ACCESS.2019.2897131

Zhai, Y., Danandeh, N., Tan, Z., Gao, S., Paesani, F., & Götz, A. W. (2018). *Parallel implementation of machine learning-based many-body potentials on CPU and GPU.* Academic Press.

Zhang, Y., Chen, H., Wei, Y., Zhao, P., Cao, J., Fan, X., ... Yao, J. (2019, October). From whole slide imaging to microscopy: Deep microscopy adaptation network for histopathology cancer image classification. In *International Conference on Medical Image Computing and Computer-Assisted Intervention* (pp. 360-368). Springer. 10.1007/978-3-030-32239-7_40

Zhou, J., Chen, W., Peng, G., Xiao, H., Wang, H., & Chen, Z. (2017, December). Parallelizing convolutional neural network for the handwriting recognition problems with different architectures. In *2017 International Conference on Progress in Informatics and Computing (PIC)* (pp. 71-76). IEEE. 10.1109/PIC.2017.8359517

Zhuravlev, S., Blagodurov, S., & Fedorova, A. (2010, March). Addressing shared resource contention in multicore processors via scheduling. *ACM SIGPLAN Notices, 45*(3), 129–142. doi:10.1145/1735971.1736036

Chapter 17
Enhancement of Toll Plaza System With Smart Features

Sagar Gupta
Vellore Institute of Technology, Vellore, India

Garima Mathur
Vellore Institute of Technology, Vellore, India

S. Purushotham
Vellore Institute of Technology, Vellore, India

Venkatesan R
M.I.E.T. Engineering College

ABSTRACT

This chapter aims to solve the problem of heavy traffic caused due to a long queue near the toll plaza. The authors design the website with the motive that it will save the maximum time of the public, reducing the problem of heavy traffic. Moreover, the website maintains the entire database containing the details of the staff, pass, receipts, vehicle details, etc., which will reduce any problem in the future. Since they are also aware of the fact that in many villages in India, there are not even proper toll booths to pay taxes, and people are doing it manually, which can result in data loss and even is time-consuming. So, keeping this mind, they aim to design the website that is simple to use such that every people working in toll booth can get habituated to it easily. They also aim to make this website fully secure such that data can be protected and citizens are comfortable providing their details to create their pass and generate receipts. The main feature is that users can also generate receipt for themselves from anywhere through website to avoid waste of time at toll.

DOI: 10.4018/978-1-7998-3335-2.ch017

INTRODUCTION

Toll booth system is available for use of both the administration, staff and the users. The administrator, staffs and users will be able to access the frontend of the webpage. The program experiences http server and the Application server deals with the association between the front end and backend. A wide range of data and information that are vital for the clients are put in database server. This system provides all the information about toll plaza. How the passenger checks in, pays the amount and how they will be provided by a receipt. With this receipt he/she can leave the toll booth without waiting for any verification. It also covers registration of staff, toll plaza collection for vehicles, date wise report entry, Vehicles entry and passing reports date wise.

It has three modules Admin, Staff and User. The system will consist an administrator login. The system will store user information like name, car number and with its details and address, administrator information like email address, password and the toll plaza that comes under the employee. The user will be able to get a receipt for them from anywhere through the website. The administrator will be able to view the transaction that occurred during the day with the transaction details and the total money collected during the day. The car will only be allowed to pass if the toll is paid through the system. The information will be stored in the data base after each transaction. The user can only view his/her own transactions details. All day-wise transactions will be displayed to the administrator.

Administrator will be able to set and update the charges of the vehicle categories. On each successful payment at the toll or at the website user will be provided by the receipt. Website will have facility to retrieve forgot password. This application is to motivate the user, staffs and the administrator to be more digitalized. System will help admin to get the statistical data for the sales on daily or monthly or quarterly or annually basis.

Survey

The main objective for the survey is to be well aware about the types of systems which are currently used for the toll plaza. Or the system which were existing, which are currently being used and also which are under development. As we are going to implement the system, we must be well aware that we should are not create something which already exists. So, to assure that we have gone through lot of research papers, found about all the existing systems and have also used the information which can help us in the implementation of the proposed system.

The paper (Fathima et al., 2018) implements the payment of the toll amount through android application. The user will be notified when he/she will be 1-2km from the toll about the upcoming toll name and toll distance. The notification process is done by using GPS. Payment can be facilitated through online gateway. A receipt is generated with the QR code which can be shown in toll to pass. A list of all the toll plaza and toll tariffs is available in the application. Hence, the wastage of time and fuel because of the large traffic jams can be solved by implementing this system which is extremely user friendly. As there are lot of mobile OS so user have to make the app for all, also this doesn't talk about staff and user. So, instead we decided to do website which can be used from all medium.

The paper (Galande, 2015) presents the concept of an Automated Electronic Toll collection (ETC) using the GPS, which is designed for an uninterrupted toll collection, an important part of an intelligent transportation system. Exchange of data information between the motorists and toll authorities can be more efficient as it eliminates the chances of human error.

The analysis of some of the current RFID toll collection systems and their practicality, has been discussed in the paper (Manjunath, 2019) all systems have tried to reduce the traffic overheads that occur at the toll plaza. It has also tried to optimize the current systems by providing some benefits to both toll authorities and facility users, in terms of time and cost-saving, improved security, and high capacity. IoT Toll Collection systems are aimed at automating the toll plazas to ensure efficient transactions during toll collections. The paper (Khan et al., 2009) helps us to better understand the RFID model, the hardware model which is implemented, this optimize the wastage of time at the toll. RFID is used as vehicle nears the toll the sensor at the toll detects the RFID card on it and deducts the money automatically from the wallet.

RFID is again used in (Mithya et al., 2019) with some upgradation over the past systems. Main focus is to collect the toll online so that time standing at toll can be reduced. The system proposed in the paper is to make a license place automated. In the proposed system, raspberry pi is used with the webcam to scan all the vehicles passing through toll. Image of the plate will be captured then image processing techniques will be used to process the image and then sent to Regional Transport Office server to get the details about the user matching with the same details. The GSM module will be using the information retrieved from R.T.O. about the image and then the toll amount will be automatically deducted from the user's account. If the amount is deducted accurately the gate will open and the vehicle is permitted to leave the tollgate. If not, the gate will stay shut.

After going through different papers, we came to know there exists a lot of systems with the hardware models to optimize the wait time at toll, but none of them had focused how can we optimize and make user friendly system through software point of view. Making system much more digitalized so that user and admin can have much more interaction with the system, everyone can use at a glance. So, to overcome all these drawbacks from the existing model we are Implementing this system.

Objectives:

The objective is to:-

1.   Develop an online system for reducing the congestion rate, fuel wastage, pollutions and man power at the toll plaza.
2.   Make the system user friendly to use.
3.   Provide toll statistics.
4.   Improve work speed and accuracy.
5.   To get instant detailed information at a terminal.
6.   Help in effective record storing and retrieving of data.
7.   To avoid fraud toll collection of money in the name of toll taxes in some areas.
8.   No paper work requirement.
9.   Reduces the scope of error.
10.   System is automated.
11.   Database management is centralized.
12.   Easy usages of the system for users.

METHODOLOGY

Related System

The Existing models are only defined for staff and admin module, with that to with limited features. Lot of model have been existing with hardware component such as RFID and GSM. There is existing model where receipt can be generated but that can only be generated by the staff at the toll booth and admin can look to the sales but not in monthly or within a given range.

Proposed System

As you have seen the early models, now we are going to implement the model which will be having user module and extra features for the staff and admin module. User can generate the receipt from anywhere through website they can generate it from the home or just a km before the toll, to avoid waiting time and extra fuel burn at toll. User just need to open the website enter the details and pay the toll amount and then receipt will be generated which can be used to pass through the toll. We are also adding the features to staff module which will make their work more digitally like applying for the leave from their login which will be latter on approved by admin. Staff can update their ban account details under profile menu which will be used to process the salary of the staff directly to the account. Admin will be able to see all the receipt generated from the website weather it is generated by staff or by the user and also the detailed analysis of the sales. Admin, staff and user all can search or view receipt by the receipt id, name or by the vehicle number. The proposed system is to make everything easier and more digitalize.

Structure for the Proposed System

It has three modules admin, staff and user.

Admin

Dashboard: Admin can see the details like total number of staffs, Total number of vehicle category, Total number of pass, Total number of receipt, Total vehicle enter today's, yesterday's, last seven days and total vehicle pass till now in toll plaza.

1. **Staff:** Admin can add and update staffs.
2. **Vehicle Category:** Admin can add and update vehicle category.
3. **Pass:** Staff can add and manage pass.
4. **Receipt:** Admin can view receipt and take print of receipt which is make by staffs
5. **Search Pass:** In this section admin can search pass with the help of his/her pass id, owner name and vehicle number.
6. **Search Receipt:** In this section admin can search receipt with the help of his/her receipt id, owner name and vehicle number.
7. **Reports of Pass:** In this section admin can view how many pass has been made in particular periods, counts of pass and sales come from making pass.
8. **Reports of Receipt:** In this section admin can view how much receipt has been made in particular periods, counts of receipt and sales come from making receipt.
9. **Leave Request:** Whenever some staff request for leave that can be seen here and can be approved also.

Admin can also update his profile, change password and recover password.

Staffs

1. **Dashboard:** Welcome page for staff.
2. **Receipt:** Staff can add and manage receipts.
3. **Search:** Staffs can search receipt with the help of receipt id.
4. **Apply leave:** Apply for leave.
5. **Update Bank Details:** For receiving the salary in the account.

Staffs can also update his profile, change password and recover password.

User

1. **Dashboard:** Welcome page.
2. **Receipt:** In this section user can generate receipt.
3. **Search:** In this section admin can search receipt with the help of his/her receipt id

REQUIREMENTS

Safety Requirements

1. Hazard analysis and other system safety analysis must be held regularly to avoid software glitches, catastrophic hazards, critical hazards etc.
2. The information in the database must be backed up in case the server crashes.
3. Provide process and product development, process evidence validating software and technical integrity.
4. This implementation is portable. So that migrating between the OS's while using the system doesn't affect much.
5. A system should be proficient to deal with many staffs and users with its proper functioning.

Security Requirements

1. Staffs should change their password provided by the admin after they login to the system. Also, the first password ought to never be reused.
2. Privacy of data, licensed innovation rights, and so on ought to be examined.
3. Every unsuccessful attempt by a client to login, view balance or adding money must be reported to an audit trial and must be immediately looked into and worked upon to be fixed.
4. Each user must undergo a verification process if they login from a different device.

5.   The user must change password after three consecutive unsuccessful login attempts. Such an event must be reported. The user must not use any previously used password.

6.   The user must not contain their first name, last name, initials or birthdate as a part of their passwords.

Development Methods

This chapter is based on the RDBMS technology. The main objective of this chapter is to computerize the manual system & reduce the time consumption.

A major purpose of a database system is to provide users with an abstract view of the data. This system hides certain details of how the data is stored and maintained. However in order for the system to be usable, data must be retrieved efficiently. The efficiency lead to the design of complex data structure for the representation of data in the database. Certain complexity must be hidden from the database system users. This accomplished by defining several levels of abstraction at which the database may be viewed.

Architectural Strategies

This system is to encourage the department in keeping up the report about the tax gathered at a particular timespan.

To give insights concerning about the one owing the Toll booth.

To give Toll Tax Rates to various sort of vehicles.

HTA (Hierarchical Task Analysis)

The figure 1 describes about the task and subtasks which will be performed in the proposed system, this is the analysis for the task to pass the toll gate. To pass through the toll gate the one must have the receipt it can be e-receipt or the receipt generated at toll. There are two ways to get the receipt the first one is it can be generated through the website or it can be generated by the person sitting at the toll. If you opt to get receipt from the toll then you need to tell the information about vehicle to toll person then he will ask you to pay the amount which can be done online or cash, on the successful payment staff will generate the receipt. But if this is not the case and user want to generate the receipt online then they can visit the website fill the information and pay the amount online, an e-receipt will be generated which when shown in the toll will allow you to pass the toll.

Interactive Design

Figure 1. HTA for passing the toll gate

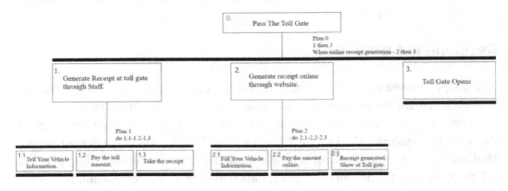

Stakeholder Identification

Any user affected by the failure or success of the system is called stakeholder. Stakeholders can be categorized into 4 categories:

- Primary Stakeholder (People who actually use this system) Staff members, a common man, Employees, Admin.
- Secondary Stakeholder (People who provide input or receive output) – Dataset providers, Developers.
- Tertiary Stakeholder (No direct involvement but affected by the system) – 2 wheeler vehicles and Government Vehicles as they don't have to pay the toll, but still have to wait sometime in the queue.
- Pacilitating (People who help developing the system) – Sagar Gupta and Garima Mathur.

Block Diagram for the System

To have better understanding on the proposed system we have figure 2, The block diagram for the proposed system. Which is an outline of the system with all the components present in it. As it can be clearly seen in the figure 2 that out system has three module and then under each module there are different components.

Figure 2. Block Diagram for proposed system

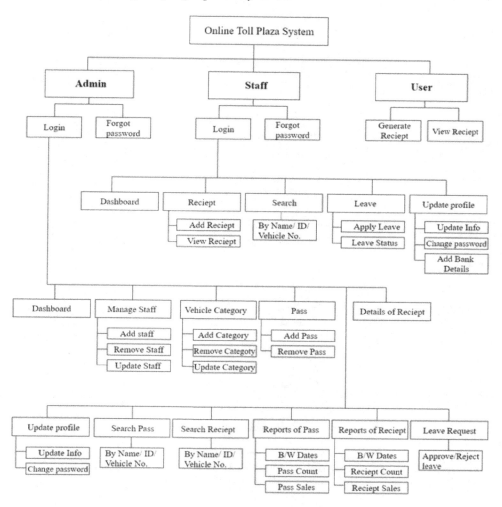

Use Case Diagram

To get the outside view of the system or to identify the external and the internal factors influencing the system. The Usecase diagram plays a role, the figure 3 depicts the use case diagram for the proposed system. In this figure we can clearly see the actors and their interaction with requirements.

Figure 3. Use Case diagram for proposed system

Test Plan

Table 1 describes about the testing done for the website login page, which is the must phase for any development. As when we get the testing results, we get to know the how well the system is performing. The testing is done keeping all the aspects in the mind, and is compared to expected result. If this phase is passed then only we can say that our system is fit for deployment. The testing is done by navigating to the login page then providing the required information as email id, password

Table 1. Login page testing

Test Case ID	001		
Priority	Medium		
Description	Verifying valid login id and password		
Module	Toll login screen		
Prepared By	Sagar	Date Prepared	04-09-2020
Reviewed / Updated	XYZ	Date Reviewed	05-09-2020
Tested By	ABC	Date Tested	06-09-2020
Test Activities			
Sl. No.	Step Description	Expected Results	Actual Results
1	Navigate to Login page	Should be able to see the login page	passed
2	Enter a valid e-mail id	Should be able to enter the credential	passed
3	Enter a valid Pass	Should be able to enter the credential	passed
4	Tap Login	Successful login	passed
Test Data Sets			
Data Types	Data 1	Data 2	Data 3
E-mail	test@gmail.com	abcd@gmail.com	admin@gmail.com
Password	Test@123	Abcd@123	Admin@123
Test Case Result	Pass		

and then clicking on the login button. If user is logged then we say that our system has passed the test. The same was done with different credentials, and we find that system has passed the test.

The information about the security testing is mentioned in Table2, we are taking different data set and then testing for the system security. How secure our system is by adding the staff details we are checking that; In the first case we are taking email id and a weak password if the system allows to create the user then system user aren't that much secured. The same we tried for the system and we have also tried with any random password and our system allowed to create the user.

Implementation of the System

The figure above is the screenshot of the implemented system, where staff can fill the credentials and login if in the case, they have forgot their password then they can click on forgot password.

Table 2. Adding new staff testing

Test Case ID		002		
Priority		Medium		
Description		Add New Staff		
Module		Admin Add Staff Screen		
Prepared By	Sagar	Date Prepared		04-09-2020
Reviewed / Updated	qwerty	Date Reviewed		05-09-2020
Tested By	ABC	Date Tested		06-09-2020
Test Activities				
S. No.	Step Description	Expected Results		Actual Results
1	Enter any email id and password with less than 8 letters and hit register button	Password is too weak please enter a complex one		failed
2	Enter valid e-mail and password and hit Register button	User Registered Successfully		passed
Test Data Sets				
Data Types	Data 1	Data 2		Data 3
E-mail	xyz1@gmail.com	xyz2@gmail.com		xyz3@gmail.com
Pass	12345	User123		Testuse123
Test Case Result		Pass		

Figure 4. Staff login page

The admin login window for the system is shown in figure 5, here admin can enter their details and get the access for the system.

Figure 5. Administrator login page

As we know system consists of staff module, when staff enter the correct credentials in the login page they are brought to staff dashboard shown in figure 6.

Figure 6. Staff dashboard

The figure 7 shows the administrator dashboard page. In dashboard admin can see the stats of toll at the glance, and can migrate to any section in the sidebar.

Figure 7. Administrator dashboard

Adding staff in the toll can only be done by the administrator, the same is shown in the figure 8. Administrator will fill the details of staff and add, latter on that details can be used to login into the system by staff.

Figure 8. Administrator add staff page

Figure 9. Add Receipt

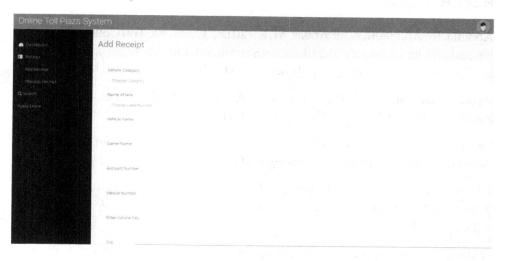

The adding receipt is the main focus of our system, the above shown figure is for generating the receipt. This will be same for staff and user, both of them can add the details and get their receipt.

CONCLUSION

Along with growing number of vehicles in major cities, Toll plaza is an option for smooth transportation. Manual toll plazas are widely used for toll fee collection in India. Manual system requires lot of paperwork and are also prone to errors. Due to manual collection, the processing time at toll plaza is very high. Manual collection causes congestion at Toll Plazas especially during festival season which leads to fuel wastage and pollution. To overcome these issues, we introduce an online system to pay toll fee. This will help to reduce the traffic at toll plaza and will also help to save time, fuel resources and reduce pollution which a major topic of concern these days. This system provides all the information about toll plaza. How the passenger checks in, pays the amount and how they will be provided by a receipt. When they are done with the payment process the receipt allotted to them can be used to leave the toll at any moment. It also covers registration of staff, toll booth collection for vehicles, report entry date wise, Vehicles entry and passing reports date wise. To make the process easy we have also given option where user can itself generate the receipt. As we have performed the testing for the website and we have found that it is having more than 95% of accuracy in terms of login, adding user and generating the receipt.

REFERENCES

Abdulla, R., Abdillahi, A., & Abbas, M. K. (2018). Electronic Toll Collection System based on Radio Frequency Identification System. *International Journal of Electrical and Computer Engineering, 8*(3), 1602-1610. Doi:10.11591/ijece.v8i3.pp1602-1610

Ayoub Khan, Manoj, & Prahbu. (2009). A Survey of RFID Tags. *International Journal of Recent Trends in Engineering, 1*(4).

Fathima, Jayamala, & Keerthika. (2018). Online Toll Payment System. *International Journal of Innovations in Engineering and Technology.*

Galande, S.D. (2015). Automated Toll Cash Collection System for Road Transportation. *International Journal of Computer Science and Mobile Computing, 4*(2), 216-224.

Kadam, Waghmare, Adhalkar, Sirsat, & Patil. (2017). A Survey on Toll Collection System Using Different Method. *IJSRTE.*

Kanthi, K., & Dontabhaktuni, J. (2013). Electronic Toll Collection System For Billing Using Wireless Communication. *IJAERS, 1*(5), 5-7.

Khali, P., Michael, C. W., & Shahriyar, H. (2007). *Toll Collection Technology and Best Practices.* Project 0-5217: Vehicle/License Plate Identification for Toll Collection Application.

Lee, Tseng, & Wang. (2008). *Design and implement of electronic toll collection system based on vehicle positioning system techniques.* Academic Press.

Mithya, V., Dharani, K. V., Nivetha, A., Praveen Rajakumari, G., & Roshel Infan, M. (2019). Smart Highway Toll Collection System. *International Journal of Innovative Technology and Exploring Engineering, 8*(5S).

National Transportation Safety Board (NTSB). (n.d.). http://www.ntsb.gov/

Omarhommadi & Mamdoohalzahrani. (n.d.). Comparison of Different toll collections system's and RFID tool collection system. *American Journal of Engineering Research, 6*(1), 118-121.

Singh. (2019). *Reduction of traffic at toll plaza by automatic toll collection using RFID and GSM technology.* doi:10.21276/ijcesr.2019.6.6.32

Chapter 18
Intelligent Driving Using Cognitive Science

Ranjani Arsu Mudaliar
Vellore Institute of Technology, Vellore, India

Sonal Sanjay Rajurkar
Vellore Institute of Technology, Vellore, India

Mythili Thirugnanam
Vellore Institute of Technology, Vellore, India

ABSTRACT

Due to negligence by drivers, there might be large number of road accidents. In order to overcome this current issue, various methodologies were used to combine the artificial intelligence theory and road traffic control system. In addition to that, researches were performed regarding driving behaviours which include intelligent driving and artificial driving. These two behaviours were based on cognitive science and as well as simulation. Cognitive science is scientific study of the mind and its processes. In the current research papers, autonomous driving system was implemented but had some drawbacks while overtaking. Therefore, this work aims to modify and implement an intelligent driving system to help the drivers and lower the accident rates.

DOI: 10.4018/978-1-7998-3335-2.ch018

INTRODUCTION

According to the current world everything should be done through machine no manual interaction should be there. To move from one place to another people use vehicles and so human thought why not machine only takes us to the destination without driving so, the self- driving vehicles came into picture. The human just has to give the instruction that he/she has to reach this destination and the vehicle will drive itself and will reach that destination.

The machine has to drive, make-decisions, decide the shortest path to the destination, make instant decisions while driving and much more knowledge is required while driving. These all can be done with some software, hardware, algorithms and many Machine learning methods.

While researching the papers we came across the issue like the vehicles were unable to move towards the original path after overtaking. Along with that it also had a problem of not working in complex environment. To overcome the traffic and accident problems as mentioned can be solved through Artificial and Intelligent driving. Artificial driving is the interaction between the driver and vehicle. Driver has knowledge about the surrounding using visual and auditory senses. The inbuilt software in the vehicle adjusts the direction, speed and plans the overtaking accordingly. Intelligent driving relies only on the in-vehicle intelligent devices with computer system. It uses sensors such as laser, radar etc to perceive the environment around the vehicle. According to the sensors the vehicle controls the steering speed and plans according to the environment. For simulation MATLAB software is used for designing vehicle dynamics model. To visualize this, scene simulation is done in three parts.

LITERATURE SURVEY

GAP ANALYSIS

Theoretically intelligent driving system seems to be similar to artificial driving system. But practically, during overtaking intelligent vehicle say A slows down, perceives environment, makes decisions accordingly and accelerate to overtake, then decreases to normal speed but fails to return to its original lane. This is not the case in artificial driving as there is presence of driver in the system.

Another important problem will be that while driving the automated system even there can be some issues like it cannot identify the objects by mistake, this will

Table 1.

Author & Year	Title	Observation/Technique/Methodology	Limitation & Future work
Mikhail B et al, 2019	Orientation a of the driverless car at a loss of aa satellite a signal	There are different alternative approaches for this first is creating the 3-D map of environment for navigating for this 3-D Euclidian space was used for finding the exact location. The implementation was done in C++ and Visual Studio 2010 (Mikhail et al., 2019)	To make useful not only in the android devices but also in all most all devices.
Kanwaldeep K et al, 2018	Trust in a driverless car: Investigating key factors influencing a the adoption of driverless cars	This paper draws the attention towards the key factors that influence the adoption of driverless cars.(Kaur & Rampersad, 2018)	To find hackers that are intervening during location tracking.
Naujoks F et al, 2018	From partial a and high automation to a manual driving	In this automated driving system drivers are allowed to take their smart phones where they read or browse some social media till that time they might reach their destination.(Naujoks et al., 2018)	To overcome the partial automation into fully automated.
Hebbar A, 2017	Augmented Intelligence Enhancing Human Capabilities	In this sensors are used to capture the surrounding environment and simulation is carried out according to the required output. In this the experiment was carried out on VIPC's(Visual information processing characteristics). (Gao et al., 2011)	So to make the design that can have a better arrangement.
Ching C, 2017	Advancement, prospects and impacts of automated, a driving systems	This paper starts with the review of the start-of-the-art in the field of automated driving system and its deployment path.(Chan, 2017)	To overcome the drawback and improve the system using cognitive study.
Braunagel C, 2017	A New a Driver a Assistance System for a an Automated Classification a of Driver a Take-Over a Readiness	This paper introduces advanced driver assistance system which classifies the driver's readiness to takeover in scenarios like automated driving. The results shows that they combined the linear SVM with a feature selection step (Braunagel et al., 2017)	To achieve the better accuracy new method can be adopted.
Zhang X et al, 2016	A study a on a key techno-logies Of unmanned a driving	In this paper the authors tried to implement the driverless concept using sensors and studying the cognitive behaviour of the human even many fields like automatic control, ground mapping, sensor technology and some other fields.(Zhang et al., 2016)	Future scope of this was to overcome this and also develop unmanned sports car.
Schömiga N, et. Al, 2015	The interaction a between highlya automated a driving and a the development of drowsiness	In this paper there was an interaction shown between automated driving and the drowsiness level. The factor drowsiness was assessed constantly during the drive using eye lid closure measurements. It was classified into 4 different levels.(Schömig et al., 2015)	To increase the test time so that the drowsiness level increases to check that the sensors work.
Luzheng B et al, 2015	Development a of a Driver Lateral Control Model by Integrating a Neuromuscular Dynamics into the a Queuing Network-Based a Driver a Model	This paper describes about the control of steering wheel over the driver. It is QN based driver control model. The interaction between the automated steering system and driver neuromuscular system (Bi et al., 2015)	To adapt new method to overcome the problem using the cognitive science.
Chen R et al,2015	Driver Behaviour During Overtaking a Maneuvers a from the a 100-Car Naturalistic Driving a Study	In this paper related to the lane change after overtaking the other vehicle. Due to this there may be one problem i.e. Forward collision warning(FCW) designs. (Chen et al., 2015)	This study will improve the overall FCW systems by providing active safety system.
Gao X et al, 2015	Research on Intelligent Driving Behaviour a Based on Cognitive a Science and a Scene Simulation	This is the base paper that contains research on the Intelligent driving behaviour using the concept of cognitive science and scene simulation. (Gao, n.d.)	But further improvement needs to be performed. This improvement can be done with some ML techniques.
Fernandes C et al, 2016	Development a of a convenient wireless control of an autonomous a vehicle using Apple a iOS a SDK	The main aim of the paper is to present a convenient method for wireless control of a car using iPhone. It used Black Widow 1.0 microcontroller for this purpose and the software used was written on iOS SDK platform. They also used 802.11b Wi-Fi standard for the experiments purpose. (Fernandes et al., 2011)	Their future scope is to enable a close loop control of the system in opposition to the current open loop implementation.

continued on following page

Table 1. Continued

Author & Year	Title	Observation/Technique/Methodology	Limitation & Future work
Wang M et al,2015	iDriver – Human Machine Interface for Autonomous Cars	This paper describes an iPad software which was developed to navigate and remote-control autonomous cars, to give access to live sensor data and useful data about the car state, as there are, e.g., current speed of the engine and gear state. **(Reuschenbach et al., 2011)**	We can make the software flexible to use in all platforms.
Urmson C et al, 2009	Autonomous a Driving a in Urban a Environments: Boss and a the Urban Challenge	Boss here is automated driving system. The automated driving is based on sensors such as cameras, GPS, radar. In this there is a three layer system i.e. mission, behavioural and motion planning for driving in urban environments. First layer is to find which street is the destination. **(Urmson et al., 2008)**	To overcome this problem, can use different approaches.
Desmond P,et.al,	Fatigue and Automation-Induced a Impairments a in SimulatedaDrivinga	This paper basically compares between two conditions of driving which includes manual driving and the automated driving. These conditions were performed under fatiguing driving conditions.**(Desmond et al., 1998)**	To overcome the failure, drivers were forced to control the vehicle manually.

be a major problem because this may cause many accidents while the automated system is in the motion. To identify the objects there can be some vibrations from the objects that can be sensed and the vehicle will try to stop or divert its position.

The limitation in the current system is that it is only applicable in ideal conditions and it can mislead in the complex environments. So, through our research we will try to break this gap and overcome the issue. More work will be done on Intelligent behaviour of driving so that the limitation can be resolved.

DATASET

No particular dataset is used because mainly here stimulation is done in MATLAB where the vehicle is being modelled and stimulated to check in trial and error based.

Figure 1. Architecture of Intelligent driving systems

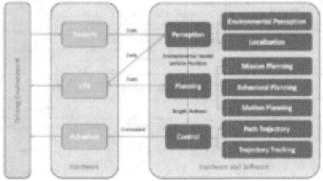

PROPOSED ARCHITECTURE

Architecture that can be followed to achieve the motion of the vehicle by its own using its sensors. Architecture will give the overall idea about the motion of the vehicle, its sensors and the ability to sense like the humans while driving.

Many Hardware related things are involved in this kind of approach like different sensors to sense the vehicles.

As shown in the above figure to build an autonomous driving system hardware and software systems are required, the above shown hardware systems are mostly known to us as sensors, actuators and some vehicle to vehicle connection.

Figure 2. Overview of the approach

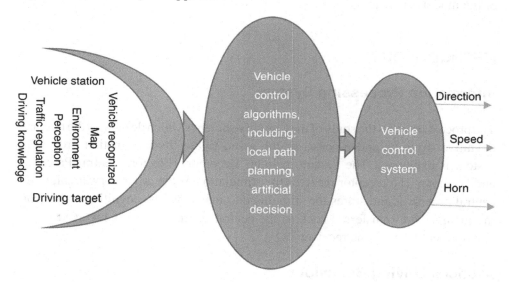

Sensors will try to sense the objects nearby and also will help to drive the vehicle; actuators will give the output accordingly what it senses i.e. if the vehicle sense any object nearby as obstacle it will give the action of stop using its actuators.

The vehicle will try to percept all the data and it has to plan according to the situations so it has to learn from the experience and has to take some times the instant decisions while driving. The vehicle also has to control all the actions that it has to perform. To do all those work by the machine itself it has to be well trained and also have to feed many data which will help to make some decisions using the previous experiences and has to think instantly. This approach is the reinforcement learning which is one of the terms in Machine learning.

These all techniques are required to do the behavioural planning, path trajectory, mission planning, it also has to environmental perception, the machine just have to mimic the human tendency of driving any vehicle.

The vehicle be programmed in such a manner that it can do all the above works with its own without the human interference. The algorithms used for planning for path, any decision-making algorithms also should give the best or average result.

The algorithm for finding the shortest path for the destination allocated should be able to find using the best approaches made by the system using the algorithm.

The architecture proposed will give an overall idea about the system how it should work and how it should be managed when applied in real so that if any situation rises where we are not able to understand then the model or the architecture will help us to find a way for the problem. Thus, architecture for every new technology or the model it is required.

METHODOLOGY

Information Processing System

The process involves the study of the Cognitive Science which deals with the human's cognitive structure and process. In the given figure the information processing system is explained. The system includes Receptor, Effector, Central Processor and Memory. The receptor receives the stimulation as the input, forwards it to the central processor and stores the stimulus into memory. The cognitive codes from the memory are transferred back to the central processor and is received by the environment through the receiver.

Artificial Driving Behaviour

There is an interaction between driver and vehicle in artificial driving model. The driver can use sensors to perceive the environment. The Artificial Driving behaviour can be incorporated into Information driving system using the below workflow. The receptors perceive the driving environment with the help of visual sensory organs. This perceived information is transferred to the Central processing unit which acts as a brain. The system acts to the environment by identifying the incoming information and takes some decision with the help of Memory. In return the appropriate decisions are provided as output through effectors.

INTELLIGENT DRIVING BEHAVIOUR

As in artificial driving system, driver was involved in the process which is not the case in intelligent driving system. In this, system is fully automated without the interaction of the driver. It perceives the environment using the sensors, odometer etc. The workflow can be explained as follows: The information is perceived through the sensors and is forwarded to electronic control unit. In this ECU some processing is performed and the appropriate decisions are taken with the help of memory. The output is acquired by the environment through the controller.

IMPLEMENTATION

In this model has to be created and stimulated in MATLAB for easier view and testing purpose. In this actually no dataset is used as just we are stimulating the model of car and for testing like is the model able to make decisions, reaches the destination or meets with an accident or not or able to manage the situations or not.

MATLAB helps to see the virtual image of the model of the self-driving car.

RESULTS

Artificial Driving Behaviour

For the simulation system we used the latitudinal distance as one of the parameters. The latitudinal distance is computed as the distance between the centre line of the test vehicle and that of two-way four lane road. For this instance, the width was considered as 15 m for the two-way four lane road.

While overtaking, the velocity of the vehicle reduces and then after overtaking velocity increases. While overtaking the latitudinal distance lowered to 1.5 m and the distance increased up to 5.5 m while returning to the original lane.

INTELLIGENT DRIVING BEHAVIOUR

In Intelligent Driving System, vehicle A gets the information about the forward moving object and it took some time for taking decisions. This time is also known as reacting time which is necessary for taking some decision as humans.

The vehicle overtakes it tries to speed up first and falls to the original speed after crossing the vehicle. The latitudinal distance earlier was 5.5m that decreased to 2m in order to perform overtaking.

CONCLUSION

We compared the accuracy of both the driving behaviours that is artificial driving and intelligent driving. As artificial driving systems includes human interaction, it can perceive the forward moving object easily and accurately. But in intelligent driving system there is no interaction and it has autonomous driving capacities. As a result, it takes some time in taking decisions and this might cause traffic problems. So intelligent driving system seems to be less accurate.

FUTURE WORK

To increase the accuracy of intelligent driving system and overcome its issue, further studies will be carried out. It will include reducing of delay time which is termed as reacting time for taking the appropriate decisions. The reacting time is the most vital part as it may also rise an accident issue if the decision is not taking at proper time.

The decisions taken by the system should be more accurate and appropriate so that no life is harmed as it is very crucial work that can be implemented in real with required accuracy. The approaches, algorithms, hardware devices, software related data, programs should be tested twice or thrice to achieve the required accuracy of the system.

REFERENCES

Bi, L., Wang, M., Wang, C., & Liu, Y. (2015). Development of a driver lateral control model by integrating neuromuscular dynamics into the queuing network-based driver model. *IEEE Transactions on Intelligent Transportation Systems, 16*(5), 2479–2486. doi:10.1109/TITS.2015.2409115

Braunagel, C., Rosenstiel, W., & Kasneci, E. (2017). Ready for take-over? A new driver assistance system for an automated classification of driver take-over readiness. *IEEE Intelligent Transportation Systems Magazine, 9*(4), 10–22. doi:10.1109/MITS.2017.2743165

Chan, C. Y. (2017). Advancements, prospects, and impacts of automated driving systems. *International Journal of Transportation Science and Technology, 6*(3), 208-216.

Chen, R., Kusano, K. D., & Gabler, H. C. (2015). Driver behavior during lane change from the 100-Car naturalistic driving study. In *24th International Technical Conference on the Enhanced Safety of Vehicles (ESV)* (No. 15-0423). Academic Press.

Desmond, P. A., Hancock, P. A., & Monette, J. L. (1998). Fatigue and automation-induced impairments in simulated driving performance. *Transportation Research Record: Journal of the Transportation Research Board, 1628*(1), 8–14. doi:10.3141/1628-02

Fernandes, C., Ng, K. Y., & Khoo, B. H. (2011, November). Development of a convenient wireless control of an autonomous vehicle using apple iOS SDK. In TENCON 2011-2011 IEEE Region 10 Conference (pp. 1025-1029). IEEE. doi:10.1109/TENCON.2011.6129266

Gao, X. (n.d.). Research on Intelligent Driving Behaviour Based on Cognitive Science and Scene Simulation. *International Conference on Intelligence Science and Information Engineering*. DOI 10.1109/ISIE.2011.15

Gao, X., Gao, L., & Dong, G. (2011, August). Research on intelligent driving behavior based on cognitive science and scene simulation. In *2011 International Conference on Intelligence Science and Information Engineering* (pp. 226-229). IEEE. 10.1109/ISIE.2011.15

Kaur, K., & Rampersad, G. (2018). Trust in driverless cars: Investigating key factors influencing the adoption of driverless cars. *Journal of Engineering and Technology Management, 48*, 87–96. doi:10.1016/j.jengtecman.2018.04.006

Mikhail, B., Anna, D., Igor, I., & Natalia, K. (2019, July). orientation of the driverless car at loss of a satellite signal. In *2019 42nd International Conference on Telecommunications and Signal Processing (TSP)* (pp. 548-551). IEEE.

Naujoks, F., Höfling, S., Purucker, C., & Zeeb, K. (2018). From partial and high automation to manual driving: Relationship between non-driving related tasks, drowsiness and take-over performance. *Accident; Analysis and Prevention, 121*, 28–42. doi:10.1016/j.aap.2018.08.018 PMID:30205284

Reuschenbach, A., Wang, M., Ganjineh, T., & Gohring, D. (2011, April). iDriver-human machine interface for autonomous cars. In *2011 Eighth International Conference on Information Technology: New Generations* (pp. 435-440). IEEE.

Schömig, N., Hargutt, V., Neukum, A., Petermann-Stock, I., & Othersen, I. (2015). The interaction between highly automated driving and the development of drowsiness. *Procedia Manufacturing, 3,* 6652–6659. doi:10.1016/j.promfg.2015.11.005

Urmson, C., Anhalt, J., Bagnell, D., Baker, C., Bittner, R., Clark, M. N., ... Gittleman, M. (2008). Autonomous driving in urban environments: Boss and the urban challenge. *Journal of Field Robotics, 25*(8), 425–466. doi:10.1002/rob.20255

Zhang, X., Gao, H., Guo, M., Li, G., Liu, Y., & Li, D. (2016). A study on key technologies of unmanned driving. *CAAI Transactions on Intelligence Technology, 1*(1), 4–13. doi:10.1016/j.trit.2016.03.003

Compilation of References

Aamir, M., & Syed, M. A. Z. (2019). DDoS attack detection with feature engineering and machine learning: The framework and performance evaluation. *International Journal of Information Security, 18*(6), 761–785. doi:10.100710207-019-00434-1

Abbas, A., Abdelsamea, M. M., & Gaber, M. M. (2020). *Classification of COVID-19 in chest X-ray images using DeTraC deep convolutional neural network.* arXiv preprint arXiv:2003.13815

Abbasy, M. B., & Quesada, E. V. (2017). Predictable influence of IoT (Internet of Things) in the higher education. *International Journal of Information and Education Technology (IJIET), 7*(12), 914–920. doi:10.18178/ijiet.2017.7.12.995

Abdel-Basset, M., Manogaran, G., Mohamed, M., & Rushdy, E. (2019). Internet of things in smart education environment: Supportive framework in the decision-making process. *Concurrency and Computation, 31*(10), e4515. doi:10.1002/cpe.4515

Abdulla, R., Abdillahi, A., & Abbas, M. K. (2018). Electronic Toll Collection System based on Radio Frequency Identification System. *International Journal of Electrical and Computer Engineering, 8*(3), 1602-1610. Doi:10.11591/ijece.v8i3.pp1602-1610

Ackovska, Kirandziska, Tanevska, Bozinovska, & Božinovski. (2017). Robot - assisted therapy for autistic children. *SoutheastCon 2017*, 1-2. doi:10.1109/SECON.2017.7925401

Agarwal, S., Verma, A. K., & Dixit, N. (2014). Content based image retrieval using color edge detection and discrete wavelet transform. In *2014 International Conference on Issues and Challenges in Intelligent Computing Techniques* (pp. 368-372). IEEE. 10.1109/ICICICT.2014.6781310

Aldowah, H., Rehman, S. U., Ghazal, S., & Umar, I. N. (2017, January). Internet of Things in higher education: a study on future learning. Journal of Physics: Conference Series, 892(1). doi:10.1088/1742-6596/892/1/012017

Alhamad, M., Dillon, T., & Chang, E. (2010, September). The SLA-based trust model for cloud computing. In *2010 13th international conference on network-based information systems* (pp. 321-324). IEEE.

Ali, M., Bilal, H. S. M., Razzaq, M. A., Khan, J., Lee, S., Idris, M., Aazam, M., Choi, T., Han, S. C., & Kang, B. H. (2017). IoTFLiP: IoT-based flipped learning platform for medical education. *Digital Communications and Networks, 3*(3), 188–194. doi:10.1016/j.dcan.2017.03.002

Ali, S., Mehmood, F., Dancey, D., Ayaz, Y., Khan, M. J., Naseer, N., Amadeu, R. D. C., Sadia, H., & Nawaz, R. (2019). An Adaptive Multi-Robot Therapy for Improving Joint Attention and Imitation of ASD Children. *IEEE Access: Practical Innovations, Open Solutions, 7,* 81808–81825. doi:10.1109/ACCESS.2019.2923678

Anagnostopoulou, P., Alexandropoulou, V., Lorentzou, G., Lykothanasi, A., Ntaountaki, P., & Drigas, A. (2020). Artificial Intelligence in Autism Assessment. *International Journal of Emerging Technologies in Learning, 15*(06), 95. doi:10.3991/ijet.v15i06.11231

Anderborght, Simut, Saldien, Pop, Rusu, Pintea, & Lefeber. (2012). Using the social robot probo as a social story telling agent for children with ASD. Interact. Stud., 13.

Apostolopoulos, I. D., & Mpesiana, T. A. (2020). Covid-19: automatic detection from x-ray images utilizing transfer learning with convolutional neural networks. *Physical and Engineering Sciences in Medicine, 1.*

Archibald, R., & Fann, G. (2007). Feature selection and classification of hyperspectral images with support vector machines. *IEEE Geoscience and Remote Sensing Letters, 4*(4), 674–677. doi:10.1109/LGRS.2007.905116

Ashour, S. A., Samanta, S., Chakraborty, S., & Salem, M. (2015). Principal Component Analysis in Medical Image Processing: A Study. *International Journal of Image Mining, 40,* 65–86.

Ayoub Khan, Manoj, & Prahbu. (2009). A Survey of RFID Tags. *International Journal of Recent Trends in Engineering, 1*(4).

Baccianella, S., Esuli, A., & Sebastiani, F. (2010). *SentiWordNet 3.0: An enhanced lexical resource for sentiment analysis and opinion mining* (Vol. 10). LREC.

Bagheri, M., & Movahed, S. H. (2016, November). The effect of the Internet of Things (IoT) on education business model. In *2016 12th International Conference on Signal-Image Technology & Internet-Based Systems (SITIS)* (pp. 435-441). IEEE.

Baig, Sivakumar, & Nayak. (2020). Optimizing Performance of Text Searching Using CPU and GPUs, Progress in Computing, Analytics and Networking. *Advances in Intelligent Systems and Computing, 1119,* 141-150.

Banerjee, M., Lee, J., & Choo, K. K. R. (2018). A blockchain future for internet of things security: A position paper. *Digital Communications and Networks, 4*(3), 149–160. doi:10.1016/j.dcan.2017.10.006

Banica, L., Burtescu, E., & Enescu, F. (2017). The impact of internet-of-things in higher education. *Scientific Bulletin-Economic Sciences, 16*(1), 53–59.

Bass. (1997). *Conveners report of CHI ' 97 Workshop on Wearable Computers.* Personal Communication to attendees. http:// www.bham.ac.uk/ManMechEng/ieg/w1.html

Behmann, J., Mahlein, A., Rumpf, T., Romer, C., & Plumer, L. (2015). A review of advanced machine learning methods for the detection of biotic stress in precision crop protection. *Precision Agriculture, 16*(3), 239–260.

Bell, N., & Garland, M. (2008). *Efficient sparse matrix-vector multiplication on CUDA.* Nvidia Technical Report NVR-2008-004, Nvidia Corporation.

Bernabeu, S. R., Puzyrev, V., Hanzich, M., & Fernandez, S. (2015). Efficient Sparse Matrix-vector Multiplication for Geophysical Electromagnetic Codes on Xeon Phi Coprocessors. *Second EAGE Workshop on High Performance Computing for Upstream.* 10.3997/2214-4609.201414033

Bhatt, J., & Bhatt, A. (2017). IoT techniques to nurture education industry: scope & opportunities. *International Journal on Emerging Technologies,* 128-132.

Bi, L., Wang, M., Wang, C., & Liu, Y. (2015). Development of a driver lateral control model by integrating neuromuscular dynamics into the queuing network-based driver model. *IEEE Transactions on Intelligent Transportation Systems, 16*(5), 2479–2486. doi:10.1109/TITS.2015.2409115

Bindra, N., & Sood, M. (2019). Detecting DDoS attacks using machine learning techniques and contemporary intrusion detection dataset. *Automatic Control and Computer Sciences, 53*(5), 419–428. doi:10.3103/S0146411619050043

Bishop, C. (2006). *Pattern recognition and machine learning.* Springer.

Blake, G., Dreslinski, R. G., & Mudge, T. (2009). A survey of multicore processors. *IEEE Signal Processing Magazine, 26*(6), 26–37. doi:10.1109/MSP.2009.934110

Blelloch, G. E., Koutis, I., Miller, G. L., & Tangwongsan, K. (2010). Hierarchical diagonal blocking and precision reduction applied to combinatorial multigrid. In *IEEE conference on High Performance Computing* (pp. 1–12). Networking, Storage and Analysis. doi:10.1109/SC.2010.29

Bradley, P., Keller, S., & Weinmann, M. (2018). Unsupervised feature selection based on ultrametricity and sparse training data: A case study for the classification of high-dimensional hyperspectral data. *Remote Sensing, 10*(10), 1564. doi:10.3390/rs10101564

Brassard & Siu. (2005). *Sniper Detection Using Wireless Sensor Networks EE-194WIR.* Wireless Sensor Networks Tufts University.

Braunagel, C., Rosenstiel, W., & Kasneci, E. (2017). Ready for take-over? A new driver assistance system for an automated classification of driver take-over readiness. *IEEE Intelligent Transportation Systems Magazine, 9*(4), 10–22. doi:10.1109/MITS.2017.2743165

Brodersen, C., Kalis, B., Leong, C., Mitchell, E., Pupo, E., Truscott, A., & Accenture, L. (2016). *Blockchain: Securing a new health interoperability experience.* Accenture LLP.

Buratti, C., Conti, A., Dardari, D., & Verdone, R. (2009). An Overview on Wireless Sensor Networks Technology and Evolution. *Sensors (Basel)*, *9*(9), 6869–6896. doi:10.339090906869 PMID:22423202

Burd, B., Barker, L., Divitini, M., Perez, F. A. F., Russell, I., Siever, B., & Tudor, L. (2018, January). Courses, content, and tools for internet of things in computer science education. In *Proceedings of the 2017 ITiCSE Conference on Working Group Reports* (pp. 125-139). Academic Press.

Bustamam, A., Burrage, K., & Hamilton, N. A. (2012). Fast parallel Markov clustering in bioinformatics using massively parallel computing on GPU with CUDA and ELLPACK-R sparse format. *IEEE/ACM Transactions on Computational Biology and Bioinformatics*, *9*(3), 679–692. doi:10.1109/TCBB.2011.68 PMID:21483031

Çakmakç, S. D., Kemmerich, T., Ahmed, T., & Baykal, N. (2020). Online DDoS attack detection using Mahalanobis distance and Kernel-based learning algorithm. *Journal of Network and Computer Applications*.

Cao, W., Yao, L., Li, Z., Wang, Y., & Wang, Z. (2010). Implementing sparse matrix-vector multiplication using CUDA based on a hybrid sparse matrix format. *IEEE International Conference on Computer Application and System Modeling (ICCASM)*, 11, V11-16.

Cao, X., Xiong, T., & Jiao, L. (2016). Supervised band selection using local spatial information for hyperspectral image. *IEEE Geoscience and Remote Sensing Letters*, *13*(3), 329–333.

Carlos-Mancilla, López-Mellado, & Siller. (2016). Wireless Sensor Networks Formation: Approaches and Techniques. *Journal of Sensors*. doi:10.1155/2016/2081902

Centers for Disease Control and Prevention. (2020). *Treatment | Autism Spectrum Disorder (ASD) | NCBDDD | CDC*. https://www.cdc.gov/ncbddd/autism/treatment.html

Ceylan, E., Kutlubay, F., & Bener, A. (2006). Software defect identification using machine learning techniques. *Software Engineering and Advanced Applications. SEAA '06. 32nd EUROMICRO Conference on*, 240-247.

Chan, C. Y. (2017). Advancements, prospects, and impacts of automated driving systems. *International Journal of Transportation Science and Technology, 6*(3), 208-216.

Charmisha, K. S., Sowmya, V., & Soman, K. P. (2018). Dimensionally reduced features for hyperspectral image classification using deep learning. In *International Conference on Communications and Cyber Physical Engineering 2018* (pp. 171-179). Springer.

Chen, R., Kusano, K. D., & Gabler, H. C. (2015). Driver behavior during lane change from the 100-Car naturalistic driving study. In *24th International Technical Conference on the Enhanced Safety of Vehicles (ESV)* (No. 15-0423). Academic Press.

Chen. (2014). *Smart Wearable Change the World: The Next Business Tides*. Benjing: Publishing House of Electronics Industry.

Chen, D. Y. (2000). The Evolution and Trend of Wearable Computer (2). [Natural Science Edition]. *Journal of Chongqing University, 23*(4), 142–148.

Chen, S., Cheng, X., & Xu, J. (2012). Research on image compression algorithm based on Rectangle Segmentation and storage with sparse matrix. *Proc. 9th IEEE International Conference on Fuzzy Systems and Knowledge Discovery (FSKD)*, 1904-1908. 10.1109/FSKD.2012.6233969

Choi, J. W., Singh, A., & Vuduc, R. W. (2010). Model-driven autotuning of sparse matrix-vector multiply on GPUs. *ACM SIGPLAN Notices, 45*(5), 115–126. doi:10.1145/1837853.1693471

Chong, S. K., Abawajy, J., Ahmad, M., & Hamid, I. R. A. (2014). Enhancing trust management in a cloud environment. *Procedia: Social and Behavioral Sciences, 129*, 314–321. doi:10.1016/j.sbspro.2014.03.682

Cooper, G. F., Hennings-Yeomans, P., Visweswaran, S., & Barmada, M. (2010). An efficient bayesian method for predicting clinical outcomes from genome-wide data. *AMIA 2010 Symposium Proceedings*, 127 – 131.

Crosby, M., Pattanayak, P., Verma, S., & Kalyanaraman, V. (2016). Blockchain technology: Beyond bitcoin. *Applied Innovation, 2*(6-10), 71.

Dagar, V., Verma, A., Govardhan, K. (2019). *Sentiment analysis and sarcasm detection (using emoticons)*. Academic Press.

Dahl, G. E. (2013). Large-scale malware classification using random projections and neural networks. In *2013 IEEE International Conference on Acoustics, Speech and Signal Processing*. IEEE. 10.1109/ICASSP.2013.6638293

Dankar, F. K., & El Emam, K. (2012, March). The application of differential privacy to health data. In *Proceedings of the 2012 Joint EDBT/ICDT Workshops* (pp. 158-166). 10.1145/2320765.2320816

Dass, R. (2018). Pattern Recognition Techniques: A Review. *International Journal of Computer Science and Telecommunications, 24*, 25–29.

Datta, D., Mittal, D., Mathew, N. P., & Sairabanu, J. (2020a, February). Comparison of Performance of Parallel Computation of CPU Cores on CNN model. In *2020 International Conference on Emerging Trends in Information Technology and Engineering (ic-ETITE)* (pp. 1-8). IEEE.

Datta, D., David, P., Mittal, D., & Jain, A. (2020b). Neural Machine Translation using Recurrent Neural Network. *International Journal of Engineering and Advanced Technology, 9*(4), 1395–1400. doi:10.35940/ijeat.D7637.049420

Deng, L. (2012). The MNIST database of handwritten digit images for machine learning research. *IEEE Signal Processing Magazine, 29*(6), 141–142. doi:10.1109/MSP.2012.2211477

Desmond, P. A., Hancock, P. A., & Monette, J. L. (1998). Fatigue and automation-induced impairments in simulated driving performance. *Transportation Research Record: Journal of the Transportation Research Board, 1628*(1), 8–14. doi:10.3141/1628-02

Dey, M., Raman, B., & Verma, M. (2016). A novel colour-and texture-based image retrieval technique using multi-resolution local extrema peak valley pattern and RGB colour histogram. *Pattern Analysis & Applications, 19*(4), 1159–1179. doi:10.100710044-015-0522-y

Diehl & Schmitt. (2012). The clinical use of robots for individuals with Autism Spectrum Disorders: A critical review. *Research in Autism Spectrum Disorders, 6*. PMID:22125579

Dijkstra, K., van de Loosdrecht, J., Schomaker, L. R. B., & Wiering, M. A. (2019). Hyperspectral demosaicking and crosstalk correction using deep learning. *Machine Vision and Applications, 30*(1), 1–21. doi:10.100700138-018-0965-4

Dongarraxz, J., Lumsdaine, A., Niu, X., Pozoz, R., & Remingtonx, K. (1994). A sparse matrix library in C++ for high performance architectures. Academic Press.

Dorazio, T., Distante, A., Pianese, V., Cavaccini, G., Leo, M., & Guarag-nella, C. (2008). Automatic ultrasonic inspection for internal defect detection in composite materials. *NDT & E International, 41*(2), 145–154.

Dormehl. (2017 November). *8 Major Milestones in the Brief History of Virtual Reality.* www.digitaltrends.com

Doshi, R., Apthorpe, N., & Feamster, N. (2018, May). Machine learning ddos detection for consumer internet of things devices. In *2018 IEEE Security and Privacy Workshops (SPW)* (pp. 29-35). IEEE. doi:10.1109/MILCOM.2018.8599738

Drown, D. J., Khoshgoftaar, T. M., & Seliya, N. (2009). Evolutionary sam-pling and software quality modeling of high-assurance systems. *IEEE Transactions on Systems, Man, and Cybernetics. Part A, Systems and Humans, 39*(5), 1097–1107.

Dryden, N., Maruyama, N., Benson, T., Moon, T., Snir, M., & Van Essen, B. (2019, May). Improving strong-scaling of CNN training by exploiting finer-grained parallelism. In *2019 IEEE International Parallel and Distributed Processing Symposium (IPDPS)* (pp. 210-220). IEEE. 10.1109/IPDPS.2019.00031

Duff, I. S., Grimes, R. G., & Lewis, J. G. (1989). Sparse matrix test problems. *ACM Transactions on Mathematical Software, 15*(1), 1–14. doi:10.1145/62038.62043

Düking, P., Achtzehn, S., Holmberg, H. C., & Sperlich, B. (2018). Integrated Framework of Load Monitoring by a Combination of Smartphone Applications, Wearables, and Point-of-Care Testing Provides Feedback that Allows Individual Responsive Adjustments to Activities of Daily Living. *Sensors (Basel), 18*(5), 1632. doi:10.339018051632 PMID:29783763

Duquette, A., Michaud, F., & Mercier, H. (2007). Exploring the use of a mobile robot as an imitation agent with children with low functioning autism. *Autonomous Robots, 24*(2), 147-157.

Dziekonski, A., Lamecki, A., & Mrozowski, M. (2011). A memory efficient and fast sparse matrix vector product on a GPU. *Progress in Electromagnetics Research, 116*, 49–63. doi:10.2528/PIER11031607

Eack, S. M., Greenwald, D. P., Hogarty, S. S., Bahorik, A. L., Litschge, M. Y., Mazefsky, C. A., & Minshew, N. J. (2013). Cognitive enhancement therapy for adults with autism spectrum disorder: Results of an 18-month feasibilitystudy. *Journal of Autism and Developmental Disorders*, *43*(12), 2866–2877. doi:10.100710803-013-1834-7 PMID:23619953

Ekblaw, A., Azaria, A., Halamka, J. D., & Lippman, A. (2016). A Case Study for Blockchain in Healthcare:"MedRec" prototype for electronic health records and medical research data. Proceedings of IEEE open & big data conference, 13.

Elie, S. (2013). *An overview of Pattern Recognition*. Academic Press.

El-Said, S. A., & Hassanien, A. E. (2019). Artificial Eye Vision Using Wireless Sensor Networks. In Wireless Sensor Networks: Theory and Applications. CRC Press, Taylor and Francis Group.

Ergul, U., & Bilgin, G. (2019). MCK-ELM: Multiple composite kernel extreme learning machine for hyperspectral images. *Neural Computing & Applications*, 1–11.

Esteban. (2017). *How to Build a Supervised Autonomous System for Robot-Enhanced Therapy for Children with Autism Spectrum Disorder*. Academic Press.

Ester, M., Kriegel, H.-P., Sander, J., & Xu, X. (1996). A density-based algorithm for discovering clusters in large spatial databases with noise. *KDD-96 Proceedings*, 226-231.

Faes, L., Wagner, S. K., Fu, D. J., Liu, X., Korot, E., Ledsam, J. R., ... Moraes, G. (2019). Automated deep learning design for medical image classification by health-care professionals with no coding experience: A feasibility study. *The Lancet Digital Health*, *1*(5), e232–e242. doi:10.1016/S2589-7500(19)30108-6

Falck-Ytter, T., Bölte, S., & Gredebäck, G. (2013). Eye tracking in early autism research. *Journal of Neurodevelopmental Disorders*, *5*(1), 28. doi:10.1186/1866-1955-5-28 PMID:24069955

Fan, K., Ren, Y., Wang, Y., Li, H., & Yang, Y. (2017). Blockchain-based efficient privacy preserving and data sharing scheme of content-centric network in 5G. *IET Communications*, *12*(5), 527–532. doi:10.1049/iet-com.2017.0619

Fan, W., & Perros, H. (2014). A novel trust management framework for multi-cloud environments based on trust service providers. *Knowledge-Based Systems*, *70*, 392–406. doi:10.1016/j.knosys.2014.07.018

Fathima, Jayamala, & Keerthika. (2018). Online Toll Payment System. *International Journal of Innovations in Engineering and Technology*.

Feil-Seifer & Matarić. (2009). *Toward Socially Assistive Robotics for Augmenting Interventions for Children with Autism Spectrum Disorders*. Academic Press.

Feil-Seifer. (n.d.). *Robot assisted therapy for children with Autism Spectrum Disorders*. Academic Press.

Feil-Seifer, D., & Matarić, M. J. (2011). Socially Assistive Robotics. *IEEE Robotics & Automation Magazine, 18*(1), 24–31. doi:10.1109/MRA.2010.940150

Feng, J., Chen, J., Liu, L., Cao, X., Zhang, X., Jiao, L., & Yu, T. (2019). Cnn-based multilayer spatial–spectral feature fusion and sample augmentation with local and nonlocal constraints for hyperspectral image classification. *IEEE Journal of Selected Topics in Applied Earth Observations and Remote Sensing, 12*(4), 1299–1313. doi:10.1109/JSTARS.2019.2900705

Fernandes, C., Ng, K. Y., & Khoo, B. H. (2011, November). Development of a convenient wireless control of an autonomous vehicle using apple iOS SDK. In TENCON 2011-2011 IEEE Region 10 Conference (pp. 1025-1029). IEEE. doi:10.1109/TENCON.2011.6129266

Fickas, S., Kortuem, G., & Segall, Z. (1997). Software organization for dynamic and adaptable wearable systems. Wearable Computers. *Digest of Papers, First International Symposium on. IEEE, 1997*, 56-63

Galande, S.D. (2015). Automated Toll Cash Collection System for Road Transportation. *International Journal of Computer Science and Mobile Computing, 4*(2), 216-224.

Gandhi, S. L. (2017, April). Smart education service model based on IOT technology. *International Interdisciplinary Conference on Science Technology Engineering Management Pharmacy and Humanities.*

Ganesan, P., Sivakumar, S., & Sundar, S. (2015). An Experimental Analysis of Classification Mining Algorithm For Coronary Artery Disease. *International Journal of Applied Engineering Research, 10*(6), 14467–14477.

Gao, X. (n.d.). Research on Intelligent Driving Behaviour Based on Cognitive Science and Scene Simulation. *International Conference on Intelligence Science and Information Engineering.* DOI 10.1109/ISIE.2011.15

Garofalakis, M., Hyun, D., Rastogi, R., & Shim, K. (2003). Building decision trees with constraints. *Data Mining and Knowledge Discovery, 7*(2), 187–214. doi:10.1023/A:1022445500761

Gewali, U. B., Monteiro, S. T., & Saber, E. (2018). *Machine learning based hyperspectral image analysis: a survey.* arXiv preprint arXiv:1802.08701

Ghoneim, S. (2020). *Accuracy, Recall, Precision, F-Score & Specificity, Which To Optimize On?* Medium. Available at: https://towardsdatascience.com/accuracy-recall-precision-f-score-specificity-which-to-optimize-on-867d3f11124

Gibert, D. (2016). *Convolutional neural networks for malware classification.* University Rovira i Virgili.

Goharian, N., El-Ghazawi, T., & Grossman, D. (2001). Enterprise text processing: a sparse matrix approach. *Proc. of IEEE International Conference on Information Technology: Coding and Computing,* 71-75. 10.1109/ITCC.2001.918768

Golovko, V. (2010). Neural network and artificial immune systems for malware and network intrusion detection. In *Advances in machine learning II* (pp. 485–513). Springer. doi:10.1007/978-3-642-05179-1_23

Goparaju, B., & Bandla, S. R. (2020). *Distributed Denial of Service Attack Classification Using Artificial Neural Networks (No. 3201)*. EasyChair.

Gordon, W. J., & Catalini, C. (2018). Blockchain technology for healthcare: Facilitating the transition to patient-driven interoperability. *Computational and Structural Biotechnology Journal*, *16*, 224–230. doi:10.1016/j.csbj.2018.06.003 PMID:30069284

Grama, A. Y., Gupta, A., & Kumar, V. (1993). Isoefficiency: Measuring the scalability of parallel algorithms and architectures. *IEEE Parallel & Distributed Technology Systems & Applications*, *1*(3), 12–21. doi:10.1109/88.242438

Greathouse, J. L., & Daga, M. (2014). Efficient sparse matrix-vector multiplication on GPUs using the CSR storage format. *Proc. IEEE International Conference on High Performance Computing, Networking, Storage and Analysis*, 769-780. 10.1109/SC.2014.68

Guedjou, Boucenna, Xavier, Cohen, & Chetouani. (n.d.). *The Influence of Individual Social Traits on Robot Learning in a Human-Robot Interaction*. Academic Press.

Guedria, S., De Palma, N., Renard, F., & Vuillerme, N. (2019, December). Auto-CNNp: a component-based framework for automating CNN parallelism. In *2019 IEEE International Conference on Big Data (Big Data)* (pp. 3330-3339). IEEE. 10.1109/BigData47090.2019.9006175

Gunasekera, K., Borrero, A. N., Vasuian, F., & Bryceson, K. P. (2018). Experiences in building an IoT infrastructure for agriculture education. *Procedia Computer Science*, *135*, 155–162. doi:10.1016/j.procs.2018.08.161

Gundersen, G., & Steihaug, T. (2004). Data structures in Java for matrix computations. *Concurrency and Computation*, *16*(8), 799–815. doi:10.1002/cpe.793

Guo, D., & Gropp, W. (2011). Optimizing sparse data structures for matrix-vector multiply. *International Journal of High Performance Computing Applications*, *25*(1), 115–131. doi:10.1177/1094342010374847

Guo, P., Wang, L., & Chen, P. (2014). A performance modeling and optimization analysis tool for sparse matrix-vector multiplication on GPU's. *IEEE Transactions on Parallel and Distributed Systems*, *25*(5), 1112–1123. doi:10.1109/TPDS.2013.123

Guo, R., Shi, H., Zhao, Q., & Zheng, D. (2018). Secure attribute-based signature scheme with multiple authorities for blockchain in electronic health records systems. *IEEE Access: Practical Innovations, Open Solutions*, *6*, 11676–11686. doi:10.1109/ACCESS.2018.2801266

Habib, S. M., Ries, S., & Muhlhauser, M. (2011, November). Towards a trust management system for cloud computing. In *2011 IEEE 10th International Conference on Trust, Security and Privacy in Computing and Communications* (pp. 933-939). IEEE. 10.1109/TrustCom.2011.129

Harito, C., Utari, L., Putra, B. R., Yuliarto, B., Purwanto, S., Zaidi, S. S. J., Bavykin, D. V., Marken, F., & Walsh, F. C. (2020). Review—The Development of Wearable Polymer-Based Sensors: Perspectives. *Journal of the Electrochemical Society, 167*(3), 037566. doi:10.1149/1945-7111/ab697c

Hassanien, A. E., Mahdy, L. N., Ezzat, K. A., Elmousalami, H. H., & Ella, H. A. (2020). *Automatic x-ray covid-19 lung image classification system based on multi-level thresholding and support vector machine.* medRxiv.

He, Z., Zhang, T., & Lee, R. B. (2017, June). Machine learning based DDoS attack detection from source side in cloud. In *2017 IEEE 4th International Conference on Cyber Security and Cloud Computing (CSCloud)* (pp. 114-120). IEEE. 10.1109/CSCloud.2017.58

He, J. S., Ji, S., & Bobbie, P. O. (2017, April). Internet of things (iot)-based learning framework to facilitate stem undergraduate education. In *Proceedings of the SouthEast Conference* (pp. 88-94). 10.1145/3077286.3077321

Hill, M. D., & Marty, M. R. (2008). Amdahl's law in the multicore era. *Computer, 41*(7), 33–38. doi:10.1109/MC.2008.209

Hou, J., Fu, P., Cao, Z., & Xu, A. (2018, October). Machine learning based DDoS detection through netflow analysis. In MILCOM 2018-2018 IEEE Military Communications Conference (MILCOM) (pp. 1-6). IEEE.

Hsu, P. (2004). Feature extraction of hyperspectral images using matching pursuit. *Proc. of the XXth ISPRS Congress.*

Hsu, P. (2004). Feature extraction of hyperspectral images using matching pursuit. *Proc. Of the XXth ISPRS Congress.*

Huang, H., Li, Z., & Pan, Y. (2019). Multi-Feature Manifold Discriminant Analysis for Hyperspectral Image Classification. *Remote Sensing, 11*(6), 651. doi:10.3390/rs11060651

Hugues, M. R., & Petiton, S. G. (2010). Sparse matrix formats evaluation and optimization on a GPU. In *High Performance Computing and Communications (HPCC), 2010 12th IEEE International Conference on* (pp. 122-129). IEEE. 10.1109/HPCC.2010.85

Hwang, K., & Faye, A. (1984). *Computer architecture and parallel processing.* Academic Press.

Idika & Mathur. (2007). *A survey of malware detection techniques.* Purdue University.

IEEE Sight. (2018). Humanoid Robots for Therapeutic Treatment of Autism Spectrum Disorder (ASD). *Children.*

Im, E. J., & Yelick, K. (2001). Optimizing sparse matrix computations for register reuse in SPARSITY. *Proc. Conference on Computational Science (ICCS), 2073,* 127-136. 10.1007/3-540-45545-0_22

Inchingolo, F., & Stanfill, C. W. (2008). *U.S. Patent No. 7,467,383*. Washington, DC: U.S. Patent and Trademark Office.

Irtaza, A., Jaffar, M. A., Aleisa, E., & Choi, T. S. (2014). Embedding neural networks for semantic association in content based image retrieval. *Multimedia Tools and Applications, 72*(2), 1911–1931. doi:10.100711042-013-1489-6

Ivan, D. (2016, August). Moving toward a blockchain-based method for the secure storage of patient records. In *ONC/NIST Use of Blockchain for Healthcare and Research Workshop. Gaithersburg, Maryland, United States: ONC/NIST* (pp. 1-11). Academic Press.

Jain, A. K., Duin, P. W., & Mao, J. (2000). Statistical Pattern Recognition: A Review. *IEEE Transactions on Pattern Analysis and Machine Intelligence, 3632*(1), 4–34. doi:10.1109/34.824819

Jeffers, J., & Reinders, J. (2015). *High performance parallelism pearls volume two: multicore and many-core programming approaches*. Morgan Kaufmann.

Jiao, Y., Chen, R., Ke, X., Chu, K., Lu, Z., & Herskovits, E.H. (2009). Predictive models of autism spectrum disorder based on brain regional cortical thickness. *Neuroimage, 50*(2), 589-599. doi:10.1016/j.neuroimage

Jiménez, M., Torres, M. T., John, R., & Triguero, I. (2020). Galaxy Image Classification Based on Citizen Science Data: A Comparative Study. *IEEE Access: Practical Innovations, Open Solutions, 8*, 47232–47246. doi:10.1109/ACCESS.2020.2978804

Joshi, R. (2020). *Accuracy, Precision, Recall & F1 Score: Interpretation Of Performance Measures - Exsilio Blog*. Exsilio Blog. Available at: https://blog.exsilio.com/all/accuracy-precision-recall-f1-score-interpretation-of-performance-measures/

Kadam, Waghmare, Adhalkar, Sirsat, & Patil. (2017). A Survey on Toll Collection System Using Different Method. *IJSRTE.*

Kanthi, K., & Dontabhaktuni, J. (2013). Electronic Toll Collection System For Billing Using Wireless Communication. *IJAERS, 1*(5), 5-7.

Karakasis, V., Goumas, G., & Koziris, N. (2009). A comparative study of blocking storage methods for sparse matrices on multicore architectures. *Proc. of IEEE International Conference in Computational Science and Engineering*, 1, 247-256. 10.1109/CSE.2009.223

Karbowski, A. (2008). *Amdahl's and Gustafson-Barsis laws revisited*. arXiv preprint arXiv:0809.1177

Kaur, K., & Rampersad, G. (2018). Trust in driverless cars: Investigating key factors influencing the adoption of driverless cars. *Journal of Engineering and Technology Management, 48*, 87–96. doi:10.1016/j.jengtecman.2018.04.006

Ke, F., Choi, S., Kang, Y. H., Cheon, K., & Lee, S. W. (2020). Exploring the Structural and Strategic Bases of Autism Spectrum Disorders With Deep Learning. *IEEE Access: Practical Innovations, Open Solutions, 8*, 153341–153352. doi:10.1109/ACCESS.2020.3016734

Khali, P., Michael, C. W., & Shahriyar, H. (2007). *Toll Collection Technology and Best Practices.* Project 0-5217: Vehicle/License Plate Identification for Toll Collection Application.

Khan, A., & Farooq, H. (2012). Principal Component Analysis-Linear Discriminant Analysis Feature Extractor for Pattern Recognition. *International Journal of Computer Science Issues, 42,* 267–270.

Khan, S. M., & Hamlen, K. W. (2012, June). Hatman: Intra-cloud trust management for Hadoop. In *2012 IEEE Fifth International Conference on Cloud Computing* (pp. 494-501). IEEE. 10.1109/CLOUD.2012.64

Khodatars. (2020). *Deep Learning for Neuroimaging-based Diagnosis and Rehabilitation of Autism Spectrum Disorder.* Academic Press.

Kim, M., & Park, S. O. (2013). Trust management on user behavioural patterns for mobile cloud computing. *Cluster Computing, 16*(4), 725–731. doi:10.100710586-013-0248-9

Kiranyaz, S., Ferreira, M., & Gabbouj, M. (2006). Automatic object extraction over multiscale edge field for multimedia retrieval. *IEEE Transactions on Image Processing, 15*(12), 3759–3772. doi:10.1109/TIP.2006.881966 PMID:17153949

Kleinaki, A. S., Mytis-Gkometh, P., Drosatos, G., Efraimidis, P. S., & Kaldoudi, E. (2018). A blockchain-based notarization service for biomedical knowledge retrieval. *Computational and Structural Biotechnology Journal, 16,* 288–297. doi:10.1016/j.csbj.2018.08.002 PMID:30181840

Kodagali, J. A., & Balaji, S. (2012). Computer vision and image analysis based techniques for automatic characterization of fruits-a review. *International Journal of Computers and Applications, 50*(6).

Kolchyna, O., Souza, T. T. P., Treleaven, P. C., & Aste, T. (2015). *Twitter Sentiment Analysis: Lexicon Method, Machine Learning Method and Their Combination.* arXiv preprint arXiv:150700955

Koza, Z., Matyka, M., Szkoda, S., & Miroslaw, L. (2014). Compressed multirow storage format for sparse matrices on graphics processing units. *SIAM Journal on Scientific Computing, 36*(2), 19–39. doi:10.1137/120900216

Kozima, H., Nakagawa, C., & Yasuda, Y. (2005). Interactive robots for communication-care: a case-study in autism therapy. *ROMAN 2005. IEEE International Workshop on Robot and Human Interactive Communication,* 341-346, 10.1109/ROMAN.2005.1513802

Kreutzer, M., Hager, G., Wellein, G., Fehske, H., & Bishop, A. R. (2014). A unified sparse matrix data format for efficient general sparse matrix-vector multiplication on modern processors with wide SIMD units. *SIAM Journal on Scientific Computing, 36*(5), 401–423. doi:10.1137/130930352

Kumar, Anbazhaghan, Razia, Sivani, Pravalika, & Harshini. (n.d.). Prediction of cardiovascular disease using classification techniques with high accuracy. *JARDC, 12*(2), 1134-1139.

Kumar, R. E., & Rao. (2020). Suicide Prediction in Twitter Data using Mining Techniques: A Survey. *International Conference on Intelligent Sustainable Systems (ICISS 2019),* 122-131.

Kumar, A., Kim, J., Wen, L., Fulham, M., & Feng, D. (2014). A graph-based approach for the retrieval of multi-modality medical images. *Medical Image Analysis, 18*(2), 330–342. doi:10.1016/j.media.2013.11.003 PMID:24378541

Kumar, R. (2020). Suicidal ideation prediction in twitter data using machine learning techniques. *Journal of Interdisciplinary Mathematics, 23*(1), 117–125. doi:10.1080/09720502.2020.1721674

Kumar, V. (2002). *Introduction to parallel computing.* Addison-Wesley Longman Publishing Co., Inc.

Kuo, T. T., Kim, H. E., & Ohno-Machado, L. (2017). Blockchain distributed ledger technologies for biomedical and health care applications. *Journal of the American Medical Informatics Association, 24*(6), 1211–1220. doi:10.1093/jamia/ocx068 PMID:29016974

Kushwah, G. S., & Ranga, V. (2020). Voting extreme learning machine based distributed denial of service attack detection in cloud computing. *Journal of Information Security and Applications, 53*, 102532. doi:10.1016/j.jisa.2020.102532

Kyrkou, C., & Theocharides, T. (2019, June). Deep-Learning-Based Aerial Image Classification for Emergency Response Applications Using Unmanned Aerial Vehicles. doi:10.1109/CVPRW.2019.00077

Lainhart, J. (2015). Brain imaging research in autism spectrum disorders. *Current Opinion in Psychiatry, 28*(2), 76–82. doi:10.1097/YCO.0000000000000130 PMID:25602243

Landage, J., & Wankhade, M. P. (2013). Malware and malware detection techniques: A survey. *International Journal of Engineering Research & Technology (Ahmedabad), 2*(12).

Langr & Tvrdik. (2015). Evaluation Criteria for Sparse Matrix Storage Formats. *IEEE Transaction on Parallel and Distributed Systems*, 1-14.

Lanillos, Oliva, & Philippsen, Yamashita, Nagai, & Cheng. (2020). A review on neural network models of schizophrenia and autism spectrum disorder. *Neural Networks, ●●●*, 122.

Lee, J. S., Su, Y. W., & Shen, C. C. (2007). A comparative study of wireless protocols: Bluetooth, UWB, ZigBee, and Wi-Fi. Industrial Electronics Society, *IECON 2007. 33rd Annual Conference of the IEEE*, 46-51.

Lee, S., Agrawal, A., Balaprakash, P., Choudhary, A., & Liao, W. K. (2018, November). Communication-Efficient Parallelization Strategy for Deep Convolutional Neural Network Training. In *2018 IEEE/ACM Machine Learning in HPC Environments (MLHPC)* (pp. 47-56). IEEE.

Lee, Tseng, & Wang. (2008). *Design and implement of electronic toll collection system based on vehicle positioning system techniques.* Academic Press.

Leo. (2015). *Automatic Emotion Recognition in Robot-Children Interaction for ASD Treatment.* Academic Press.

Li, J., Zhong, Y., & Ouyang, G. (2018). Identification of ASD Children based on Video Data. *2018 24th International Conference on Pattern Recognition (ICPR)*, 367-372. 10.1109/ICPR.2018.8545113

Li, J., Zhang, L., Wu, Z., Ling, Z., Cao, X., Guo, K., & Yan, F. (2020). Autonomous Martian rock image classification based on transfer deep learning methods. *Earth Science Informatics*, 1–13.

Li, K., Yang, W., & Li, K. (2015). Performance analysis and optimization for SpMV on GPU using probabilistic modelling. *IEEE Transactions on Parallel and Distributed Systems*, *26*(1), 196–205. doi:10.1109/TPDS.2014.2308221

Li, M., Tang, H., Chan, M. D., Zhou, X., & Qian, X. (2020). DC-AL GAN: Pseudoprogression and true tumor progression of glioblastoma multiform image classification based on DCGAN and AlexNet. *Medical Physics*, *47*(3), 1139–1150. doi:10.1002/mp.14003 PMID:31885094

Lin, C. H., Chen, R. T., & Chan, Y. K. (2009). A smart content-based image retrieval system based on color and texture feature. *Image and Vision Computing*, *27*(6), 658–665. doi:10.1016/j.imavis.2008.07.004

Lin, T. K., & Chien, S. Y. (2010). Support vector machines on gpu with sparse matrix format. *IEEE Ninth International Conference on Machine Learning and Applications*, 313-318. 10.1109/ICMLA.2010.53

Li, Q., Zhong, Z., Liang, Z., & Liang, Y. (2015). Rail inspection meets big data: Methods and trends. *International Conference on Network-Based Information Systems*, 302–308.

Li, T., Leng, J., Kong, L., Guo, S., Bai, G., & Wang, K. (2019). DCNR: Deep cube CNN with random forest for hyperspectral image classification. *Multimedia Tools and Applications*, *78*(3), 3411–3433. doi:10.100711042-018-5986-5

Liu, S., Bruzzone, L., Bovolo, F., & Du, P. (June 2012). Unsupervised hierarchical spectral analysis for change detection in hyperspectral images. In *2012 4th Workshop on Hyperspectral Image and Signal Processing: Evolution in Remote Sensing (WHISPERS)* (pp. 1-4). IEEE. 10.1109/WHISPERS.2012.6874245

Liu, Y. C., Ma, Y. T., Zhang, H. S., Li, D. Y., & Chen, G. S. (2011). A method for trust management in cloud computing: Data colouring by Cloud watermarking. *International Journal of Automation and Computing, 8*(3), 280.

Liu, C. C., Zhang, Y. C., Chen, P. Y., Lai, C. C., Chen, Y. H., Cheng, J. H., & Ko, M. H. (2019). Clouds classification from sentinel-2 imagery with deep residual learning and semantic image segmentation. *Remote Sensing*, *11*(2), 119. doi:10.3390/rs11020119

Liu, D., Zeng, X. A., & Sun, D. W. (2015). Recent developments and applications of hyperspectral imaging for quality evaluation of agricultural products: A review. *Critical Reviews in Food Science and Nutrition*, *55*(12), 1744–1757. doi:10.1080/10408398.2013.777020 PMID:24915395

Liu, G. H., & Yang, J. Y. (2013). Content-based image retrieval using color difference histogram. *Pattern Recognition*, *46*(1), 188–198. doi:10.1016/j.patcog.2012.06.001

Liu, J., Wang, H., Wang, D., Gao, Y., & Li, Z. (2015, March). Parallelizing Convolutional Neural Networks on Intel $$^{\textregistered}$$ Many Integrated Core Architecture. In *International Conference on Architecture of Computing Systems* (pp. 71-82). Springer. 10.1007/978-3-319-16086-3_6

Liu, P., Liu, X., Liu, M., Shi, Q., Yang, J., Xu, X., & Zhang, Y. (2019). Building Footprint Extraction from High-Resolution Images via Spatial Residual Inception Convolutional Neural Network. *Remote Sensing, 11*(7), 830. doi:10.3390/rs11070830

Liu, W., & Vinter, B. (2015). CSR5: An Efficient Storage Format for Cross-Platform Sparse Matrix-Vector Multiplication. *Proc. of the 29th ACM International Conference on Supercomputing,* 339-350. 10.1145/2751205.2751209

Liu, X., Smelyanskiy, M., Chow, E., & Dubey, P. (2013). Efficient sparse matrix-vector multiplication on x86-based many-core processors. *Proceedings of the 27th international ACM conference on International conference on supercomputing,* 273-282. 10.1145/2464996.2465013

Liu, X., Sun, Q., Meng, Y., Fu, M., & Bourennane, S. (2018). Hyperspectral image classification is based on parameter-optimized 3D-CNNs combined with transfer learning and virtual samples. *Remote Sensing, 10*(9), 1425. doi:10.3390/rs10091425

Liu, Y., Khoshgoftaar, T. N., & Seliya, N. (2010). Evolutionary optimization of software quality modelling with multiple repositories. *IEEE Transactions on Software Engineering, 36*(6), 852–864.

Li, W., He, C., Fang, J., Zheng, J., Fu, H., & Yu, L. (2019). Semantic Segmentation-Based Building Footprint Extraction Using Very High-Resolution Satellite Images and Multi-Source GIS Data. *Remote Sensing, 11*(4), 403. doi:10.3390/rs11040403

Lohr, K. N., & Donaldson, M. S. (Eds.). (1994). *Health data in the information age: use, disclosure, and privacy.* National Academies Press.

Luján, M., Usman, A., Hardie, P., Freeman, T. L., & Gurd, J. R. (2005). Storage formats for sparse matrices in Java. In *Computational Science–ICCS 2005* (pp. 364–371). Springer Berlin Heidelberg. doi:10.1007/11428831_45

Magesh, G., Muthuswamy, P., & Singh, B. (2015). Use of Information Technology among school students in the State of Tamil Nadu, India. *International Journal of Applied Engineering Research, 10*(1), 2201–2209.

Maksimović, M. (2017). Transforming educational environment through Green Internet of Things (G-IoT). *Trend, 23,* 32–35.

Mallick, P. K., Ryu, S. H., Satapathy, S. K., Mishra, S., Nguyen, G. N., & Tiwari, P. (2019). Brain MRI image classification for cancer detection using deep wavelet autoencoder-based deep neural network. *IEEE Access: Practical Innovations, Open Solutions, 7,* 46278–46287. doi:10.1109/ACCESS.2019.2902252

Mannaro, K., Baralla, G., Pinna, A., & Ibba, S. (2018). A blockchain approach applied to a teledermatology platform in the Sardinian region (Italy). *Information*, *9*(2), 44. doi:10.3390/info9020044

Manning, Surdeanu, Bauer, Finkel, Bethard, & McClosky. (2014). The Stanford CoreNLP Natural Language Processing Toolkit. Association for Computational Linguistics (ACL).

Manuel, P. (2015). A trust model of cloud computing based on Quality of Service. *Annals of Operations Research*, *233*(1), 281–292. doi:10.100710479-013-1380-x

Marchi, E., Ringeval, F., & Schuller, B. (2014). *Voice-enabled assistive robots for handling autism spectrum conditions: An examination of the role of prosody.* Academic Press.

Marinetti, S., Grinzato, E., Bison, P., Bozzi, E., Chimenti, M., Pieri, G., & Salvetti, O. (2004). Statistical analysis of ir thermographic sequences by pca. *Infrared Physics & Technology*, *46*(1-2), 85–91.

Markall, G. R., Slemmer, A., Ham, D. A., Kelly, P. H. J., Cantwell, C. D., & Sherwin, S. J. (2013). Finite element assembly strategies on multi-core and many-core architectures. *International Journal for Numerical Methods in Fluids*, *71*(1), 80–97. doi:10.1002/fld.3648

Marquez, J., Villanueva, J., Solarte, Z., & Garcia, A. (2016). IoT in education: Integration of objects with virtual academic communities. In *New Advances in Information Systems and Technologies* (pp. 201–212). Springer. doi:10.1007/978-3-319-31232-3_19

Marwa, C., Haythem, B., Ezahra, S. F., & Mohamed, A. (2014). Image processing application on graphics processors. *International Journal of Image Processing*, *8*(3), 66.

Marzano, G., Martinovs, A., & Usca, S. (2019). Mechatronics Education: Needs and Challenges. In *Proceedings of the 12th International Scientific and Practical Conference*. Volume II (Vol. 214, p. 217).

Mather, P. M., & Koch, M. (2004). *Computer processing of remotely-sensed images: an introduction.* John Wiley & Sons.

Mathews, S. P., & Gondkar, D. R. (2017). Solution Integration Approach using IoT in Education System. *International Journal of Computer Trends and Technology*, *45*(1), 45–49. doi:10.14445/22312803/IJCTT-V45P109

Matin & Islam. (2012). Overview of Wireless Sensor Network. In *Wireless Sensor Networks - Technology and Protocols*. IntechOpen. Doi:10.5772/49376

Mena, J. B. (2003). State of the art on automatic road extraction for GIS update: A novel classification. *Pattern Recognition Letters*, *24*(16), 3037–3058. doi:10.1016/S0167-8655(03)00164-8

Mettler, M. (2016, September). Blockchain technology in healthcare: The revolution starts here. In *2016 IEEE 18th international conference on e-health networking, applications and services (Healthcom)* (pp. 1-3). IEEE.

Michahical, S. (2016). Image Compression using Singular Value Decomposition. *International Journal of Advanced Research in Computer and Communication Engineering, 7*, 208–211.

Michel, P. (2004). *The Use of Technology in the Study*. Diagnosis and Treatment of Autism.

Mikhail, B., Anna, D., Igor, I., & Natalia, K. (2019, July). orientation of the driverless car at loss of a satellite signal. In *2019 42nd International Conference on Telecommunications and Signal Processing (TSP)* (pp. 548-551). IEEE.

Mithya, V., Dharani, K. V., Nivetha, A., Praveen Rajakumari, G., & Roshel Infan, M. (2019). Smart Highway Toll Collection System. *International Journal of Innovative Technology and Exploring Engineering, 8*(5S).

Mohamed, A., Hamdi, M. S., & Tahar, S. (2015). A machine learning approach for big data in oil and gas pipelines. *International Conference on Future Internet of Things and Cloud*, 585-590.

Mokeev, A. V., & Mokeev, V. V. (2015). Pattern Recognition by Means of Linear Discriminant Analysis and the Principal Components Analysis. *Pattern Recognition and Image Analysis, 3*(4), 685–691. doi:10.1134/S1054661815040185

Montagne, E., & Ekambaram, A. (2004). An optimal storage format for sparse matrices. *Information Processing Letters, 90*(2), 87–92. doi:10.1016/j.ipl.2004.01.014

Moritz, P., Nishihara, R., Wang, S., Tumanov, A., Liaw, R., Liang, E., . . . Stoica, I. (2018). Ray: A distributed framework for emerging {AI} applications. In *13th {USENIX} Symposium on Operating Systems Design and Implementation ({OSDI} 18)* (pp. 561-577). Academic Press.

Mostafa, S., Tang, L., & Wu, F. (2019). Diagnosis of Autism Spectrum Disorder Based on Eigenvalues of Brain Networks. *IEEE Access: Practical Innovations, Open Solutions, 7*, 128474–128486. doi:10.1109/ACCESS.2019.2940198

Mrabet, H. E., & Moussa, A. A. (2017). Smart Classroom Environment Via IoT in Basic and Secondary Education. *Transactions on Machine Learning and Artificial Intelligence, 5*(4).

Muchahari, M. K., & Sinha, S. K. (2012, December). A new trust management architecture for a cloud computing environment. In *2012 International Symposium on Cloud and Services Computing* (pp. 136-140). IEEE. 10.1109/ISCOS.2012.30

Mukaddes, A. M., Shioya, R., & Ogino, M. (2014). Comparative Study of Sparse Matrix Storage Format in the Finite Element Analysis of Thermal-Structure Coupling Problem. *Proc. International conference on computational methods*, 1-9.

Munshi, A. (2008). OpenCL: Parallel Computing on the GPU and CPU. *Proceeding of 35st International Conference and Exhibition on Computer Graphics and Interactive Techniques*.

Nakamoto, S. (2008). *Bitcoin: A peer-to-peer electronic cash system*. Retrieved from https://bitcoin.org/ bitcoin.pdf

Namal, S., Gamaarachchi, H., MyoungLee, G., & Um, T. W. (2015, December). Autonomic trust management in cloud-based and highly dynamic IoT applications. In 2015 ITU Kaleidoscope: Trust in the Information Society (K-2015) (pp. 1-8). IEEE.

Narkhede, S. (2020). *Understanding AUC - ROC Curve*. Medium. Available at: https://towardsdatascience.com/understanding-auc-roc-curve-68b2303cc9c5

Nasridinov, A., Lee, Y., & Park, Y. (2014). Decision Tree Construction on GPU: Ubiquitous Parallel Computing Approach. *Computing, 96*(5), 403–413. doi:10.100700607-013-0343-z

National Transportation Safety Board (NTSB). (n.d.). http://www.ntsb.gov/

Naujoks, F., Höfling, S., Purucker, C., & Zeeb, K. (2018). From partial and high automation to manual driving: Relationship between non-driving related tasks, drowsiness and take-over performance. *Accident; Analysis and Prevention, 121*, 28–42. doi:10.1016/j.aap.2018.08.018 PMID:30205284

Nguyen, H. (2007). *GPU Gems 3*. Addison-Wesley Professional.

Nickolls, J., Buck, I., Garland, M., & Skadron, K. (2010). Scalable Parallel Programming with CUDA. *ACM Queue; Tomorrow's Computing Today, 6*(2), 40–53. doi:10.1145/1365490.1365500

Nikolopoulos. (2011). *Robotic Agents used to Help Teach Social Skills to Children with Autism: The Third Generation*. Academic Press.

Ning, H., & Hu, S. (2012). Technology classification, industry, and education for Future Internet of Things. *International Journal of Communication Systems, 25*(9), 1230–1241. doi:10.1002/dac.2373

Noor, T. H., & Sheng, Q. Z. (2011, December). Credibility-based trust management for services in cloud environments. In *International Conference on Service-Oriented Computing* (pp. 328-343). Springer. 10.1007/978-3-642-25535-9_22

Noor, T. H., & Sheng, Q. Z. (2011, October). Trust as a service: A framework for trust management in cloud environments. In *International Conference on Web Information Systems Engineering* (pp. 314-321). Springer. 10.1007/978-3-642-24434-6_27

Noor, T. H., Sheng, Q. Z., Yao, L., Dustdar, S., & Ngu, A. H. (2015). CloudArmor: Supporting reputation-based trust management for cloud services. *IEEE Transactions on Parallel and Distributed Systems, 27*(2), 367–380. doi:10.1109/TPDS.2015.2408613

Novak, P. K., Smailović, J., Sluban, B., & Mozetič, I. (2015). Sentiment of emoticons. *PLoS One, 10*, 12.

Ntaountaki, P., Lorentzou, G., Lykothanasi, A., Anagnostopoulou, P., Alexandropoulou, V., & Drigas, A. (2019). Robotics in Autism Intervention. *International Journal of Recent Contributions from Engineering Science & IT, 7*(4), 4–17. doi:10.3991/ijes.v7i4.11448

Nunes, R., & Almeida, J. A. (2010). Parallelization of sequential Gaussian, indicator and direct simulation algorithms. *Computers & Geosciences, 36*(8), 1042–1052. doi:10.1016/j.cageo.2010.03.005

NVIDIA Corporation. (2010). *CUDA Best Practices Guide*. NVIDIA Corporation.

NVIDIA Corporation. (2014). *CUDA C Programming Guide*. NVIDIA Corporation.

O'Shea, K., & Nash, R. (2015). *An introduction to convolutional neural networks*. arXiv preprint arXiv:1511.08458

Obeidat, I. (2019). *Intensive pre-processing of kdd cup 99 for network intrusion classification using machine learning techniques*. Academic Press.

Oberhuber, T., Suzuki, A., & Vacata, J. (2010). New row-grouped CSR format for storing the sparse matrices on GPU with implementation in CUDA. Acta Technica Journal, 436-440.

Omarhommadi & Mamdoohalzahrani. (n.d.). Comparison of Different toll collections system's and RFID tool collection system. *American Journal of Engineering Research, 6*(1), 118-121.

Ortaç, G., & Özcan, G. (2018, October). A Comparative Study for Hyperspectral Data Classification with Deep Learning and Dimensionality Reduction Techniques. *Uludağ University Journal of The Faculty of Engineering, 23*(3), 73–90.

Pai, S. S. (2017). IOT Application in Education. *International Journal for Advance Research and Development, 2*(6), 20–24.

Palestra, G., Carolis, B.D., & Esposito, F. (2017). Artificial Intelligence for Robot-Assisted Treatment of Autism. *WAIAH@AI*IA*.

Pathuri. (2019). Feature-Based Opinion Mining for Amazon Product's using MLT. *International Journal of Innovative Technology and Exploring Engineering, 8*(11), 4105–4109. doi:10.35940/ijitee.K1837.0981119

Pavithra, L. K., & Sharmila, T. S. (2018). An efficient framework for image retrieval using color, texture and edge features. *Computers & Electrical Engineering, 70*, 580–593. doi:10.1016/j.compeleceng.2017.08.030

Perez, L., & Wang, J. (2017). *The effectiveness of data augmentation in image classification using deep learning*. arXiv preprint arXiv:1712.04621

Pervez, S., ur Rehman, S., & Alandjani, G. (2018). Role of Internet of Things (IOT) in Higher Education. In *4th International Conference on Advances in Education and Social Sciences* (pp. 792-800). Academic Press.

Peter & Perttunen. (2014). *Network Topologies*. https://www.stl.tech/sterlite-live/application_notes/1/original/Network_Topologies.pdf?1499156038

Peterson, K., Deeduvanu, R., Kanjamala, P., & Boles, K. (2016, September). A blockchain-based approach to health information exchange networks. In *Proc. NIST Workshop Blockchain Healthcare (Vol. 1,* No. 1, pp. 1-10). Academic Press.

Pilkington, M. (2016). Blockchain technology: principles and applications. In *Research handbook on digital transformations.* Edward Elgar Publishing. doi:10.4337/9781784717766.00019

Polat, H., Polat, O., & Cetin, A. (2020). Detecting DDoS Attacks in Software-Defined Networks Through Feature Selection Methods and Machine Learning Models. *Sustainability, 12*(3), 1035. doi:10.3390u12031035

Prabhu, B., Sudhir, S., Maheswaran, S., & Navaneethakrishnan, M. (2013). Real-World Applications of Distributed Clustering Mechanism in Dense Wireless Sensor Networks. International Journal of Computing. *Communications and Networking., 2,* 99–105.

Pradeepini, G., Pradeepa, G., Tejanagasri, B., & Gorrepati, S. H. (2018). Data classification and personal care management system by machine learning approach. *IACSIT International Journal of Engineering and Technology, 7*(32), 219–223. doi:10.14419/ijet.v7i2.32.15571

Prasanth, Y., Sreedevi, E., Gayathri, N., & Rahul, A. S. (2017). Analysis and implementation of ensemble feature selection to improve accuracy of software defect detection model. *Journal of Advanced Research in Dynamical and Control Systems, 9*(18), 601–613.

Qin, J., Chao, K., Kim, M. S., Lu, R., & Burks, T. F. (2013). Hyperspectral and multispectral imaging for evaluating food safety and quality. *Journal of Food Engineering, 118*(2), 157–171. doi:10.1016/j.jfoodeng.2013.04.001

Ramuhalli, P., Udpa, L., & Udpa, S. (2002). Electromagnetic nde signal inversion by function approximation neural networks. *IEEE Transactions on Magnetics, 38,* 3633–3642.

Rasti, P., Ahmad, A., Samiei, S., Belin, E., & Rousseau, D. (2019). Supervised image classification by scattering transform with application to weed detection in culture crops of high density. *Remote Sensing, 11*(3), 249. doi:10.3390/rs11030249

Reddy, B. M., & Shanthala, S. (2017). *Performance Analysis of GPU V/S CPU for Image Processing Applications.* Issue II. *International Journal for Research in Applied Science and Engineering Technology, 5*(II), 437–443. doi:10.22214/ijraset.2017.2061

Reuschenbach, A., Wang, M., Ganjineh, T., & Gohring, D. (2011, April). iDriver-human machine interface for autonomous cars. In *2011 Eighth International Conference on Information Technology: New Generations* (pp. 435-440). IEEE.

Ricks, D. J., & Colton, M. B. (2010). Trends and considerations in robot-assisted autism therapy. *2010 IEEE International Conference on Robotics and Automation,* 4354-4359. 10.1109/ROBOT.2010.5509327

Russell, S., & Norvig, P. (2003). *Artificial Intelligence: A Modern Approach* (2nd ed.). Prentice Hall.

Sadek, A. R. (2012). SVD Based Image Processing Applications: State of The Art, Contributions and Research Challenges. *International Journal of Advanced Computer Science and Applications, 101*, 26–34.

Sahoo, K. S., Tripathy, B. K., Naik, K., Ramasubbareddy, S., Balusamy, B., Khari, M., & Burgos, D. (2020). An Evolutionary SVM Model for DDOS Attack Detection in Software Defined Networks. *IEEE Access: Practical Innovations, Open Solutions, 8*, 132502–132513. doi:10.1109/ACCESS.2020.3009733

Sahu, K. K., & Satao, K. J. (2013). Image Compression Methods using Dimension Reduction and Classification through PCA and LDA: A Review. *International Journal of Science and Research, 4*, 2277–2280.

Sanders, J., & Kandrot, E. (2011). CUDA by Example: An Introduction to General-Purpose GPU Programming. Addison-Wesley.

Sanders, J., & Kandrot, E. (2010). *CUDA by Example: An Introduction to General Purpose GPU Programming.* Addison - Wesley.

Sandhu, K., & Singh, M. (2018). Image compression using singular value decomposition (SVD). *International Journal of Latest Research in Science and Technology, 15*, 5–8.

Saule, E., Kaya, K., & Çatalyürek, U. V. (2014). Performance evaluation of sparse matrix multiplication kernels on intel xeon phi. In *Parallel Processing and Applied Mathematics* (pp. 559–570). Springer Berlin Heidelberg. doi:10.1007/978-3-642-55224-3_52

Savas, O., Jin, G., & Deng, J. (2013, May). Trust management in cloud-integrated wireless sensor networks. In *2013 International Conference on Collaboration Technologies and Systems (CTS)* (pp. 334-341). IEEE. 10.1109/CTS.2013.6567251

Saxe, J., & Berlin, K. (2015). Deep neural network based malware detection using two dimensional binary program features. In *2015 10th International Conference on Malicious and Unwanted Software (MALWARE).* IEEE. 10.1109/MALWARE.2015.7413680

Saxena, S., Sharma, S., & Sharma, N. (2017). Study of Parallel Image Processing with the Implementation of vHGW Algorithm using CUDA on NVIDIA'S GPU Framework. In *Proceedings of the World Congress on Engineering (Vol. 1).* Academic Press.

Scassellati, B. (2005). How Social Robots Will Help Us to Diagnose, Treat, and Understand Autism. *Procs. 12th Int. Symp. on Robotics Research.*

Schömig, N., Hargutt, V., Neukum, A., Petermann-Stock, I., & Othersen, I. (2015). The interaction between highly automated driving and the development of drowsiness. *Procedia Manufacturing, 3*, 6652–6659. doi:10.1016/j.promfg.2015.11.005

Scudellari, M. (2017). AI Predicts Autism From Infant Brain Scans. *IEEE Spectrum.*

Sen, A., Rudra, K., & Ghosh, S. (2015). Extracting situational awareness from microblogs during disaster events. *2015 7th International Conference on Communication Systems and Networks (COMSNETS).* 10.1109/COMSNETS.2015.7098720

Seth, R., & Shantaiya, S. (*2013*). A Survey on Image Compression Methods with PCA & LDA. *International Journal of Science and Research,* 274-277.

Shahnaz, R., Usman, A., & Chughtai, I. R. (2005). Review of storage techniques for sparse matrices. In *9th International Multitopic Conference, IEEE INMIC 2005* (pp. 1-7). IEEE. 10.1109/INMIC.2005.334453

Shamila, S. N. S., Mahendran, D. S., & Sathik, M. M. (2019). Image and Video Frame Extraction System Based on Improved Deep Learning Technique. *International Journal on Emerging Technologies, 10*(3), 384–390.

Sharma, Verma, Sandeep, & Sharma. (2013). Network topologies in wireless sensor networks: A review. *Int. J. Electron. Commun. Technol., 4,* 93–97.

She, T., Kang, X., Nishide, S., & Ren, F. (2018). Improving LEO Robot Conversational Ability via Deep Learning Algorithms for Children with Autism. *2018 5th IEEE International Conference on Cloud Computing and Intelligence Systems (CCIS),* 416-420.

Shi. (2019). The Application of AI as Reinforcement in the Intervention for Children With Autism Spectrum Disorders (ASD). *Journal of Educational and Developmental Psychology, 9.*

Simecek, I. (2009). Sparse matrix computations using the quad tree storage format. *Proc. 11th International Symposium on Symbolic and Numeric Algorithms for Scientific Computing (SYNASC),* 168-17.

Simecek, I., Langr, D., & Tvrdík, P. (2012). Space-efficient sparse matrix storage formats for massively parallel systems. *Proc. IEEE International Conference on Embedded Software and Systems,* 54-60.

Simon, H. D. (1991). Partitioning of unstructured problems for parallel processing. *Computing Systems in Engineering, 2*(2-3), 135–148. doi:10.1016/0956-0521(91)90014-V

Singh, Y., & Chauhan, A. (2005). Neural networks in data mining. *Journal of Theoretical and Applied Information Technology,* 37-42.

Singh. (2019). *Reduction of traffic at toll plaza by automatic toll collection using RFID and GSM technology.* doi:10.21276/ijcesr.2019.6.6.32

Sivakumar, S., Ganesan, P., & Sundar, S. (2017). A MMDBM Classifier with CPU and CUDA GPU computing in various sorting procedures. *The International Arab Journal of Information Technology, 14*(7), 897–906.

Skalski, P. (2020). *Gentle Dive Into Math Behind Convolutional Neural Networks.* Medium. Available at: https://towardsdatascience.com/gentle-dive-into-math-behind-convolutional-neural-networks-79a07dd44cf9

Sophian, A., Tian, G., Taylor, D., & Rudlin, J. (2003). A feature extraction technique based on principal component analysis for pulsed eddy current ndt. *NDT & E International, 36*(1), 37–41.

Sreedevi, E., PremaLatha, V., & Sivakumar, S. (2019). A Comparative Study on New Classification Algorithm using NASA MDP Datasets for Software Defect Detection. *2ⁿᵈInternational Conference on Intelligent Sustainable Systems (ICISS 2019),* 312-317.

Sreedevi, E., & Prasanth, Y. (2017). A novel class balance ensemble classification model for application and object oriented defect database. *Journal of Advanced Research in Dynamical and Control Systems, 9,* 702–726.

Srivastava, P., Binh, N. T., & Khare, A. (2014). Content-based image retrieval using moments of local ternary pattern. *Mobile Networks and Applications, 19*(5), 618–625. doi:10.100711036-014-0526-7

Stone, H. S. (1971). Parallel processing with the perfect shuffle. *IEEE Transactions on Computers, 100*(2), 153–161. doi:10.1109/T-C.1971.223205

Stoyanov, Cardie, & Wiebe. (2005). *Multi-perspective Question Answering Using the OpQA Corpus.* doi:10.3115/1220575.122069

Su, B. Y., & Keutzer, K. (2012). clSpMV: A cross-platform OpenCL SpMV framework on GPUs. In *Proceedings of the 26th ACM international conference on Supercomputing* (pp. 353-364). ACM. 10.1145/2304576.2304624

Suja, K.V., & Rajkumar, K.K. (2019). Classification of Abnormalities in Medical Images Based on Feature Transformation- A Review. *International Journal of Scientific & Engineering Research,* 1304-1308.

Sun, X., Zhang, Y., Wang, T., Long, G., Zhang, X., & Li, Y. (2011). CRSD: application specific auto-tuning of SpMV for diagonal sparse matrices. InEuro-Par 2011 Parallel Processing, 316-327.

Sun, X. H., & Chen, Y. (2010). Reevaluating Amdahl's law in the multicore era. *Journal of Parallel and Distributed Computing, 70*(2), 183–188. doi:10.1016/j.jpdc.2009.05.002

Sun, X., Chang, G., & Li, F. (2011, September). A trust management model to enhance the security of cloud computing environments. In *2011 Second International Conference on Networking and Distributed Computing* (pp. 244-248). IEEE. 10.1109/ICNDC.2011.56

Swetha, Santhosh, & Sofia. (2018). Wireless Sensor Network: A Survey. *IJARCCE, 7,* 114-117. doi:10.17148/IJARCCE.2018.71124

Syberfeldt, A., & Ekblom, T. (2017). A comparative evaluation of the GPU vs. the CPU for parallelization of evolutionary algorithms through multiple independent runs. *International Journal of Computer Science & Information Technology, 9*(3), 1–14. doi:10.5121/ijcsit.2017.9301

Tahir, R. (2018). A Study on Malware and Malware Detection Techniques. *International Journal of Education and Management Engineering, 8*(2).

Tang, W. T., Zhao, R., Lu, M., Liang, Y., Huyng, H. P., Li, X., & Goh, R. S. M. (2015). Optimizing and auto-tuning scale-free sparse matrix-vector multiplication on Intel Xeon Phi. *International Symposium on Code Generation and Optimization (CGO)*, 136-145. 10.1109/CGO.2015.7054194

Tang, W., Tan, W., Goh, R. S. M., Turner, S., & Wong, W. K. (2015). A Family of Bit-Representation-Optimized Formats for Fast Sparse Matrix-Vector Multiplication on the GPU. *IEEE Transactions on Parallel and Distributed Systems, 26*(9), 2373–2385. doi:10.1109/TPDS.2014.2357437

Tharwat, A., Gaber, T., Ibrahim, A., & Hassanian, A. E. (2017). Linear discriminant analysis: A detailed tutorial. *AI Communications, 127*, 1–22.

Thomas, T., Vijayaraghavan, A. P., & Emmanuel, S. (2020). *Machine Learning Approaches in Cyber Security Analytics*. Springer. doi:10.1007/978-981-15-1706-8

Too, E. C., Yujian, L., Njuki, S., & Yingchun, L. (2019). A comparative study of fine-tuning deep learning models for plant disease identification. *Computers and Electronics in Agriculture, 161*, 272–279. doi:10.1016/j.compag.2018.03.032

Tuan, N. N., Hung, P. H., Nghia, N. D., Tho, N. V., Phan, T. V., & Thanh, N. H. (2020). A DDoS Attack Mitigation Scheme in ISP Networks Using Machine Learning Based on SDN. *Electronics (Basel), 9*(3), 413. doi:10.3390/electronics9030413

Tuan, T. A., Long, H. V., Kumar, R., Priyadarshini, I., & Son, N. T. K. (2019). Performance evaluation of Botnet DDoS attack detection using machine learning. *Evolutionary Intelligence*, •••, 1–12.

Tvrdík, P., & Šimeče, I. (2006). A new diagonal blocking format and model of cache behavior for sparse matrices. Parallel Processing and Applied Mathematics, 164-171. doi:10.1007/11752578_21

Umuroglu, Y., & Jahre, M. (2014). An energy efficient column-major backend for FPGA SpMV accelerators. In *Computer Design (ICCD), 2014 32nd IEEE International Conference on* (pp. 432-439). IEEE. 10.1109/ICCD.2014.6974716

Urmson, C., Anhalt, J., Bagnell, D., Baker, C., Bittner, R., Clark, M. N., ... Gittleman, M. (2008). Autonomous driving in urban environments: Boss and the urban challenge. *Journal of Field Robotics, 25*(8), 425–466. doi:10.1002/rob.20255

Vázquez, F., Ortega, G., Fernández, J. J., & Garzón, E. M. (2010). Improving the performance of the sparse matrix vector product with GPUs. *IEEE 10th International Conference on Computer and Information Technology (CIT)*, 1146-1151. 10.1109/CIT.2010.208

Veeramanickam, M. R. M., & Mohanapriya, M. (2016). Iot enabled futurus smart campus with effective e-learning: i-campus. *GSTF Journal of Engineering Technology (JET), 3*(4), 8-87.

Vishwakarma, G., & Thakur, G. S. (2019). Comparative Performance Analysis of Combined SVM-PCA for Content-based Video Classification by Utilizing Inception V3. *International Journal on Emerging Technologies, 10*(3), 397–403.

Volchok, B. A., & Chernyak, M. M. (1968). Transfer of microwave radiation in clouds and precipitation. *Transfer of Microwave Radiation in the Atmosphere, NASA TT, F-590*, 90–97.

Waltz, E. (2018). Therapy Robot Teaches Social Skills to Children With Autism. *IEEE Spectrum*.

Wang, H., & Song, Y. (2018). Secure cloud-based EHR system using attribute-based cryptosystem and blockchain. *Journal of Medical Systems*, *42*(8), 152. doi:10.100710916-018-0994-6 PMID:29974270

Wang, J., Yang, Y., Mao, J., Huang, Z., Huang, C., & Xu, W. (2016). Cnn-rnn: A unified framework for multi-label image classification. In *Proceedings of the IEEE conference on computer vision and pattern recognition* (pp. 2285-2294). 10.1109/CVPR.2016.251

Wang, M., Lu, Y., & Qin, J. (2020). A dynamic MLP-based DDoS attack detection method using feature selection and feedback. *Computers & Security*, *88*, 101645.

Wang, X. Y., Yu, Y. J., & Yang, H. Y. (2011). An effective image retrieval scheme using color, texture and shape features. *Computer Standards & Interfaces*, *33*(1), 59–68. doi:10.1016/j.csi.2010.03.004

Wang, X., Zhang, H., & Peng, G. (2017). A chordiogram image descriptor using local edgels. *Journal of Visual Communication and Image Representation*, *49*, 129–140. doi:10.1016/j.jvcir.2017.09.005

Wang, Y., Yan, H., Pan, C., & Xiang, S. (2011). Image editing based on sparse matrix-vector multiplication. *Proc. IEEE International Conference on Acoustics, Speech and Signal Processing (ICASSP)*, 1317-1320. 10.1109/ICASSP.2011.5946654

Wieland, M., & Pittore, M. (2014). Performance evaluation of machine learning algorithms for urban pattern recognition from multi-spectral satellite images. *Remote Sensing*, *6*(4), 2912–2939. doi:10.3390/rs6042912

Wilheit, T. T., Chang, A. T. C., & Rao, V., M. S., Rodgers, E. B., & Theon, J. S. (1977). A satellite technique for quantitatively mapping rainfall rates over the oceans. *Journal of Applied Meteorology*, *16*(5), 551–560. doi:10.1175/1520-0450(1977)016<0551:ASTFQM>2.0.CO;2

Williams, S., Oliker, L., Vuduc, R., Shalf, J., Yelick, K., & Demmel, J. (2009). Optimization of sparse matrix–vector multiplication on emerging multicore platforms. *Parallel Computing*, *35*(3), 178–194. doi:10.1016/j.parco.2008.12.006

World Health Organization. (2019). *Autism spectrum disorders*. WHO.

Wu, T., Wang, B., Shan, Y., Yan, F., Wang, Y., & Xu, N. (2010). Efficient pagerank and spmv computation on amd gpus. In *Parallel Processing (ICPP), 2010 39th International Conference on* (pp. 81-89). IEEE. 10.1109/ICPP.2010.17

Xie, X. (2008). A review of recent advances in surface defect detection using texture analysis techniques. *ELCVIA. Electronic Letters on Computer Vision and Image Analysis*, *7*(3).

Yalla, P., Mandhala, V. N., Abhishiktha, V., Saisree, C., & Manogna, K. (2019). Machine Learning Techniques to Predict Defects by using Testing Parameters. *International Journal of Recent Technology and Engineering*, *8*(4), 7829–7834. doi:10.35940/ijrte.D5396.118419

Yang, A., Yang, X., Wu, W., Liu, H., & Zhuansun, Y. (2019). Research on feature extraction of tumor image based on convolutional neural network. *IEEE Access: Practical Innovations, Open Solutions*, *7*, 24204–24213. doi:10.1109/ACCESS.2019.2897131

Yang, C., Bruzzone, L., Zhao, H., Tan, Y., & Guan, R. (2018). Superpixel-based unsupervised band selection for classification of hyperspectral images. *IEEE Transactions on Geoscience and Remote Sensing*, *56*(12), 7230–7245. doi:10.1109/TGRS.2018.2849443

Yang, W., Li, K., Liu, Y., Shi, L., & Wan, L. (2014). Optimization of quasi-diagonal matrix–vector multiplication on GPU. *International Journal of High Performance Computing Applications*, *28*(2), 183–195. doi:10.1177/1094342013501126

Yang, W., Li, K., Mo, Z., & Li, K. (2015). Performance Optimization Using Partitioned SpMV on GPUs and Multicore CPUs. *IEEE Transactions on Computers*, *64*(9), 2623–2636. doi:10.1109/TC.2014.2366731

Yang, X., Parthasarathy, S., & Sadayappan, P. (2011). Fast sparse matrix-vector multiplication on GPUs: Implications for graph mining. *Proceedings of the VLDB Endowment International Conference on Very Large Data Bases*, *4*(4), 231–242. doi:10.14778/1938545.1938548

Yavits, L., Morad, A., & Ginosar, R. (2015). Sparse matrix multiplication on an associative processor. *IEEE Transactions on Parallel and Distributed Systems*, *26*(11), 3175–3183. doi:10.1109/TPDS.2014.2370055

Yue, J., Li, Z., Liu, L., & Fu, Z. (2011). Content-based image retrieval using color and texture fused features. *Mathematical and Computer Modelling*, *54*(3-4), 1121–1127. doi:10.1016/j.mcm.2010.11.044

Yue, X., Wang, H., Jin, D., Li, M., & Jiang, W. (2016). Healthcare data gateways: Found healthcare intelligence on blockchain with novel privacy risk control. *Journal of Medical Systems*, *40*(10), 218. doi:10.100710916-016-0574-6 PMID:27565509

Yun, Kim, & Choi. (2016). A robot-assisted behavioral intervention system for children with autism spectrum disorders. *Rob. Auton. Syst.*

Zhai, Y., Danandeh, N., Tan, Z., Gao, S., Paesani, F., & Götz, A. W. (2018). *Parallel implementation of machine learning-based many-body potentials on CPU and GPU*. Academic Press.

Zhamanov, A., Sakhiyeva, Z., Suliyev, R., & Kaldykulova, Z. (2017, November). IoT smart campus review and implementation of IoT applications into education process of university. In *2017 13th International Conference on Electronics, Computer and Computation (ICECCO)* (pp. 1-4). IEEE. 10.1109/ICECCO.2017.8333334

Zhang, P., White, J., Schmidt, D. C., & Lenz, G. (2017). *Applying software patterns to address interoperability in blockchain-based healthcare apps*. arXiv preprint arXiv:1706.03700

Zhang, B., Huang, W., Li, J., Zhao, C., Fan, S., Wu, J., & Liu, C. (2014). Principles, developments, and applications of computer vision for external quality inspection of fruits and vegetables: A review. *Food Research International, 62,* 326–343. doi:10.1016/j.foodres.2014.03.012

Zhang, J., Liu, E., Wan, J., Ren, Y., Yue, M., & Wang, J. (2013). Implementing Sparse Matrix-Vector Multiplication with QCSR on GPU. *International Journal of Applied Mathematics and Information Sciences, 7*(2), 473–482. doi:10.12785/amis/070207

Zhang, L., Su, H., & Shen, J. (2019). Hyperspectral Dimensionality Reduction Based on Multiscale Superpixelwise Kernel Principal Component Analysis. *Remote Sensing, 11*(10), 1219. doi:10.3390/rs11101219

Zhang, N. (2012). A Novel Parallel Scan for Multicore Processors and Its Application in Sparse Matrix-Vector Multiplication. *IEEE Transactions on Parallel and Distributed Systems, 23*(3), 397–404. doi:10.1109/TPDS.2011.174

Zhang, X., Gao, H., Guo, M., Li, G., Liu, Y., & Li, D. (2016). A study on key technologies of unmanned driving. *CAAI Transactions on Intelligence Technology, 1*(1), 4–13. doi:10.1016/j.trit.2016.03.003

Zhang, Y., Chen, H., Wei, Y., Zhao, P., Cao, J., Fan, X., ... Yao, J. (2019, October). From whole slide imaging to microscopy: Deep microscopy adaptation network for histopathology cancer image classification. In *International Conference on Medical Image Computing and Computer-Assisted Intervention* (pp. 360-368). Springer. 10.1007/978-3-030-32239-7_40

Zheng, C., Gu, S., Gu, T. X., Yang, B., & Liu, X.-P. (2014). BiELL: A bisection ELLPACK-based storage format for optimizing SpMV on GPUs. *Journal of Parallel and Distributed Computing, 74*(7), 2639–2647. doi:10.1016/j.jpdc.2014.03.002

Zhou, J., Chen, W., Peng, G., Xiao, H., Wang, H., & Chen, Z. (2017, December). Parallelizing convolutional neural network for the handwriting recognition problems with different architectures. In *2017 International Conference on Progress in Informatics and Computing (PIC)* (pp. 71-76). IEEE. 10.1109/PIC.2017.8359517

Zhu, Z. T., Yu, M. H., & Riezebos, P. (2016). A research framework of smart education. Smart learning environments, 3(1), 4.

Zhuravlev, S., Blagodurov, S., & Fedorova, A. (2010, March). Addressing shared resource contention in multicore processors via scheduling. *ACM SIGPLAN Notices, 45*(3), 129–142. doi:10.1145/1735971.1736036

Zimmermann, T., & Nagappan, N. (2009). Predicting defects with program dependencies, in Empirical Software Engineering and Measurement. *ESEM 2009. 3'd International Symposium on,* 435-438.

Zou, D., Dou, Y., Guo, S., & Ni, S. (2013). High performance sparse matrix-vector multiplication on FPGA. *IEICE Electronics Express, 10*(17), 20130529–20130529. doi:10.1587/elex.10.20130529

Zyskind, G., & Nathan, O. (2015). Decentralizing privacy: Using blockchain to protect personal data. In 2015 IEEE Security and Privacy Workshops (pp. 180-184). IEEE.

About the Contributors

P. Swarnalatha is an Associate Professor, in the School of Computer Science and Engineering, VIT University, at Vellore, India. She pursued her Ph.D. degree in Image Processing and Intelligent Systems. She has published more than 130 papers in International Journals/International Conference Proceedings/National Conferences. She is having 19+ years of teaching and research experience. She is a member of IACSIT, CSI, ACM, IACSIT, IEEE (Senior Member), ACEEE. She is an Editorial board member/reviewer of International/ National Journals and Conferences. Her current research interest includes Image Processing, Remote Sensing, Artificial Intelligence, Big data Analytics and Software Engineering.

S. Prabu has completed B.Engg. in Computer Science and Engineering from Sona College of Technology (Autonomous) and M.Tech in Remote Sensing from College of Engineering Guindy, Anna University Chennai and one more M.Tech in Information Technology at School of Computer Science and Engineering, Bharathidasan University Trichy. Did Doctoral studies on Integration of GIS and Artificial Neural Networks to Map the Landslide Susceptibility from College of Engineering Guindy, Anna University, Chennai under faculty of Civil Engg. Was a Post-Doctoral Fellow at GISE Advanced research lab, Department of Computer Science and Engineering, Indian Institute of Technology Bombay. Has more than 100 publications in national and international journals and conferences. Has organized 3 International Conferences which includes one IEEE Conference as chair and also participated in many workshops and seminars. Is a member of many professional bodies and is a senior member of IACSIT, UACEE and IEEE. Has more than 15 years of experience in teaching and research. Currently is working as a Professor and Head, School of CSE, Vellore Institute of Technology Vellore.

* * *

S. Anandakumar holds a PhD degree in the field of computer science from VIT University. He possesses one decade of experience in teaching and worked as Project Assistant in IIT Kharagpur. His areas of interest include QoS in Wireless Sensor Networks, Green computing, Mobile computing, Ad-Hoc networks, MANET, Data Mining, IoT. He has published numerous articles in SCOPUS and SCI-indexed journals. He presented his chapters in various national and international conferences and attended many faculty development programs to keep pace with changing teaching environment. He is a member of multiple scientific and professional bodies. Apart from teaching, he is passionate about social services and rural development activities.

Lahari Anne is graduated from VIT University. She is a security and machine learning enthusiast. She has worked as a UI developer and software testing engineer with Nutantek and as a software developer with ExxonMobil. She enjoys writing blogs on security and cutting edge technologies.

Magesh R. Babu has a Ph.D., MIMSA., Professor & Head, C' Block, 4th Floor, Sri Sakthi Amma Institute of Biomedical Research, Sri Narayani Hospital and Research Center.

Samarth Bhutani is a Software developer at Cerner Corporation. He was a student of B. Tech CSE in the Vellore Institute of Technology.

Vibhu Dagar is pursuing Computer Science And Engineering from Vellore Institute of Technology.

Debajit Datta is an engineering student pursuing B.Tech degree in computer science branch, enrolled in Vellore Institute of Technology, Vellore campus. He has got wide industrial exposure from five internships. He was born in Kolkata on March 31, 2000 and in his nineteen years. He did his schooling from Kendriya Vidyalaya, Barrackpore (Airforce Station). He had been actively participating in various clubs and chapters of VIT; he is currently a core committee member of Venturesity and is a former frontend developer in DSC Vellore which is powered by Google Developers. He has secured first position amongst entire computer science engineering students of VIT Vellore in his first year, and is amongst top five currently.

Sreedevi E. received her M.Tech degree in Computer Science and Engineering from Acharya Nagarujuna University. She completed her Phd in Computer Science and Engineering with a specialization Software Engineering from Koneru Lakshmaiah University, Guntur. She is working as an Associate Professor in Dept of C.S.E, K.L.E.F, Vaddeswaram, Guntur A.P. Her area of Interest are "software engineering" and "software agents".

Gyasi Emmanuel Kwabena received his BSc. Computer Science degree from Catholic University College of Ghana (CUCG), Sunyani-Ghana, and his MPhil. Computer Science degree from Kwame Nkrumah University of Science and Technology (KNUST), Kumasi-Ghana. He is currently a Ph.D. Computer Science Scholar and Teaching cum Research Assistant at School of Computer Science and Engineering (SCOPE) at Vellore Institute of Technology (VIT) University - India. He maintained an active appointment at Ghana Meteorological Agency (GMet), Ghana as a Meteorologist for more than 15 years. Gyasi has attended several courses which include MESA/PUMA 2015 System Administration in July 2016 at Mauritius; Training Course on the Use and Maintenance of Meteorological Instruments for Developing Countries, in June 2017 at Nanjing University of Information Science and Technology (NUIST), Nanjing-China; Information and Communication Technology for Meteorological Services in July 2018 at Korea Meteorological Administration (KMA), South Korea. He has served on several committees and boards and has also attended seminars and conferences with a couple of publications. His research interest is in Artificial Intelligence (AI), Machine Learning (ML), Big Data Analytics, and many more.

Muhammad Rukunuddin Ghalib is an Associate Professor at School of Computer Science & Engineering, Vellore Institute of Technology (VIT), Vellore, India. Completed his B.Tech, M.E, PhD in Computer Science & Engineering from Anna University, Chennai. He is actively involved in research related to Big Data Analytics, Soft Computing and Artificial Intelligence. A Senior IEEE member and also a life member of CSI. He has founded the SIAM student chapter at VIT Vellore. He has authored & co-authored on various research chapters in International peer-reviewed journals & Conferences. Also, an active reviewer in SCI & SCOPUS journals.

Uttam Ghosh joined Vanderbilt University as an Assistant Professor of the Practice of Electrical Engineering and Computer Science in January 2018. He obtained his PhD in Electronics and Electrical Engineering from the Indian Institute of Technology Kharagpur, India in 2013, and has Post-doctoral experience at the University of Illinois in Urbana-Champaign, Fordham University, and Tennessee State University. His main research interests include Cybersecurity, Computer Networks, Wireless Networks, Information-Centric Networking and Software-Defined Networking. Dr Ghosh is selected for Junior Faculty Teaching Fellow for 2018-19 at Vanderbilt University. He is also serving as Associate Editor and Reviewers of reputed journals and conferences. He is a Senior Member of the IEEE. Member of Sigma Xi, AAAS, ASEE, and ACM.

Sagar Gupta is currently pursuing B-tech in CSE from Vellore Institute of Technology, Vellore.

D. Haritha working as a Professor & HOD in Department of Computer Science and Engineering at K L University, Guntur, AP-522502. Her received Doctor of Philosophy degree in Department of Computer Science and Engineering in Acharya Nagarjuna University, India. She completed M.Tech & B.Tech Computer Science and Engineering from K L University, India, Her research program focuses on Data mining and areas of interest are parallel computing (GPU), Classification and analysis, Image processing.

Saira Banu Jamalmohammed is working as a faculty at the School of Computer Science and Engineering, VIT University, Vellore. She completed her Ph.D. in the domain of parallel computing in multicores from VIT University. She has publications in the domain of parallel computing with good citations. She has Fourteen years of teaching experience. Her areas of interest include parallel computing, computer architecture, Image Processing, and Multicore Programming.

Latha M. is currently working as associate professor of computer science in Sri Sarada College for Women (Autonomous), Salem - 16. She has 24 years of teaching experience. Her area of research includes Software Engineering and Digital Image Processing. Her h-index is 5 and i10 index.

Anand Mahendran received his Ph.D. (computer science and engineering) from VIT University, India, in 2012, his M.E. (computer science and engineering) from Anna University, India, in 2005, and his B.E. (computer science and engineering) from VIT University, India, in2003. His research interests include formal language theory and automata, and bio-inspired computing models. He has published more than 20 papers in international journals and refereed international conferences. He worked as an assistant professor in the College of Computer Science and Information Systems, Jazan University, Kingdom of Saudi Arabia. Currently, he is working as an Associate Professor in School of Computer Science and Engineering, VIT Vellore.

Anbarasi Masilamani received a Ph.D from Vellore Institute of Technology, Vellore, Tamilnadu, India. She is an Assistant Professor (Senior) in the School of Computer Science and Engineering at Vellore Institute of Technology, Vellore,

Tamilnadu, India. Her research interests include Database, Data Mining, Soft Computing and Bioinformatics.

Garima Mathur is currently pursuing Btech . CSE from Vellore Institute of Technology, Vellore.

Ranjani Mudaliar is Pursuing M.Tech CSE Spl in Artificial Intelligence and Machine Learning from Vellore Institute of Technology.

Aritro Paul is a Computer Science Student, VIT University, Vellore.

Sonal Rajurkar is currently pursuing her master's in Computer Science with specialization in Artificial intelligence and Machine learning from VIT university, vellore. She completed her bachelor in Computer Science itself in year 2019 with overall cgpa as 9.64.Since childhood she was keen in learning new things and always liked learning. This was one of the reason to achieve good grades throughout her educational phase. She has the ability to mold herself according to the situations. She can grasp things quickly and can handle extreme conditions. Along with academics she has published two research papers, one in IEEE Xplore and other in IJATCSE journal. She also participated in Smart India Hachathon and her team was one of the finalist. She also volunteered in many rotaract events and was director of Rotaract club in college. To freshen up her mind she loves singing and listening to music.

Jaya S. is currently pursuing Ph.D Research Scholar (Full Time) in Department of Computer Scicence at Sri Sarada college for Women (Autonomous), Salem-16. She has published 3 research papers and 1 conference proceedings in IEEE. Her area of interest is Digital Image Processing.

Sivakumar S. is working as an Associate Professor in Department of Computer Science and Engineering at K L University, Guntur, AP-522502. I received Doctor of Philosophy degree in Department of Mathematics, College of Engineering Guindy Campus, Anna University, Chennai, India in the year of 2015. I have completed M.Sc Computer science from Periyar E.V.R College and M.Phil computer Science from St.Joseph's College of Bharathidasan University, India, My research program focuses on Data mining and areas of interest are parallel computing (GPU), Classification and analysis, Image processing and CUDA Programming.

Ramani Selvanambi is an Assistant professor (Senior) in the School of Computing Science and Engineering at VIT, Vellore, India. He received his BE (Computer Science and Engineering) from MNM Jain Engineering College, Madras University and M.Tech (Computer Science and Engineering) from Bharathidasan University and Ph.D. (Computer Science and Engineering) from VIT, Vellore. He has 10 years of experience in teaching and 2 years of experience in the Consultancy and Software Industry. He has published about 30 papers in International Journals on Data Mining, Nature-Inspired Algorithms, and Health Care. His research interest includes Data Mining, Database Systems, Optimization Techniques, Internet, and Web Technology. He is a life member of the Computer Society of India.

Lavanya Sendhilvel is currently working as an Associate Professor in the School of Computer Science and Engineering(SCOPE) in VIT University, Vellore. She received her Ph.D. degree in Computer Science and Engineering from VIT University, Vellore, on August 2015 [July 2011 - August 2015]. She completed MTech in Computer Science and Engineering from VIT University, Vellore, in the year 2011. She also received BE degree in Computer Science and Engineering from the Anna University, India, in 2005. Her current research interests includes Computational Intelligence, Data Science, NoSQL databases, Data Mining and Warehousing, Machine Learning.

Brijendra Singh received a Ph.D from VIT University, Vellore, Tamilnadu, India. He is an Assistant Professor (Senior) in the School of Information Technology and Engineering at VIT University Vellore, Tamilnadu, India. His research interests include Health Informatics, Soft Computing Techniques, Artificial Intelligence, Rough Set, Knowledge Representations.

Sumaiya Thaseen is an Associate Professor with fourteen years of teaching and research experience in the School of Information Technology and Engineering, Vellore Institute of Technology, Vellore, Tamil Nadu, India. Few of her publications in the domain of intrusion detection are indexed in Springer, Elsevier and SCI. Sumaiya has 443 citations in Google Scholar and the H-Index is 9. Her areas of research are Cyber Security, Machine Learning and Cyber-Physical Systems.

Mythili Thirugnanam is an Associate Professor Senior in the School of Computer Science and Engineering at Vellore Institute of Technology, Vellore, India. She received her Master's in Software Engineering from VIT University. She has been awarded a Doctorate in Computer Science and Engineering at VIT University in 2014. She has a teaching experience of around 13 years and research experience of three years in handling sponsored projects funded by the Government of India. Her area of specialization includes image processing, software engineering, and machine learning. She has published more than 45 papers in international and national journals and presented around 20 papers in various national and international conferences.

Biju Vasudevan is an Assistant Professor in the Department of General Studies, Jubail University College, Jubail Industrial City, KSA. He has a total of 16 years of experience in teaching and research. He has published many research articles in various peer reviewed international journals and most of them are indexed in Scopus and some are in Springer. His areas of interest are Algebra, Linear Algebra, Homological Algebra, Fuzzy topology, Algebraic Cryptography and Algebraic geometry. He has published three text books in Engineering mathematics and has delivered many invited talks. He is a member of editorial boards for many international journals and Editor in chief of the international journal "Asia Mathematika".

PremaLatha Velagapalli received her B.Tech degree in Computer Science and Engineering from P.V.P.Siddhartha Institute of Science and Technology(JNTU-H) A.P. She Completed her Postgraduation M.Tech degree in Computer Science and Engineering from Karunya University, Coimbatore, T.N. She is working as an Assistant Professor in Dept of C.S.E,K.L.E.F, Vaddeswaram, Guntur, A.P. She is a Phd Scholar in KL UNIVERSITY, Vaddeaswaram, Guntur, A.P. She is an author of seven research papers in International Journal's. Her area of Interest is in "Software Agents in Internet of Thing's."

Komal Veauli is a Software developer. He was a student of B. Tech CSE in the Vellore Institute of Technology.

Amber Verma is a student of VIT University, Vellore pursuing B.Tech in Computer Science.

Akila Wijethunge is a lecturer in Mechatronics at University of Sri Jayewardenepura.

Prasanth Yalla received his B.Tech Degree from Acharya Nagarjuna University, Guntur (Dist), India in 2001, M.Tech degree in Computer Science and Engineering from Acharya Nagarjuna University in 2004, and received his Ph.D. degree in CSE titled "A Generic Framework to identify and execute functional test cases for services based on Web Service Description Language" from Acharya Nagarjuna University in April 2013.

Index

Ensure Quality Research is Introduced to the Academic Community

Become an IGI Global Reviewer for Authored Book Projects

Premier Reference Source

Emerging GIS Applications for Emergency and Disaster Management

Premier Reference Source

Managerial Strategies and Green Solutions for Project Sustainability

Premier Reference Source

Comparative Approaches to Using R and Python for Statistical Data Analysis

Premier Reference Source

Solutions for High-Touch Communications in a High-Tech World

The overall success of an authored book project is dependent on quality and timely reviews.

In this competitive age of scholarly publishing, constructive and timely feedback significantly expedites the turnaround time of manuscripts from submission to acceptance, allowing the publication and discovery of forward-thinking research at a much more expeditious rate. Several IGI Global authored book projects are currently seeking highly-qualified experts in the field to fill vacancies on their respective editorial review boards:

Applications and Inquiries may be sent to:
development@igi-global.com

Applicants must have a doctorate (or an equivalent degree) as well as publishing and reviewing experience. Reviewers are asked to complete the open-ended evaluation questions with as much detail as possible in a timely, collegial, and constructive manner. All reviewers' tenures run for one-year terms on the editorial review boards and are expected to complete at least three reviews per term. Upon successful completion of this term, reviewers can be considered for an additional term.

If you have a colleague that may be interested in this opportunity, we encourage you to share this information with them.

Publisher of Peer-Reviewed, Timely, and
Innovative Academic Research Since 1988

www.igi-global.com

IGI Global's Transformative Open Access (OA) Model:
How to Turn Your University Library's Database Acquisitions Into a Source of OA Funding

In response to the OA movement and well in advance of Plan S, IGI Global, early last year, unveiled their OA Fee Waiver (Read & Publish) Initiative.

Under this initiative, librarians who invest in IGI Global's InfoSci-Books (5,300+ reference books) and/or InfoSci-Journals (185+ scholarly journals) databases will be able to subsidize their patron's OA article processing charges (APC) when their work is submitted and accepted (after the peer review process) into an IGI Global journal. *See website for details.

How Does it Work?

1. When a library subscribes or perpetually purchases IGI Global's InfoSci-Databases and/or their discipline/subject-focused subsets, IGI Global will match the library's investment with a fund of equal value to go toward subsidizing the OA article processing charges (APCs) for their patrons.

   Researchers: Be sure to recommend the InfoSci-Books and InfoSci-Journals to take advantage of this initiative.

2. When a student, faculty, or staff member submits a paper and it is accepted (following the peer review) into one of IGI Global's 185+ scholarly journals, the author will have the option to have their paper published under a traditional publishing model or as OA.

3. When the author chooses to have their paper published under OA, IGI Global will notify them of the OA Fee Waiver (Read & Publish) Initiative. If the author decides they would like to take advantage of this initiative, IGI Global will deduct the US$ 2,000 APC from the created fund.

4. This fund will be offered on an annual basis and will renew as the subscription is renewed for each year thereafter. IGI Global will manage the fund and award the APC waivers unless the librarian has a preference as to how the funds should be managed.

Hear From the Experts on This Initiative:

"I'm very happy to have been able to make one of my recent research contributions, "Visualizing the Social Media Conversations of a National Information Technology Professional Association" featured in the *International Journal of Human Capital and Information Technology Professionals*, freely available along with having access to the valuable resources found within IGI Global's InfoSci-Journals database."

– **Prof. Stuart Palmer**,
Deakin University, Australia

For More Information, Visit: www.igi-global.com/publish/contributor-resources/open-access/read-publish-model
or contact IGI Global's Database Team at eresources@igi-global.com.

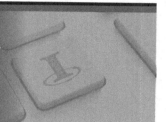

Printed in the United States
By Bookmasters